Bosnia Warriors

Bosnia Warriors
Living on the Front Line

Major Vaughan Kent-Payne

ROBERT HALE · LONDON

ISBN 0 7090 6158 7

Robert Hale Limited
Clerkenwell House
Clerkenwell Green
London EC1R 0HT

2 4 6 8 10 9 7 5 3 1

Photoset in North Wales by
Derek Doyle & Associates, Mold, Flintshire.
Printed in Great Britain by
St Edmundsbury Press Limited, Bury St Edmunds
and bound by
WBC Book Manufacturers Limited, Bridgend.

Contents

This book is dedicated to the men of
C Company Group, 1st Battalion The Prince of Wales's
Own Regiment of Yorkshire, Operation GRAPPLE 2,
May–November 1993.

Acknowledgements

This book covers the deployment of First Battalion The Prince of Wales's Own Regiment of Yorkshire to Bosnia in 1993. The story is focused on the actions of C Company, the sub-unit I commanded. It is not intended to be read as a record of the battalion's activities but as a personal account of the tour. As such, similar stories could have been written by many members of the regiment.

Several people helped me with the proof-reading of the manuscript: Squadron Leader Ian Phillips, Captain John Parrott, Corporal Stu Hunt and Lance-Corporal Paul Ryan from the staff of British Forces headquarters in the Falkland Islands. Also, Gordon, Danny, Mike, Steve, Dave and all the other officers of the Royal Fleet Auxiliary Gold Rover who gave me a civilian perspective on the book.

Furthermore, I'd like to thank Flight Lieutenant Sean Cunningham for rescuing the manuscript several times when I crashed the word processor. Thanks also to Ronna Turley and David Howcroft who redrew the maps and sketches after my children asked if I'd drawn them when I was at primary school. I am indebted to the *Daily Telegraph* and *Guardian* newspapers who very kindly allowed me to quote from some of their articles. Their journalists, who risked their lives alongside us, have described the events in Bosnia in a manner far beyond my own powers of expression. Thank you especially to Judith Caul of the *Guardian* who helped me to trace the photograph used on the jacket. I am also most grateful to James Mason for his kind permission to use his photograph of the Bosnian Warriors.

Special thanks go to Captain Mark Bower QGM for taking the trouble to correct the mistakes made by my goldfish-like memory. Thank you also to John Harding of the Army Historical Branch for his most helpful comments and to John Hale for his support of this virgin author. My biggest thanks go to my wife, Dawn, whose understanding and tolerance persuaded me to go ahead with this project. It was her support that ensured that I didn't give up when the words refused to flow.

Finally, thank you to the men of C Company 1 PWO. For this is their story.

Preface

This book is an account of early United Nations Operations in Bosnia. My regiment deployed on Operation GRAPPLE 2 in April 1993 to relieve the Cheshire Regiment. I commanded C Company 1 PWO and it is within this small group that the action is concentrated.

Because of the nature of the tour we rarely operated at company strength and, indeed, it was unusual for more than two vehicles to operate together. Thus, when I describe the actions of soldiers in my platoons I've based this on eyewitness accounts and notes I wrote at the time.

Most of the book, however, describes the activities of myself and the crew of my Warrior, callsign Zero Bravo (hereafter referred to as 0B). Our actions are described in some detail to give the reader a feel for the intensely localized nature of the UN operations. I make little attempt to analyse the UN mandate or the successes and failures of the organization. Indeed, where I have commented, the views are entirely my own and not, necessarily, those of the Ministry of Defence.

Much has been written about the various ethnic groups. To avoid confusion, when I mention Serbs, I refer to Bosnian Serbs, and Croats as Bosnian Croats unless I explain to the contrary. The BiH refers to the Army of Bosnia Herzegovina, which is mainly Muslim. As such, I sometimes refer to them as the Muslims. There are Croats in the BiH but there were few in our area. Finally, by Muslims I mean Bosnian Muslims. These people often have a very different interpretation of Islam to those in many other Muslim countries. Throughout the tour I kept a detailed diary recording what I saw, what I did and how I felt. As such, this book is, inevitably, of a personal nature. Our work for the UN in Bosnia was a totally new environment for most of us. We'd trained to kill the Queen's enemies

11

and the tasks we were required to perform were alien to us. We coped as best we could through all the stresses of being in the middle of someone else's war. We made some mistakes either through ignorance, incompetence, or, through simply not caring enough. I've tried to avoid naming individuals but have attempted to analyse my own mistakes to the best of my ability. The reader may judge whether I was right or wrong. However, in the end God will judge whether any of us did enough.

Maps

Illustrations

Illustration Credits

Maj. Roy Hunter: 6, 32. S/Sgt. McLeod: 9. Crown Copyright: 19, 34. Capt.
Peter Edwards: 29. WO2 Mick Clark: 40. C Company 1 PWO: 46.

All other photographs are from the collections of the author and the men of
C Company Group.

Introduction

Crack, crack! The high velocity shots were fired from somewhere close to our left.

'Fuck me!' I cried as I ducked down inside the Warrior until only my eyes peered over the top of the sight, like a Mister Chad. 'What no cease-fire?'

Thwack! Another round hit the side of the wagon. Someone here didn't like us. I swung the turret to the left, and traversed around trying to locate the firing point. There he was! A man dressed in camouflage fatigues and a blue baseball cap was pointing a Soviet-style AK 47 assault rifle at me. A small, bright orange flash briefly lit up the muzzle and another round struck the side of the vehicle.

'Can you see him?' I shouted to my gunner, seated to my left.

'Yeah!' came back the laconic reply.

'Chain Gun loaded! Fire!'

As the gunner was about to open fire, the Warrior suddenly swerved violently to the right then left. When I looked up again, the man with the AK had ducked out of sight. I looked back to see what had caused the driver to take such violent evasive action. Lying in a huddle on the road was a small boy. The breeze tugged at his curly brown hair and at the hood of his yellow coat. He was very still, and very dead. A teddy bear lay just beyond the reach of one, tiny, out-stretched hand. Beside the road was a burned out house and, out-side, the body of his mother. She lay on her back, her white blouse stained red with blood and her skirt hitched up around her waist. These people had been ethnically cleansed, which is just a posh name for murder.

Twenty minutes later I was sitting in an armchair sipping coffee and reading a newspaper. Outside, a sniper was plying his trade and the odd high-velocity shot was loosed off at some unsuspecting vic-tim. Was this all part of a surreal, Daliesque, nightmare?

17

Unfortunately not, or the mother and child would wake up, return to their undamaged house and live happily ever after. This was Bosnia and I was in the middle of someone else's civil war. How the hell did I get here?

The story starts in the middle of 1992 and I was serving as the Chief of Staff of the 107th (Ulster) brigade in Ballymena. Well over half way through my posting, I was looking forward to returning to my regiment early the next year.

I'd been commissioned into The Prince of Wales's Own Regiment of Yorkshire in 1978, the fulfilment of a childhood ambition. My father was a career soldier and my grandfather had died in the First World War while serving with the East Yorkshire Regiment. I only ever wanted to be a soldier and finally entered Sandhurst in 1977. My chosen regiment was the product of an amalgamation of the West and East Yorkshire Regiments. Like so many others in small county regiments, I came from a regimental family into the family of the regiment. It is this closeness that marks the Infantry Battalion out from all the other units in the Army. You join with people and serve with them for most of your career. You or they may be posted away for a while but you always return and, inevitably, meet up again. It's this family ethos that is at the heart of the regimental system.

I left Sandhurst with two other officers, David Hill and Roy Hunter and joined D Company. Three of the company characters were Lance-Corporal Mick Clark, known to everyone as Zippy, from the children's television 'Rainbow' character, Lance-Corporal Tez Cook and Private Paul Dobson, known simply as Dobby. These fine soldiers will appear again in fifteen years time. My career followed the normal pattern for an infantry officer with stints away at the Recruit Training Depot and, later, teaching tactics to corporals. After a year at the Staff College I was posted to Northern Ireland.

It was during this tour that the Balkans started to dominate the news.

The situation in the former Republic of Yugoslavia had deteriorated and, by 1992, a state of open warfare existed in many areas. Several books have been written about the causes of the conflict and I don't intend to use my peanut-size brain to add my own analysis. Suffice it to say that the death of Tito, in 1980, had left a vacuum with no one strong enough to hold the disparate peoples together. Gradually, the State fragmented into breakaway republics and, inevitably, squabbles started over who owned what. The flashpoint was the area of Bosnia–Herzegovina where there were three distinct ethnic groups, all vying for a share of a finite amount of territory. The Bosnian Serbs were by far the strongest side and, supported by Serbia itself, they started to carve out a new nation with the aim of a link-up with Serbia. Territory was taken off Croatia and heavy fighting erupted in Bosnia. The Bosnian Serbs had stockpiled much of the weaponry of the Yugoslavian National Army, the JNA. Therefore, they quickly pushed aside the mainly Muslim Army of Bosnia-Herzegovina (BiH) and the mainly Croat, Bosnian Croat Defence Organization (HVO). Soon Sarajevo was under siege and pictures of atrocities were filling the television screens of the world. The Bosnian Serbs drove the Croats and Muslims from the captured territory. Hundreds of thousands of displaced persons were created and the term ethnic cleansing was born. The world's media descended on Bosnia and beamed back images of suffering to the comfort of suburban homes. What shocked the world was not so much the atrocities themselves but that they were happening in Europe. Perhaps inevitably, people had become used to viewing strife on the other side of the world. To many, the sight of a few more starving black kids was hardly newsworthy. However, here were little blond kids with mothers in Benetton frocks in the refugee camps. People demanded action because the media demanded action. This was a conflict a little too close to home and the fear was that the newly liberated, former Communist states could go the same way. In reality, there was little reason for many UN members to become involved but they felt they had to be seen to be doing something. Never before has there been intervention on such a scale generated largely by the power of the media.

Once the UN decided to deploy it was inevitable that Britain would become involved. In early 1992, the decision was made to send 1st Battalion The Cheshire Regiment, an armoured infantry battalion. The battalion was due to go in November 1992 for a six-month tour. I took little more than a passing interest in this although I knew that I was due back to my Regiment in February 1993. This suddenly changed when I happened to notice an article in the *Sunday Telegraph* in late October telling that the Cheshire Regiment would be relieved by The Prince of Wales's Own Regiment of Yorkshire in May 1993. I phoned the Adjutant of the battalion in Germany and asked if the story was true. He told me this was the first the regiment had heard of it and the Commanding Officer was away trying to confirm the story. Indeed, the CO was not officially told the battalion was to go to Bosnia until January 1993, three months after the story appeared in the papers.

I left 107 Brigade in late December 1992 and flew to England to attend the Combined Arms Tactics Course. The course was for officers about to command a sub-unit and was like a reunion of many of the old Camberley cronies who'd finished their staff jobs. Roy Hunter was on the course and was going to take over A Company. We were due a week's leave after the course but, in true army fashion, this was snatched away at the last moment. The current OC of C Company, Richard Watson, was due to take over as the regimental second-in-command and I was required early to relieve him on the battalion exercise.

Chapter 1
The Wrong Trousers

Two days later, I arrived at Belfast Barracks, Osnabrück, Germany. The place was deserted, which was not surprising as most of the soldiers were on exercise. I found my room, which contained, to my amazement, my boxes of kit from Northern Ireland. However, before I could contemplate unpacking, a soldier appeared and told me that transport would arrive to take me out to the exercise area in an hour's time. Ten minutes later my orderly pile of boxes had been transformed into a heap of twelve crates of kit in the middle of the floor! Soon, having spent less than ninety minutes in Osnabrück, I was heading for the Soltau training area.

The two soldiers who picked me up were Lance-Corporal Dave Latus and Private 'Billy' Dainty. It was great to be back in the company of Yorkshire soldiers and, although I hadn't met the two before, we were soon chatting away. It appeared that the battalion had finally received the order to go to Bosnia but hadn't yet started specialist training. The exercise was the final stage of conversion to the Warrior, Infantry Fighting Vehicle, and it was bloody cold!

I reached Soltau training area at eight o'clock in the evening of 14 February 1993. My period as OC C Company 1 PWO had almost begun.

It was pitch black but I eventually found Richard and the Company Sergeant Major, Zippy Clark. I'd seen Richard only six months before and was surprised at the change in him. He was once described in the regimental magazine as 'the hit-man for Mothercare' but he had, by now, gone extremely grey. He was obviously very tired, for the CO had been working the battalion hard, and kept nodding off during our handover. Nevertheless, we sat in the back of a Warrior, for the best part of six hours, and talked about company personalities and the aspects peculiar to a Warrior company.

The following morning, Richard departed and I gave a short talk to the assembled soldiers. Giving them a quick insight to my background, I told them what I expected from them. I said I only knew one way to lead. As long as I was out in front I expected them to follow and I wouldn't ask them to do anything that I wouldn't do myself.

I spent the first day getting to know the company hierarchy. The oldest man in the company was the Warrior Captain, Phil Stainthorpe, known as 'Pop'. Phil had been commissioned from the ranks having been the RSM of a battalion. His role was to oversee all specialist aspects of the Warrior within the company. His immediate job was as the gunner in my vehicle and, as such, he sat next to me. Phil had a wealth of experience and was just the sort of guy that a somewhat wilful company commander needed in close proximity. I soon grew to trust Phil and use him as a sounding board for any new ideas. Phil was one of those lucky folk who appear to look younger the older they get. He had a good head of jet black hair and wore glasses that made him look like a university professor rather than an ex-RSM.

Zippy Clark was another blessed with apparent eternal youth. Barely five foot six he had the build of a teenager and was skinny as a beanpole. It seemed impossible that he could impose discipline over some of the hulks in the company, yet he ruled them with a rod of iron. Not for him the mindless shouting of many sergeant majors. Zippy rarely raised his voice but would deliver such stinging bollockings that the recipient would slink away blushing with the embarrassment of having let the CSM down. We'd known each other for years and appeared to hit it off right from the start.

The platoon commanders were a mixed bunch. Tom Crowfoot was the senior and commanded Nine Platoon. The son of a general he was always relaxed and very popular with his men. However, he commanded a platoon with a deeply-rooted discipline problem. The platoon had run riot on a recent Northern Ireland tour. Several RAF policemen and a dog had been injured in the resulting scuffle. The platoon had great morale but the boys were not nearly as good as they thought they were.

John Reeve commanded Seven Platoon. Short and stocky, John

looked like a pocket-sized version of Jean-Claude van Damme. He was a university graduate and had a certain arrogance that was unusual for one so inexperienced. He had clearly made a good start and his platoon seemed in good shape.

The final platoon commander was Colour Sergeant 'Tez' Cook. He was slightly overweight, with a wispy moustache. Although he was coming to the end of his army service it soon became clear that Cooky was out to prove himself to be as good a platoon commander as any officer.

The CQMs was Colour Sergeant Andy Goy. Even thinner than Zippy, he caught any germ that passed within a mile and spent most of the exercise in bed with flu. When he was up and about I soon realized that I had an exceptionally good man running the stores. The final member of the company I saw closely during those first days was Corporal Paul Dobson. Dobby was the Company Warrior Equipment Storeman. This was not a particularly demanding job but then Dobby didn't appear to be the sort who could hold down a high-pressure post. He'd been in the Army for about eighteen years and most of his contemporaries were sergeant majors. Dobby didn't give a stuff and seemed quite content to serve his time out as the classic underachiever. Well over six feet, seventeen stones at least and with a huge moustache, he looked as hard as hell but was, in reality, the archetypal gentle giant.

Each company was organized into three platoons, each equipped with four Warriors. The radio call sign of the vehicle was painted on the wagons. The platoon commander of Seven Platoon was One Zero, written as 10, Eight Platoon, 20 and Nine Platoon, 30. The rifle sections were then 11, 12, and 13 followed by 21, 22 etc. The company symbol was a circle that surrounded the callsign. This system is Army-wide and so a triangle with 10 inside it would be the vehicle of the first platoon commander in A Company. A square with 31 inside it would denote the first section vehicle of the third platoon in B Company. My vehicle was 0B, the company 2/ic was 0C. Confused? The Bosnians took months to get used to it!

During that first couple of days I also familiarized myself with the Warrior. Weighing in at around twenty-seven tons, it is the first British infantry fighting vehicle. It offers the classic trio of firepower, mobility and protection. The armour is aluminium and, if the back door is anything to go by, about 50 mm thick. The engine is enormous and located at the front right. The turbo makes a deafening roar and the whole outfit has a top speed in excess of eighty kilometres per hour. On the front left sits the driver in a high tech seat that reclines into a sort of bed. Needless to say, this is the most comfortable place in the house. The rifle section consists of seven men sitting on bench seats in the rear.

The turret is roughly central on the top of the vehicle, with the commander on the right and the gunner on the left. The main armament is the 30 mm RARDEN Cannon. Although of an old design, the weapon has many good points. The gun fires out to about 2000 metres with great accuracy. It is loaded with six rounds in clips of three. These can be fired either as single shots or in an automatic burst. The rounds are loaded and then wound into the gun by means of three turns of a small handle. The first round is rammed into the breech with a clunk that is clearly audible from outside the vehicle. Little did I know that this feature was to lead to some hairy moments a few months later.

The gunnery is a bit steam driven compared with other systems. Both gunner and commander have a times-one and times-ten magnification sight. There are no lasers or computers in the system but, in the hands of a good crew, it works.

Fitted coaxially to the main armament is the 7.62 mm Hughes Chain Gun with a rate of fire of over six hundred rounds a minute. The seats are a better feature of the Warrior and can be raised and lowered hydraulically. However, I had a pathological fear of the wagon tipping over and me being unable to get back inside the hatch. I therefore collapsed my seat and stood on the turret floor. Being a short-arse, I could just see over the top of the sights and, when the need arose, bend down and talk face-to-face with the crew in the back.

After a couple of days trundling around the training area, I soon appreciated that, at last, the infantry had a vehicle that was world class.

I had a REME fitter section attached to the company of around a dozen men and three vehicles. This section was led by the Artificer (a staff sergeant). My 'Tiffy', Staff Sergeant Tim Mackareth, was clearly very intelligent and determined to keep the vehicles on the road. This became almost an obsession and he delighted in having the best availability record in the battalion. To assist him he had a sergeant and a variety of mechanics, electricians, instrument technicians and armourers. During this period I met the commanding officer. Lieutenant Colonel Alastair Duncan had commanded the battalion for over two years already and had been extended in post to take it to Bosnia. He'd commanded during a highly successful tour of West Belfast the year before and there were rumours that he might be awarded the OBE. A tall and imposing figure, he wore gold-rimmed glasses and looked younger than his forty years. I'd known him for about thirteen years but we'd never served closely. First impressions are always important. Therefore, when I drew to a halt beside him and dismounted I was keen to get off to a good start. I saluted smartly and we shook hands. I was then fixed with a withering stare that I later found out was known as 'the look'.

'Why are you wearing jungle combats?' were his first words to me. I thought better of pointing out that I had only an hour to sort out my kit for the exercise and meekly mumbled some form of apology.

I should've anticipated that this would happen. My regiment has always insisted on issue kit only and woe betide anyone who transgresses this unwritten rule. I'd been away from the battalion for five years and had forgotten this characteristic and I cursed myself for setting off on the wrong foot.

The exercise finally ended and the battalion received the tick-in-the-box for successfully completing the conversion to armoured infantry. We were ready to commence Bosnia training.

Chapter 2
Innocents Abroad

Back in Osnabrück, the dates for the advanced reconnaissance were confirmed. Bosnia had started to appear in the news with increasing frequency as UNPROFOR struggled to escort humanitarian aid convoys. These convoys frequently came under fire either from the warring factions or from bandit groups. The media took a great interest in the activities of the British Battalion and focused on their commanding officers, Lieutenant Colonel Bob Stewart in particular. Hardly a day went by without Stewart appearing on the news to deliver some punchy message. He seemed to have the knack for dealing with the media.

The recce party assembled at Düsseldorf Airport on 27 February 1993 and boarded a Croatian Airlines Boeing 737 bound for Split. After a couple of hours we arrived over the city. It looked like a scene straight from a holiday brochure with the sun shining over the clear azure waters of the Adriatic. The airport stood on the coastal plain and the mountains to the north were capped with snow.

We reclaimed our baggage and queued to clear their customs. The customs officer was a hatchet-faced woman in her forties, backed-up by three guards toting AK 47 assault rifles. She scrutinized my passport for at least a minute, examining every page and flicking her eyes from the book to me every few seconds. She eventually decided I posed no threat to the State and, with an air of reluctance, stamped my passport, Aerodrom Split. I'd forgotten that the Communists have an obsession with restricting travel and insisting on correct paperwork. I would be involved in similar scenes scores of times in the coming months.

Transport was waiting for us in the form of two white-painted Land Rovers, which sped us off to the British HQ.

Divulje Barracks was a Croatian army camp with part leased to the UN. We were shown into the headquarters and briefed on all aspects of the UN operations in Former Yugoslavia.

One of the most obvious problems was that the mandate to UNPROFOR from the UN was not the best one for the job. Basically, the UN forces were to escort humanitarian aid convoys. There was no mention of patrolling, peace-keeping, hearts-and-minds operations, route-maintenance, distribution of aid or mediation in local disputes. All of these tasks were implied in the mission and helped to make it work. There was, however, no laid-down policy on these matters. Thus, the Spanish Battalion, SPANBAT, did little other than escort convoys, whereas the Cheshires, BRITBAT, were carrying out all the implied tasks, and more. The briefings gave me a lot to ponder and it seemed clear the task we faced was not going to be easy.

The battalion was due to take over from the Cheshires in Vitez and the journey would take about five hours. I travelled in the lead Land Rover with the CO, David, Roy, and Graham Binns, B Company Commander. As we travelled north, the terrain became first hilly and then mountainous as we left Croatia and entered the Bosnian-Croat controlled area of Bosnia. Roy commented that we were passing through classic karst scenery. I didn't know then that this meant a limestone region with many cavities and passages caused by the dissolution of the rock. In fact I only know now because I just looked it up in the dictionary. Either way, I wasn't going to admit my ignorance so I said, 'What, as in half-caste? Is that because the rocks are a light-brown colour?'

Roy was just about to commence one of his, 'no you idiot, the answer is' routines when Binnsy butted in.

'No, it's as in open-cast mining because the rocks look like they've been quarried'.

Once again, Roy puffed out his chest and seemed about to put yet another Philistine in his place, when David interjected.

'No way. Anyone knows that it's as in worm-cast, because the hills resemble them.'

Then the CO added, 'I personally believe that it's as in cast-iron, because of the rusty hue of the rock.'

Roy finally clicked that we were taking the mickey. With a mutter, he settled down to sulk for the next hour.

The route was initially a metalled road. However, once we reached the town of Tomislavgrad, known as TSG, it narrowed into a dirt track. The track was called Route Diamond and was the main supply route into Central Bosnia. Each MSR was named and marked with a symbol every couple of kilometres. Much of Diamond had been a muddy path but had been significantly widened by the Royal Engineers.

One of the spin-offs for the locals was that they too had a reasonable route to use and there were several cars and lorries about. The cars were all filthy and seemed to be clapped out, emitting great clouds of exhaust fumes. They were mostly of Eastern European origin with the most common being home-produced copies of Italian cars, made by Yugo or Zastava. There were a few Western vehicles, mostly Volkswagens, as proof that the collapse of Communism had heralded the introduction of the free market. The newer cars were driven by men in uniform. The driving was atrocious, especially considering the road conditions, and we were almost forced off the track by four armed men in a Golf GTI.

The lorries were in an appalling state of repair and all seemed to be manufactured by a firm called Raba. Several trucks lay abandoned by the side of the track. Stripped of anything of value, the shells mouldered away like the carcasses of dinosaurs.

North of TSG, the track entered a huge forest and a few miles on we arrived in the small town of Prozor. It was here that we encountered our first evidence of the War.

The Croats had recently driven the Muslim population out of the town in a carefully orchestrated bout of ethnic cleansing. This was part of a campaign of territorial acquisition between the two sides that thrust the Cheshires back into the limelight. There were several burned-out buildings, many of them with bullet holes around the doors and windows. Their blackened walls sharply contrasted with the untouched Croat houses and we could only guess as to the fate of the occupants. The town centre was full of swaggering youths, carrying the ubiquitous AK 47, who glowered at us as we passed. After Prozor, the track again rose into the hills and there were frequent signs of ethnic cleansing in the small villages that lined the route. We discussed why the Croats would want to burn the houses and the consensus was that they must've wanted to ensure that the displaced people had nothing to return to.

The next major town on the route was Gornji Vakuf. The town had witnessed a flare up in ethnic violence earlier in the year with the Croats fighting to gain control of the town. As we crossed over the bridge in the town centre, we passed several bunches of wilted flowers by the side of the road. The driver told us this was where Lance-Corporal Wayne Edwards had been killed a few weeks earlier. He was the first British soldier to die in the Bosnia conflict and I was determined to bring all of my company back alive.

In Gornji Vakuf, or GV as it was known to the UN, the Cheshires had a company stationed in a disused factory. This had been the quietest area and had been selected to provide a secure 'back door' for the rest of the battalion. The fighting of the previous month had changed all this and it looked like GV was going to be the front line, with Vitez instead, the quiet backwater. Colonel Alastair had selected B Company, under Graham Binns, to station GV. As this was likely to be the most prestigious area, he'd allowed him to recruit from the other companies to bring his own up to strength. We pulled into the sprawling complex and were briefed by the Company Commander, a guy from the Royal Irish Regiment. The Cheshires, in common with most infantry battalions, were under-strength and had received around a hundred Royal Irish. We were in the same position, with A and C Companies about thirty men short. We knew that reinforcements were due to arrive from three other regiments. Leaving Binnsy behind, we headed north once more for the final part of the journey to Vitez.

After about an hour, we started to see much more evidence of civilization. We were entering the Lasva Valley, the most densely populated area of Central Bosnia. To our left I noticed the lights of a large town that the driver said was Novi Travnik. A little further on we came to a prominent junction, the Novi Travnik T-junction. The spot marked the confluence of the roads to Novi Travnik, Travnik and Vitez and had a large checkpoint. The area was of some local importance and was to be the site of much heavy fighting over the next few months. I was to get to know this place very well and have some of the luckiest escapes of my tour here. We'd passed through several checkpoints already and the CO, having already visited the area on his initial recce, told us of their significance.

The whole of the Lasva Valley was a patchwork of ethnic mixes with Croat, Muslim and mixed villages all along the same road. Checkpoints were designed to regulate access to the villages and

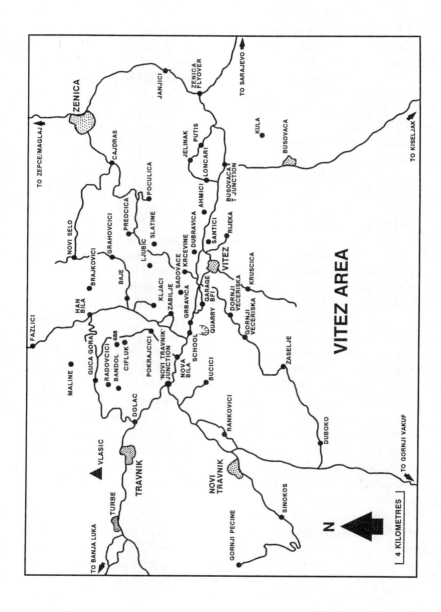

prevent the ingress, or indeed escape, of other ethnic groups. This obsession with controlling movement is very Communist and, although the party was no longer in control, old habits die hard. The checkpoint was the tool and it was not unusual to have one every couple of kilometres.

The Novi Travnik checkpoint consisted of a hut about the size of an ISO container providing some degree of shelter from the bitter cold. Two soldiers sat on stools in front of a brazier, smoking and drinking clear liquid from a bottle. Their uniform was a collection of old American cast-offs, with training shoes completing the air of consummate professionals. One had a shoulder flash with HVO written on a shield decorated with a red-and-white checkerboard pattern. Roy informed us that the HVO was the Bosnian Croat Militia. The CO also told us that the bottle probably contained Slivovitz, a local brew made from plums. Apparently it was the sort of fluid tried by NASA as propulsion for their Saturn Five rockets. The prospect of dealing with armed men who were also drunk didn't fill me with glee. However, it would soon become part and parcel of the job.

The guard waved us through the chicane. I thought the driver was going a little too slowly for the situation but then I noticed the mines.

Interspersed between the barriers were about half a dozen anti-tank mines. Looking like upturned green dinner plates, they lay, seemingly innocuously, on the road. I recognized them as copies of the Soviet TMA 3 mine but resisted the temptation to get one-over on Roy by telling everybody. They were at the bottom end of the lethality scale for anti-tank mines. Nevertheless, TMA 3 would happily send us all to the great regimental reunion in the sky. Fortunately, the driver skilfully negotiated the chicane and we went on our way. I couldn't help wondering how on earth the Warriors managed the tight turns.

Finally, well after last light, we entered Vitez school. The school was actually in the village of Stara Bila, the town of Vitez being about four kilometres away. The location had been chosen to provide a base for the 500 or so troops stationed there and was, with hindsight, far from ideal. The school was an unimpressive, two-storey concrete structure. The main building housed the offices, operations room and communications setup. There were some areas where soldiers lived, often thirty to a room. Most of the men, how-

ever, lived in tiny Portakabins the size of an ISO container and able
to fit on the back of a flatbed lorry.

After a quick orientation we were taken to Bob Stewart's house. I
didn't really twig exactly where the house was, in relation to the camp,
because it was dark and I was sitting in the back of the Rover. We
unloaded our kit and the next-door house was pointed out to us. This
was where the Press Information, or P Info, team lived and worked.
Our house was a large three-storey chalet affair that wouldn't have
looked out of place on a postcard from Switzerland. The light was provided by a generator that puttered away in a corner of the front garden and the place looked almost inviting.

Over supper in the cookhouse we met several of the officers,
including Bob Stewart, who had, by this time, become something of
a media star. The Army has prided itself on producing generations
of low-profile senior officers. However, here was a man who spoke
his mind in simple language and the media loved him. He was
always there with a quotable quote and was therefore much sought
after by the numerous reporters in Vitez. Not since Colonel Colin
'Mad Mitch' Mitchell in Aden, in the 1960s, had the Army had a
senior officer who was prepared to speak his mind on film. Mitchell
had paid the price and I wondered if Stewart would go the same way.

The other officers seemed a good bunch. Hardly surprising as
they were from a county regiment, the same as us. I knew one of the
company commanders quite well. Philip Jennings and I had been at
Camberley together.

After the meal, we wandered over to the mess. It was now that I
began to get some idea of the crazy nature of the base. The officers'
mess was actually outside the perimeter wire and we walked past the
guard position to get to it. The place was some fifty metres away
from the nearest sentry and about twenty from the main road past
camp. Across the narrow access road to the base were more houses,
occupied by civilians. It all seemed to be extremely vulnerable to
anyone wishing to attack the mess. Inside, the walls were painted a
mottled cerise colour and the woodwork was either black or red.
There were several garish marble tables, long padded benches along
the walls and banks of lights attached to the rafters. Phil must've
noticed my open mouth. 'This used to be the local disco', he
explained. To add further to the surreal air, the Cheshires had
brought their regimental colours, some paintings and several items
of regimental silver. There was, however, a well-stocked bar and I

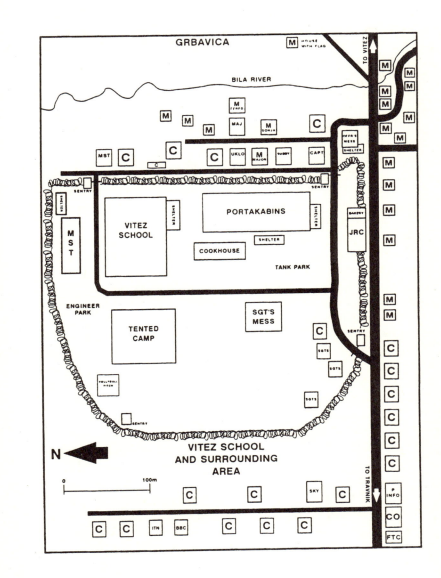

GRBAVICA

BILA RIVER

PORTAKABINS

VITEZ
SCHOOL

COOKHOUSE

TANK PARK

SGT'S
MESS

ENGINEER
PARK

TENTED
CAMP

VITEZ SCHOOL
AND SURROUNDING
AREA

N

0   100m

was soon presented with a can of Boddington's beer. This was a momentous occasion as the bright yellow can, proclaiming its contents to be the cream of Manchester, was the first of many to be held to the K-P lips over the next few months. As I savoured the amber nectar I looked around at some of the Cheshires.

The more I looked, the more some of them appeared to be decidedly odd. One fellow came up to me and introduced himself as one of the LOs. He was wearing a pistol in a shoulder holster over the top of his jumper. I started behaving like I was talking to a girl with a massive cleavage. I just couldn't take my eyes off it. It wasn't the fact that I was talking to someone silly enough to parade around the mess wearing a pistol, it was the size of the magazine on the weapon. Normally the 9 mm Browning takes a thirteen-round magazine, which fits snugly into the butt. This guy had a mag which, he proudly told me, held 25 rounds and was several centimetres longer than normal. Every time he turned round it bumped against the corner of the bar with an audible clank. However, he was totally oblivious to the fact that he looked a complete prat. He was posing around with this thing with not a word said by anyone.

Above all, however, the oddest fact was the huge amount of drink that everyone was consuming. I thought I could handle my beer but, after five in an hour, I was forced to slow down. Meanwhile, everyone carried on as if nothing was out of place. Roy and I discussed this and we decided that many of them appeared to have gone barking-mad. We reflected that it must be down to poor leadership and that there was no way we would become like that. What a naïve and pretentious sentiment this proved to be.

Another extraordinary aspect of the mess was that reporters were allowed to come and go as they pleased. At one stage, Stewart held an impromptu press conference, complete with quotable quotes. As Roy and I were chatting, a figure sidled up to us and started to ask us what we thought of the situation in Bosnia. Before we realized what was happening we were giving an interview to Robert Fox of the *Daily Telegraph*. Fortunately, we were sober enough not to say anything crass. The press, like police officers, are never really off duty and are always on the lookout for some scoop. Having them in our midst was surely courting disaster.

By around one o'clock, the place was starting to thin out and Phil gave us directions to walk back to the house. Clutching our rifles, we lurched, somewhat unsteadily, into the freezing night air. The route took us back into the camp and past the tank park, where the Warriors stood, waiting for their next tasks. We then walked by a number of houses, where the S/NCOs lived, before arriving at another sentry position. Sensing we'd gone wrong, we asked the soldier on duty for directions. Instead of pointing us back into camp he simply said, 'Nine houses down the road on the left'.

Feeling extremely vulnerable, and suddenly very sober, we ducked under the barrier and into the middle of Central Bosnia. The silence was oppressive and we started to hard-target towards our house. I crouched down and prepared to give Roy covering fire. He sprinted forward a few metres and then he crouched down. After a couple of rounds of this we both squatted, side by side, to listen. I expected the noise of the generator to guide us towards the house but all I could hear was the pounding of my own heart. Crack! a single high-velocity shot rang out, not close, but the still air made it seem near enough. Like two startled rabbits we both took off and sprinted together in what we thought was the right direction.

After a few seconds, we stopped again. The sky was overcast and there were no lights visible. Crouching in the road, we could not even see the houses to our left, let alone tell which one was ours. Panting from our exertions, our breath hung in clouds in the still night air, like spectral fingers providing a convenient pointer for the snipers who must surely have us in their sights.

Finally, we were reduced to creeping up every garden until we located first the P Info house and then our own. I checked the silent generator. It was cold and we only later discovered that it was turned off at midnight. Still expecting further shots, I covered Roy as he fumbled with the key. Finally, we entered the house. The place was in darkness and totally silent as we crept upstairs, still expecting to be ambushed at every turn of the corridor. We reached the room and shut the door behind us. I pushed a chair against it while Roy checked under the beds using a small torch. Only then did we collapse into a series of nervous giggles. The room was freezing and I slept, fully dressed, in my maggot with my rifle inside with me.

The next morning I took stock of our surroundings. The CO's house and P Info were, indeed, located a couple of hundred metres outside the camp. They were not wired off and the only way of differentiating them from the others on the street was by the small UN stickers on the windows. Apparently, Colonel Stewart had chosen the house, one of the best in the area, after spending several weeks living in his office in the school. The owners had moved out to allow the UN to rent the house for several hundred deutschmarks a month. This was a king's ransom in a country where the average wage was around ten marks a month. The place was ideal for putting up guests to the battalion but seemed a security nightmare.

At breakfast, we mentioned our escapades of the night before. The officers chuckled and told us there were shots from the militiamen around camp all the time. Most of these were either drunken soldiers loosing off, or nervous sentries firing at shadows. The totally blasé attitude confounded me as I'd served many years in Northern Ireland, where every shot is a major incident. They all seemed so utterly cool that it only served to compound my 'barking-mad' theory.

The first activity of the day was a brief on the general situation in the area. The camp was situated on the edge of a plain with high ground on all sides. Although hardly the best place for a defended area, the school had been one of the few available buildings in the initial days of the UN deployment. Most schools were used as military HQs by one side or another. The risk from a stray shell landing on a crowded classroom was so great that all formal education had been suspended.

To the north, open fields led to the hills either side of the Bila Valley. This was a mixed Muslim and Croat area. To the south, lay the main Travnik to Vitez road, lined on the far side with houses. These too were mixed Muslim and Croat and included the P Info and CO's houses. Further to the south was the River Lasva and a range of hills held by the Croats. To the west, lay a street known as Press Row. The houses were Croat and several of these had been rented out to the various press agencies. Further to the west were Croat settlements with Nova Bila being the largest. Past the Novi Travnik T-junction, lay the town of Travnik. Rising above this, and dominating the camp, was the Vlasic Mountain feature. This was held by the Serbs and we were within range of their heavy guns. Finally, to the east, were more houses of mixed ethnic ownership, the Bila River, then a hill with a Muslim village on top called Grbavica. Further still to the east was Vitez Garage, housing the Cheshires support elements, and then the town of Vitez itself. The Muslims and Croats had coexisted reasonably happily for the early part of the War, united in a fight against a common enemy, the Serbs. After startling initial success, the BSA offensive had run out of steam. Halted by a combination of the appalling winter weather and a lack of manpower to hold their new territory, they were forced to dig in. However, cracks were starting to appear in the Muslim–Croat alliance. There'd already been some fighting and ethnic cleansing, particularly around the town of Busovaca. The situation around the camp mirrored the Lasva Valley in miniature with the two factions seemingly inextricably mixed all around the school. There was an uneasy calm that threatened to be the lull before the storm.

The mandate given to the commanding officer was simply 'to escort humanitarian aid convoys'. This had, however, been impossible to adhere to as, in order to achieve this, the battalion was sucked into a number of other tasks. For instance, the CO became involved in negotiations with the various parties to facilitate free passage through checkpoints. This was often the only way convoys could reach certain areas. Stewart had, in the best traditions of what the Army calls Mission Command, analysed his task. He then produced a whole list of duties that enabled his men to complete it. He called this 'the creation of the conditions by which humanitarian aid can pass freely through the area'. As this involved a peaceful area, he had, in effect become a peace-maker. This was definitely not what the UN had in mind. However, it was probably Stewart's greatest legacy that he understood the nature of the problem and was prepared to change the rules to get the job done. This was a radical departure from the role assumed by many other UN battalions.

The aid arrived, usually via Route Diamond. It was then escorted through some areas and stored in the warehouse in Zenica, a city some twelve kilometres to the north-east. From there, it was distributed to various sub-depots and then, we believed, to the people. This process could be upset at any time should further fighting erupt. Stewart and his officers were, therefore, at great pains to smooth the ruffled feathers of the various local leaders. They attended an endless series of meetings, arranged medical assistance and conducted hearts-and-minds operations, such as visits to orphanages. The amount of aid being distributed paid testimony to the fine efforts of the Cheshires during this period. They were doing a cracking job and I was immensely impressed by their achievements. They'd set the whole show up from nothing and were efficiently going about their business as if they'd been in the country for years.

The outside agencies were also impressed and representatives from several of them lectured us. The actual movement and distribution of the aid was carried out by the UNHCR. Their trucks carried the aid and distribution took place under the supervision of their field operatives. There were, however, many other agencies. Some carried and distributed aid such as Médicins Sans Frontières and Feed the Children. These were known as non-governmental organizations and received a varying degree of support from the UN. Others, such as the International Commission for the Red Cross, the ICRC, were concerned with helping the sick.

There were also several agencies apart from the Cheshires, who were monitoring the conflict. The European Community Monitoring Mission was the strongest. The ECMM wore white overalls causing them to be known as the 'cricket team' or the 'ice-cream sellers'. They were heavily involved in mediation in local disputes. There were also United Nations Monitors or UNMOs. Recruited multinationally, they worked for the UN at the worst trouble spots. Both groups were unarmed. Finally, the United Kingdom Liaison Officers, UKLOs, worked, via the battalion, to Brigade Headquarters in Split.

The CO also had several LOs from within his own organization. These were captains, supported by a small team of soldiers, and fell into two groups. The largest was made up of LOs for the various areas around the patch. LOs for the UNHCR HQ and the 'G5' team completed the setup. The G5 LO was, basically, mister hearts-and-minds, responsible for winning over the locals. We followed this system and most of our own LOs had already been chosen. Finally, we were briefed that there was a sub-unit deployed about 150 km to the north in the town of Tuzla. Phil told me, the night before, that his company was to change over in Tuzla in the near future. All of this was fascinating stuff but, after a morning's worth, I was glad to get out and wander round the camp.

Rather selfishly, we went to see our own accommodation first and received our biggest shock of the day. Running down the eastern perimeter of the camp was a gravel track with a line of houses on the far side. Some of these had been rented out to the UN and they were, from north to south: the medical personnel house, three Croat civilian houses and a little kiosk, the UKLO's house, a Muslim civilian house, the subaltern's house, and finally the captain's house. The track then ended at the front guard sangar and was used by military and civilian traffic alike. As with the CO's house there were small UN stickers on the windows. The major's house was behind the subaltern's and right in the middle of the village. Its location seemed crazy to us as the place couldn't be seen from the camp. This house was rented from a man called Fered, who'd moved into a partly completed house next door. Outside was a concrete verandah about four metres by three. The front door led into a small hall, to the right was a small room with a bath and lavatory, neither of which worked. To the left was what had once been the kitchen. It was quite large with two single beds, a couple of lockers, table and chair and the cooker and sink. Upstairs was another bathroom and four bedrooms. It was a setup that clearly had major pros and cons.

On the plus side, the house was away from the bustle of camp life and we could chill-out there. It was comfortable enough and much better than many places I'd stayed in Northern Ireland. The Cheshires assured us it was absolutely safe as the locals were very friendly. On the down side, the plumbing was atrocious and the walk to the showers involved trudging 500 metres or so, through the mud. I was still concerned about the security but the Cheshires were so insistent that I figured I was displaying the paranoia of the new boy. Eventually, we decided to recommend that we kept the house and Roy and I agreed to share the kitchen. The other houses were much the same, with the captain's being the best of the lot. The subbies were living four or five to a room in the usual squalor that only young officers and chimpanzees seem able to create. As there was no room within the main perimeter for the extra officers it looked like we'd be forced into carrying on with the same system. It was a messy arrangement with the potential pitfall of having most of the officers asleep outside the camp, unable to get in during some emergency. This seemed odd but then there was no threat and the UN was, after all, impartial. We were going to be safe as houses living there, or so we thought.

The S/NCO's lived under similar arrangements except that their houses were inside the perimeter. Their mess was also a converted disco and somewhat larger than ours. The soldiers had use of the junior ranks club, yet another converted disco. The JRC was large and provided bar, snack, pool-table and television for well over a hundred soldiers. Part of the building housed the local bakery and this was, itself, part of the camp perimeter.

Also inside the wire was another house still occupied by locals who'd refused to move out and rent the place to the UN. The lure of cash had, however, tempted many other families. Some had gone to stay with relatives but others continued to live in the area in the most bizarre circumstances. The owners of the subaltern's house moved into a shed in the garden, where they lived, with their numerous children. The captain's house still had a family living in the garage and I was initially amazed at the lengths that some people would go to for money. The more I thought about it, however, it made sense if the cash enabled them to buy goods that would normally be beyond their pocket. In a country with little work and appalling wages, maybe they were the lucky ones.

We then toured the soldier's accommodation. The Portakabins were tiny and contained two sets of bunk-beds, two lockers and very little else. The boys told us they were infinitely better than the tents and were easy to keep warm. Providing everyone got along together there were few problems. There were four rows of about twenty Portakabins with showers and toilet blocks dotted around the place. The walkways were paved by duckboards laid in the mud and had been given names by the soldiers such as Coronation Street and Albert Square. Their rooms were cosy, secure, close to the facilities and the boys seemed happy with their lot.

Their one complaint was that because they didn't know what to expect when they deployed, few had brought any home comforts. Everyone we spoke to wished he'd packed a duvet and indeed most spent the tour festering in their issue sleeping-bags. Every room we entered had a lingering odour of damp doss-bag.

The dining room was another, much larger, Portakabin. All ranks ate together with a small partition to separate the officers and S/NCOs from the men. The food was absolutely excellent and all the more superb because it was cooked in the most rudimentary conditions. Dotted around the camp were hardened shelters in case of artillery or air attack. These were ISO containers covered in earth and rocks and surrounded with similarly-filled wire gabions. They were proof against a direct hit from a 155 mm shell but it seemed highly unlikely we would ever need them. At the start of the Cheshire's tour in November 1992 the majority of the boys were accommodated in the tented city. This was still present although, as more Portakabins arrived, fewer and fewer soldiers lived there. The rows were, again, paved with duckboards and many tents were flooded to a depth of several centimetres. It must have been hell spending weeks on end in what was basically a muddy field. My admiration for their achievements increased further.

Most of the remaining open ground was taken up with parking space for well over a hundred vehicles. The tank park was home to the Warriors, Scimitar Light Tanks and other tracked vehicles. The ground had been pulverized over the months and was ankle deep in fine mud that penetrated every little fissure of my boots. I was still cleaning it out weeks after the recce.

The outside area was a hive of activity with armoured vehicles, UNHCR Land Rovers, ICRC, ECMM and press vehicles all coming and going. Soldiers slopped through the mud, as their grandfathers had done on the Somme. Meanwhile other brave souls ran, or to be more precise, slithered, around the short perimeter track in a bid to keep fit. Finally, the locals using the route through camp, some pushing prams, added to the air of a gigantic circus. I was reminded of some of the shots of Saigon I'd seen and hoped this wasn't going to be Britain's very own Vietnam.

The school itself had marble floors and downstairs was the ops room, the nerve centre of the battalion. Here, communications were maintained with the troops on the ground, the other company locations, UNPROFOR HQ in Kiseljak, the brigade HQ in Split and the UNHCR. There were also normal telephones and the local commanders knew the numbers should they need to arrange a meeting with one of the LOs. The ops room was brightly lit, but windowless, with the ceiling shored-up by wooden posts. Next door was the Military Information Cell. Milinfo was a euphemism for intelligence and, indeed, was based upon the Regimental Intelligence Cell. The change of name was due to the fact that, as we weren't supposed to be fighting anyone, there was, supposedly, no need to collect Intelligence. Either way, that's exactly what Milinfo did and they had a mass of details on the three sides, their weapons, equipment and leaders.

There was also some accommodation downstairs in the school and soldiers were crammed into the former classrooms in preference to the tents. Upstairs was more accommodation and the offices of the battalion staff. Every available space in the school appeared to be utilized and the whole camp was a seething mass of humanity. As we strolled back to the mess we encountered a small gang of kids, the oldest about ten.

'*Bon bon! Bon bon!*' they cried, pointing to their mouths in a parody of hunger. I was all for barging past, they couldn't possibly be starving this close to camp. However, Roy was full of the milk of human kindness.

'I'm terribly sorry boys, I don't have any sweets but I'll bring you some later.'

The kids didn't have a clue what he'd said but figured it was 'No!'

'Fuck off! Cheesy bell end!'

That's what you get after four months of rubbing shoulders with the descendants of Shakespeare and Wordsworth!

Early that evening, we were driven down the road to Vitez Garage. This location was, as its name implied, a requisitioned garage and the sign outside still identified its former allegiance to Renault. The QM's department, for clothing and equipment, and the TQM's, dealing with weapons and spares, were situated there. I caught a fleeting glimpse of Byron Cawkwell and Dave Thompson who'd be running these for us. My fitter section would work out of here and, judging by the amount of Warriors standing in various stages of repair, would be kept busy.

On the way back to the school, we were briefed on the bulk fuel installation. The BFI held thousands of gallons of diesel in several massive tanks. It was surrounded with wire and sentries stood guard and patrolled the lines of hundreds of stacked petrol jerrycans. Fuel was a scarce commodity and there'd been several small thefts from the compound.

Back in the CO's house, Roy and I reflected that the Cheshires may appear to be a little mad but they were doing a superb job in the most difficult circumstances. When they arrived, there'd been nothing but a disused school in the middle of a field, in the middle of a war. Now, there was a well-oiled machine that was assisting with the distribution of aid and mediating in local disputes. It seemed that they would be a hard act to follow.

That night in the mess was a repeat of the first with more outlandish quantities of beer consumed. Phil offered to take us around the area the next day and we were grateful for the excuse to have a moderately early evening.

Next morning, we drove a round-robin of the tactical area of operations. The GV and Tuzla sub-units had their own TAORs within the general battalion area. The Vitez area started from the front line with the Serbs at Turbe in the west. It followed the Lasva Valley east until it joined the Bosna River and then on to the front line with the Serbs a few kilometres further east. In the north, there was one main road which passed through Zenica and on to Maglaj where the front line again started. Finally, in the south, the TAOR stretched until it met that of the GV Company some thirty km from Vitez.

The area was vast, covering several thousand square kilometres. It was clearly impossible to fully patrol it and Phil admitted there were many places where the UN had never been. The countryside was hilly, with deep valleys and few good roads. Luckily, the task was made easier as there was relative peace, enabling a comparatively free passage of aid. There were few contacts with the Serbs and the general situation appeared to be fairly simple. When I ventured this opinion, Phil was a little sceptical and suggested I reserve my judgement until I'd visited Busovaca in the afternoon.

Our first port of call was Travnik, some eight kilometres to the west. The view on entering the town was breathtaking, with the place being located in a steep-sided valley. A huge Crusader castle dominated the skyline and several minarets pointed to the heavens. I immediately assumed the town to be Muslim. However, the proportion was about 60 per cent of Muslims with the remainder being mostly Croat. Unfortunately, the initial beauty of the town soon gave way to the normal dreary concrete apartment blocks. The centre was a mish-mash of faded, early twentieth century, architecture and Tito's finest concrete flats. There were several unfinished buildings and the rusting cranes of abandoned building sites competed with the minarets for skyline space.

The town was only a few kilometres from the front line and at one stage had looked likely to fall to the Serbs. There'd been heavy shelling and several buildings bore the pockmarks of shrapnel. However, the streets were busy and people were going about their normal business. We passed through several checkpoints and I noticed two flags at some of them. The red-and-white check of the HVO hung alongside the blue-and-white fleur-de-lys of the BiH. This was the strongest symbol of cooperation between the two factions I'd yet seen, a stark contrast to the surly troops at the Novi Travnik T-junction.

Several kids surrounded the Land Rover. I had half a packet of Polo Mints in my pocket and beckoned to a little blond urchin to take it. In an instant, he was upon me and snatched it with the practised eye of an Artful Dodger. He sprinted off, pursued by a baying mob of children. The kids looked just like any other little Europeans and it was no wonder that the images of their suffering had so touched the public conscience.

The road to Turbe was under sporadic shell fire so Phil decided to head east, a decision that I heartily applauded.

Our next port of call was Vitez. After a five-minute drive around I was sure that this was possibly the ugliest town I'd ever seen. There was nothing old or stylish about the place and it was like Milton Keynes without the concrete cows. Row upon row of dreary, drab, apartment blocks lined the streets and I rather shabbily thought that a good war could only improve the place.

Just to the east of town was the Dutch Transport Battalion at a village called Santici. Their role was to assist in the carriage of aid and their base was grouped around a factory complex. The road followed the Lasva valley until the river flowed into the larger Bosna River. Here, there was a massive bridge known as the Zenica flyover and the road forked left for Zenica and right for Sarajevo. Zenica straddled the Bosna River and was as architecturally pleasing as any other Communist-built city. The usual apartment blocks dominated the skyline together with a massive steelworks. The local BiH Corps had its HQ in the city and Phil told us the Commander was a man named Enver something-or-other.

After a quick look at the UNHCR depot, which looked as interesting as any other warehouse, we headed back towards Vitez. A couple of kilometres past the Zenica flyover we turned left at a place called the Busovaca T-junction. I began to see that imagination had not been a great consideration when the Cheshires had named the various reference points around the patch.

Busovaca was a drab town not unlike Vitez with another Dutch UN base in a hotel in the centre. As we headed south the evidence of recent fighting became more widespread. Phil told us the local leader was a man called Dario Kordic. He was the President of the HDZ, the Bosnian Croat political party and, as such, influenced the actions of the HVO. This sounded like the relationship between Sinn Fein and the IRA except Kordic made Gerry Adams look pleasant. He'd been a lawyer before the war and, with his bottle-bottom specs, apparently looked like Joe 90. Kordic had whipped up opinion against the Muslims, resulting in a bout of ethnic cleansing. He sounded like a nasty piece of work, and this opinion was further reinforced when I actually met the man.

The valley was now divided into small pockets of one ethnic group or the other with an uneasy state of peace existing between them. Phil described it as a powder keg waiting to blow and one spark would spread the conflict throughout our area. It looked like it might be an interesting tour after all.

We stopped for lunch at the UN Bosnia-Herzegovina Command HQ in Kiseljak. The place was centred on a huge Alpine-style hotel built as accommodation for visitors to the Sarajevo Winter Olympics. Over lunch the interpreter told us she'd been in her last year at medical school when the War started. She now worked for the UN, for about 400 marks a month, and hoped, one day, to finish her studies. There were around a dozen local interpreters working for the Cheshires. Their skill was vital as Serbo-Croat isn't an easy language to learn and few, if any, of the local leaders spoke English. Without interpreters, there would be little or no business done.

That evening we attended Bob Stewart's daily conference, a wash-up of the day's events and a look forward to the next. The Milinfo NCO, Sergeant Connolly, gave an excellent update of the situation in the whole of Bosnia and highlighted the details of the latest Vance-Owen Peace Plan.

Stewart then held court for ten minutes. He was scathing about several people and wasn't afraid to humiliate them in public. It was a bit like going to a Bernard Manning show where the whole audience cringes and waits for their turn to be singled out. Finally, the company commanders, Phil and Martin Thomas, had their say and the conference split up.

Later that evening, I talked to a fellow called Alan Cheshire, the field co-ordinator of FTC. This small charity was trying to distribute aid, independently of the UNHCR, directly to children in inaccessible villages. They occupied the house next door to the CO and enjoyed the special support of the Cheshires, but not always the UNHCR. Tomorrow, they were being escorted to a couple of villages in the hills and we were invited along. It struck me as odd that there appeared to be a kind of snobbery amongst the aid organizations. It seemed to me that as long as an agency didn't endanger lives by its actions, it should be treated as being on the same side. I remarked to Alan that he had a rather fortunate name given the regiment he was working with. Would his replacement be called Yorkshire?

'No, I don't think so. I believe his name's Ryan.'

The next morning, Roy and I walked over to the P Info house for a chat with the staff and were given a brief on their role. The media was still taking an intense interest in the activities of the British Battalion. After the brief we walked down Press Row to the BBC house. Inside, we were met by Martin Bell and his news team. Tall, with curly grey hair, Bell was dressed in his trademark white linen jacket. He seemed to be very lame, the result of a wound earlier in the conflict. He was most friendly and, over a coffee, showed us how the news was filmed and then edited, before being transmitted, via a satellite link, to the UK. He stressed that the decision to screen a piece always rested with the news editor in London and there was never any guarantee of making the programme. All he could do was to put the piece together as skilfully as possible to give it the maximum chance. I began to appreciate just how short the time could be between an event happening and it actually appearing on the news. After half an hour or so I left to get ready for the afternoon's journey.

We left at midday in a convoy of four Land Rovers, a four-ton truck and two FTC vehicles. Matthew Dundas-Whatley, one of the LOs, was in charge. The journey took us to the flyover, where we turned left and along the main road past Zenica. As we drove north the weather became worse and snow started to fall. We followed the course of the Bosna River towards our first destination, the town of Zepce. This was right in the north of the Cheshires' area and it was only a few more kilometres further on to the front line at Maglaj.

Our first stop was the local BiH brigade HQ. Here we were shown into the commander's office and seated round a large table. The main man came in and Matthew introduced us. Coffee was brought in, a murky brown liquid in tiny cups. I didn't usually drink coffee so I shovelled sugar in to mask the taste. The stuff was thick and bitty with a centimetre of sludgy sediment in the bottom. I also noticed that everyone was smoking. Even Roy, who didn't usually smoke, had produced a packet of cigars. Puffing away, he soon added his contribution to the rapidly developing fug. I'd stopped some twelve years before and could see that if I didn't start again on the tour I'd probably die of secondary smoking anyway.

Matthew was explaining the purpose of our visit and I had a chance to sit back and notice his technique with the interpreter. He didn't look at her at all but kept his gaze firmly fixed upon the brigade commander. He talked away in short sound-bites, roughly corresponding to a sentence. The interpreter then translated, emphasizing words in the same way that Matthew had done. The replies were spoken to the interpreter who then relayed them, in English, to Matthew. Svetlana was a girl of about twenty with long blonde hair who seemed to be very good at her job. Occasionally she would stop Matthew and ask for clarification on a point before continuing.

I realized this was a skill in itself and any discussion was going to take at least twice as long as usual. The one obvious advantage was that the speakers had longer to think of a reply or to anticipate the next question. After ninety minutes of this, my first introduction to the Bosnian pace of life, the meeting closed.

Leaving Zepce, we headed south again before turning up a narrow track that ended a few miles later in the almost unpronounceable village of Zeljezno Polje. The convoy halted in the village square and the FTC aid was taken into a store. We had yet more coffee with the local commander, a ferret-faced man of about twenty-five, who chain-smoked Marlboros. Once again, I endured the coffee and the smoke as he explained that his village was about five kilometres from the Serbs. The BSA had pushed as far as it could and had gone firm for the winter. The advance had been carried out by Serbs from another area but now the line was garrisoned by locals who had no interest in further attacks. Thus there existed a state of truce with only the occasional sniping and shelling to remind people there was a war on. This concept of bussing soldiers away from their local area to fight was a new one to me. It made sense, given the previous harmony in which all the groups had lived, and all three ethnic groups employed this tactic.

It was not long before some delicious little sticky cakes were brought in. It seemed a strange way to conduct business where you took aid to a village and then ate all their food. However, I soon realized this was the Bosnian way of life and hospitality was second nature to them.

We bade farewell to the Cheshires the next morning and set off back to Split via a different route. We drove to the Zenica flyover and then turned south following the course of the Bosna River. This, in effect, took us down the right hand side of the non-Serb area of Bosnia and past the historic town of Mostar.

Back at Divulje, there was an immediate air of hostility as we entered the officers' mess. Clearly, the regulars, in their cushy little hole, resented the intrusion of us rough boys from up-country. This seems to be the attitude of many base-rats towards anyone who actually gets his hands dirty and I'd seen a similar attitude in Northern Ireland.

During the flight back I had time to collect my thoughts about the recce. We'd been very well looked after by the Cheshires and had seen a lot. They were all very tired and had begun to take sides with the Muslims, probably due to the natural British concern for the underdog. I wondered if this would affect their dealings with the other factions and thought it would be interesting to see how things developed. There was clearly an immense amount of tension in the Lasva Valley and it was only a matter of time before the pot over-boiled. We were likely to have a busy tour under the constant scrutiny of the world's media. The tension and potential danger made me more sure than ever that our final weeks of training were vital if we were to be effective right from day one. My abiding memory of the recce was just how strange the War was. The situation around the camp was surreal with the Cheshires just accepting the sporadic shooting as no reason to spoil a good pint. We had a lot to learn. They took it all in their stride while we were truly innocents abroad.

Chapter 3
Please Don't Let Him Die!

Right from the moment we returned from Bosnia in early March 1993 the pace of life hotted up. With less than two months to go before the advance party deployed, there was still an awful lot to do. The priority was to pass on the details from the recce so the soldiers would have some idea of what to expect.

I made up two large photo boards with suitable captions. These went on the wall in the corridor outside my office where small groups of soldiers soon congregated around them. In fact, the boards were so popular that someone nicked them a few weeks later.

The next major event was the arrival of the Chobham armour. It is, without doubt, the best armour in the world and is still top secret. In fact, you'll probably be killed for just reading the word Chobham. The exact composition is the secret bit as other Armies have similar, but slightly inferior, armour.

The fitting involved drilling holes in the armour of the Warrior and literally bolting the Chobham on. There were several plates, each individually numbered, and they fitted together like a giant Airfix kit. The Chobham itself was hidden inside a box of thin steel called the cosmetic plates. The whole thing stood out about half a metre on each side of the Warrior. Because the boxes could be knocked off if the vehicle scraped an obstacle, there were small, angled, deflector plates at the front and back. These were to become a complete pain in the arse and were, themselves, always falling off. We knew we'd have to carry out a lot of driver training as the Warrior was now wider and an extra three tons heavier. This was planned for our specialist training package a couple of weeks later. The battalion received around a hundred reinforcements to bring us up to full wartime establishment. Three complete platoons arrived, one each from the Argylls, the Gordons and the QLR. I received around thirty Gordons.

The Argylls and QLR platoon commanders, Chris McCabe and Paul Davies, were employed as watchkeepers in the ops room and the senior Gordons officer, Angus Hay, as an LO. This left the Gordons platoon commander, Jason Calder, to become my company 2/ic. The Jocks were a tough-looking bunch but were well controlled by their senior NCO, Sergeant Cunningham. Zippy, Jason and I debated whether to split them up but the deciding factor was that none of them had any Warrior experience. In the end, the platoons received about ten men each. A couple of the NCOs had fired the RARDEN and could be used as turret crew but the majority of them would be dismounts in the rifle sections.

As the specialist training approached it was time to sort out my own crew. In 0B, Phil would be the gunner. However, the driver was a major problem, and we examined all the options. It was vital we had one of the best drivers but, above all, one who could think for himself. In the end, we chose Lance-Corporal Graham Chapman. Chappy was one of the attached NCOs drafted in to add experience when the battalion had initially received the Warriors. He was from The King's Own Royal Border Regiment and was a madcap character. He'd run a radio show in Belize and made 'Good Morning Vietnam' look like 'The Archers'. If nothing else, we were going to be kept amused. Perry Whitworth, the signals Officer, came up trumps and sent me Corporal Martin Knight as my signals detachment commander. I'd known Knight for years and thought very highly of him.

The most difficult post to fill was that of close-protection NCO. Both Cheshires company commanders mentioned the need to have a tough-looking soldier close by when dismounted. This enabled the commander to concentrate on negotiation without worrying about his own personal safety. Both used their CSMs and Bob Stewart, his RSM, in this role. However, Zippy was one of the rare breed of sergeant major who'd reached the top without actually looking the part. He understood the problem and freely admitted that, while he could handle himself in a fight, his appearance was unlikely to strike fear into the hearts of stroppy militiamen. We therefore looked around the company and decided on two complete opposites.

Dobby was an obvious choice. He was the biggest man in the

company and certainly looked the part. His moustache would be a great asset as it was, apparently, a status symbol in Bosnia. Dobby was a kind and gentle family man and I hoped he wouldn't be put to the test. Hopefully, his appearance would be enough to discourage would-be troublemakers.

The second NCO we selected was Corporal Alan Donlon. Now he really was hard. He had the same build as Zippy but there the similarities ended. Donlon was one of the Gordons NCOs. Shaven-headed, with several teeth missing, his head was crisscrossed with the scars from countless fights. The archetypal Glaswegian, he had the colourless eyes of a shark and made me nervous just to look at him. Whereas Dobby accepted the job somewhat reluctantly, Donlon jumped at the chance to get out of a platoon. He was relishing the chance to 'brek a few heeds!'

The selection of these two was a major headache and I had reservations about their ability to handle a real crisis. There just wasn't the raw material to choose from. I firmly believe that Yorkshire soldiers are as good as any in the world but, the ones in my company were, essentially, nice guys. The majority were under twenty and had little experience. While they could handle themselves in a pub brawl, they didn't ooze aggression. Instead, they went about their business in the self-effacing, no-nonsense manner of the northerner. I was tempted to sack the idea altogether as the two NCOs mightn't be up to it. Anyway, they'd probably have a quiet tour as we were, after all, only there to escort convoys. How very wrong I was.

There was some mirth from the company at the concept of a CP NCO and we tried to avoid the term bodyguard. Nevertheless, Dobby took a lot of stick as he was not exactly a Kevin Costner lookalike. Eventually, after the umpteenth soldier asked him, 'Oy Dobby! Where's Whitney?' he resorted to violence. The ribbing stopped!

In Jason's vehicle was Private 'Daz' Erwin as the driver and Lance-Corporal Ricky Holtom as signaller. Holtom was as qualified as Knight but younger and less experienced. He'd work with my crew if we needed another signaller. Zippy would also command this vehicle on occasion and there was also the CQMS as an alternate commander. Completing the crews were the spare signallers, Private Nash from the Signal Platoon and Private McCloy, who was our solitary Argyll.

Finally, on the support front, I had Corporal 'Mo' Mowforth running the Warrior stores and Lance-Corporals Dave Latus, 'Watty' Watson and private 'Wally' Waltham assisting Goy. Last, but not least, Lance-Corporal Carl Braithwaite ran the company office and Private Allan drove the ambulance.

The week before we deployed to Sennelager for our specialist training the Warriors were painted white, making them dazzling in the sunlight. The callsigns were also painted on the turret sides and on the left rear stowage bin.

The UN signs were not painted on at this stage as it was supposed to upset the Germans. However, when all the Warriors suddenly turned white, even Jerry may have twigged where we were going. We finally deployed to Sennelager where the training was conducted by a newly-formed team. The first two days were filled with lessons on everything from convoy drills to road safety. The Cheshires hadn't had the benefit of a detailed training package and we, in the end, had little advantage over them. The operations were so unlike anything the Army had done before, no one really knew what to teach us. They therefore played safe and plumped for the UN mandate. Thus, we spent nearly two weeks learning how to escort convoys.

The method of convoy escort was straight out of the manual and bore little relation to reality. Each convoy was supposed to have a UN vehicle between every three trucks or so, as well as a scouting vehicle out in front. Anti-tank and mortar assets were mixed in as well. Roy and I worked out that each company could escort only two convoys at any one time with this method.

The package ended with a dinner in the mess. Brigadier Robin Searby was the main guest; he was to be the new Commander of British Forces in Bosnia, COMBRITFOR. He smoked long cheroots that looked like they'd been borrowed from the prop department of a spaghetti western. The other guest had been in more fights than Clint Eastwood and Lee Van Cleef put together.

The war in Bosnia had attracted all the main television stations and many of the reporters were household names. Few were more famous than Kate Adie, a lady with the habit of being wherever the trouble was. She was very sceptical of the chances for peace. In her hour-long talk, she was full of praise for the British soldiers. She was, however, scathing about every other nation involved except the French. We giggled over stories about the Egyptians stealing the cutlery from UN headquarters because they thought it was silver. The Ukrainians, apparently, were unable to leave camp because they'd sold all their fuel on the black market. Above all, however, she was scathing about the Bosnian people whom she described as lying, cheating and ungrateful. I was prepared to differ on that one, but, in the end, events were to prove her right.

The Sennelager package was of some use but suffered from the lack of a clear aim and a poor connection with what the troops actually did in Bosnia. However, the Army is generally quick to learn and the CO asked us for a list of recommendations on how to improve the training. Many of these were incorporated in subsequent courses. However, if all we did was escort convoys in Bosnia, we were going to be bloody good at it.

The period saw final adjustments on the battalion organization and a confirmation of appointments. At company level I was given a section from the Anti-Tank Platoon, commanded by Sergeant Terry Smith. They would be equipped with three of the ageing FV 432 tracked vehicles. I would also have a section from the Mortar Platoon under Sergeant Nigel White with two more 432s. Finally, I'd have a troop of four Scimitar light tanks from the LD Squadron attached to the battalion.

At battalion level, the LO posts had all been filled, as follows:

UNHCR	Captain Dominic Hancock
G5	Captain Mark Bower and Colour Sergeant Ginner Burton
Tuzla	Captain Andrew Jackson
Zenica	Captain Cameron Kiggel
Travnik	Captain Angus Hay
Busovaca	Captain Boris Cowan
Vitez	Captain Perry Whitworth
Gornji Vakuf	Captain Simon Holden

Other key posts were:

Operations Major	Major David Hill assisted by Sergeant Major Byrne
Watchkeepers	Lieutenants Jane Brothwell, Chris McCabe and Paul Davies
Milinfo	Captain Simon Harrison and Staff Sergeant McLeod
Light Dragoons	Major Marcus Browell

With the whole team assembled and briefed there only remained final gunnery training. But first, three weeks Easter leave.

The return to work in early April 1993 was a definite return to reality. I was due to deploy three weeks later and there was still a hell of a lot to do. We loaded the Warriors onto the rail-flats and boarded the coaches bound for Hohne Ranges in northern Germany.

The training was in earnest, for the next time we fired the weapons could be for real. We were coached by the company gunnery instructors led by Sergeant Geoff Barratt from the King's Regiment. Barratt was a real gunnery enthusiast and a great teacher who knew how to get the best out of us. If you could stand his Brummy accent, he was great company as well. He was the Eight Platoon Warrior Sergeant. With Seven Platoon was Sergeant 'Choo Choo' Huskisson from the QLR. The unusual nickname was a piece of history in itself. One of Huskisson's ancestors had the dubious distinction of being the first man to be killed by a train. He was knocked down by Stephenson's Rocket. The final Warrior sergeant was Corporal Stu Foote.

I hadn't fired for some years but was determined to set a good example on the ranges. I wasn't sure how Phil would shape up and, as we sat in the turret ready for the first shoot, I feared the worst.

Taking off his rather trendy civilian glasses, he donned a pair of black-rimmed, bottle-bottom specs that made him look like an inmate from 'One Flew Over the Cuckoo's Nest'. It was going to be a disaster, why did I have to be lumbered with a blind gunner? The first shoot was the CAB F – a three-round group at 600 metres to check whether the cannon is firing correctly. I gave the fire control order and Phil laid-onto a dot in the centre of the white screen. On my order he fired the first shot, and the practice round sped towards the target, its red tracer content indicating its passage. However, there was so much smoke from the gun that neither of us observed the fall of shot.

There was nothing for it but to take the same point of aim and fire again. This time we both blinked simultaneously and missed this one as well. The final shot was definitely on target but the heat-shimmer from the exhaust partly obscured the view.

Once everyone had fired we all dismounted and walked forwards to inspect the target. I stopped in my tracks a few metres from our screen and stared incredulously. Phil, meanwhile, just stood there and looked smug. There, on our target, were three holes, right in the centre, in an area the size of a saucer. One had passed through the black spot explaining why we couldn't see it. It was superb shooting for a blind geriatric and I knew my fears were totally unfounded.

None of the other crews came near this standard and we taped the target to the side of 0B as a challenge to the boys.

Zippy and I had the chance that day to have a good look at the platoons and assess their various strengths and weaknesses.

Seven Platoon was probably the best. Although the most inexperienced of the platoon commanders, John ran a tight ship. Sergeant Cunningham had fitted in well and the two of them were developing a good rapport. The soldiers were well motivated and their gunnery results were excellent.

Eight Platoon was suffering from not having an officer platoon commander. Cookie was doing a grand job and tried harder than anyone in the company. However, the soldiers were always playing tricks on him. On one occasion they had him jumping up and down on top of the Warrior while one of them pretended to adjust the suspension. How Cookie believed he was going to get thirty tons of Warrior to move I can't imagine.

He never let me down and was always coming up with new ideas, which certainly kept John and Tom on their toes. Nevertheless, I wanted an officer platoon commander. The chances were that he wouldn't do as good a job as Cookie. However, I strongly believed there was no future for the battalion unless there was a regular supply of young officers coming in. The CO promised I would receive one in mid-April. I had a soft spot for old Cookie and didn't just want to put him out to grass so I told the boss I was happy to take him to Bosnia until another job could be found for him.

Nine Platoon was an enigma. The soldiers collectively revelled in their reputation as a wild bunch. New recruits were imbued with this spirit and soon started to act like the old sweats. The platoon had excellent morale and did everything as a total entity, which was fine if they did well. However, they couldn't get their act together and the constant cry was: 'We'll be all right in Bosnia, you'll see'. One day, we'd finished firing and the boys were picking up the empty cases. The Chain Gun sprays fired cases several metres in front of the Warrior and they were lying in the long grass. (They are melted down to make new ones so they have to be picked up.) Phil, Zippy and I were helping the boys with this boring task, being seen to muck in.

Suddenly, there was an outbreak of loud, raucous, laughter from the direction of the Warriors. Zippy and I wandered over and there, in the back of one, was Tom and all his NCOs having a coffee, while their soldiers were grafting. Zippy blew his top and took the NCOs off for a one-sided conversation.

That evening, I took Tom to task. I reminded him there was a great difference between being liked and being respected.

Tom listened intently and agreed with most of what I'd said. He had the courage of his convictions to point out that he was scared to approach me because I was so gruff. Only then did I realize just how hard I'd been driving the company and I resolved to lighten up a bit. I thanked Tom for pointing that out to me and we had a laugh about how even old dogs can learn new tricks. I hated having to talk to Tom like this but it did the trick and a new, dynamic, platoon commander was on the ranges the next day. He had an excellent tour of Bosnia and his platoon produced outstanding results. Even after he gripped his men they still liked him and he was the most popular platoon commander I've ever come across.

The next day was one of the worst of my life.

I'd been summoned, along with the other company commanders, to take lunch with General Sir Charles Guthrie, who was visiting for the day.

I intended to get away as soon as possible and told Phil to be ready to fire again at two o'clock. The general was on good form and was quizzing me about the earlier recce to Bosnia when I was called away. One of my men had been crushed by a Warrior and an air ambulance was on its way.

Twenty minutes later, my Land Rover screeched into the range and I was out and running before the wheels had stopped. I sprinted over to the huddle of men grouped around a figure on a stretcher, just as the rotors were being switched off on the helicopter. As I forced myself through the tight knot of men I saw Phil, his face ashen white, kneeling down, holding the hand of the figure on the stretcher. Looking down I saw, to my horror, it was Chappy. He looked in a terrible way. His coveralls had been pulled off his chest and there were several large grazes running up his body. His breathing was laboured and he was unconscious. I'd feared the worst and expected to see a soldier who'd been mangled by the huge Warrior tracks. Chappy wasn't obviously maimed but I knew enough about internal injuries to know this was serious. I couldn't figure out how the accident had happened and I asked Phil.

Fighting back tears, he told me how Chappy had been working on one of 0B's road wheels in the gap next to an Eight Platoon Warrior. The other vehicle was due on the firing point and the crew jumped in and moved off, without checking the area. Chappy was caught between the two Warriors as he stood up and tried to escape. Apparently he'd been picked up and rolled between the two vehicle sides. The grazes had been caused by the bolt-heads protruding from the Chobham boxes. He'd somehow survived being smeared between sixty tons of metal.

I took his other hand and Phil and I mopped the dirt away from his forehead. There were tears in both our eyes and the boys kept a respectful distance. The female doctor from the helicopter arrived and started to work on Chappy. Suddenly, he opened his eyes. Looking up at me he whispered: 'Please don't let me die, sir!' I instantly had a huge lump in my throat and reassured him that he was going to be OK. It was touching that, in his desperate moment of need, he should turn to me for help. I wasn't a doctor but, for the first time in my life, I prayed, and really meant it.

Turning to the doc, I pleaded with her, 'Please don't let him die!' She dismissed me with a typically Teutonic: 'In Germany ve are not in the habit of letting our patients die!' However, that's exactly what did happen.

Chappy gave a shudder and just stopped breathing. I was still holding his hand and there was a moment of vice-like grip, then nothing. The doctor swept me out of the way and inserted a large tube into his left side. She then pounded on his chest and, just as suddenly, he spluttered and started breathing again. He was only gone for a few seconds but it seemed like an hour.

Having stabilized him, the doc wheeled Chappy to the chopper and he was whisked off to the hospital in Celle.

That evening, I drove to the hospital where I met up with Chappy's wife. Joanne Chapman had just heard she was pregnant and now her husband was on the critical list. As we waited to see the doctor I told her what had happened. Without hesitation, she asked me to tell the Warrior crew she didn't blame them at all. She'd been in the Army herself and knew what the two lads must be going through. She was one very tough lady.

Eventually, the doc arrived and told us that Chappy had a collapsed lung, crushed chest and several broken ribs. He'd been operated on and was in intensive care.

Chappy lay there, connected to various tubes and wires that led to a multitude of drips and monitors but obviously alive. He was kept artificially unconscious to allow the injuries to heal without causing him undue pain. Joanne remarked: 'It's the first time I've ever seen him so quiet.'

That same evening, Private Broomhead, one of the young lads from Eight Platoon, collapsed. He was diagnosed as having a brain tumour and I was back to Celle the next day to see a second unconscious soldier.

The company was at a pretty low ebb on the penultimate day and I saw how affected everyone was at the loss of two men. I wondered how we'd cope in Bosnia if the company started suffering casualties. As I pondered the problem, Tom wandered over. He looked nervous and, after beating about the bush for a couple of minutes, still hadn't told me what the problem was.

'For God's sake Tom, what is it?'

Finally, he admitted that a delegation of soldiers from his platoon had asked to see me. Zippy had just appeared and nearly exploded.

'What! A bloody deputation! I'll give them a bloody deputation to the bloody jail! Who do they think they are, bloody commies?'

I'd never seen him so angry, he was absolutely apoplectic, jumping up and down.

'What exactly is it they want?'

Tom told me his boys were annoyed that I'd bollocked him and wanted to tell me so.

'Right, that's it! They're off to bloody jail!'

Calming Zippy down, I agreed to talk to them.

'Sir, it's not a good idea. Why don't you let me deal with them?'

I told Tom I'd speak to them and selected a patch of grass, in the shade of a tree. The boys would sit on a bank with the sun in their eyes. Zippy stalked off muttering about how soft I was getting.

Tom returned with the deputation. They all looked shifty and uncomfortable and I thought they must have deliberated long and hard before asking to see me. They were sweating profusely and I felt a bit of a heel for sitting them in the sun. I asked Tom to stay and the discussion opened.

I told them it was rather un-British to form a delegation but, now they'd done it, I'd hear what they had to say.

'Why are you always picking on Nine Platoon? And why are you always picking on Mr Crowfoot?'

'The answer to your first question is because Nine Platoon is quite the worst platoon it has ever been my misfortune to serve with. The answer to your second is that Mr Crowfoot will continue to get it in the neck from me until you stop dropping him in the shit.'

My answer completely stunned them so I continued by listing around a dozen incidents where the platoon had failed to come up to standard. The boys hadn't expected so many home truths and a couple looked as if they'd rather be anywhere else at that time.

I asked them to come back at me on every point and the recurring theme was: 'Yeah, that's true, but we worked well in Northern Ireland and we'll produce the goods in Bosnia.'

'Are you telling me you can't hit the targets on these ranges but you'll suddenly become better gunners when you go to Bosnia? Are you saying that you can't be bothered to maintain the vehicles properly when we train for Bosnia but it'll be all right when we actually get there?'

As this went on their responses became more disjointed and there was a lot more nodding rather than shaking of heads.

They were miffed because I was always praising the other two platoons, especially Seven. They then tried to give me a list of supposed Seven Platoon misdemeanours that had gone undetected. This was only clouding the issue and they were, collectively, like a child that wants praise but hasn't realized that it has to deserve it first.

Zippy was hovering in the background, just out of earshot, straining to catch what was being said. I summed up by telling them that things would improve for them, and their platoon commander, only if they all put in the work to deserve it. They all agreed the meeting had cleared the air and now we all knew where we stood. The four scuttled away and made a large detour around Zippy. He gave them his best glare then joined me.

We sat and discussed the platoon. The meeting made me resolve to praise Nine Platoon for any little thing in the future. I was also sure the word would get back to the soldiers and the gang of four would ensure things improved. Above all, however, I was glad that Tom had been there. He was now not going to have to carry the burden for any future bollockings. He could make his guys do all sorts of unpopular things and all the blame would fall on me. If that raised the standard of his platoon, it was OK by me.

I realized Nine Platoon did have a special spirit and it had taken guts to have a head-to-head with the company commander. It was also touching to see how much they thought of Tom. Time would tell whether the meeting had been worth it.

The proof was not long in arriving. Nine Platoon was a different organization on the last range days. Their shooting improved and they doubled-around like men possessed. There were still cock-ups but this time Zippy and I ignored most of them. I was at great pains to tell them when they'd done well and I could see this was a new experience for them. The platoon had such a bad reputation that they were scapegoats for any unsolved crime within the battalion. I wondered how long it had been since anyone had taken time to look for their good points. I'd almost fallen into the same trap.

I was now driverless as there was no way Chappy was going to be fit to deploy with us. In fact, it was touch and go whether he'd ever be fit for anything again. Phil and I eventually selected Lance-Corporal Andy Tooke.

Tookey was a somewhat swarthy-looking individual and the boys called him Mario. He'd joined in his mid-twenties and had been a wild man for his first two years. He'd committed all the available crimes and was a squaddie going nowhere until he met his wife. Amanda was the daughter of an RSM and made it her mission to sort out her errant fiancé. Now, with his first tape on his arm, and a Warrior DMI course under his belt, he was on the up.

0B joined on a couple of the platoon battle runs as a spare vehicle and I was pleased to note that Tookey was as good a driver as his predecessor. He didn't quite have Chappy's comedy repertoire but he did have the most outrageous laugh to keep me amused.

The gunnery camp was a great success marred only by the tragic loss of two trained soldiers. The standard of both gunnery and general soldiering had improved dramatically and I was confident that C Company could handle anything thrown at it.

The Warriors were finally loaded onto low-loaders ready for their journey to Emden docks. We still weren't allowed to paint the letters UN on them. The German involvement in the Balkans during the War had made them ultra-sensitive about the region. Anyway, our white Warriors were whisked away to the docks and the Germans, presumably, never guessed where they were heading!

My last few days in Osnabrück were livened up by the arrival of my new platoon commander. Second Lieutenant Stephen Lees was straight out of Sandhurst and arrived with that stunned look that a mullet has when you club it over the head.

I introduced myself to him and chatted away, welcoming him to the battalion. He kept calling me sir, about eight times in every sentence, so I politely told him: 'Please don't call me sir again. If you do, I'll have to hit you!'

'Right, sir. Sorry, sir. Won't happen again, sir. I'm really sorry to have ...'

His apologies were interrupted by a swift dig in the ribs. I could see him thinking: 'Hm, they didn't teach this at Sandhurst.'

I took an immediate liking to Stephen. He was keen and spoke confidently and I was sure he'd do well.

Later that afternoon, I'd gone for a run and a group of us were sitting having afternoon tea in the sun. Stephen emerged from the mess and walked over to us. Spying a track-suited officer he didn't recognize he followed the correct Sandhurst procedure: 'Good afternoon sir, I don't believe we've met.'

He immediately regretted his error as his Company Commander gave him yet another dig!

The news from Bosnia in the last days before we deployed wasn't good. Fresh fighting had erupted between Muslims and Croats around Vitez with the Croats appearing to have the upper hand. The centre of the Muslim part of Vitez was devastated by a huge bomb. The most shocking atrocity, however, was the massacre of nearly a hundred Muslim civilians in the village of Ahmici, close to the Cheshires' base. The pictures on the news were harrowing and Bob Stewart had appeared on the TV several times.

He'd won praise in the popular press for the way he'd harangued the Croat militiamen in the area calling them 'Bloody HVO'. I did wonder how the Croat leadership would react to this and it hardly seemed to advertise the British Battalion as a neutral force. We were clearly in for an interesting tour.

The training was now over, the team was complete and the Battalion was raring to go. After a long weekend with my girlfriend, Dawn, I left for Bosnia on the advance party on the 27 April 1993. The great adventure had begun.

Chapter 4
New Kids on the Block

The advance party consisted of over a hundred of us including the company commanders and LOs.

Alastair Duncan was at Hanover Airport to see us off and he stepped on to our coach to say a few words of encouragement. He would be flying out to join us in a few days.

A couple of hours later, we were ready to board. The aircraft waited on the pan and the cry came up from the soldiers: 'I'm not flying in that!'

Standing there was an ancient, propeller-driven, Russian-built Ilyushin IL 18. The aircraft was painted in a faded blue and white and had been operated by an East German company.

The aircraft was falling to pieces and several seats were broken. There was also a large crack running around the window and I imagined Roy being sucked out into space like Goldfinger in the Bond movie. It was no wonder Eastern European Airlines had the worst accident record in the world and I hoped I wouldn't become a statistic in next year's Flight Safety magazines.

One good point was that the stewardesses were quite the prettiest I'd ever seen. They were also the surliest and every request was followed by a prominent tut.

Still, at least the officers in the front were fairly well behaved. The boys at the back were being served by the campest air steward in the whole of the western hemisphere. The boys were giving him stick and I hoped his English didn't run to arse bandit and pink-oboe player. Either way he didn't seem to mind and revelled in the attention. He wasn't the only one being attended to. Two of the boys had their shaving mirrors out, looking up one of the stewardess's skirts. It was like going to war with a rugby club.

The aircraft droned on and every part of the old crate seemed to be rattling and vibrating. It was rather soporific and I'd just nodded off when something hit me on the head. Searching around my feet, I located the offending item. A large screw had worked itself loose from the ceiling and landed on me. For some reason I couldn't get back to sleep again.

After two and a half hours of shake, rattle and rolling we landed at Split. Above the terminal door was a balcony with dozens of Cheshires soldiers lining the rails, jeering at us as we passed: 'Welcome to the arse-end of the world! See you in six months!'

We were driven to Divulje Barracks again, where we received several briefings to update us on the situation up country. We were then issued with twenty rounds of ammunition and a flak jacket. These wonderful garments have saved hundreds of soldiers' lives over the years and we'd been told to wear them all the time. The latest model came with a separate camouflage cover that could be removed for washing. The one I picked up smelled like it had spent six months at the bottom of a gorilla's cage.

We set off after breakfast in a large convoy of Land Rovers and eight-ton trucks and eventually drew into the factory at GV. After bidding our farewells to Binnsy and the B Company lads we set off once more. As darkness fell, there was sporadic shooting close by and the occasional burning house illuminated the valleys. There was an air of tension both inside the Rover and outside at the checkpoints we passed. The whole area seemed ready to blow at any time. Finally, after eleven hours on the road, we reached Vitez school.

We threw our gear into a transit Portakabin and headed off to the mess. The Cheshires were even more tired than when I'd last seen them and the events of the last few days had taken their toll. One of the captains told me about the scenes in Ahmici and how most of those killed were old people, women and children. As he described how he'd discovered the charred remains of four children, he drew deeply on a locally-made cigarette.

It was easy to be glib as a fresh outsider, but many of them seemed so involved with the problem they were actually part of it. Their hatred of the Croats was vehement and some favoured arming the Muslims. I wondered if there were any good Croats at all. Again, I doubted whether we'd get like this and they simply appeared to be following the lead of their CO. One thing was certain, they were sure glad to see us.

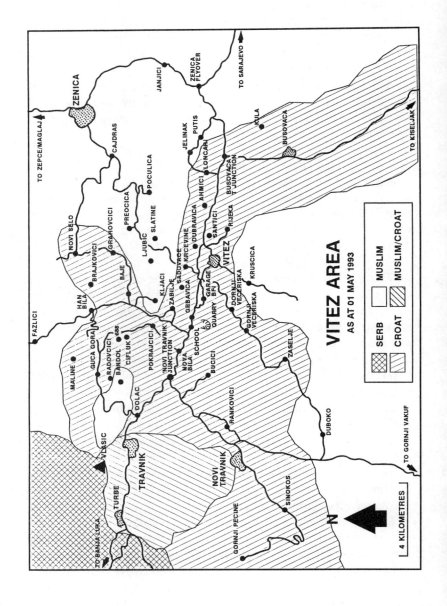

There was little to do on the first day so I moved my kit over to the major's house. Again, I thought how strange it seemed to have the majors so isolated and out of contact with the rest of the camp. Byron Cawkwell told us there was no room for all the officers in the main camp and we'd only be moved if the threat increased. Some comfort. The house was now festooned with small UN flags and stickers and the threat had, quite clearly, increased since we were last here.

The kitchen was still occupied. Phil Jennings's kit was there and he hadn't yet returned from Tuzla. Alan Abraham, the outgoing squadron leader, was lying in his sleeping-bag, nursing a cold. The room smelled of vapour-rub and I was glad when Roy strode in and dumped his stuff on the other bed. I found a bed upstairs in a room with a couple of the Cheshires. They too, had spent the last six months with only an army sleeping-bag. One of these had split and there were feathers everywhere. Either that, or one of them had a chicken fetish.

Roy and I wandered over to P Info where Martin Bell shuffled in and invited us over to the BBC house. There, we chatted with Robert Fox, of the *Daily Telegraph*. A skinny fellow with glasses, Fox was a respected journalist who'd covered the Falklands and Gulf Wars. He reported for one of the most pro-military papers. Also there was Mark Laity of BBC Radio. Laity was a jolly fellow who looked as if any exercise would probably kill him. I quizzed him about how hard it must be to portray the horror of the War without the advantage of pictures. He disappeared away into a back room and returned with a large, old-fashioned, tape recorder. Setting it on the table, he played back a piece he'd submitted for BBC Radio Four.

He'd accompanied a patrol, in the back of a Warrior, and there'd been some trouble. The quality was excellent and the sounds of the gunshots may as well have been in the room with us. He described the scene both outside and inside the Warrior. The soldiers were asked for their thoughts and their tension came across clearly. A further burst of gunfire rang out from the machine and I involuntarily ducked. The clarity was amazing. The atmosphere in that Warrior almost oozed from the box and Laity's skill brought the moment alive. Because I was robbed of the power of sight, all my senses concentrated on the sounds coming from the player and my imagination filled in the gaps. I knew exactly what it must've been like in that Warrior. Laity was, indeed, a master of his craft. Bell looked absolutely shattered and sank wearily onto the sofa. He told us the Muslims wouldn't tolerate the Ahmici massacre and there was sure to be further fighting. He described the scene inside the charnel houses with the same, faraway, stare as the Cheshires' Captain.

At five o'clock we attended Bob Stewart's conference. As usual, he held court and the primary source of discussion was the release of someone called Mackenzie. Apparently, the plan was to free him and transport him to Split.

That night I went out on my first patrol. One of the LOs was visiting the joint checkpoint to check on reports of tension in the town. We left, after dark, in two Warriors. I acted as gunner with the LO in the commander's seat. The regular crew looked extremely hacked off at having two officers in the turret. The captain fumbled his way up the glacis plate and into the hatch, clearly not familiar with the beast. I made a show of carrying out all the turret, firing-circuit and gun checks and one of the lads said: 'Bugger me, sir. That's the first time I've ever seen an officer do all them checks!'

Hopefully, I'd restored a modicum of faith in the Officer Corps. The LO, meanwhile, was trying to put his helmet on, digging me in the ribs as he thrashed around in the confines of the turret. Eventually, he realized he hadn't detailed anyone to walk in front of the Warrior to keep the speed down until we were out of camp.

'Get out and do it for me!' he snapped.

I was about to tell him to poke off, but bit my tongue and dismounted, muttering to myself.

I walked the vehicle past the front gate to the mess and halted it outside. As I clambered up again, I noted, with satisfaction, that he had his helmet on at an angle and I hoped it was uncomfortable. We set off and sped towards Travnik. Two miles from the town, at a place called Dolac, we halted at a checkpoint manned by both BiH and HVO police. They surrounded the vehicle and the LO barked over the intercom, 'Svetlana out!' He dismounted and joined the interpreter who'd emerged from the rear of the Warrior. They chatted with the police for ten minutes or so and he gave them what looked like a packet of Marlboro. Clearly, he'd succeeded as the barrier was moved aside. He clambered back up again and tripped over one of the bolts on the engine louvres. As he sprawled over the front decks I heard the driver chuckling and I couldn't resist joining in.

I asked the LO about the cigarettes and was told it was a way of showing friendship to the locals as tobacco was scarce and very expensive. Each LO was given a monthly allowance to buy small gifts for the locals.

Travnik was quiet, and very dark. The power supply was intermittent and people were ordered to minimize on usage. We reached another joint checkpoint and he again ordered: 'Svetlana out!' I wondered if he'd ever heard of the word please. The two of them walked over to another group of police and began chatting. I noticed there was a second group of men standing a few metres away from them, staring with an air of open hostility. The LO totally ignored this group and the meeting ended with another packet of cigarettes changing hands.

Aided by the moonlight, he was considerably more agile and successfully negotiated the ascent up to the turret. He then ruined the image by attempting to put his helmet on back-to-front. I asked him about the second group and he spat out the word: 'HOS.' Even I knew he wasn't referring to Ben Cartwright's sidekick, as not one of them was wearing an outrageous ten-gallon hat. This organization was the political police wing of the HVO and were so right-wing they probably considered Hitler a pinko commie. They'd taken over from the regular HVO military police earlier that day and had been openly hostile to the BiH men. This was a bad development and was likely to lead to trouble. He was scornful of the Croats and reckoned them to be the cause of all the trouble in the area. The HOS was suspected of involvement in the Ahmici massacre. There was no middle ground with him and he was totally pro-Muslim. I knew we were supposed to be impartial but it did seem the Croats were the instigators. With typical British support for the underdog, I began to agree with him.

The journey back was uneventful and I wandered back to the house at around midnight. I was surprised to see two armed men standing outside who asked me something that I guessed was a request for cigarettes. I wished I had one of the LO's packets but they seemed amiable enough when I indicated I didn't smoke. I figured they must be guarding their own homes and didn't seem much of a threat to us. As I lay in bed, there were a few bursts of small-arms fire about a couple of hundred metres away. I jumped the first time and felt for my rifle beside the bed. The two Cheshires didn't stir and I soon dozed off as well. Funny how quickly you get used to it.

Next morning, I joined Mike Dooley, a Royal Signals subaltern on attachment, for a convoy escort. Martin Thomas was the overall commander and he explained that we would escort the vehicles through areas of potential Croat interference as far as the UNHCR depot in Zenica.

On the way back from Zenica I was shown an alternative to the long route via the flyover. The mountain road wound its way through the hills, south west, through a series of villages until it emerged near Vitez.

Mike took me for a look at the village of Ahmici. As we drove in I noticed nearly all the houses had been burned out. The roofs had collapsed inwards and the glass in the windows had shattered with intense heat. Their gaping windows were blackened with soot from the fires. In some buildings, the heat had been so intense they were burned to the ground. There can have been little left of anyone caught in any of them.

The most striking image, however, was of the mosque. The Croats had blown up the minaret and it lay across the main building of the mosque. With its shiny, pointed top virtually undamaged, it looked as if a Scud missile had crash-landed on the place. There'd clearly been a concerted effort to destroy the mosque and it was the Croat way of saying to any survivors: 'There is nothing here for you now.'

The burned buildings had numerous bullet holes around the windows and doors. It was easy to imagine the helpless occupants being dragged out and shot, before being thrown into the conflagration. It was no wonder the Cheshires were so pro-Muslim when they'd witnessed the consequences of such barbarity. There had been other witnesses, however. Dotted around the village were several Croat houses. These were totally untouched and some were sandwiched between two gutted shells. The people were working in their gardens or hanging washing out seemingly without a care for the fate of their neighbours. It was only then that I began to realize the level of hatred between the sides.

Back in camp, we again attended Colonel Stewart's nightly conference. As usual, Sergeant Connolly stood up to give his brief: 'Right sir, if I may begin with the picture of the north in the Posavina Corridor ...'

'Sit down! We'll go straight on to the company commanders.'

'Well sir. We always start with the Milinfo picture and we do have our guests from the PWO here.'

'Bloody well sit down!'

'But sir. We have the new PWO Milinfo rep here and he's due to give his first brief tomorrow. It's important that he sees how it's done. Now if I may turn to events in the north ...'

At this stage the unbelievable happened. Stewart lurched to his feet, pulled his pistol from its holster and pointed it directly at Connolly. I could clearly see the magazine on the weapon indicating that it was loaded. More to the point, so could Connolly. He blanched and started to shuffle nervously from foot to foot.

'I said bloody sit down!'

Funnily enough, Connolly did.

I felt sorry for the NCO as he was trying to do his job in a professional manner, setting a good example to the new unit.

As the conference progressed there were further references to Mackenzie and I eventually sussed out that he was a bear. Apparently, he'd belonged to a local restaurant owner who kept him in a cage in the garden. The fellow had fled the area and the Cheshires had renamed the bear after the first commander of the UN in Bosnia. They'd been feeding the animal and were mounting an operation to move it down to a zoo in Split. A charity called Libearty were providing a special cage for the journey. Every opportunity was used to gain maximum media coverage and most of the discussion centred around how to involve as many reporters as possible. The great Bear Removal Exercise was scheduled for the next week to coincide with a visit from the *Soldier Magazine* team.

Next day, 1 May, I acted as the gunner of a Warrior in a patrol led by Bob Stewart. The Colonel spied me as he walked towards his Warrior, or Juliet as he called it.

'Hey you! Are you a qualified gunner? And if not, what the hell are you doing in one of my Warriors?'

I was a little taken aback by this friendly greeting aimed at an officer from the new regiment but, by this time, we'd all had enough of this treatment.

'Yes sir! I bloody well am, and would you care to challenge me to a few timed drills on the gun stand?'

There was a pregnant pause and I thought: 'Whoops! Overstepped the mark there.' Instead, his face split into a huge grin.

'Good for you! I'll maybe take you up on it later.'

He was still grinning as he walked off and I didn't have a run-in with him again. He never did take me up on the offer of a competition. We trundled off towards the Zenica flyover and turned off to the left some three kilometres short of it, through the village of Putis, to a hamlet called Jelinak. On the way, we crossed over a tiny bridge. It swayed and creaked under our weight and one of the Cheshires told me it was only a class three-ton structure. This was typical of the positive attitude of the regiment. They were prepared to take the risk of overloading the bridge by 27 tons in order to complete a task.

The village had been devastated and several of the houses torched. Even from the height of the turret I could see hundreds of empty cases littering the ground. We slowly negotiated the narrow track and I saw Stewart had already dismounted and was being led by a group of militiamen to a charred house. As we passed there was a repulsive stench of rotten meat that could only have come from a dead cow, or something similar. We parked at the top of the lane and I noticed several BiH soldiers occupying the surrounding buildings. A couple of vehicles arrived, both painted white and with the word 'Press' prominently displayed. There'd already been more journalists killed in Bosnia than there'd been in Vietnam and nearly all the agencies operated in armoured vehicles. At this stage they were relatively free to travel throughout the Lasva Valley. However, there'd been some threats, especially from the Croats who resented the pro-Muslim media coverage following Ahmici.

Stewart appeared to be giving an interview, surrounded by a mixture of camera crew and British and BiH soldiers. Martin Bell's tall, distinguished figure stood out in the crowd. Feeling a little bored I dismounted, retrieved my rifle from one of the boys in the back, and wandered down a narrow lane. The same smell greeted me and I nervously approached the garage of one building. The flies were everywhere but especially on the carcass of a calf lying on the floor. It was heaving with thousands of shiny, black insects and appeared to be rippling on the surface. My presence must have disturbed them, for they rose, as one, into a swarming black miasma. I noticed that the poor creature had been shot several times before beating a hasty retreat to the door. A few flies pursued me, hopefully not as a potential source of food, and one flew into my mouth. It flew out quickly enough when I gave an enormous retch. Feeling very queasy, I scuttled back to the Warrior. I hoped I was giving my best impression of a UN tough guy and not some bloke who's nearly swallowed a rotting flesh-encrusted insect.

After a suitable pause, I continued to wander around. There was clearly little or no threat. There'd been no shots fired and some of the boys were giving a few rations to the BiH. We were heavily outnumbered but there was at least one man in every turret. The BiH hadn't the will to capture the Warriors, or, indeed, any of us. It was clearly a fine art to judge whether the situation was hostile or not.

Rounding the corner of a building where I'd seen the press earlier, I smelled the same sickly stink of putrefaction and expected to see another cow. That was, until I almost tripped over the bodies.

There were three of them, not that I could tell at first, lying jumbled up in a shallow pit. They'd been hacked to pieces and then burned. The largest body part was a head and torso, lying on its back. Its skin was burned to a crispy black and the empty eye sockets stared at the sun. The lips were burned away, revealing the teeth, and the whole face was set in a ghastly, grinning, rictus. There were also four or five other limbs and a pair of boots. One fellow's legs had obviously been sticking out of the fire and had survived the worst. The boots were undamaged and still contained the owner's feet with the charred shin bones protruding from each one. There were a lot of sludgy cinders and a few other bits and pieces that only a pathologist would've recognized.

The smell was stronger than I'd have thought possible, given the obvious intensity of the blaze, but it did become bearable after a while. I bent down for a closer look, transfixed in a kind of morbid fascination. It was horrific, but only if you used your imagination and thought of the suffering these poor people must've gone through. I'd seen worse in horror films. In fact, the scene was like 'Night of the Living Dead', with odour.

I was surprised at my reaction, especially after the scene in the shed earlier and didn't feel in the least bit nauseous. I kept shutting my eyes and was almost disappointed that I had no after-image of the scene. Some part of my brain seemed to click in as a sort of defence mechanism, probably to safeguard my sanity. I was blessed throughout the tour in that I could witness horrible sights and describe them later in graphic detail. However, when I shut my eyes, there was just a blank.

Roy had also wandered over. He was obviously shocked and remarked that only an animal could do this to a human being. The squaddy sense of humour then surfaced and I asked him if he thought I'd be able to get the feet out of the boots. He fell for it, hook, line and sinker.

'Why?'

'Because I'm sure those boots will fit me!'

After calling me an animal as well, Roy told me he'd listened to the television interview. Apparently the Croats had attacked the village on 14 April and discovered the three men hiding in a cellar. They'd been shot, then mutilated and burned. The wall of the house was peppered with splat holes and there was what looked like dried blood on the floor.

We were clearly there at the invitation of the BiH and the bodies had obviously been left there for us to see. The whole thing smacked of cynical manipulation at all levels. The bodies could've been buried long ago but were an essential ingredient of the circus. The press got their story, the BiH got sympathetic coverage in the world's news and the British Battalion received yet more publicity.

More vehicles turned up in the form of two French armoured cars and an armoured saloon car. It was no coincidence that General Morrillon, the UN Commander, was passing by. He joined the circus, providing even more weight to the media coverage. Everyone had a field day and it was no wonder the world appeared to be solidly behind the BiH. It was skilful use of the media and, by the afternoon, there must have been more than fifty people milling around.

I soon tired of the circus and sauntered back to the Warrior. One of the boys handed me a piping hot can of chicken curry from the army compo rations. Sitting on top of the turret I devoured the stringy meat, washed down with a can of Coke. I was pleasantly surprised that I could wolf down food so soon after seeing such horror. In fact I was still feeling pleased with myself as I attempted to tidy up by forcing the drink can inside the meat can. The inevitable happened and I was suddenly covered in a fine spray of curry juice. This was more disgusting than anything I'd witnessed and I smelled like the dustbins outside an Indian takeaway.

Back in the mess, I met Morrillon. He was very tall with spectacles and close-cropped, iron-grey hair. I noticed he had a withered finger, which stuck out at an odd angle. The general looked every inch the Gallic warrior and seemed a good man to have on your side in a crisis. He spoke English with an outrageous French accent that could've been straight from a Monty Python film. Instead of telling me that my father was a hamster and my mother smelled of elderberries he chatted about the difficulties facing the UN in the coming summer. The tradition in the region was to fight in the summer months and consolidate in the winter. He was sure there was going to be a fresh outbreak of serious fighting in the near future. How right he was.

In the evening, Roy and I walked down to a barbecue at the BBC house. Despite the clear skies, there was a definite chill in the evening air. The meat was a whole lamb roasted over a large fire. The lamb looked identical to the bodies in the ditch and when I mentioned it to Roy I could see he was having the same thoughts. Nevertheless, I tucked into the tough, greasy meat while my friend, for some reason, ate a plate of salad.

I chatted to the various people there and spent several minutes discussing the War with Mark Laity. As we were talking, a heavy machine gun opened up about 600 metres away. The rounds were coming from Croat positions and heading for a Muslim village. In the twilight the green tracers looked almost pretty as they delivered their message of death. All conversation stopped as we watched when suddenly there was more firing from some houses only a hundred metres or so from us. I instinctively reached for my rifle as Laity reached for another beer. With an 'If you can't beat 'em, join 'em!' I followed suit. The cameraman set up his equipment to film the firing, but was so pissed that I doubt if he captured much usable footage. He gave up as darkness suddenly descended and joined the rest of us in totally ignoring the shooting. Laity again predicted that the powder keg was going to blow any day and I hoped my company was there when it did. I could think of nothing worse than being a spare part in another regiment's war.

A major in the newly-formed Princess of Wales's Royal Regiment introduced himself. James Myles was the new guy in charge of the P Info setup. He'd arrived that afternoon on the latest convoy. At the next conference, our Milinfo guy, Staff Sergeant McLeod, gave his first brief. He had a strong Jock accent but was easily understood. Stewart kept interrupting him: 'Speak up! I can't understand a word you say, with that stupid accent of yours!'

McLeod was, understandably, nervous and this was the last thing he needed.

That evening, one of the Cheshires, very much the worse for drink, let slip that Bob Stewart and the ICRC worker, Claire Podbielski, were very close.

Their friendship was common knowledge throughout the Battalion and it was a measure of the men's loyalty that this was the first I'd heard of it. They'd closed ranks to protect their colonel. Whatever they might think of him, he'd probably saved their regiment. The Cheshires had been due to amalgamate with the Staffords under the latest round of defence cuts. Stewart had relentlessly lobbied for a reprieve and the high media profile of the regiment had kept the issue in the public eye. Eventually, when the government announced an add-back of two battalions the Cheshires was one of those spared.

It had to be a matter of time before the whole story emerged. With so many press in the mess every evening, someone else must have been as indiscreet as the guy I was talking to. I mentioned this and he gleefully remarked: 'You'll see. When he's gone from here and they no longer need him, the press will crucify him!'

How right he was.

The next morning I was on the road again acting as the gunner to a Cheshires subby, Tudor Ellis. The task was Operation SLAVEN, one of the most heartbreaking of the tour.

The Serbs had captured a large town called Banja Luka, to the north west. They advertised for Muslim families to head off for a better life in BiH-held territory. The generous Serbs would provide the bus and arrange safe passage along the route. They would also ensure that Muslim bandits on the front line would not molest them.

People were so desperate to leave the Serb-held areas they accepted further conditions. First, they had to sign over the rights to their house and car. To 'place them in the care of the Bosnian Serb Government so they are well looked after for when you return'. They also paid for a place on the bus and could take only two bags each … 'to allow more space for people on the buses'.

It was, of course, ethnic cleansing on a grand scale with people actually paying for the privilege. Once they'd signed the papers, they had nothing to return to. I don't know whether people actually believed the Serb lies but they were certainly desperate enough to give it a go. The UN, of course, was actually assisting with Serb ethnic cleansing by enabling the people to pass freely through the lines. I reflected that it wasn't quite as simple as that. In reality, it was better that these people reached relative safety rather than be cleansed in the same way as the victims of Ahmici.

Tudor told me the exchange took place in Serb territory. The people were taken off the buses and had to walk to waiting UN transport. Often, the Serbs fired over their heads in a final gesture of humiliation. Our task was to guard the crossing point on the BiH line at Turbe, ready to rush to the assistance of the UN personnel over the lines if necessary. As such, we would see nothing of the exchange and I made a note to try to accompany our first SLAVEN after we'd taken over.

Turbe was some seven kilometres west of Travnik. The place was in ruins and had been very heavily shelled. The only occupants were BiH soldiers who lurked in the ruins, and a few scabby dogs, doing the same. Two Scimitars parked up in the village as a reserve and our two Warriors drove a further kilometre west to the front line. The proper war, which had ground to a standstill here, seemed far removed from the localized trouble around Vitez. There was a very real sniper threat so we closed the hatches and sat observing the area through the sights.

In front of us was the Banja Luka road, littered with TMA 3 anti-tank mines. All the houses were wrecked, not from the fires of eth-nic cleansing but from the ravages of high explosives. Several build-ings had been mangled and clawed by artillery and tank fire and many trees reduced to stumps. Curtains flapped from several shat-tered windows, and doors hung at crazy angles. The people from these houses were just as homeless as the ones arriving on the buses.

The first sign that the operation was on was the arrival of a green VW Golf with a yellow flashing light on the roof. Following it was a Land Rover that I knew belonged to Matthew Dundas-Whatley. The vehicles stopped and two men, in BiH uniform, trotted over to the mines. They then slid them to the side of the road before scamper-ing back to the car.

Both vehicles roared off and silence once more descended. The atmosphere in the closed down Warrior was stifling and I could feel the sweat dripping down my back. Soon, the gorilla's cage smell from my flak vest returned.

After an hour or so, during which time the LOs had negotiated with the Serbs to allow the crossing, eight Cheshires lorries arrived and slowly drove past the mines. A further ninety minutes followed while the people were transferred and then the trucks returned. Craning my neck to look through the rear vision port I could just make out the sad faces of some of the people in the crowded lorries.

After the last had passed there were four, high-velocity shots. They appeared to pass close to us and came from the direction of the

Serb lines. Tudor was very cool and mature and said there was no point firing back as it would only create problems for the LO party over the lines. We were not under any threat so we just sat there. After a while, the LOs returned and the mines were replaced. Ten minutes later, we received the order to return to Vitez.

Two hundred and fifty Muslims were taken to the refugee centre. It was an operation that amply showed the cynical way the Bosnian Serbs manipulated the UN.

Back in Vitez I sought out the other members of the company advance party. Colour Goy had almost finished taking over the stores and was pleased with the assistance he'd received from the Cheshires. I would also take over an office in the school when they departed. Corporal Knight had taken over the signal store that was in a broom cupboard in the school. On closer inspection, the tiny store turned out to have once been a toilet. A large pile of radios obscured the urinal but the lingering odour of Jeyes Fluid was the real giveaway.

Every nook and cranny in the school seemed to have been put to some use. While I was in the store I asked Knight to give me a hair-cut. The stuffy atmosphere in the Warrior earlier and the confines of my helmet had matted my hair. Knight duly ran his clippers over the K-P scalp and I emerged, five minutes later, with a number four crew cut.

The Vance-Owen peace plan had recently been signed and was the talking point in the mess. This laid down how the country would be partitioned and involved the Serbs giving back some territory they'd captured. It remained to be seen whether they would agree to the terms.

Roy and I had started a moustache-growing race. I'd never tried to grow one before and wasn't doing at all well. Roy, on the other hand, had much darker hair and already had a prominent smudge adorning his top lip. My father, who has the most outrageous handlebar moustache, would've recommended rubbing chicken manure onto the offending area.

As I awoke to the insistent buzzing of my alarm clock I suddenly realized I'd been in Bosnia for a week. If the time passed as quickly as this it was going to be a short tour indeed. I accompanied Alex Watts, one of the platoon commanders, back to Ahmici. Our task was to escort an ECMM team who were searching for more bodies. Ahmici was much as before with the odd HVO soldier skulking, keeping an eye on us. The monitors were acting on a tipoff and together we did, indeed, find three more bodies.

The house, in which they were found, was one of those that had burned almost to the ground, which was why they'd not been found on the initial search. Around two metres of wall remained with the inside littered with charred debris and thousands of pieces of the roof tiles. We discovered the remains of an adult and two children. It was impossible to judge the sex or ages of any of them for they'd been all but destroyed by the intense heat. The limbs had disintegrated and the heads and torsos had fused with the tiles and other debris. A monitor accidentally kicked one of the smaller bodies and it was fused to the floor as well. It was only the size that suggested they were children. I prayed they were dead before the fire overcame them but I suspected not as the debris showed they'd been huddled under the stairs. Roy's words came back to me: 'Only an animal would do this.' I knew then that these people were worse than any animal.

I was deeply shocked at seeing the bodies of the children. My own two were six and three and I knew that somewhere there was probably a father, just like me, grieving for his family. I was thankful the bodies were just so unrecognizable. It was hard for my mind to make the link between the things in front of me and living human beings. Nevertheless, I could feel my anger rising and knew how Colonel Stewart had felt when he'd called them 'Bloody HVO!'

Back in camp it was over to the mess for a curry lunch for the Cheshires to say farewell to some local commanders. The majority were BiH but there were a couple of HVO who looked very nervous in the company of the Muslims. They'd brought a team of bodyguards with them and one of them was toting an automatic grenade launcher. He looked like Rambo, with the body of Woody Allen. The locals placed great store on bodyguards as they were a sign of importance. If we were expected to compete with the local warlords I was glad I had Dobson and Donlon.

After lunch, I was back out with Alex, this time to Vitez. A lorry bomb had exploded in the centre of the Muslim area, totally destroying several houses. The remains of the chassis lay in the road where it had been hurled and a large crater marked the actual site of the blast. There was no one about but several BiH flags fluttered defiantly in the breeze. Judging by the number of bunkers, the Muslims were determined to defend their homes. Again, I got the distinct impression that something was about to happen, much as I'd done in Travnik a couple of nights before.

We linked up with an ECMM team and followed them about as they shuttled between several local HQs in the area. They were arranging prisoner exchanges and each meeting took at least an hour. I chatted to one of the 'cricket team' and he gleefully informed me he earned around £200 a day. Goodness knows what Jacques Delors was on if that were the case.

During one of these interminable waits we drove over to see the bear. Mackenzie was pacing up and down his cage. The cage was barely, if you'll excuse the pun, big enough for such a large animal. He stood up and lumbered towards us and we both took an involuntary step back. The bear was more than two metres tall and towered over us. His coat was a wiry brown, rubbed away in places from constant chafing against the bars. Alex told me it was due to be moved tomorrow and the special cage had already arrived. I thought it was a hell of a lot of effort for just one animal. However, it would be great publicity and people always seemed to care more about animals than other people. There's no doubt this was a carefully-orchestrated public relations coup. The Cheshires appeared in several newspapers and publications with the incident supposedly displaying the caring nature of the soldiers. Such was the high regard for the Cheshires that I never read any criticism of the time and energy wasted over this creature.

We finally escorted the monitors back to the Zenica flyover. When we returned, I learned that one of the subbies had been summoned for an interview without coffee with James Myles.

President Clinton had proposed bombing the Serbs to the conference table. A Reuters reporter asked the officer, in the mess, for his views. The subby said that, in his opinion, there was a possibility the Serbs would retaliate by shelling the base at Vitez from their positions on the Vlasic feature. The next day, the *Sun* carried a headline along the lines of: 'Army spokesman says our boys will suffer if Clinton bombs Serbs.' James really laid into the guy and I couldn't help agreeing with him. However, the incident was a clear indication of the dangers of living, and above all socializing, with the media.

That evening, I moved downstairs into the kitchen and spread my kit around the room, much to Roy's chagrin.

The great Bear Rescue day dawned. I accompanied a patrol to

Zenica, to the headquarters of Third BiH Corps. We passed the café and there were around a dozen assorted reporters clustered around the bear. Several soldiers were attempting to entice Mackenzie into the Libearty cage.

The HQ in Zenica was a requisitioned office block. We waited outside and, about half an hour later, four grey-haired, middle-aged men emerged. They all wore the rank of officers in the BiH, a system of yellow bars that was unlike anything I'd seen before. None wore hats and all carried what I can only describe as satchels. The corps commander carried the biggest bag and it looked like the sort of item I used to take to primary school. I soon sussed that the satchel was a sort of status symbol. In the Russian forces, the more important you are, the bigger, and sillier, hat you have. In the BiH the same clearly applied to satchels.

The commanders climbed into the two Warriors and settled down onto the bench seats. They seemed cheerful enough and had obviously done this many times before. This was an important function of the UN as these men could not travel freely now that lines of Croat and Muslim confrontation had been drawn up. By taking them to and from meetings we were at least creating the conditions where dialogue could continue between the sides. It was also a duty that couldn't be taken lightly as the French had found to their cost. Only a few days before, the Bosnian deputy president had been assassinated as he sat in the rear of a French APC.

As we passed the café the bear was still in his cage. The crowd of reporters and hangers-on had dwindled to a handful. Mackenzie was resisting every attempt to coax him into the transport cage. Maybe he wasn't keen on the idea of living in Croatia.

We dropped the commanders off in Travnik, for a meeting with the HVO, and headed back to the school.

I learned that, after several hours, the bear had finally been enticed into the transit cage. He was still in there, now on the back of a lorry in camp, so I popped over to see him.

The lorry stood against a wall, ready to join the next morning's convoy south. I lifted the tarpaulin and was presented with a graphic view of Mackenzie's backside. He steadfastly refused to move, and I couldn't get round the other side. Oh well, life's a bear's arse anyway.

The other new arrival in camp was the Commanding Officer. I bounced into the mess full of the joys of spring and gave him my best cheerful greetings. The Colonel took one look at my hair and his lips immediately formed themselves into 'the look'.

His first words were: 'I don't like your hair cut.'

'I'm sorry, sir. I'll try to grow it quickly!'

Bad mistake! The lips pressed even more tightly together and I wished I'd said something like: 'Terribly sorry, sir. It's that bloody local barber. Rest assured, I won't be going to him again.'

'By the way, I hope you're not trying to grow a moustache. I don't like them, they're un-officer like.'

Somehow, I bit back the retort: 'Well it was good enough for Bill Slim!'

However, the damage was already done and, once again, I'd got off to a bad start.

Eventually I stalked back to the house and met up with Roy on the patio. He was sitting with a short swarthy man who introduced himself as Fered, the owner of our house. His English wasn't up to much but he was clutching a bottle of Ballantyne's whisky. He was OK for me. His two children were sitting on the floor. Dalma, the elder, was a girl of about sixteen, with lush dark hair worn in a bob. She still had a bit of puppy fat but would undoubtedly be a stunner in a couple of years. She spoke pretty good English with an American accent. The boy was about twelve and had more puppy fat than a litter of Jack Russells. Dalmin spoke much less English but seemed to know lots of words like 'rifle' and 'grenade'. His sister told me he spent his time chatting to the soldiers guarding the camp. They'd been born in Dalmatia, hence the silly names. Roy and I told Fered we'd do our best to get along with the locals and this seemed like an excellent start.

The latest convoy arrived from Split bringing another hundred or so members of the battle group. These were mostly members of the LD on their way north to Tuzla. However, the platoon commanders had also arrived.

I was sitting in the mess reading a newspaper when, suddenly, the room went quiet and all eyes were on the CO. The lips pursed again and I turned to see what the latest cause of annoyance was. Thankfully it wasn't me this time.

To my horror I spied the subbies standing in the doorway. Each was sporting the shortest haircuts I'd ever seen. They were only one stage up from bald, but that wasn't all. Each of them wore the most appalling attempts at facial fungus. I'd seen more hair on a lot of women, particularly Bosnian ones. John Reeve's was the worst and was the original 'eyebrow popped down for a drink'. In fact, it was a miracle none of the growths had blown away during the trip up. The subbies didn't notice 'the look' and bounded over like excited puppies. There was only one thing to do at a time like this. Start drinking heavily.

It was about twenty minutes to midnight, and we were well ensconced in a company huddle at the end of the bar. Suddenly, there was a loud explosion and one of the upstairs windows shattered. Moments later, came a second, even closer, bang. The building shook and bits of the ceiling fell off. There was a moment of panic and several people threw themselves under tables. The subbies, on their first night, were about to do the same but I cried: 'Stand still C Company!'

We all stood there, shielding our pints from the falling dust, and surveyed our surroundings. There was no need to flap as no one was hurt. Apart from a fresh covering of dust, the building appeared to have survived. One of the majors was nowhere to be seen. He'd been there when the first explosion occurred but then disappeared. He emerged from the toilets to a chorus of raucous abuse. Amid cries of 'Wimp!' he attempted to explain that it was purely a coincidence he just happened to run out of the room at the moment of the first bang.

A soldier arrived. Breathlessly, he explained that a car had stopped outside the mess and the passenger had thrown two hand grenades at the building. Before the guard could react, the car sped off in the direction of Nova Bila. It was almost certainly a Croat attack and displayed exactly the sort of regard the HVO held for the British Battalion. The subbies giggled about the incident for days and how certain people had not been 'steadfast'. The scene reminded me of 'Carry on up the Khyber' where the officers continue to dine while their camp is under attack.

At breakfast, the talk was of whether the Croats were going to launch an offensive in the area to clear the Muslims from around camp. How would the battalion react to fighting around our own perimeter? The UN rules were fairly clear on this one. We were not allowed to intervene in conflict between soldiers but could do so when civilians were at risk. All we could do was to move the civvies to safety. There was no question of taking sides with one or other of the warring factions. Unfortunately, the HVO didn't believe in our neutrality.

I accompanied a patrol with the subbies to show them some of our

patch. We travelled on a new route, one that was to become extremely familiar over the coming months. After leaving camp, we headed in
the direction of Travnik but turned right a few hundred metres past
the CO's house. The narrow road followed the Bila River valley, peter-
ing out into a dirt-track clinging to the side of a steep, wooded hill. We
halted at an HVO checkpoint where the track was mined. Several
TMA 3s lay scattered around, totally blocking the route. The Sergeant
in charge waved at the sentry and the fellow, who must have been at
least sixty, shuffled out of his little shelter. Carefully, he proceeded to
move the mines. Each mine was picked-up and gingerly placed at the
side of the road until the route was clear. We drove slowly past and,
looking down, I saw there were only a few centimetres between a sheer
drop on one side and the mines on the other. Again, the driver negotiated the gap without a moment's hesitation.

The Bila Valley was a microcosm of Central Bosnia. From the
HVO checkpoint at the head of the valley we passed a Croat village
on the left and a Muslim village on the right. We were again stopped
at another checkpoint where the river crossed under the road. The
BiH soldiers waved us through and, a few kilometres further on, we
entered the Muslim village of Han Bila. We turned right and I asked
the Sergeant what was straight on. He told me the BiH had asked
that the UN avoid the area. He didn't know why.

A little further on we were again stopped at another checkpoint.
This time it was HVO guarding the village of Brajkovici. The guards
were little short of hostile and only reluctantly let us pass. As we
edged past their barrier they glared at us in a show of Latin machismo. The difference between the friendly BiH soldiers and the surly
HVO men seemed a reflection of their regard for the British. If we
were going to operate effectively throughout this area, we were going
to have to build up a far higher level of trust with the Croats. Cooky
was with us as Stephen Lees would not join us for a few days. I'd
decided that the Colour Sergeant would eventually assist Jason in
our ops room.

Back at the house, Roy was sitting on the patio at a red-and-white
metal garden table. Fered had brought it, and four chairs, across.
Our place was beginning to feel like home already.

The Cheshires were rapidly thinning out now. The Light
Dragoons Squadron was almost in place and would soon move to
Tuzla. I'd briefly met the Commander of the troop attached to my
company, Jimmy Cliffe.

I took one of Jimmy's Scimitars on a short patrol to Turbe to see an alternate SLAVEN crossing point. I sat in the Gunner's seat and the Milinfo Officer, Simon Harrison, was in notional Command. The driver was a jolly Geordie corporal who'd volunteered to come along to look after what must have been the worst turret crew in Bosnia. Simon was known as 'Snapper' as he had a very volatile temper. As we left camp there was a huge explosion off to our left about five hundred metres away, clearly audible above the clatter of our tracks. The Croats had a 152 mm gun, nicknamed Nora, hidden in the quarry south of the school. It was sited so it could engage either Serb or BiH positions. In this case, we later learned the target was Zenica. The UN was powerless to prevent this and the weapon loosed off a couple of shells most days during the early part of our tour.

The quarry was overlooked by a small hill topped by a prominent white church. Charlie Stevens, the RSM of the Cheshires, had published several poems penned during his tour and some of these appeared in the *Sun*. This caused our RSM, Andy Adair, to remark to the CO: 'I hope you don't expect me to start writing no bloody poems!'

We decided to follow old Charlie's example and a group of us agreed to pen verses about the church. It seemed like a good idea over a couple of beers but, with the deadline approaching, I was experiencing writer's block.

That evening, Roy and I had our first tiff since sharing the room. I was being my usual slobby self and had taken over most of the one table with my junk. Roy was trying to find a letter that, of course, I'd buried. Suddenly, he blew his top and started calling me for all the untidy bastards under the sun. I countered by reminding him how unpleasant his snoring was and then my dirty boots on his side of the room were mentioned. I'd just replied that it wasn't very pleasant sharing a room with someone who chewed raw garlic when we suddenly caught on. We were behaving like kids, or more likely 'the odd couple' and we started to laugh about it. If it was bad for us what must it be like for the boys, four to a Portakabin.

The Warriors had arrived in Split and Phil had appeared on the BBC news talking about the future task. This was ironic as he'd always maintained he hated journalists and would never give an interview. He was caught on the quay with nowhere to hide and had no choice. He was in for a ribbing when we saw him.

On the 9 May, Roy disappeared south to collect his Warriors and

I took the subbies to Kiseljak. The purpose of the journey was to show them the route for the mail run. When we returned, I was delighted to find that, for the first time, there was hot water in the house. This was too good a chance to miss so I filled the bath with piping hot but very rusty looking, water. As I wallowed, the windows shook as Nora fired again and suddenly the inspiration came. I paddled across the hall into the room, found a piece of paper in my heap, returned to the bath and wrote:

The Church

The Church sits high upon a hill
The ancients built it stone by stone,
Its aisles, the faithful used to fill
Now the Priest prays all alone.

The Church has seen it all before
The German followed on the Turk,
Croat and Muslim now make War
And save the Serbs the dirty work.

The Church surveys the hiding place
As the big gun fires another shell,
Symbol of the twisted face
Of Ethnic War, a man-made hell.

The Church has stood a thousand years
Another thousand will it stand,
Now it sheds a thousand tears
For the rape of its beloved land.

It wasn't exactly William Wordsworth but then he couldn't drive a Warrior.

Roy arrived back in the early evening. He'd led the first group of Warriors north. The second group arrived at GV after dark and stayed there for the night.

At seven the next morning I set off to meet my own Warriors. Our wagons were carried from Split on low-loaders as far as TSG and then driven north. However, the other armoured vehicles remained in theatre and were handed on to the next unit. The Warriors were changed over with each Regiment to keep the wear and tear on the wagons to a minimum. The Cheshires vehicles were looking very shabby and reflected the enormous amount of kilometres they'd travelled. Roy's Warriors looked dazzling compared to Martin Thomas's outgoing vehicles.

We arrived at TSG at about the same time as the first packet of eight Warriors. Phil, our resident TV star, was there, sporting a magnificent black drooping Zapata moustache. He'd also had an outrageously short haircut and looked lean and mean. It was he who'd shamed the subbies into their haircuts and I hadn't the heart to tell him about all the angst it had caused.

There was a problem: there were too few low-loaders. They had to go back to Split for the rest of my Warriors and the round trip would take six hours. This was bad news as there was no way the second packet would reach even GV by dark. There wasn't a way round it so I sent Jason off with the first group.

The last of the low-loaders finally arrived at four in the afternoon and we bombed-up the vehicles with brand new ammunition. After a few last-minute checks on 0B I briefed the commanders and we trundled out of TSG at 5.30.

Tookey hadn't driven for two weeks and was very rusty. Every time a car came the other way he swerved to the right and we left the road several times, nearly tipping over on one occasion. I was getting hacked off with this and contemplated driving myself. On one of the halts Phil calmed me down, like he usually did, and assured me Tookey would soon get the hang of driving on the narrow tracks. He told me that Chappy was out of the coma but still very ill. There was a slight chance he might join us for the last part of the tour. I certainly wished I had him driving for me now.

By the time we reached the hills above Prozor it was nearly dark. The drop on our right was over a hundred metres and it would not be a smart move to leave the road here. Tookey knew this as well and he hugged the middle of the track. Every time something came the other way he would edge dangerously close to the yawning drop. I doubted if my nerves could take six months of his driving. However, we survived and reached GV around ten at night. I popped in for a quick chat with Binnsy and told him I intended to press on.

As we neared the Novi Travnik T-junction, there'd been no problems with the wagons, a sure sign for the future. Even Tookey was seeming more confident.

The HVO checkpoint was the first chicane we'd encountered. I wasn't going to tell Tookey about the mines but he'd already seen them. We slowed to a crawl and attempted to negotiate the barriers. He was keeping so far from the mines there was no way we were going to succeed. Eventually, after several attempts, he clipped the guard hut, drawing howls of protest from the Croats. Three of them ran out and I thought we were in for trouble. Instead, they moved the barrier and the mines and we passed through to a chorus of jeers and catcalls. I felt such a prat and was seething. However, Phil said he'd take Tookey through some manoeuvres in the camp, and I calmed down again.

Tired, cold, stiff and hungry we finally rolled into camp at just after midnight. Goy was there to allocate rooms to everyone so I retired to the mess for a nightcap. There were still a couple of the Cheshires about and they were due to leave in the morning.

The handover period was two weeks and far too long. After a week we just wanted to get on with the job without having the old sweats cluttering the place. They also wanted to get away and must have viewed our enthusiasm in the same way we viewed their cynicism.

The Cheshires had done a superb job. They'd undertaken a task that was totally unlike any the Army had done before. Constantly under the glare of the media they had operated under a mandate that was, to say the least, vague. They'd coped with the harsh Bosnian winter and safeguarded the delivery of thousands of tons of aid. Without their efforts, hundreds of people would, undoubtedly, have died.

The regiment had its faults, as does any. They'd alienated the Croats and were leaving us a legacy of distrust that would be hard to overcome. Many of them had 'gone native' and become too involved with the problems, but, after just two weeks, I could see how that could happen. Bob Stewart was a maverick who appeared almost to be manipulating the press as much as they were manipulating him. However, he deserved the credit for the massive achievements of his battalion. Without his inspiration and foresight far less would have been achieved. He was, undoubtedly the man of the moment.

I found most of their officers charming, and the soldiers were cheerful and very professional. They were a hard act to follow for us, the new kids on the block.

Chapter 5
First Blood

On Tuesday 11 May Alastair Duncan finally assumed command. There was a short ceremony at the entrance to camp and 'Bosnia Bob' departed. The change-over had been gradual and quite leisurely and all the key players had been in the chair for a few days. The battlegroup was not yet complete as the riflemen from A and C Companies had still not arrived.

I'd lost a platoon on temporary detachment to the LD in Tuzla. The LD were equipped with Scimitar light tanks armed with the RARDEN cannon, also several Spartan light APCs. The Spartan was fine for carrying four or five people but didn't have the offensive capability or, more importantly, perceived clout, of the Warrior.

I chose John Reeve's platoon to go. It was a toss-up between Seven and Nine Platoons – Eight was out of the question as Stephen had no experience and would need as much help and guidance as we could give him. Tom was my first choice as I trusted him to work away from the company. However, I wasn't sure if I fully trusted Nine Platoon away from the supervision of Zippy and me. Therefore, I plumped for the middle option of John's platoon. John was still quite inexperienced but I felt sure that he and Sergeant Cunningham would cope.

Roy's company was to be the first on operations. The CO had decided to follow the same ops cycle as the Cheshires. The two Vitez companies would work a system of alternate operations and guard weeks. The engineers would guard the camp until my full company arrived. This slack couple of days gave me an ideal time to take the vehicle crews out to familiarize them with the area.

It was a great feeling as I commanded my first patrol. After a fortnight of being in other people's vehicles, analysing their good points and faults, I wanted to see if I could do any better.

I reported in to the A Company ops room and spoke to James Hurley the 2/ic. The procedure was to list the occupants of each vehicle giving their individual 'zap' number and blood-group. In an emergency the details of an injured soldier could be radioed back so that the surgical team could stand by. The zap code was to stop the man's name being revealed and perhaps leaked to the press before the Army had time to notify the next of kin. Having passed this on, I gave the time out and in and the route. This became standard practice before every patrol.

Out on the tank park I briefed the patrol members on the task, route and order of march and we walked the vehicles to the gate. The road running down the eastern side of the school had been concreted, which greatly cut down on the quagmire.

My first patrol consisted of four Warriors and was a round robin of most of the local towns. We travelled with the mortar hatches at the back open and four men could stand and look to the sides and rear. This 'top cover' proved to be invaluable as there was a huge blind spot to the rear that the turret crew could only view with difficulty. We deployed with the turret hatches in the up position. This gave physical protection to the crew from the rear, an area where most of the contacts came from. However, we soon found that four in the rear were too many and usually made do with two.

We passed through Travnik, Vitez and Zenica and then took the mountain road back. In the village of Poculica, 20 (Two Zero) had a problem with a track-ram and careered off the road. The driver managed to stop the Warrior under some semblance of control a metre short of a steep drop. Cookie was shaken, to say the least.

I halted and we deployed sentries as we awaited the arrival of the fitter section. Dobby and I strolled over to investigate a smouldering house. The village had been mainly Muslim and now looked like it was totally Muslim. The building was a Croat house, judging by the number of crucifixes about, and the occupants had been driven away. Only a couple of the upstairs rooms were gutted as the fire hadn't fully taken hold. The place had been ransacked and looted and there was nothing of any value remaining. The family photograph album was strewn about the yard and snapshots of little children were fluttering around in the breeze. It was a sharp reminder that a happy family had lived in this place until a couple of days ago.

Now, they were added to the ever-growing list of displaced persons and were, by now, probably in the refugee centre in Vitez. They had, presumably, lived alongside their Muslim neighbours for generations and now were simply victims of the spreading disease of ethnic cleansing. A further four houses along the same lane had also been torched. It was the first positive sign I'd seen that the Croats were not the only aggressors in our area.

The REME deployed in force to their first call-out. All three vehicles arrived in a clatter of tracks. Staff Mackareth and his deputy, Sgt Pratt, assessed the damage. The recovery was simple. Two Zero was dragged into the road and repaired by half a dozen very enthusiastic fitters. Half an hour later, we were ready to go. I was pleased the system had worked. My radio call to the Ops room had been passed to the garage and the REME had found the correct location first time. It was great to have teamwork like this in our first week and I knew we were always going to receive the best possible service from the 'grease monkeys'. As we left to the waves of the locals I wondered what they thought about the UN and whether they felt guilty that we'd seen the burned out houses. I was soon to learn that they didn't give a toss.

Tookey's driving was improving. He still had the odd glitch and we hovered dangerously close to the edge of some pretty fearsome drops on occasion. However, he was definitely getting the hang of it. We drove down to the Novi Travnik T-junction and negotiated the chicane, turned round and tried again. It was still slow and the HVO guards looked on with amusement, but at least we didn't hit anything this time.

In camp, I attended the five o'clock conference. David Hill briefed us on the following day's operations then, with a deadpan face, told us that the bear cage had been brought back up from Split the previous evening. It had taken ten men to coax him in but Bob Stewart had finally been taken back down to civilization!

I retired to bed early but Roy and I were woken by a furious firefight close to the house. We grabbed our rifles and crouched beneath the window and listened to the activity outside. With the shutters down, it was impossible to see anything but we both kept a wary eye on the door. Our room was the nearest to the front door and would be the first port of call for anyone raiding the house. Several hundred rounds were fired from the houses around ours and return fire seemed to be coming from the Croat houses over the main road. At one stage, two men fired several shots from the verandah and I distinctly heard the sound of bullets hitting the house. We pulled a locker over the door as a makeshift barricade and sat it out like breathless school children hiding from a teacher. Neither of us felt like going outside for a closer look as this was definitely a matter between the local militias. There was no telephone in the house and thus no way of alerting the guard to our situation. It further highlighted how isolated we were in the Major's house.

After an hour or so the firing died away and I slept under my duvet with my rifle for company.

The next morning, I wasn't surprised to see three splat marks on the front of the house. Roy and I decided to build a wall around the verandah to give a little more protection. I read the guard log and the entry simply stated: 'Firing from the direction of Muslim houses. No threat to the camp, no further action.' The firing was in our front garden yet not visible from camp and only merited a single line. We discussed moving out and decided to give it a week to see if things got any better.

Our first day of operations was Friday 14 May. There were several convoy escort tasks and all my vehicles were employed. The company, at this stage, comprised ten Warriors, four Scimitars and the MFC Spartan. In addition, I had five FV 432s, three in the anti-tank section and two in the mortar detachment as well as the three fitter section vehicles.

There were nearly twenty tasks throughout the day and Jason and I had to devise a programme that would fulfil our commitments. The convoys all arrived at different times and there was little chance of combining any two. Eventually, we arranged to hold three at the school for an hour until escorts became available. This first day turned out to be the busiest of the tour and I was always able to have spare callsigns on every other day. There was clearly no chance of adopting the tactics taught at Sennelager as there were not enough AFVs to intersperse them throughout the convoy. It was one at the front and one at the back and that's how it remained for the rest of our time in Bosnia.

I took a patrol into the area of Putis and Jelinak. The attitude of the BiH soldiers was noticeably more hostile, as if they didn't want us there any more. The track was blocked by a farm cart and we had to stop. I had no interpreter with me so negotiation was going to be difficult. The local commander was a thin, weasel-faced man, wearing a dirty brown vest and an old East German Army helmet, about six sizes too big. He carried an ancient bolt-action rifle and didn't seem keen to let us through. There was no point in getting down so I pointed at the cart and indicated that I wanted him to move it. He refused at first and kept shouting *'Papiers, papiers'*. They were obsessed with us having papers for every journey and, of course, we didn't have them. Eventually I told Tookey to drive right up to the cart and gently nudge it. He accomplished this rather skilfully. The fellow got the message and three of his cronies pulled the cart aside.

The villages were deserted save for scores of BiH soldiers, far more than had been there the week before. They seemed surprised to see us, clearly expecting their checkpoint to do a better job. However, they were friendly enough. I counted over two hundred soldiers, that was quite a concentration for the area and I knew they were building up to something big.

I wasn't going to hang around so we moved on, down the lane where I'd found the dead calf, and into the hills. We passed through the small Croat village of Loncari, and someone shot at us. There was a 'crack!' clearly audible above the noise of the engine, and a splash on the rock wall to my right. Phil ducked into the gunner's seat and I ordered him to traverse on. Tookey closed down and Dobby and Knight bobbed down into the safety of the Warrior. Phil told me he could clearly see a soldier pointing an AK at us from a trench about two hundred metres away.

This area was where Bob Stewart had returned fire when he'd been shot at. I remembered seeing the incident on the news and recalled that he fired over fifty rounds of Chain Gun. By the rules of the orange card, I too was entitled to return fire. The card was carried by everyone and laid out the rules of engagement. The gunman had fired at us, close enough to endanger life and seemed likely to fire again. Phil was waiting for the order to fire.

I could see the guy through the times-ten sight. He was aiming at us and probably thought the log in front would protect him. In reality the 7.62 mm rounds would punch through the wood and, at this range, it should all be over in one burst of fifteen. I was about to give the word when I had the sort of session you see in cartoons with an angel and devil on some bloke's shoulders.

'Go on Vaughan, kill him.'

'Come on, what's the point? You're all under cover now, he can't harm you.'

'But he shot at you. You're allowed to kill him.'

'But can you be sure it was actually him? Did you see him fire?'

'Who cares, it'll discourage the others anyway.'

'No! There's enough bodies in this country already. Why create more?'

The moral debate lasted a split second. I knew I could've killed him and doubted if I would suffer any pangs of guilt. It was more the fact that to fire back was to place myself in the same category as this Neanderthal. I told Phil to deselect and he looked at me quizzically. I knew he expected good old gung ho Vaughan to waste the guy and I think he was surprised.

Instead, I raised myself chest-out of the turret and gave him the finger. It was childish but I felt I needed the last word. I hoped he could see the disdain on my face as we drove off.

I reported the troop concentration to Snapper who told me this tied in with the indications coming in from the LOs. The BiH was winding up for an attack of its own. This was not just as a result of Ahmici but also in response to the Croat attack on Mostar. The latter attack had closed the road we'd travelled down on the recce and it was not opened again during our tour. Now, almost all aid into Central Bosnia had to come up Route Diamond.

At the conference, the CO told us that the practice of throwing sweets from the vehicles was to cease. This was a sound decision. There was nothing nicer than chucking a handful of goodies to some appealing little waif as we passed. The danger was, however, that one would run under the tracks. Already the children living on Route Diamond were chasing after every UN vehicle. They would point to their mouths and shout *'Bon bon! Shockolade!'* They were out night and day and were probably the best fed kids in the region. After the conference I held my own 'O Group' to pass the points down to the soldiers. This became a nightly occurrence. Jason, the platoon commanders and Sergeants, Zippy and the CQMS, Sergeant Barratt as the gunnery rep, Corporals Mowforth and Knight and Staff Mackareth all attended. It was a useful time to get together and discuss the events of the day and plan for the next. We had an office in the school opposite the gym. It was small but adequate and a place for the mail to be distributed and briefings held.

That evening, I went through the nightmare of phoning Dawn. There were only three telephones between over five hundred soldiers. During the day, the lines were all used for official business but three were opened up for private calls between six at night and eight in the morning. Two phones were in what had been a toilet. One was in the toilet part and the other in the wash basin part. Each room was no bigger than a metre-and-a-half square. The third phone was in another ex-toilet, about the same size. You could hear everything said by the other two callers as the walls were paper thin. The lines went to the MOD operator in London and were then forwarded, at the local rate. They were not cheap and I had two horrendous quarterly bills. There was a slight time delay and the lines were always faint and interspersed with the sort of bleeps that used to accompany transmissions from astronauts on the moon. All these factors made holding a private conversation virtually impossible as three people shouted to their loved ones in stuffy cubicles that smelled of decades of urine and bleach.

The next day was a lot slacker as fewer convoys travelled at the weekends. Staff Sergeant McLeod wanted information on rumours of troop movements north of Han Bila. This was the area where the BiH had told the Cheshires not to go.

I was again taking 0B and 0C and this time I had an interpreter with me. She was just eighteen years old and had studied English at school. At around five feet nothing, her shiny new combat uniform hung off her. There were no boots in the stores small enough for her so a pair of daps completed the ensemble. In fact, she was scruffier than the local soldiers. She was in her first week of the job and was very nervous.

I decided to put several callsigns into the area. Cookie was a few kilometres to the east in the hills above Travnik and Corporal John Hutchinson was a couple of kilometres away, in a place called Guca Gora. There was a small degree of mutual support and we were all on the radio. Still, it shouldn't be necessary as we were the UN and there to help people. What could possibly go wrong?

We had no problems at the Croat checkpoint at the foot of the valley. A young HVO man nonchalantly booted the mines off the track. However, we were stopped in Han Bila when we tried to go straight on instead of turning right to Zenica. This was clearly a departure from the norm and the BiH reacted like startled ants. A dozen or so ran out of the buildings and stood in front of the Warrior. I halted and several others emerged from the 'woodwork' until there were around thirty of them. Few of the soldiers had weapons but those who did were pointing them at me. Tookey closed down and I dismounted. I felt a bit lonely leaving the safety of my thirty-ton armoured box to surround myself by hostile natives. I walked round to the back where Dobby and the interpreter were climbing out. The locals parted when they saw Dobby, as he was carrying a GPMG with an outrageously long belt of ammunition wrapped over his shoulder. He had more firepower than all the locals put together.

I asked to see their commander and we were shown into a house a few metres away. Dobby eclipsed the doorway while I talked to the village commander, a balding man in his late forties. He asked why I was there and I told him I wanted to check the villages to the north to see if food aid was getting through. This wasn't true but I could hardly say I was there to spy on his army. He assured me aid was getting through but I said I needed to check and it was in his interest as they were all Muslim villages. This went on for around ten minutes by which time I was getting the hang of looking at him and talking via the interpreter. She was quite effective although her command of military words was not good. But then it was her first week. I soon noticed there was an optimum 'sound bite' which she could cope with so I started to use shorter sentences. The Commander had no such skill and rabbitted on so she was forced to halt him several times to translate for me. Eventually, just as I thought it was going to be a wasted journey he suddenly capitulated. An aide entered and whispered something to him and he informed us that higher command had allowed us to proceed. We shook hands and went back to the Warrior. The locals had organized themselves by now and there were a couple of RPG 7 anti-tank rocket launchers around. Nevertheless, they stepped aside and we were on our way.

We'd almost reached our first destination, the village of Fazlici, when we encountered a barrier across the road. This wasn't the normal makeshift affair but was solid, with a small sentry box at the right-hand end. As we approached, the barrier was swung shut and around twenty, heavily armed men gathered in the road. Most held AKs but there were also a few light machine guns. There was a large earth bank on the right and a stream with steep sides to the left. There was no way we could manoeuvre.

We halted about ten metres in front of them and, on an order, they all cocked their weapons. This was the first time I'd witnessed any semblance of discipline and these people looked like they meant business. I told Barratt in OC to stay to the rear and cover me. Again, I dismounted, this time feeling extremely small and vulnerable. I walked down the glacis plate straightening my beret and trying to look as nonchalant as possible. Tookey had closed down so I couldn't even look at his spiccy features to cheer myself up. I jumped to the ground and studied them. They all glared at me and I felt my bowels turn to water. I clenched my butt cheeks together and tried not to show how scared I was. Cornered animals crap themselves and, of course, birds do before they fly. It's a natural reaction to lighten the load before fleeing and man is, after all, a mammal. I now understand the expression, 'He crapped himself with fright'.

I sauntered round to the back doors of the Warrior and Dobby handed me my rifle. Out of sight of the BiH, I cocked the weapon and Dobby did the same with the GPMG. I also took off the safety catch and selected automatic. Between the two of us we could probably take most of them, especially with surprise on our side. As soon as I started doing something the fear subsided and I relaxed a little. As we approached the crowd I briefed Dobby and the interpreter to dive under the Warrior if shooting started and I assured them I wouldn't be far behind. This would protect us from the sides and narrow the angle from which we could be fired at. The three of us approached the barrier and I asked to see the local commander. A tall fellow with greasy black hair and a pockmarked face stepped forward and I asked him if we could pass. He demanded to see my papers and told me I couldn't proceed without them as the area was 'restricted', whatever that meant. We debated this for several minutes and I just knew we weren't going to succeed. The atmosphere gradually relaxed and soon we were almost passing polite conversation. By this time there were around fifty soldiers and about a hundred civilians. It was obvious they'd rarely, if ever, seen a UN vehicle. I was just about to call it a day when a white Toyota Land Cruiser arrived and three men got out. There was a murmur of excitement as they approached. The leader was a short man of about five-foot-five dressed in combat fatigues, with a pistol holster on his belt. As he drew closer I saw he was from the Middle East, with a neatly cut beard that was slightly greying. He screamed at the civilians and his two henchmen started to prod them with their AKs. The BiH soldiers instantly started to bristle with aggression again and we were back to square one.

The Arab pushed himself to the front of the group and stared at me. His brown eyes held a malevolent glint and I forced myself to meet his glare. I held out my hand and said in my best Serbo-Croat:

'*Dobar Dan. Kakoste?*' (Hello. How are you?) The interpreter was a little confused and repeated the phrase while I stood with my hand outstretched. In near-perfect English he replied:

'I will not shake the hand of an infidel and I will not talk to a woman.'

I figured he probably wasn't going to win an award as 'nineties man'. Nevertheless, I sent the interpreter back to the Warrior and the poor wee girl's sigh of relief could probably be heard in Sarajevo.

The guy then objected to Dobby who was standing to one side, looking mean.

'What is he doing there? He is threatening my men.'

This sounded a bit rich from someone with over a hundred of the bastards on his side and I told him so. By this time the group of armed men had swollen to almost a company worth and there were several faces that were clearly not Bosnian. There were at least three blacks, one of whom carried a 64 mm rocket launcher. Little did I know that I'd been sent straight into the training camp of the foreign mujahideen.

This bunch of fanatics was running a jihad of their own. They were drawn from all over the Muslim world and over thirty countries were represented in their small group. There were only around a hundred of them but their fanaticism and ruthlessness acted as a force multiplier. They often spearheaded attacks and rarely took prisoners. It was hardly surprising the Croats were scared stiff of them.

The mujahideen also trained soldiers, which was what they were doing here. The BiH didn't like their fanaticism as the Bosnian Muslim is usually very easy going. The last thing the BiH wanted was Tehran in the Balkans. However, these people were useful and so were kept out of the way and only used sparingly. They'd not fought in the Lasva Valley as yet and there was, until now, no indication that they were in the area. The question was, would I get back alive to spread the information? I stood my ground and tried to reason with the fellow. He would not let me pass without papers but I got the impression that even a document signed by the Ayatollah himself wasn't going to get me through. I was getting nowhere, in fact, all I was getting was hard-sell and I listened for a couple of minutes to a tirade about the decadent West.

My brain was racing, trying to weigh up my options while still trying to negotiate with the guy. I was very vulnerable out on my

'Bosnia Warrior'   With my Warrior, callsign Zero Bravo, on the tank park at Vitez School. The tank park was home to the seventy or so armoured vehicles at the UN base. It was also the starting point for all patrols and the meeting place for those involved

'The nerve centre of the battalion'   Lieutenant Paul Davies and his signaller Stag-on in the Vitez operations room. The Ops room was always manned and kept a constant link with the troops on the ground as well as the multitude of higher headquarters. Most of the officers took their fair share of duties in this and the smaller company Ops room

'The boys called him Mario'   Corporal Andy Tooke, Warrior driver callsign Zero Bravo, was nicknamed after his supposed resemblance to the Super Mario Brothers. Tookey was one of the best Warrior drivers in the battalion. He drove more miles than any other driver and helped to ensure that my Warrior had the best maintenance record of any at Vitez

'Every house had been burned ...' The militia held the Croats up for long enough for the majority of the villagers to flee. Only this prevented Bandol from becoming another Ahmici. Even so, there were several casualties and the village was burned. The HVO occupied the high ground around the place only to be pushed back a few weeks later

'The fellow was a BiH soldier and had been dead for several days' Body of Muslim militiaman tortured then murdered by the HVO at Bandol. He had been strung up by a clothes-line and beaten before being stabbed and shot. I filled in several forms for the War Crimes Commission but it is unlikely the culprits will ever be brought to justice

'I presented the caring face of the UN' Photo of me taken by Sergeant Geoff Barratt shortly after a brush with the Mujahideen near Guca Gora, 17 June 1993. We usually dismounted to talk to the militias face to face. However, there were times when reason gave way to force and a scowl from an anonymous figure in a helmet followed by thirty tons of Warrior often did the trick!

own. The edges of the crowd had gradually spread to either side of me and I was now, effectively, surrounded on three flanks. The group had swelled to well over 150 and there were many more foreigners about. A small knot of about six men, all dressed in Arab headdress, were stirring things up crying '*Allah Akhbar!*' I was sure I heard a north-country voice shout 'Death to the infidel!' It was time to do something. The leader was still peddling his brand of fanaticism but he knew I was thinking of a way out. He continued to talk but was now eyeing me like a cat looking at a mouse. His eyes were flecked with tiny black spots and seemed to be boring into my soul.

I knew I had to walk away. There were still no clear grounds for opening fire and there was no way I would make it back to the Warrior. Dobby was still covering me and, by now, had the GPMG pointing at the mob. Phil was also trained onto the checkpoint and we'd worked out a procedure where he would open fire if I threw myself to the deck. It was still nearly a hundred to one and it was the soldiers on either flank that were the problem. It would be fun if the firing started as both flanks would almost certainly fire at me and hit each other. I doubted if I'd live long enough to witness this but it did give me comfort to know that most of the militiamen were a complete bunch of prats.

If I could make it back to the Warrior we might be able to carry on. We had a task to do but I reckoned we would have to kill an awful lot of people to complete it. If they fired first, which they inevitably would, we could return fire. They weren't going to give in and we would probably have to kill the lot. I could imagine the reception back in Vitez.

'Good afternoon colonel. We got the job done, sir, and visited all the villages. Oh yes, we had to kill a hundred people to do it!'

On a more practical note, I remembered from the map there was just this one road in and out of the valley. The Serb lines lay to the north and west and there were mountains to the east. We were going to have to come back through here, and, even if we completed that, there was still Han Bila to negotiate. We were up Shit Creek without a paddle.

I asked if I could turn the Warrior round in the village square as it would be difficult in the narrow road.

'That's your problem!' was the reply. Out of the corner of my eye I could see the almost imperceptible move to further cut me off.

There was also the black man with the 64 mm standing at the side of the road pointing it at 0B. It was time to go, and quickly.

Looking the leader in the eye, I told him:

'We mean you no harm and we are a peaceful organization.'

At that precise moment Phil loaded six rounds of High Explosive (HE). The barrel was pointing directly at the leader and we both clearly heard the 'clank, clank, clunk!' as the rounds were fed into the gun. The sound was audible to most of the crowd as well and those who hadn't cocked their weapons did so now.

Phil had seen the men outflanking me and, quite rightly, decided he was going to need every bit of firepower he'd got. The leader eyed me with an 'Oh really!' look and I knew it was act or die.

'It has been a pleasure talking to you. You command a very professional group of men, but, as you have heard, my gunner is very professional too. I will go before there is bloodshed on both sides. You will not shake my hand but I will salute you as a fellow fighting man.'

With that, I swung him my best Sandhurst salute and smartly turned on my heel. Keeping my back to the crowd, I deliberately sauntered towards the Warrior. My bowels swung into action to remind me there was a good chance I was going to get a bullet in the back. Trying to look as nonchalant as possible, and as disdainful, I walked the longest thirty paces of my life. Tookey was closed-down but I knew he was watching me and I signalled him to start up. The engine exploded into life with a roar that sent a flock of crows skyward from a near by copse. Feeling very small and vulnerable, I marshalled Zero Bravo round in what was at least a ten-point turn. I was more scared than a big box of fear with 'Terrified' written on the side.

I was about to call something crass after them like, 'I'll be back', but thought better of it. They'd probably never seen a Schwarzenegger movie anyway.

I was never so glad to see the inside of a Warrior in my life. As I was putting my helmet on the crowd were cheering each other and jeering us. Suddenly, the black man raised the 64 mm to his shoulder and, just as suddenly, Phil traversed the turret to the rear, directly at the centre of the crowd. To a man they hit the deck, many trying to burrow under their mates in a vain attempt to find bullet-proof cover. Good old Phil. His spontaneous reaction had given us just the way to depart with a little dignity and I gave them another, rather more mocking, salute as we left. As we trundled back towards Han Bila, Phil's only comment was:

'I couldn't eat a Ritz cracker for a million pounds!'

I knew what he meant as my mouth was bone-dry as well. We stopped a couple of kilometres down the road and I climbed through the turret cage into the rear. The interpreter had regained a little of her colour but still looked as if she'd faint at any moment. Dobby just looked as phlegmatic as usual. I scrounged a cigarette from him, an Embassy Regal. It was the first I'd had for years and I smoked it, and half the filter as well. Up in the turret, Phil was puffing away on his brier and, judging by the fug emerging from the driver's tunnel, Tookey was smoking as well. My hands had stopped shaking and I was feeling a little light-headed from the nicotine. The silence, and the tension, was broken when Dobby asked me:

'Sir. What the hell's an infidel?'

After I explained, I climbed back into the turret, chuckling to myself. I'd been called a few things on the streets of Belfast, but never an unbeliever.

We returned to camp and I vented my spleen on Snapper. To be fair, it wasn't his fault as this was the first indication that the mujahideen was in the area. Nevertheless, it showed how easy it was to become sucked into a situation where violence is the only way out. I was unlucky to encounter this bunch on my first ops week. As the tour progressed I became far better at reading people's moods and never again had so much trouble at a checkpoint. I'd been lucky to walk away from this one. Walking away from trouble is usually an alien concept to the soldier but, in Bosnia, it was one we had to master quickly.

That evening, we received a call from the CO of the Dutch Transport Battalion in Busovaca. He'd been approached by Dario Kordic who had asked for help as a BiH attack seemed imminent. This was rich seeing as it was Kordic who'd started the ethnic war in the Lasva Valley. Now he wanted protection from the UN. In the end I sent Tom's platoon, more to look after the lightly-armed Dutch than the locals. The attack didn't materialize but Tom's men were fed like royalty by the 'Cloggies'.

The Colonel had banned the press from the mess when he took over. This was done in the nicest way possible but, nevertheless, the hacks were hacked off. This was an excellent move because it meant that the mess was our home again. We could speak easily and freely without worrying about the dangers of a conversation appearing in the papers.

James Myles held daily briefings that kept all the journalists in the area right up to date with the latest developments. This annoyed many journos at first as they were now all being fed the same information. There was much less chance of a scoop resulting from some unguarded comment. Nevertheless, most of them seemed to realize that the situation of them having free use of the mess couldn't go on. After an initial period of whingeing they settled down to their new routine and we had little trouble with the majority of the media. It took courage to risk upsetting the press in his first week, but the boss definitely had the right idea on this one. I was informed at the conference that I was to run an Op SLAVEN the next day, the 17 May. I gave my orders in the company office to all the commanders concerned. Altogether the briefing took around two hours and I hoped I'd covered every eventuality. I was delighted to meet up with Zippy, who'd arrived with the last of my company. These soldiers were easily identifiable by their bright, shiny berets. The ones belonging to us 'old sweats' of all of three weeks, were already filthy and oil-stained from constant exposure to the Warriors.

Stephen Lees had just arrived and was told by Tom that he'd better introduce himself to those people he didn't know. Over he bounded to a very short-haired, moustached Major whom he didn't recognize. His 'Hello, sir. I don't believe we've met ...' was cut short by yet another dig in the ribs.

The SLAVEN was scheduled for 11.30 in the morning. An hour or so beforehand I deployed Tom's platoon to watch over the front line in much the same way as I'd done with Tudor Ellis. Eight trucks from the MT Platoon were parked up ready for the call forward. Sergeant Major Kev Debnam was in the lead truck with a radio link forward to me.

I travelled in my Land Rover with Zippy, Dobby and Tookey. We followed our LO and the BiH LO who was introduced to me as Beba Salko. Beba was a short, stocky fellow in his mid-thirties. He had a friendly smile and spoke quite good English, which was unusual. Again, we halted at the mines and Beba gingerly placed them to one side. The Serb front line was stoutly constructed and seemed much stronger than its BiH counterpart. The buildings on the Serb side were just as shell-blasted and there were hardly any birds in the twisted and gnarled trees. It was almost as if the wildlife had fled along with the locals.

A couple of kilometres further on we halted at the side of an undamaged house that was flying the Bosnian-Serb flag. The LO and Beba disappeared inside. I made to follow but was told in no uncertain terms that there were difficult negotiations ahead and I'd only get in the way. I was livid. I could keep my gob shut as well as the next man and had managed to negotiate myself out of a pretty difficult situation a couple of days before. Still, this was his call and I didn't press the point. Looking back, it was the first sign of the power-mad LO syndrome that had so afflicted the Cheshires.

We sat outside for the best part of an hour during which time I studied the dozen or so BSA soldiers who were wandering about. They seemed taller than the BiH ones. Whether the Serbs picked the ones on show for their physical presence or not I don't know, but they were head and shoulders above the average Muslim. They were all bearded and all wore ridiculous little side hats perched on their huge heads. These looked like the little pork-pie hats that two-tone bands used to wear in the late seventies.

The Serbs had perfected the art of looking surly and glowered at us in an intimidating way as we stood around the Land Rover. It was hard not to feel intimidated as there was little chance of the reserve actually reaching us even if I did manage to call them.

Eventually our LO emerged, swaggered over to me and told me to call up the trucks. Again it was his attitude that hacked me off and I asked him what arrangements had been made. He said that I didn't need to know as he was in overall command, so I started to walk to the Rover.

'OK mate, you just carry on, I'll take my Warriors and trucks back to Vitez. You give us a call when you're prepared to tell me what's going on.'

His bluff was called, and he hastily explained that the buses were about twenty minutes away. Please would I call the trucks up now, so they would be in position in time to meet the coaches. The buses would halt and the Serbs would usher the refugees off and herd them towards the lorries. We would help them aboard and assist the old and infirm into the ambulance.

Now that wasn't hard was it? No state secrets given away there? I now knew exactly what the form was and could brief everyone on what to expect. That way, if something out of the ordinary happened, we might just have a chance of reacting to it.

The trucks arrived and, one by one, turned around in a lay-by and parked, facing back toward Turbe. A few minutes later, four civilian coaches halted about four hundred metres from the lorries. They were absolutely packed with people. The Serbs surrounded the coaches and the LO, and his interpreter, boarded each vehicle in turn and briefed the occupants on what was going to happen.

While he was on the third bus the Serbs started to, none too gently, herd the people off the first one. A stream of humanity issued forth from the front door, most of them clutching battered fibreboard suitcases or bundles of blankets tied up with string. They stood in the road in a daze with anxious eyes and fearful expressions. The only movement was from the young children who strained at their mother's arms, glad to be free from the confines of the coach. Meanwhile, the adults were totally passive and stood there like sheep. Most of them were well dressed, with the men in suits and the women in smart coats. They reminded me of films of Jewish people meekly waiting to walk to the gas chamber. Indeed, they were the same sort of person, mostly middle-class professionals. Just as most of the Jews hadn't resisted, aggression wasn't in the nature of these people either. It was a lesson in the psychology of controlling people. The Serbs were in the same total command as the Germans had been, and there was no resistance. The only difference was that these people would, hopefully, live to see another day.

On an order from one of the Serbs the guards started to prod the leading group towards the waiting trucks. There was little discernible movement and the group seemed rooted to the tarmac. The road was slightly uphill and the lorries were still a long way off. It was as if they feared the worst and the apparent safety of the coach was preferable to that walk into the unknown.

Something had to happen as the Serbs were getting frustrated and were being decidedly more liberal in their interpretation of the word 'prod'. I stepped forward and gently took a little girl of about three from a lady in her late twenties. The woman had short dark hair and three other children aged between about four and seven clung to the hem of her blue skirt. Both child and mother hung on for a second before the girl transferred her limpet-like grip to around my neck. I started to walk towards the buses and the mother and children followed. It was as if the spell was broken and the remainder streamed after us.

The girl had beautiful blonde hair with pink ribbons tying it into pigtails. She was wearing a purple coat that was obviously expensive and would not have looked out of place on the shelves of

'Mothercare'. Her brown eyes were enormous and she had long lashes that made her look like a newly-born doe. She reminded me of my own daughter, Aimee, and I felt a huge lump rising in my throat. Within seconds she accepted this change to her surroundings, as only the very young can, and started playing with the UN badge on my beret.

The boys from the trucks had now dismounted and came toward us. They moved past me and, looking over my shoulder, I saw them lifting children and bundles of clothes from those civilians who were staggering under the weight. This was the British Tommy, reviled in times of peace by smug civilians safe in their snug suburban houses. These men who drink too much and fight all-comers helping those poor people with a compassion that most people back home couldn't begin to comprehend. It was so natural, there was no need to tell them. They just saw people in trouble and rushed to help. It is this combination of aggression and compassion that makes Tommy the best in the world. They are also the qualities that make him the best UN soldier in the world.

I reached the trucks and continued to the first one. At least if they were on this one they might be in time to get a bed in the refugee centre. The driver lifted the three oldest children up into the back where they ran about, clambering over the wooden seats. Meanwhile, the mother was watching the oncoming mass. She broke away, returning a few moments later with a distinguished looking couple in their sixties. The man was grey-haired and, with his silver-rimmed spectacles, he could've been a lawyer. The driver helped them to climb up and I noted, with satisfaction, that he'd had the foresight to bring a small ladder. Those two metres up to the rear of the eight-tonner must have been a mountain to some of the elderly. Several people were pressing around me and I didn't want the woman to become separated from her children. There were no young men on the buses and I wondered if she'd ever see her husband again. I motioned for her to climb up and she gripped my hand and whispered 'Hvala' (Thank you) to me. As I was handing her over, the little girl suddenly reached across and, with a grubby finger, wiped a tear from the corner of my eye.

The lump in my throat had grown to the size of a cricket ball so I distracted myself by briskly walking back down to the coaches. Dobby had also dropped off a family and joined me. The interpreter had been talking to one family and was told they'd paid a fortune for

places on the bus. They'd signed away their home and the small factory that they ran near Banja Luka. These people had lost everything bar their lives and faced a very uncertain future.

Our friendly neighbourhood Serbs treated the occasion as a huge
joke and were jeering the civilians and shouting something that
sounded like 'Bally Oh!' The funniest part of the joke was centred
around the last bus and we went to investigate. This coach was
empty save for an old man who was fussing over a white-haired
woman lying on the floor. Three Serbs were lounging around the
door and jeering at them, laughing at the man's feeble attempts to
pick his wife up. We elbowed past them and they glared at us. I carefully stepped over the woman and gasped as I saw the poor old dear
had no legs. She'd lost them above the knee and a blanket was
pinned over the lower part of her body. The man was sobbing and
obviously believed they were going to be left behind. The bastards
in the doorway wouldn't lift a finger to even let us know they were
in trouble.

Cursing my lack of Serbo-Croat, I gave my best impression of
miming picking someone up. It wouldn't have won first prize in a
game of charades but he eventually got the message. Reluctantly, he
stepped aside and Dobby and I lifted her. She was light as a child,
her arms frail as sticks but her eyes were bright and sparkling. She
must have been a pretty lady in her youth. We edged to the front of
the coach where the pond-life blocked our way for a moment before,
reluctantly, stepping aside. One of them gave a loud tut as if we'd
spoiled his fun for the afternoon, which we probably had.

We carried her to the ambulance and the old man held her hand
the whole way.

All the refugees had, by now, moved from the buses to the lorries
and they crowded the tail-gates. Many wore expressions that, while
not exactly happy, certainly looked like relief. One little mite wore a
yellow T-shirt bearing the slogan 'Happy World' ... If only.

Leaving the LO to conduct more top-secret, high-level negotiations, I led the convoy back towards Turbe. As we crossed the lines
a volley of shots was fired over our heads and I ducked involuntarily. The Serbs were not content with making the poor folk walk to the
trucks when they could've parked the buses next to them. They
weren't content with harassing them all the way to the lorries. Now
they just had to have the last word and I imagined the panic in the
trucks as the shots were fired.

I dropped off the people at the refugee camp in Travnik, a huge school in the middle of town. There was a reception committee to usher the dazed and bewildered into the building. I caught a glimpse of the little girl running along hand-in-hand with one of her sisters and I knew she'd be OK. We drove back to camp in silence, each of us lost in his own thoughts. That day, I helped to ethnically cleanse two hundred and fifty people.

I was not best pleased to be tasked by Snapper to investigate reports of fighting in the hills above Poculica. I just wanted to have a drink and put images of those poor souls out of my mind. Instead, I climbed into 0B and hit the road again.

A little north of Poculica was a BiH checkpoint at a track that led to the village of Preocica. The fighting was supposed to have taken place near the villages of Ljubic and Slatine, a kilometre or so to the south. The guards were definitely local militia and were mostly middle-aged. Their leader was a stout, balding man with more chins than the Hong Kong telephone directory. He was sweating profusely in the afternoon heat but wouldn't let us pass, so I dismounted.

I'd soon learned that it was impossible to negotiate from the turret of a Warrior. First, the height of the vehicle and the noise of the engine were intimidating and impersonal. Equally impersonal was the checkpoint-eye view of the commander, two metres up and masked by helmet and dark glasses. Whatever the danger, the only way to negotiate was face to face, at ground level.

For once, towering over the opposition, I pointed out that it was the BiH who reported the fighting in the first place and what was the point in him not letting us through. He tried to tell me that it was for my own safety as we would run near to the Croat lines. I laughed and asked what they could do to me in my 'big white tank'. He was wavering and I was losing patience. I'd spent all morning helping his side and now they were preventing me from carrying out my duties. This was a gross over-simplification but the situation was, nevertheless, frustrating. The guy clearly wanted a quiet life and would've let me through if I'd pressed the issue. However, I wasn't prepared to use force as this was one of the main routes into Zenica. We would undoubtedly need to use the route again. We'd reached a stalemate when I hit on a cunning plan that Edmund Blackadder would have been proud of.

'I demand to see your brigade commander. He is an old friend of mine.'

This was untrue. I hadn't a clue who the man was as I hadn't been in Bosnia long enough to make any friends. The guard didn't know this and began to sweat even more at the mention of his boss. His shirt was now black and dripping. A cloud of flies buzzed around him and, unfortunately, around me as well.

Eventually, he nodded and scuttled off into a nearby house to make a phone call. Twenty minutes later a battered white Zastava 500 bowled up. Smart staff cars these Bosnian leaders had.

The brigade commander was a wiry man in his forties. He had a shock of black hair and a handlebar moustache that made him look like Zebedee from the 'Magic Roundabout'. As he walked towards me I caught a glimpse of gold teeth. He stopped in front of me and eyed me over.

'Good afternoon, sir! I am very pleased to meet you again so soon.' He was flummoxed and stopped in mid-sentence.

'You remember, sir. We met at a recent meeting when we were taking over from the Cheshires.'

The Commander looked confused for a moment and I could see the wheels turning as he desperately tried to figure out who I was.

'Oh I do apologise, sir. I've just started growing this moustache and that must have confused you. I'm afraid I've a long way to go until I have such a magnificent one as yours!'

He was hooked. His face split into an enormous grin and the sun glinted off his teeth. He started to preen his whiskers, which were obviously his pride and joy.

Within minutes we were chatting away like old friends. I don't think he could figure where he'd met me but I was so confident he certainly wasn't going to query it. He told me he'd approached the corps commander expressing his concern over the amount of sniping in his area. A local cease-fire had been negotiated and it appeared the Croats were regularly breaking it. I asked about the size of his brigade and he proudly told me he had over four hundred men under his command. When you consider there are over four thousand men in a British brigade it gives some idea of the small, localised nature of the conflict.

The guy was charm itself and told me he'd been a major in the JNA Artillery. He had no objections to me visiting his front line but did warn me to beware of Croat snipers. As he departed, he called the guard over and subjected him to a finger-pointing session and I thought the guy was going to melt. The fellow, and his swarm of flies, came over and apologised for the misunderstanding. Yes, of course, we could pass any time. As we returned to the Warrior the interpreter said:

'Major Vaughan. You are a better liar than most Bosnians!'

We drove up the track towards Preocica and turned off for Slatine a few hundred metres short of the village. There was a tiny chapel on the corner.

The track narrowed and eventually we had to stop. I dismounted, and saw the clearance was no more than ten centimetres on each side. To the right of 0B was a small cliff and to the left was a sheer drop of about fifty metres. I walked backwards, giving Tookey minor corrections to keep him as close to the rock wall as possible. Our left track sent stones and small boulders cascading down the slope. The path narrowed to about nothing on the right and five centimetres on the left. With a vicious rasping the Chobham plates scraped along the rock and I was on the verge of turning back when the track suddenly widened. I clambered back up the glacis and paused for a quick word of encouragement with Tookey. His face was glistening with sweat that collected in droplets on his moustache; he was doing a great impression of the man on the checkpoint.

We slowly passed through Ljubic where hordes of grimy children ran out to gawp at us. It was clear most of them had never seen a Warrior before and, given the state of the road to their village, it was hardly surprising. Not one of them begged for sweets and I realized it was the UN's fault there was such a problem on Route Diamond. If nobody handed over goodies the kids never knew what they were missing.

We passed a knot of about twenty soldiers ranging in age from about sixteen to sixty. Some were handing weapons over to their colleagues. I'd heard rumours there was a chronic shortage of weapons in the BiH and that the same rifle could be used by several men. Three or four were already heading back to the village and a similar number were walking the other way, slinging AKs over their shoulders.

A young man, with a green bandanna wrapped around his head, stopped us just short of the front line. I dismounted and Dobby and I went to meet him. He was irate and demanded to know how I'd reached the front line. I threw in that I'd seen the brigade commander but, if he was impressed, he didn't show it. He wanted us to turn back and I pointed out this was impossible given the lack of room.

We would go forward, as agreed with his commander, or we would stay there. It was obvious we were on a fairly hairy part of the line as all the BiH ran from cover to cover. In front of me, the guy I was talking to was squatting down and looking around nervously. I asked him what the matter was and he told me there was a Croat sniper who'd killed five men in the last two weeks. I said I wasn't scared, which was a lie, and that my blue beret would protect me, another lie. He lightened up then and I sat in his dugout for half an hour while he told me about the cease-fire violations. He told me they happened every evening at last light. I said I'd like to witness this and would be there the following evening. However, he thought the Croats would hear the Warrior and wouldn't fire. When I asked how far the lines were apart, he replied: 'Fifty metres!'

Eventually, I agreed to visit, on foot, the next evening. The guy seemed surprised I would take the risk but I told him that was what we were there for. I arranged the details and he said he'd leave a guide at the chapel to meet us.

We had to move on and the only way was forward. This part of the line was on the crest of a hill where there was a small farm. The house was on the right of the track and bore all the usual scars of life close to the line. The BiH soldiers moved their tables and chairs from the track, which was in dead ground to the Croats. However, there was still precious little room between the wall of the house on one side and a bunker on the left. There was no way I was going to demolish their dugout; they may have to fight from that tonight. As an infantryman, I thought how annoyed I'd be if some git in a tank came and trashed my dugout. I therefore plumped for the other option and we scraped down the side of the house. Masonry and dust fell over me and a window that was open was dragged off its hinges. The soldiers pulled part of the roof of the bunker to one side and we were through.

As we rounded the corner by the barn, the ground sloped away to a hedgerow partially concealing the brown line of the HVO trenches. There was a sudden 'crack' and both Phil and I ducked. We'd soon learned there were two types of small-arms contacts. The first was a 'Fuck you!' This was where a bullet passed close enough for the crew to be aware it had been fired at them but not close enough to be too dangerous. The automatic response to this was to raise the finger and shout 'Fuck you!'

The second was a 'Fuck me!' This was where the round was

extremely close, or hit the vehicle. Here the human self-defence mechanism took over producing an involuntary duck for cover, and a cry of 'Fuck me!'

This was definitely in the 'Fuck me' category. The round was high velocity and the crack of the bullet breaking the sound barrier overhead was instantly followed by the thump of the rifle firing.

The firer was very close and I was learning to judge the distance from the interval between the crack and thump.

We drove until we were out of sight of the BiH front line and then stopped. A crowd of scruffy HVO soldiers surrounded us and I dismounted to talk to them. They were a sorry looking bunch and all glared at me while they were swaggering about holding their AKs on the hip like gunslingers. There was a sickly stink of booze and I could also smell cannabis smoke on the air. There was no way I was going to get much sense out of this lot. They were the perfect example of the Croat machismo and were poles apart from the friendly, disciplined, lot on the other side of the line.

I asked them who'd fired the shot and why and they all laughed and blamed the Muslims. This was a bit rich unless the BiH had developed boomerang bullets. The Croats didn't want us in the area and accused me of taking weapons to the Muslims. I asked how they knew this and they said I'd been seen in the area several weeks before. Unless I had a double in the Cheshires this was a little unlikely. I asked about the cease-fire and they laughed again. They said they always respected it but the Muslims broke it every night. Funnily enough they rejected my offer to return and see this for myself.

I was beginning to see just why the Cheshires had formed the opinions they had. The Croats seemed to be a bunch of thugs who had the upper hand and were determined to rid the whole area of all Muslims. I'd not seen a single redeeming feature about these people. If these were my feelings so early on in the tour, how impartial was I going to be after six months?

I was glad to leave this bunch of scum and headed back to Vitez. Just north of the town, at a village called Krcevine, an HVO man tried to block the track with mines. He put the first one in the middle and ran back for more. We drove straight over the top of the mine. There was a metre clearance on each side and I judged it to be quite safe. I looked back and 0C was already through, leaving the poor guy standing in the road holding an armful of TMAs.

Back in camp there was still no peace for the wicked. First I went to see Snapper. I told him about the supposed violations and he said it was important that this was verified. The HVO commander, Colonel Tihomir Blaskic, was meeting the CO in a couple of days. Blaskic was always quick to blame the BiH for breaking the cease-fire and had insisted it was never his men that fired first. He'd gone on to say that he would personally investigate any proven Croat violations. This was the ideal opportunity to provide proof. The consequences could be a crackdown by the HVO leadership on rogue elements in their army. This might, in turn, lead to greater peace and stability in the area and freer movement of aid convoys. There seemed to be all to play for and I set about planning the operation.

I was sitting in the office writing my orders when Roy entered to remind me about the local liaison meeting. Here was something I could do without.

The Cheshires had started a series of meetings with the local community leaders over matters in the immediate vicinity of the school. This had worked well at first and had been a good opportunity for the community leaders of both sides to meet on neutral ground. However, after Ahmici, the Croats had attended once and received an understandably hostile reaction from the Muslims. Thereafter, they boycotted the event. The meetings had continued and become a forum for a one-sided airing of grievances. I couldn't see the point in this as all it served to achieve was to further polarize BRITBAT and the Croats.

Roy however, had entered into the spirit of the meetings and had already held three. They were on Mondays and Thursdays and were chaired by the guard company commander. Roy had done my last one and now it was pay-back time. I'd had a long day and didn't want to chair the bloody meeting. Still, a deal was a deal.

The forum was scheduled for 7 p.m. and five Muslims arrived five minutes before. They were all in their forties and fifties and were the village elders for the Stara Bila area. All were dressed in crumpled suits and had obviously made the effort to look smart for the occasion. Their spokesman was a fellow called Munib, a man of medium height with fair, curly hair. He had an open, honest face and a firm handshake and I immediately took a liking to him. He could've passed for the average German and was a reminder how different the average Bosnian Muslim was to the fanatic I'd met a couple of days earlier.

We waited for over thirty minutes making small talk and it seemed the Croats weren't going to appear again. However, a couple of minutes later one of the guard announced that three had arrived at the guardroom.

I met them at the front door to the school and was not impressed by what I saw. All had been drinking and all wore pistols, which they had to hand in to the guard. They were all in their twenties and were dressed in a mixture of combat trousers, sweatshirts and training shoes.

We returned to the conference room and I cut my way through the thick smoke to reach my chair. There were cursory handshakes between the two parties before both sides launched into vitriolic verbal attacks on each other. The interpreter was slaving away trying to relay the various sides to the arguments. In a nutshell, an HVO sniper had killed two people earlier in the day and a BiH sniper had killed one Croat. In the end I bellowed:

'Shut the fuck up!'

There was an instant, shocked silence. None of them had a clue what I'd said but the intention was clear. I then went on to ask each in turn for his comments and then asked the other side for their views. They were obviously used to speaking all at the same time and it was no wonder things took so long to accomplish in this part of the world. However, it was impossible to conduct business via an interpreter in this way. They soon got the hang of it and a couple of them even reverted back to school days and held their hand up when they wanted to speak. These men were neighbours and all knew each other well. They were all, however, falling into the spiralling cycle of mistrust and ethnic hatred. Both sides had legitimate grievances and I struggled to find a solution. All were concerned about snipers who were preying on the unwary and people were afraid to leave their houses during the day. This was an embarrassment as it was happening under the very noses of the battalion. Eventually, I agreed to send the occasional patrol through the village to discourage snipers and both sides agreed that it might work. At least I'd achieved something and I was just starting to feel smug when the oldest Muslim said:

'We are concerned about armed Croat gangs moving through our area and we believe they will attack us in our homes.'

The Croats were on their feet even before the interpreter had finished relaying the sentence to me. I tried to calm them down but all

I received was a stream of insults about how the British were supporting the BiH. They had 'information' that we were smuggling
weapons to the Muslims in Kruscica. This was all rubbish but the
Croats were in machismo mode and were determined to storm out
whatever else was said. I walked with them to the door and they
retrieved their pistols in silence. As they departed I tried to reassure
them that this battalion would be impartial but I could see I was
fighting against months of anti-British propaganda. It would be an
uphill struggle to get them on our side.

Back in the conference I immediately rounded on the Muslims.
They sat in silence while I berated them like naughty schoolboys. In
fact I pointed out that it was rather apt that we were in a school as
they were behaving like children. They hung their heads and eventually I calmed down. Munib repeated the concern that the Muslim
houses around the camp were to be the targets of Croat gangs. I
asked what we could do to help and he replied they would take care
of themselves.

It was easy to become pro-Muslim as the five were so reasonable.
The volatile Croats had stormed out amid a stream of threats and
there seemed no way they would attend any further meetings.
Munib told me they would be here again on Thursday and I said we
would patrol the local area more frequently. Little had been
achieved apart from widening the gulf between the two sides and I
couldn't see a future for one-party meetings. My dislike for the
Croats was growing by the day and tonight had only served to
heighten this. As they left, Munib gripped my hand and thanked me
for my patience. I told him if ever any of the people in the area were
in trouble they should come to the camp and ask for me personally.
I repeated my name and they looked bemused at the words 'Kent-
Payne'. In a flash of inspiration I remembered what the interpreter
had called me earlier:

'Just ask for Major Vaughan.'

Little did I realize how soon this promise of help would be called
upon.

I returned to the mess in a foul mood. Stephen Lees bounded
over to me and I thought for a moment that he was going to introduce himself again. Standing just out of punching range, he told me
about his first day in Bosnia. He'd been on patrol with Cooky and
had a contact at the Busovaca T-junction. There was a large factory
called the Mediapan on the corner and they'd been sniped at from

the rooftop. I retired to a corner and chatted to the subbies and gradually the place thinned out.

I was just about to leave when there was a frantic banging at the
door. Looking at my watch, I saw it was half past midnight. Pulling
the door open, I surprised a teenage boy in mid-knock. He rapped
three times on my chest before, with a look of horror, he realized
what he'd done. I gave him my best 'come here little boy, I'm not
going to hurt you' smile and he grabbed my arm. Jabbering away in
Serbo-Croat, he dragged me outside.

Leaving the light of the mess I couldn't see a thing outside and I
stumbled over something soft. Looking down I could just make out
a figure lying in the gutter. This was nothing unusual, just like Hull
on a Saturday night. The fellow was obviously drunk and was keeping me from my own drink. I gave him a rather uncharitable prod
with the toe of my boot but he didn't move. I bent down, prodded
him in the cheek and found he was warm. He still hadn't stirred and
I still couldn't see a thing. I slapped him on the chest and snatched
my hand away as I felt the sticky wetness. My first thought was:
'The bastard's puked-up.'

My hand was covered in something and I brought it up to my face
for a closer inspection. All I could see was a darker colour on the
palm but I could smell the unmistakable metallic odour of blood. I
ran back inside and retrieved a small Maglite torch from my flak
jacket and returned to the man, hotly pursued by those left in the
mess.

The guy was unmistakably dead. That is, unless he could carry on
living with five bullet wounds to the chest. There was a group of
holes spread over the area of a dinner plate and the holes were still
oozing blood. He wore military fatigues and combat boots. The jacket was open and I pushed my hand inside and under his body. There
were no exit wounds so it was likely the weapon was low-velocity
and the bullets were still inside him. There didn't seem much point
looking for a pulse but I did anyway. Stephen held the torch while I
checked. Nothing! I also checked his eyes. They were open and
already glazed over with a thin film of dust. I tried to close them, but
they kept popping open. You never see that happen in the movies.

There was nothing else I could do so I looked around me. A couple were sobbing in the shadows and I went across to them. By now,
a small crowd had gathered, including Padre Carson Nicholson,
Stephen, and Mike Stanley, one of the military interpreters.

The couple told me they were the dead man's parents. Two Croat soldiers had burst into their house and, with pistols, shot the man. This confirmed my diagnosis and I thought that 'Quincy' wasn't so smart after all. The man was on leave from the BiH front line and was killed in a house just a few metres over the road. His family had carried him here but he'd died on the way. They were, understandably, distraught and the woman was wailing and screeching. I asked if there was anything else I could do and they asked me to take the body to the local mosque, in nearby Grbavica. This seemed the least we could do so I told one of the guards to bring the duty ambulance to the mess.

As I was organizing this Carson stepped forward and asked the parents if they wanted him to perform the last rites on their son. They immediately agreed as the imam was away from the village. I then witnessed the extraordinary sight of a methodist minister administering the last rites to a Muslim via a Croat interpreter. This was the army padre at his best and his words seemed a great comfort to the family. The father was so dignified and kept thanking us. It was probably his defence mechanism and the grief would hit him later.

The ambulance arrived and we wrapped the body in a blanket and loaded it in. The damned wagon conked out and refused to be push started. This was becoming a farce so I ran to the quick reaction force (QRF) room and called out a Warrior crew. Within minutes I heard the engine starting up, over on the tank park, and the QRF wagon clattered towards us out of the darkness. The body was too tall to lie in the rear so we folded him in. Hardly the most dignified send-off.

We retired to the mess to finish our drinks. Stephen was quite shaken and Carson and I comforted him. He'd been shot at and seen a dead person on his first day in Bosnia. As I walked down the darkened lane towards the house I noticed that there were extra BiH guards patrolling around the village. Munib had been right about the hit squads. It was surreal that we could be disturbed from our pints to go and give the last rites to a murder victim and then carry on as if nothing had happened. There would be no inquiry and no trial for the perpetrators. It was amazing how quickly we'd adapted to the unreal way of life.

Next morning Roy and I built a wall around our verandah. Fered provided the breeze blocks and would've built the wall as well if we'd let him. Unfortunately, neither of us were particularly skilled builders and my comment of 'They're only like big Lego bricks' was far from the reality. We muddled on through and constructed a barrier, two blocks thick, around the concrete patio. It wasn't going to be bullet-proof but it would provide cover from view.

On the tank park, Dobby pointed out that we'd lost a deflector plate from the right rear. I hadn't noticed, but figured it happened when we scraped along the side of the house. There shouldn't be a problem as we were going back that night anyway.

That afternoon, I selected my patrol of six and wrote a complete set of orders for the cease-fire monitoring operation. They would take about three hours to deliver and I believed I'd covered every eventuality. There were dozens of 'actions-on'. Actions on there being no guide, on a contact on the walk to the front-line, on a Croat attack while we were on the line. Actions on one of us getting lost, on a loss of radio communications and so the list went on. They followed the same format as orders for a patrol in general war and I felt a tingle of anticipation for the night ahead.

I went to see Snapper to give him the time for the orders as he'd expressed a wish to accompany us, to log the violations himself.

'Sorry, I'm not coming. Richard's told me not to.'

Richard Watson walked in.

'I don't like the idea of you patrolling the lines at night,' he said.

'I might be considered to be gung-ho but I don't make a habit out of stupidity. There's no way I'm going to patrol the lines at night inviting a contact from some frightened soldier firing at sounds in the dark. This operation was in response to a specific tasking from battalion HQ and if you think it was a bad idea then why the hell was I given the job in the first place? If it's too dangerous to go out then what the hell are we doing here?' I said.

'I'm saying it's too dangerous to go there at night.'

'OK. I promise I won't risk the lives of any of my men.'

With that, I turned and stormed down to the office. The patrol was waiting for orders, sitting with notebooks at the ready, expectant for the details of the op.

'There's a change of plan. I'm going up to the lines alone now.'

I went on to explain that the risks were too great and there was a collective sigh of disappointment. Donlon voiced the thoughts of the others:

'We joined the fucking army to take risks!'

'Sorry boys, I can't let you go there.'

I finished the orders and we started to prepare the equipment. As I checked my rifle, the thought hit me that I was about to deliberately disobey an order for the first time in fifteen years in the army. I knew I was playing with semantics and that I wasn't actually risking any of my men as I'd promised. However, I knew I was disobeying the spirit of the order but thought it was worth it to complete, what I believed was, a worthwhile task.

We left the school at 6.30. Jason had volunteered to man the ops room and Stephen was on standby should we need assistance. At the Poculica checkpoint the same guard, complete with flies, waved us through with a cheery smile. We halted at the chapel and I gave Phil a final briefing. I would give a radio-check every ten minutes. If I missed a check he was to wait five minutes and then drive straight up to the line. If he heard firing and I did not confirm I was OK then the same applied. Dobby helped me on with my kit. I wore my flak vest with my chest-webbing over the top. In the pouches were five spare magazines and two hand grenades and a packet of flares. I had two torches, water bottles and a couple of packets of Marlboro I'd bought in the mess. On my back I carried a 351 Radio with a long antenna and a spare battery. Corporal Knight assured me I'd boom through to the Warrior. Finally, I wore my pistol inside my smock and had fitted an image-intensifying night-sight to my rifle. I was laden down, and felt like a Sherpa. I hadn't a clue what to expect and was having to carry the majority of kit that six of us would have taken.

At 7.15 the guide appeared, a big bear of a man with a shaggy black beard who introduced himself as Zijad. We set off on the two kilometres or so to the line, and I gave one, wistful, glance back. I was in pretty good spirits as the appearance of the guide was part of the plan I'd made with the local commander.

Zijad set a hell of a pace and I was soon dripping with sweat. It ran down my spine and collected in a puddle at the small of my back. I gasped out the radio checks. Communications were good and I was heartened to hear Jason's urbane tones loud and clear from the ops room, some five kilometres away.

Finally, we reached the line and the same commander greeted me like a long-lost brother. In the fading light, he pointed out the ground before we moved into the barn. We climbed up a rickety ladder and lay on the floor of the hayloft. Through a hole in the planks

I could clearly see the Croat lines with the occasional wisp of smoke indicating their cooking fires. Through my binoculars I saw the heads of several men and I could have shot at least one of them at this range. It made me realize that casualties were often limited by the simple weaponry available to the opponents. With more sophisticated kit, like my night-sight, there would be a greater chance to deal death on a far grander scale.

The commander showed me the body of one of his men who'd been killed earlier in the day. The man had been shot in the throat. The exiting round had taken a chunk out of his spinal column causing the head to loll at an unnatural angle. The BiH wanted me to examine the wounds. Who did they think I was, Doctor bloody Kildare? I dutifully prodded around the sludgy wound on the man's neck for a while until they seemed satisfied I'd seen enough of this evidence of cease-fire violations.

We retired to sit in his dugout. I handed over a packet of cigarettes and soldiers suddenly appeared from everywhere. Western tobacco was a much sought-after commodity. A couple of minutes later an old man appeared leading a tiny pony that was drawing a small cart. Steam was coming out of a metal container and I realized he was their equivalent of the CQMS, up with the rations.

They offered me a share of the thin gruelly stew and I poured a ladle-full into my tin mug and gingerly tasted the stuff. It was surprisingly good though God knows what the meat was! We chatted away about army life and they told me they were regular soldiers from Zenica who were billeted in the village for a week at a time. They were all sick of the War and just wanted to go home. They were equally determined there'd be no more Ahmicis and would fight to ensure that.

Darkness was falling and, at just before 8.30, the first shot came over. There was a loud crack, and no thump. It had been fired from very close by. We crawled to just below the crest of the hill and I meticulously logged each shot. I also relayed the information to Phil so at least the violations could be reported to the CO if something happened to me. The first shots were small arms and the commander pointed out the difference between the shots from the AK 47 and the even higher velocity of the sniper rifle. At around 8.45, the Croats opened up with a heavy machine gun. The first rounds flew over with a series of immense cracks, the green tracer briefly illuminating our anxious faces. I figured the weapon was probably a

14.5 mm machine gun. The thump of the firing was a few seconds later and I guessed it was from around a kilometre away. The gunner must have adjusted his aim because the next burst hit the wall of the house. The sharp detonations sent ricochets rocketing skyward with banshee wails. His third burst hit the bank above our heads and we were showered with dirt. The commander, not surprisingly, had had enough and led me back to the safety of the bunker.

The firing died down and I could hear an eerie chanting from the Croat lines: '*Balija! Balija!*'

This was the same word I'd heard at Turbe and I asked what it meant. It was the grossest insult to a Muslim. It didn't really have a translation but it was seriously rude.

I had achieved all I'd set out to do. I'd no doubt the BiH would've returned fire if I wasn't there. They would've been superhuman not to have retaliated. All over the valley I could hear little skirmishes and there was no way the cease-fire was holding.

Before I left, I asked if they'd found my deflector plate. There were lots of shrugs but no positive response. I knew it had to be there and their lies left a bitter taste.

Zijad led me down the hill. I told Phil we were on our way and heard the engine of the Warrior cough into life as Tookey switched on to charge the batteries. With about five hundred metres to go I stumbled over something white, lying on the track. By the faint moonlight I recognized our missing plate. There was no way it was there before as we'd walked up in broad daylight. The crafty beggars. They wouldn't admit they had it but they wouldn't keep it either. That was so Bosnian, a nation of unfathomable enigmas.

I tried to lift the plate and the radio slipped up my back and smacked me on the helmet. As I tried again, I was gently pushed aside and Zijad hefted the plate onto his shoulder and lumbered towards the Warriors.

Back at 0B I recounted the evening's exploits to the crew and I could tell they were hacked off at missing the show. I bade farewell to our guide and we left, returning to camp at just after 10.30.

Looking back, the operation was a waste of time. There was, in the end, very little danger but the task just wasn't worth doing. There were so many violations, on both sides, that the cease-fire agreement wasn't worth the paper it was written on. I don't know if the CO ever presented my information to Blaskic. What I do know, however, is that the Croat leadership would not have carried out an investigation. It was naïve to believe otherwise. I genuinely believed we could make a difference and save lives in the process. As the tour progressed, I saw that both sides were hell-bent on destroying each other and we were powerless to stop them.

Richard and Snapper were right to oppose the operation. However, in my opinion, they objected for the wrong reasons. Their view was that nothing in Bosnia was worth the risk. A very safe standpoint but one that was unlikely to give us the best results. We were there to do a job and, unfortunately, there was always an element of risk. It went with our profession. It was a bit like firemen standing by a blaze because they might get hurt if they tackled it. I resolved never again to be talked into such a worthless venture. I should've seen that no amount of cease-fire monitoring was going to alter the price of fish.

Back at the room, I had to borrow Roy's scrubbing brush to clean two evening's worth of dried blood from under my fingernails.

Chapter 6
Hero of Muslim Street

I awoke to the sounds of gunfire and explosions at 5.30 in the morning. There were bursts of automatic fire very close by and it appeared as if some locals were using our nice new wall as a convenient piece of cover. At one stage some Johnny loosed a whole magazine off from the patio and I heard the empty cases clinking as they hit the ground. Roy and I grabbed our weapons and listened expectantly. It sounds naff, but, with the shutter down, we hadn't a clue what was going on outside the window. With the shutter up, Roy's bed was exposed to the outside world. The kitchen door was flimsy, cheap wood and had a large glass pane that would stop an assailant for about a second. We knew there was supposed to be no threat to us. However, if there was ethnic cleansing to be done, who was going to notice a few small UN flags in the dark? Every time there was firing close by we expected the worst. Not so the boys, tucked up in their Portakabins. They slept for eight hours a night secure in the knowledge that thirty men were on guard, solely to protect them. No wonder I looked like death every morning.

This time it was far more than the normal bursts of fire and there were several loud explosions. Peeking through the shutters I noticed a large pall of black smoke in the area of the mess. There was something afoot so I pulled on my clothes and went to investigate.

I reached the corner of the mess just as the cottage opposite burst into flame. There was still a lot of shooting across the road with the occasional 'Whoosh' as some sort of rocket was fired. I ran to the room where the company headquarters boys were living and woke up the crew of 0B. Ten minutes later, six of us gingerly patrolled towards the firing. There was no point in taking the Warriors as the area was only fifty metres from the mess. We hard targeted across the road as if we were back in Belfast.

The HVO had moved into the area at dawn and cleansed the Muslims from about a dozen houses. Several were ablaze. We cleared the outside areas first and came across the body of an old man in a yard. Face up, he lay in a huge pool of blood. He wore a pair of grey trousers and a white vest. His feet were bare. He'd obviously run out of the house at the first sound of firing and been cut down in his own garden. Hit by at least a dozen bullets, he'd probably died of the three in the chest. There were also a couple of holes in his stomach and I noticed the pinky-grey snake of entrails protruding from one. There were wounds to his legs and the whole scene tallied with being sprayed at close range with an AK 47. The yard was littered with dozens of spent cases that glittered in the flames of the burning houses. Judging by the number of strike marks on the wall, these animals were better murderers than they were shots. The worst aspect of the affair was that they'd shot him in the head as he lay on the ground. Three more rounds had hit him, blowing most of his jaw away. The back of his head was also gone and his brains spattered over the concrete. I stared with a morbid fascination as the famed 'grey matter' was, actually, a light-brown colour. His white hair was matted with blood and there was a dark stain around the front of his trousers that wasn't blood. It was no way to die and brought home just how undignified death is.

A shout from Tookey brought me back to reality. He was in his element, dodging around as if pleased to be free from the confines of the Warrior. He led me to a barn, which was blazing away, and the stench of burning flesh hit me. Fearing the worst, I kicked open the door and was met by a searing blast of hot air. The cause of the smell was not another human but a cow, chained to a post. It was long gone and there was nothing we could do for the poor creature. We entered every house we could. Three were almost burned to the ground and we were beaten back by the flames. A couple had been hit by RPG rockets.

The final house I entered was well ablaze. I kicked open the front door, shielding myself from the expected blast of heat. There was, however, little fire but a great deal of smoke. It was thick and oily, with particles suspended in it that stuck to my clothes. It was impossible to see through and I remembered it was likely to be deadly to inhale. There was a clear space of about a metre, at ground level, and

I crawled on my belly across the carpet. I glanced behind for one of the others but the door was already lost in the smoke. I don't know why I went in but I just felt there was some need. The room divided into two others. One door was shut and smoke was billowing under it and adding to the dense concentration in the room. The paint at the bottom was bubbling and it would be only a matter of time before the flames burst through.

The other door was open and I hesitated on the threshold. I somehow knew there was someone inside the room. There were no indications, it was just a sixth-sense. Usually, it was the smell that alerted me to the presence of bodies but all that was in my nostrils was the whiff of smoke. As more smoke filled the room, the gap lowered and I knew it was now or never.

Leopard-crawling my way across a blue-and-white rug, my rifle clattered against the floor as I edged forward. I clashed into the feet of something and put a hand up into the smoke, groped around on the top of the object, and brought down a hand mirror. This was presumably someone's bedroom and I changed direction and felt my way around the skirting board. The gap was little more than half a metre high and I was beginning to lose my bottle. Every so often the smoke would dip to ground level forcing me to hold my breath until a space cleared again. The acrid smoke stung my eyes and I wondered if the constant streaming would wash my contact lenses out. I was just about to sack-it when I bumped into an arm.

I looked up and a finger poked me in the nostril. With a squeal, I slithered back and then felt really silly looking round to see if anyone had noticed. I thought: 'Here we go again.'

The arm was connected to a middle-aged lady lying in a bed. She wore a pink nightie with frills around the cuff. I held my breath and knelt up. She was under the bed clothes and looked as if she were asleep. Her face was bright pink and a wisp of brown hair hung down one cheek. I subconsciously pushed it behind her ear and felt that she was already cold. If I needed any further proof she was dead I accidentally leaned on her chest and a plume of smoke issued forth from her mouth. There was no need to close her eyes and it looked as if she'd died of smoke-inhalation in her sleep.

I was going to attempt to drag her outside as she would surely be consumed by the approaching flames. First, however, my lungs were bursting and I needed air. Ducking to the floor again, I drew in a deep gulp, just as the smoke dipped around me again. The stuff stung my lungs and it felt like I'd breathed in the flames themselves. I shuddered and coughed violently and inhaled yet more of the deadly smoke. I had visions of joining this poor woman in death and I panicked. Almost forgetting my rifle in my haste to get away, I floundered across the floor towards where I thought the door was. My chest was on fire and I had to get out, and bloody quickly. Suddenly, I head-butted the wall. I tried to kneel up and nutted something above me as well. My eyes were streaming and smarting and my head was spinning as I tried to figure out where I was. There was so much smoke the room was almost dark and I groped around until I realized, with relief, that I was under the dressing table. At least I knew where I was again and tried to back away. This time, the lip of my helmet caught on the underside of the table and I panicked again. I stood up and the dresser and its contents were hurled asunder. More smoke entered my lungs and I puked it out with last night's BiH gruel. I was on my feet and running now, flailing around with my rifle desperately searching for the door. There were stars in front of my eyes and a thumping in my ears that I vaguely realized was my heart. The stars gave way to a flickering and I'd reached the bedroom door. The flickering came from the other door that had been almost breached. Tongues of flame, like blowtorches, shot out from the wood in several places and I stumbled past it feeling the searing heat on my cheek. With a gasp I finally reached the front door that had shut behind me. I knew I was fading fast, and with a final burst of energy, which appeared from nowhere, I pulled it open. However, I was dismayed to find there was no instant rush of cool, sweet air but yet another lung-full of smoke. Retching up nothing, I realized I was inhaling the smoke from the house as it swirled past me. I literally fell down the concrete steps landing in a bruised and crumpled heap coughing and spluttering. It was here that Dobby found me, five minutes later. 'Ey up boss! Are you sunbathing or what?'

I was about to chew his face off for being such a cheeky git when the realization hit me that I'd bloody nearly died. Giving him a sickly grin and wiping spew from my chin, I stood up.

'Anyone in there?'

'No!' I lied, and hoped he couldn't see the guilt on my face. I didn't want to admit that I'd failed and I knew if I mentioned the woman, Dobby was the sort who'd go back in after her. She was dead and the flames were already licking out of the windows. Suddenly, they popped, showering glass over the yard. There was nothing more we could do so I kept quiet. I was a complete prat for going in alone and I realized just how bloody brave firemen are. For days afterwards I coughed up little black bits and my shame prevented me from ever reporting sick.

Half an hour later I was back in our house. Roy was still in bed and I called him for all the lazy bastards under the sun as I washed off the worst of the grime. Ten minutes later, at 7.30, I was sitting in the cookhouse eating my breakfast, while two people lay dead, less than a hundred metres away.

After scoff, I returned over the road with the same patrol. James Myles asked if I would take some members of the media along. The body of the old man had gone but the BBC crew filmed the pool of congealed blood. I avoided the woman's house, which was almost burned to the ground. The BBC reporter, Malcolm Brabant, wanted to talk to some of the locals.

We walked to the nearest house occupied by HVO soldiers. There were four of them and, after a little persuasion, they invited us inside. They were all in their early twenties and had the swagger of a group of soldiers who'd kicked arse on the battlefield. The difference was, this bunch had just kicked the arses of an old man, and a woman in her bed. They were looking down on us and giggling to each other.

One of them had a spotty face and wore a dark green beret complete with a Royal Green Jackets badge. He said he didn't want to appear on camera, which was hardly surprising considering what he'd just been part of. Spotty tried to give me the eye and I stared back. He selected a cigarette from a packet marked with the brand name 'SET' and lit it with a gold lighter. The Croat blew a stream of pungent smoke in my face before pushing past me and stalking outside, picking his nose as he went. Brabant was busy setting up his interview so I followed. We stood in the yard, eye-balling each other. He was dressed in the usual ex-American fatigues tucked into a pair of Gore-Tex boots. His shirt was opened to the navel exposing an expanse of hairless, spotty, chest. It was complemented by a large, black plastic, crucifix on a silver chain. A pair of sun glasses hung from his shirt pocket and he held the obligatory AK in his left hand. To complete the ensemble of the professional Infantryman, he wore a large combat knife on a belt with a death's head buckle. He looked like the sad gits you see in American survivalist programmes.

Something told me he was involved in the murder of the old man and I wanted to ask him. I was about to go back inside the house to fetch the interpreter when he blew smoke over me again. I inhaled some of it and it stung my sore lungs, causing me to cough involuntarily. The Croat giggled, the red mist came down, and I went for him.

The guy had been expecting it and was much quicker than me. He struck first and a straight punch, that Mike Tyson would've approved of, hit me in the chest.

There was an audible crack of broken bones, as his fist connected with the hand grenade in my top pocket. Before he could squeal, my own punch hit him in the stomach. His breath expelled with a hiss and the half-smoked cigarette was blown past my ear. He doubled-up with a grunt, still clutching his AK. I followed up with a downwards jab with all my strength. My gloved hand connected with the area above his kidneys and the shock jarred up my arm, leaving my fingers numb. Spotty fell, face first, the rest of the way to the ground. His AK clattered onto the concrete, rapidly followed by his chin. There was a slight commotion inside and I glanced up to see Dobby's bulk blocking the door like a fridge freezer. He was making sure I wasn't disturbed, and, looking around, I saw no one else had witnessed the incident.

I was sorely tempted to give the swine a good kicking and, in fact, stopped in mid-swing. Some little voice, probably the same one who'd advised me in Loncari, stopped me. Spotty was wheezing in the dust trying to hold both his stomach and back at the same time, which was no mean feat. It left him flipping about like a freshly-caught fish on the deck of a boat. I bent down and hauled him to his feet. His chin was grazed from the fall and several of his zits had burst, adding a bit of extra colour to his florid face. However, his eyes were the best bit. He was scared stiff.

They were wide as saucers and darted about looking for any possible escape. He knew he'd been felled, one on one, and he cowered there with his hands covering his groin, like a footballer awaiting a free kick. I wished I had a cigarette to blow smoke over him.

I picked up his rifle, thrust it at him noticing, with satisfaction, how he winced when his injured hand came into contact with the hard edges. His eyes narrowed, and I wondered for a moment, if he were going to try to shoot me. I gave him my best, lip-curling, contemptuous stare, turned, and sauntered off with as slow a walk as I could manage. The hairs on the back of my neck prickled but soon stopped when I noticed good old Dobby was aiming his rifle, covering the HVO's every move. Spotty had lost face, an unforgivable sin for a Croat, and I doubted if he would ever tell anyone what happened. I was also quite sure that he'd try to kill me, given half a chance.

Brabant's interview was in full swing. The three Croats had forgotten about the strange noises coming from outside and were revelling in their roles as movie stars. The reporter asked them why they burned the Muslim houses and was told the Muslims had done it themselves. However, he wouldn't let that go and kept probing until one of them admitted it was because of a sniper who lived in the area. All they'd done was to take 'military action'. They then realized they'd probably said too much and clammed up.

As we left, Brabant muttered:

'Bunch of wankers!'

The cottage opposite the mess was virtually razed. Only a couple of sections of wall remained amid the heaps of smouldering rubble. An old lady had lived there and I wondered what'd become of her.

I patrolled out, later in the day, to see the new 'tunnel' concept. David had given the problem of too many convoys and too few escorts some thought. His solution was to create a sanitized 'tunnel' through which aid could pass freely. There were two halves. One from the south of GV to a map intersection called the 81 Northing, and the second from there to the Novi Travnik T-junction. B Company manned the southern sector and the Vitez sub-units the north. Our sector was manned by four armoured vehicles. There were always two stationary vehicles at the T-junction. The other two patrolled down to the 81 and then back, where they swapped. Thus, there were eight vehicles involved in the whole of the tunnel with four roving at any one time. Anyone wishing to interfere with the convoys would never know exactly when the next patrol would come along. Also, the drivers were reassured as they were sure to see eight UN vehicles during their journey.

At a stroke, the number of vehicles on plain convoy escort was cut by at least half. There was still the need to escort the various aid agencies and monitors but now several callsigns were freed for other patrol duties. We could now start to get to know our patch. On the way back, we passed an A Company Warrior parked at the junction of the camp access road and main road. This was the guard Warrior and was there to deter further Croat aggression. At the house, I threw my kit onto my bed and started to clean my weapons. All of us carried our SA 80 Rifle, with a full magazine of thirty rounds on the weapon, at all times. I had all tracer rounds in the mag in case I was called upon to indicate any targets. I also had a second magazine that was in one of the top pockets of my flak vest. All Warrior commanders were also issued with a Browning 9 mm automatic pistol. This was in case anyone climbed onto the Warrior and threatened us. At least we could shoot them off with this as it would be difficult to deploy a rifle through the narrow turret hatch. The magazine held thirteen rounds and I kept another full one in my jacket pocket. I carried the pistol in a leather shoulder-holster that I'd used in Northern Ireland. The holster was worn immediately under the flak jacket. It was a quick and simple action to pull open the Velcro fastener of the vest and pull out the pistol. It also had the advantage of concealment. I'd tried out the issue green canvas holster that hung from the belt. However, it caught every time I climbed through the turret hatch and was a bloody nuisance. The CO had bought a rather Gucci gunslinger-type holster in camouflage fabric that fitted snugly to his belt and alleviated this problem. I was careful never to wear my holster around and I always took it off when I removed my flak vest in the mess. I knew I'd only get called a cowboy so I kept it well hidden. Finally, I carried two grenades. One of these was in a side pocket and the other, most fortuitously, in the other top pocket of the flak vest. On examining it, I noticed that the fly-off lever was dented from the force of Spotty's punch.

There was no arms store and I kept my weapons with me and always loaded. Soon they became extensions of me and I hardly noticed them. The Chain Guns on the Warrior were kept in the wagons and loaded at the start of each patrol but unloaded when we entered camp. The RARDENs were only loaded in an emergency.

I was sitting on the verandah sipping a coffee and writing home when Munib stepped into view. He had with him a lady of around thirty whom I'd seen around the houses. The woman introduced herself, in halting English, as Sonja. She was around five foot five, slim, with dark curly hair. She'd apparently learned her English in Australia.

Sonja started to tell me that it was Munib's father who'd been murdered over the road and his house was now in Croat hands. The poor fellow was grief-stricken. Earlier, he'd used the lull between my first deployment and the return of the Croats to dash back and retrieve the body. His father was dead and his house, a hundred metres away, was in Croat hands.

Munib begged me for help saying that the Muslims were worried the aggression would switch to the houses around our own. They were running scared and a group of about twenty of them had gathered to listen. I asked about the weapons I knew were around and they told me they would try to defend their homes but the Croats always came in strength. Finally, Munib said:

'You are a man of honour. I have seen the tank outside the camp and it will prevent the Croats from attacking. You told me you would do this and you were as good as your word. Please help us from further attacks.'

I didn't need this. It was Roy who was the one that was so keen on the bloody meetings. Why didn't they go and find him? At least he didn't say the Warrior was a day too late to save his Dad. I was busy listing reasons why I couldn't help. For a start, even if the Croats did attack, we were powerless to intervene unless there was a risk to life. Burning empty houses, for instance, was way outside our jurisdiction. It was a mandate minefield. I was about to speak when Munib said: 'You said that if we were ever in trouble we should ask for Major Vaughan. Well, we are in trouble now.'

Me and my bloody big mouth. Rule number one was supposed to be 'never promise the locals anything'. Eventually, I agreed to ask if I could send more patrols into the local area to help with their security. They were incredibly grateful and started showering thanks on me. This time I was more wary and told them it was not a promise, and I would only look into it. It was no good. I may as well have offered to kill half the HVO for them. They wanted to believe I'd help and I was stuck again. How the hell was I going to run this past the CO?

I went to his office in the school. He was sitting behind his desk, smoking a French cigarette that smelled like camel dung. I knocked on the door frame and he called me in. After giving him a résumé of the day's events, I told him about Munib, the liaison meeting and the deputation outside the house.

'Go on,' he said, with his lips tightening.

'Well, sir. If the Croats attack the buildings around ours it will put all the occupants of the officers' house at grave risk. The threat is probably not from a direct attack but from stray rounds, especially at night. We could be forced to move and there's no room for an extra forty officers in the camp. If we moved, then the HVO would control the access along the concrete road and perhaps prevent us using it. The mess would be untenable and a new building would have to be found. Finally, the UN would have no credibility as we cannot even prevent our own officers being driven out of their accommodation.'

'What do you propose?'

'Well, we need to continue with the guard Warrior. I also believe we should patrol the local area at first and last light to show we won't tolerate fighting on our doorstep.'

There was a pause and he smiled and said:

'Well done. Fix it.'

He looked back down to his papers, that was as good as saying 'Next!'

Jason showed me the next day's tasking and almost every vehicle was involved in escort duties. The only spare ones were from company HQ. It looked like another early start.

Back at the house there was an impromptu get together on the patio. All the occupants were there. Roy and I were the downstairs dwellers. Upstairs were Carson, who had a room to himself, and Monika, the doctor sharing with Jane Brothwell. Colin Hay, one of the UKLOs occupied a small room. He was Angus's brother and from the Queen's Own Highlanders. Finally, the big room was shared by Boris Cowan, Tom Wagstaff and Randy Rhodes. Yes, Randy Rhodes. He was the UN civil advisor attached to the battalion. He was an American who'd been a Navy Seal for many years. Randy was about six-feet-two and built like the proverbial brick shit-house. He had the sort of inverted triangle torso that only comes from decades of pumping iron.

It was up at four o'clock for me. The crew was waiting on the tank park and 0B was already rumbling away. The air was freezing and a thick mist left a fine film of moisture on the surface of the Warrior as I climbed up to carry out the turret-checks. We departed and turned left out of camp, across the bridge over the Bila River. We turned left again a little further on, and up a very steep dirt track. One side was deeply eroded and we slid precariously close to the edge. The track led us to the village of Grbavica. The house on the crest of the hill was deserted and the blue-and-white flag of the BiH fluttered from the roof-top. Our position overlooked camp and I could just pick out the white Portakabins. My house was only a hundred metres away, just over the river, and the UN flags were invisible in the mist. We needed a better form of recognition and I decided to ask about a bigger flag.

We stopped in the narrow street in full view of the newly-captured houses where Munib had lived. Down below I could hear, but not see, 0C crawling round the Croat part of the village. It was now 4.30 a.m. yet there were several people about, many of them tending gardens. We were told they only dared work the land at night, or in thick mist, for fear of the snipers. The locals all thanked us for our help in protecting them. As there'd been no firing, we'd succeeded, at least for the time we were there.

There was no firing on either side of the line that morning and we were back in by six. I was shattered and freezing cold and went back to bed for an hour.

All my vehicles were out so I went to Milinfo for tasking. Staff McLeod was there, and asked if I could take him to Kruscica to check on reports of BiH troops in the village. I went to the interpreter's office to see if one was free and encountered a wailing Muslim woman. She'd lived in one of the houses over the road and had lost all her possessions. I thought she was about to start to blame me for the death of the woman and my guilt surged up again. Instead, she asked if I would help her recover several sacks of flour from her home. There were now around thirty refugees living in the houses around ours and they needed all the food they could get. I started to give the party-line that we were unable to help and it was a matter for her leaders to resolve with the Croats. She started wailing again and I went on to say that it was a local matter anyway and that the Guard Company was responsible. I said that Major Roy would be pleased to help. Come to think of it, where was Roy? He was like a bloody policeman, never around when you needed him. Suddenly, I remembered, he'd gone off with Carson to the church in Vitez. I was on my own.

Try as I might, I always seemed to agree to help people in trouble. I had to learn to say no. Reluctantly I agreed to look at the problem and her face split into a grin, exposing a row of rotten, black teeth. She moved forward, as if to hug me but, with a body-swerve that Will Carling would've admired, I was out of the door.

Back at the house, I was confronted by Munib and the other local leaders. He too wanted me to collect the flour.

'Why can't you go and collect it?' I said.

'Because the Croats will kill us if we try.'

'Why don't you negotiate for the handover of the flour?'

'We have tried but they will not agree.'

'If I walk over with you, will you go then.'

'No. Because the snipers will shoot past you to kill us.'

'What about if I escort you over in a Warrior.'

'It would be better if we could ride inside the Warrior.'

'Now you are asking too much. It's an escort or nothing.'

I was becoming better at negotiating. I knew I was in the position of strength and started to walk off.

'OK. We will come if there is a Warrior there.'

I sent for 0B and discussed the dangers with Mike Stanley. We agreed there were many risks and the Croats were not likely to just hand over the flour. Also, the task was outside the scope of the mandate. We could be construed as interfering in the dispute and taking sides.

However, the other argument was that if we obtained the flour there would be no need for us to take it from UN stocks. It was all pretty nebulous and was a problem I was rapidly beginning to wish I hadn't become involved in.

I tried to phone the CO for advice but he was out at a meeting. I then called Richard, who told me it was an operations matter. Finally, I called David and explained the problem.

'You are the man on the ground. You are best placed to make a decision.'

I knew if this went tits-up the colonel would hang me out to dry. David's answer was in the best tradition of staff officers and I made a note to remember it for the future.

0B had arrived and I positioned it outside the mess and briefed Phil. The locals had brought along an ancient handcart and six of them stood around it. Each wore the sort of expression that said, 'I wish I'd stayed in bed this morning'.

I briefed the men that the Warrior would drive slowly across the road. They were to push the cart beside it, keeping the hull between most of the Croat houses and themselves. Mike, myself, McLeod and Dobby would walk in the open as an obvious sign that armed UN soldiers were about. We were about to set off when they bottled out. One of them suddenly bolted for the nearest house and soon all six had melted away.

'Right, sack it! If they won't show any commitment, we're not doing this on our own.'

A crowd of women had also gathered and they began to harangue their menfolk. Especially vociferous was the one who'd started the affair in the first place. The blokes looked ashamed but none made any effort to return. After a few minutes, she tossed her head in a gesture of contempt, walked over to us, and picked up one handle of the cart. Moments later three others joined her and they were back in business.

This is just typical of women the world over. Often, when the chips are down it's the fairer sex that shows us weak men the way ahead. These four were certainly a formidable bunch and possessed enough cellulite between them to keep a medium-sized power station going for a week. As we were about to go, one of the men rushed up, and I thought he'd been shamed into joining us. He said something to a woman and Mike nearly exploded, launching into what had to be a stream of Serbo-Croat insults. The man scurried away again and I asked what'd happened.

'The bastard asked his wife to collect the television set while she was in the house!'

I was about to give the order for the off when I noticed the media. God knows how they got wind of the little operation, but two of them were now standing by, watching with interest. One introduced himself as Mike Evans, of *The Times*. The other was a freelance photographer, the veteran of more wars than the rest of us put together. He'd worked in just about every major conflict, and a few minor ones, for the last decade. We called people like him 'combat groupies'. The worst of them seemed addicted to the horrors of war and were always asking about the bodies we'd seen: was there much blood? Had he crapped himself? This guy was a short, wiry man with long, greasy, curly hair. His eyes darted about with manic speed and the rest of his body wasn't far behind. He was the last person I wanted on a job like this but I could not prevent him from following us.

Finally, we were off and I walked in front of the Warrior to keep the pace down. I could hear the cartwheels squeaking above the clatter of the tracks. Soon McLeod was lending a hand as the women struggled with the cumbersome barrow. The Croats had occupied the Muslim houses and were starting to fortify them. Already, the scars of recently-dug trenches were appearing and several doorways had timbers placed over them to give protection from shell splinters.

The soldiers heard the Warrior and emerged, clutching their weapons. When they saw the women, they cocked the weapons and pointed them at us. They were only about thirty metres away and I recognized two of the Croats from the Brabant interview. Phil had traversed on and I saw the barrel was pointing at the nearest HVO man. With a sick feeling I realized this was largely my fault.

In my haste to complete the task I'd completely forgotten to tell the HVO what I was going to do. It was only a two-minute walk and would've probably taken five minutes to clear the path. Now, like a dickhead, I'd put us all in jeopardy by my stupidity. Not surprisingly, the Croats probably thought I was leading a Muslim crusade to reclaim the houses. It was my cock-up and I had to sort it quickly. I told the women to take cover, which was totally unnecessary as they were all blending themselves into the tarmac. Mike and I walked forwards and the rifles all trained on us. I was glad Spotty wasn't there as I'd probably have been ventilated by now. We talked to the Croat soldiers and explained what we wanted. There followed ten minutes of very tense negotiation until gradually the rifles were lowered. They wouldn't let the women back into the area but us soldiers could come and retrieve the flour. I was amazed, it was the first reasonable action I'd seen from a Croat. There was no reason for them to give us the flour and we had no right to take it. Had they refused, we would've had to turn around again. As it was, I was overjoyed this was actually going to work when suddenly the mood changed and the rifles were, once more, raised. This time, they were pointing past me. Looking round, I saw the cause of their anger. The freelance was squatting in a doorway filming us through a lens the size of a small cannon. I could hear the motor-drive whirring away and, with that lens, he was probably getting a good close-up of Croat nostril hair. He was in danger of ruining everything and I shouted at him:

'Get behind the bloody Warrior!'

He moved reluctantly and I called back to Dobby to escort the women back to the houses. Mike and I then returned to the cart and, together with McLeod, started to drag it towards the Croats. Dobby rejoined us, and we drew level with the HVO when the same happened again. This time, I didn't need to guess what the problem was. There was the bloody photographer, in the same bloody doorway, taking the same bloody pictures. I'd had enough and ran back to confront him. He got the message and rushed back to the Warrior.

Back at the Croats, Mike had done a great job of calming them down. I said I'd told the photographer that I'd ram the camera up his arse if I saw him again. This caused peals of laughter from them and, without further ado, they started to help push the cart.

Things were going well again and there were so many of them around the cart I didn't have to help. It was too good to be true and, sure enough, the Bosnia factor intervened.

'Crack! Crack!'

As we entered the gap before the house we were exposed to the Grbavica hill. A BiH gunman had seen the Croats clustered around the cart and the target was too good to waste. The rounds struck the path, a couple of metres in front of me raising a shower of dirt, which was caught by the breeze. I had no time to blink and the dust hit me in the face mixing nicely with my contact lenses. By the time I'd got my eyes open again the Croats had disappeared into the gardens. The gunman fired again and hit the wall behind which an HVO man was hiding. With a high-pitched whine, the bullet ricocheted away into the air like a sound effect from a B-movie. I was standing still and the cheeky git had fired right past me to hit the wall. The only possible firing point was an upstairs window of the house with the BiH flag on it.

The gunman fired again, this time at a tin shed and I thought, 'How the hell did we get caught up in all this?'

Here we were, helping the Muslims to retrieve their flour. The Croats had driven the Muslims out of the house where the flour was. The Croats were now helping us to retrieve the flour. The Muslims were shooting at the Croats, and us, as we tried to get the flour for other Muslims. It was the sort of situation that could only happen in this crazy little War.

Back on our own now, we dragged the cart to the front door. An HVO soldier appeared and demanded:

'How many sacks of flour are there?'

I hadn't bothered to find out so I made up a number.

'Six.'

'There, you see! The Muslims can't be trusted, there are eight!' We hefted the bags down from the loft to the barrow, which groaned under the weight. The cart was disintegrating under the load now and we pulled, pushed and dragged it back towards the Warrior. The sniper fired three more rounds, this time just over our heads, and I realized he probably thought we were helping the Croats. Finally, we reached the mess and several willing Muslim hands took the cart from us. Funny how they were so bloody helpful now the danger was past.

I sought out Munib and told him what I thought of the whole affair. 'You've abused my trust. While we were helping you, BiH snipers were firing at us. There'll be no more incidents like this. I'm not prepared to get any of my men killed for the sake of a few sacks of flour.'

As he hung his head in shame I noticed that Mike Evans was scribbling furiously in his notebook. He followed me into the house and we chatted while I stripped off my sweat-soaked shirt. Roy appeared and Evans asked him what life was like living in the middle of the Muslim village. Roy told him about the regular firefights and how we slept with our rifles by the beds. Finally, as an afterthought, he said:

'Oh yes, and I always keep a hand-grenade next to my bed, just in case.'

I don't know why he said this and I think he was just making polite conversation. His grenades were in his flak jacket pocket, as were mine. How these words would come back to haunt us.

After Evans had left, I went over to the school to report on the incident. Sonja stopped me and told me:

'Major Vaughan. You are the hero of all the Muslims on this street!' I wasn't a hero. I was just some idiot who'd almost got his men killed for the sake of a few sacks of flour.

At around four o'clock I went to the mess for a cup of tea. There was quite a crowd there as most of the guard company officers had little to do when the boys were on duty. It was a lovely, sunny afternoon and we sat upstairs watching Music Television on the Sky channel. The windows were open when suddenly the reverie was interrupted by high-velocity shots, very close by.

We rushed to the window and saw two HVO soldiers, not twenty metres away, blatting away at the Muslim houses on the hill. They were using the remaining walls of the burned-out cottage for cover. One of them was Spotty, his right hand covered in a grubby bandage. Here were two gunmen firing at civilian houses right past our own officers' mess. MTV continued to blare out as we sipped our tea and watched the sport outside the window. The resonant beat of an Eddie Grant reggae song filled the mess and someone shouted:

'Hey! That's us! ... "Living on the Front Line!" '

That evening I ran a line-crossing called a SLAVEN 2, which was for aid and not people. The Serbs allowed a few convoys to cross their territory and enter our sector at Turbe. The convoys originated in Zagreb and weeks of negotiations preceded each one. Not surprisingly, they were rarer than rocking horse dung.

These aid convoys used a slightly different route to the refugee convoys at Turbe. The refugees took the north route of a loop-road where there was a clear space for the exchange of transport. The aid took the southern route, which was more circuitous.

As well as the usual mines, the southern route was also blocked with an enormous earth bank. I therefore deployed four Warriors, two on the northern route and myself and 0C by the obstacle. A Combat Engineer Tractor was on standby and it squeaked and clattered into view. The operators of the CET were masters of their machine and in minutes cleared a way through the bank using the bucket on the front. The LO and Beba moved the mines and disappeared into Serb territory. Half an hour later, ten UNHCR lorries ground past, each driver waving to us.

The LOs returned, the CET replaced the bank, and we were on our way less than ninety minutes after we'd left the school.

In the morning, 21 May, it was back to Turbe. The bank was moved again and the empty trucks crossed the line without incident. I sent the CET back, escorted by two of the Warriors, and went for a quick drive around Travnik. When I returned, the cottage had gone!

A gunman had again used the ruins as cover from which to fire on the Muslims. Roy, as the Guard Company Commander, had decided to act and, together with his CSM 'Sniffer' Clarke, had run to the firing point. The Croat fled as they approached and, as Roy stood there wondering what to do next, my CET arrived from Turbe. Roy flagged the Engineers down, explained the problem, and, five minutes later, the cottage was nothing more than a slight mound of rubble. There would be no more firing from this location.

The CO wasn't exactly overjoyed and told Roy he should've asked the owner's permission first. That was hardly practicable as, for all we knew, she could still be inside it.

There were other subtle changes to the area as well. The Croats had constructed a prominent bunker at the corner of the main road and the track leading to their recently-captured houses. Stoutly constructed, this looked directly on to the mess and the houses around ours. There were also several new trenches and they were clearly intended to stay.

We had an important visitor that day, Lieutenant General Sir Michael Rose. He was the Commander of the United Kingdom Field Army. The Colonel had instructed me to prepare a tour for the General to show him the area. This wasn't as easy as it sounded as none of us had been in Bosnia long enough to have an in-depth knowledge of our patch. Also, there were some places that were virtual no-go areas to us such as where I'd met the mujahideen.

I'd worked for Rose before, and had the highest regard for him. I knew he was a man of action and would want some excitement so I decided to take him to the front line at Ljubic.

The sightseeing trip involved more people than the making of 'Ben Hur'. I led in 0B with 0C at the rear. Sandwiched in the middle was the CO's Warrior and Richard Watson's. The General travelled with me, and Brigadier Searby with the CO. There were the usual staff officers, escorts, and, of course, the RSM, to shout at everybody.

I led, as I was the only one who knew the way. Hopefully, we wouldn't have a contact as the General sat wedged in the gunner's seat. He might have commanded 22 SAS but I doubted if his gunnery drills were up to much. We drove along and I explained the situation in the area to him. He seemed very interested and was friendly and easy to talk to. He had an excellent memory and remembered me from Ulster days.

We stopped at every checkpoint to talk to the locals. Each time, the General hauled his tall frame out of the turret with the agility of a man half his age. He asked about the current Vance-Owen Peace Plan and seemed surprised at how much people understood about it. On reflection, this wasn't that strange as it was potentially the most important single thing in people's lives.

We headed for the front line and Rose remarked at the skill of the driver in negotiating the narrow track. I could almost see the hatch bulging as Tookey's head expanded with pride and I felt a slight twinge of guilt for doubting his ability. On the line, we dismounted and the General talked to the same young Commander as I'd met before, who took him into the loft to view the Croat front lines. The General asked why the Muslims didn't attack when the Croats weren't alert. The Commander looked at him as if he were an errant child and explained that it was because there was a cease-fire!

At the Croat lines the same bunch of giggling thugs greeted us. They showed no respect for the General and, in fact, were downright rude. They berated him over the way the UN, supposedly, supported the Muslims. The General was getting angry and was digging-in for an argument. However, the CO, with the skill of a Buckingham Palace courtier, intervened and reminded Rose that he had other visits back in Vitez.

We were making good time when we came across the road blocked by mines. It was at the same place as before and the Croats were not to be fooled a second time. They'd obviously heard us coming and had the mines ready to hand. We dismounted and I told the general I would negotiate them away. In an emergency, we could drive across a field of crops to avoid them. I wasn't keen to do this as it would mean damaging other people's property but, it was an option, should we need it.

I pointed out to the HVO that we'd just come from their lines so they were hardly preventing us from seeing anything we shouldn't. We were heading back now and we were only a few hundred metres away from the main road, why bother to stop us from returning to our base? Finally, in a thinly-veiled threat, I told him we'd drive over his fields if we had to.

The guy was about to move the mines when the CO butted in. He'd brought along his interpreter, Dobrila Kalaba, a raven-haired Serb girl who spoke excellent English. The boss was in a hurry to get back as the general still had the garage to visit.

'Now look here my good man! Move these bloody mines at once!' The Croats bristled. I returned to the Warrior and left him to it. Forty minutes later we finally continued.

I sat next to the general at dinner and he thanked me for an excellent day. Little did I know that I'd just hosted the future UN commander in Bosnia.

After a week on ops I was shattered. I fell into bed, was ambushed by my duvet and instantly fell into a deep sleep.

The next morning the alarm woke me at seven. I sat up in bed and was immediately aware of an acrid smell in the room. Roy was awake and I asked him if he'd noticed it. He grinned, and recounted the night's adventures.

At 1.30 in the morning, the Croats launched a raid into the Muslim houses. However, the local sentries were alert and returned fire. Eventually, they were beaten back and took cover on our verandah from where they returned yet more fire. The situation looked bleak for the Muslims.

Meanwhile, Roy had woken, walked over to his locker, opened

the metal doors and taken out a 1.5-inch rocket flare. He primed the flare, opened the shutter and then the window, and fired the device from his bed. The room filled with smoke and the rocket shot skyward with a loud 'whoosh'.

The effect outside was instantaneous. It was almost like the locals looked up and said: 'White man's magic. He make light in sky!' The shooting stopped and the Croats fled. The camp guard reported the flare but didn't know where it had come from so they deployed the Warrior to the road junction. This discouraged any further aggression.

Well, at least that explained the smoke. I still didn't believe I could sleep through such a racket until I saw the spent flare tube on the floor. So much for the roughy-toughy steely-eyed killer of the night. Roy had been the one instantly to react and had undoubtedly saved our neighbours from ethnic cleansing. There were now two heroes of 'Muslim Street'.

I was due to escort a convoy to Kruscica that morning. The village was, effectively, under siege. The Croats in Vitez were refusing to allow aid through as they'd accused the BiH of raiding houses on the outskirts of town. The convoy was important and demonstrated the UNHCR's determination to convey aid into areas of need, whatever the difficulties. I was to be the lucky chap tasked with escorting this hot potato.

James Myles called me to the P Info house and asked me if I'd take Mike Evans, the BBC with Justin Webb as the reporter, and a French TV crew.

My convoy consisted of six aid trucks, two press Land Rovers, 0B and 0C. The drop was preceded by a delivery of similar size to the Croat aid warehouse in Vitez. Our safe passage had been negotiated with the HVO in the town.

We entered Vitez and turned south for Kruscica. Five hundred metres down the track a group of civilians ran into the road, totally blocking it. They were mostly women and many had children with them. As we slowed down they held babies and small toddlers out in front of them. I weighed up the options. There was enough open ground to smartly drive around the crowd, rejoining the road later, but the lorries wouldn't be able to follow so there was no point. I could hardly run over the civilians and there was no other route round. I certainly wasn't going to emulate Brigadier Reginald Dyer at Amritsar in 1919. Machine gunning the crowd wouldn't win me too many friends! There were no other options at all, and it was negotiate or nothing.

We edged closer to the crowd and they surged forward. I was disgusted at the way they held the children in front of them. The gesture was supposed to stop me from going on. OK, it was going to work, but it's a hell of a risk to take with thirty tons of metal. I stopped and they surged round, clinging to the sides of 0B as if I was going to suddenly charge past them. One woman had a pocket camera and was snapping away with it, to report me for war-crimes against the Croats!

I dismounted and put my beret on instead of my helmet, so as not to look too aggressive. Instantly engulfed by a mob of angry civilians, I was forced back to the Warrior. The point of the glacis plate dug into my back and I thought, for a moment, the civvies were going to attack me. However, Dobby was on the periphery and I knew I'd be OK.

This wasn't getting anywhere so I tried the old, 'Shut the fuck up!' trick.

A hush descended and I was able to start speaking. The women were blocking us because they believed we were feeding their enemies. There then followed four hours of the most difficult negotiations I'd come across. It bores me just to remember it now but the general gist went as follows:

'You cannot pass because you are taking aid to the Muslims.'

'That's true but then we've delivered aid to the Croats today.'

'We do not believe you.'

'Go and check. You'll find the same amount of aid that is on these trucks is in your warehouse.'

'The UN is supporting the Muslims.'

'That's not true. We've given you the same amount of aid. This shows we are impartial.'

'No one has given you permission to come here.'

'That's not true, either. The Mayor of Vitez, Mr Santic, gave his permission.'

'We believe that you are taking arms to the Muslims.'

'That is rubbish! Where have you heard this?'

'One of my friends has seen guns in the back of a UN tank.'

'That's hardly surprising as we all carry guns.'

'We must see in the back of your vehicle.'

'That is not allowed.'

'Then you cannot pass and we will know you were trying to carry weapons to the Muslims.'

'If I prove to you that I'm not carrying arms will you let me pass?'

'Yes, but how will you prove it if we cannot see in the back?'

'I cannot allow you to see in on purpose. However, if one of you was standing at the back, when one of my men climbed out you could probably see in.'

'OK. We believe that there are no weapons inside now. But we have heard that you hide them in the petrol tank!'

'The media is watching you and recording how unreasonable the Croats are.'

'We don't care because the BBC supports the Muslims anyway.'

'Then why not state your case to the French media.'

'Because they are owned by the BBC!'

'Why are you blocking the road to Kruscica?'

'We are not. The Muslims are free to come and go as they please.'

'Then how do you know that it's the UN that is arming the Muslims?'

'Because we have closed the road!'

It was a scorching day and I was slowly broiling inside my flak jacket. The women were taking it in shifts and kept disappearing into the houses for drinks. I knew I was never going to be allowed through. The crowd would have me believe that I was a victim of people-power and they were acting on their own. However, the presence of several HVO soldiers in the area suggested that the whole thing was a set-up and the Mayor was in on it all along. The aid was safely in the Croat warehouse and there was no way the Muslims were going to get this lot.

I didn't want to give up but, after two hours, I'd got nowhere. I'd countered all their demands but the bottom-line was, they didn't want me to pass. Unless I was going to start driving over people there was no way through.

Finally, I'd had enough. I pulled out my wallet and took out a photograph of Russell and Aimee. Showing it to them, I said:

'These are my two children and are the most precious things in the whole world to me. I would never do anything to hurt them. As far as I'm concerned any group of people who would deliberately endanger the lives of their children to further a political cause are not worth talking to.'

With that, I climbed back onto the Warrior and drove back to the

school. I was fuming at the total intransigence of the people, the way
they'd duped the UN and the utter helplessness I'd felt when confronted with unarmed civilians. For days afterwards, I agonized over
how I could've handled the situation differently to get the aid
through. Roy tried another approach a few days later and attempted
to drive on. He ended up with half a dozen people clinging to his
Warrior and had to resort to fruitless negotiation as well. It was several weeks before aid finally reached the village.

In the afternoon, I was out again. Milinfo wanted an update on
some of the villages in the area of the Bila Valley. The HVO had
tried to block the road by dynamiting the rock wall. After nearly an
hour of shifting boulders we managed to clear a path. Even so, the
track was barely wide enough for the Warrior.

I meant to take a right turn to take me to the Croat village of
Grahovcici. Instead I had a 'navigational embarrassment' and
turned off three hundred metres too early. The road climbed sharply
uphill until we were stopped at a BiH checkpoint. I jumped down to
talk to them. They were not particularly friendly and if it hadn't
been for the fact I didn't want to admit I'd only arrived at their village by mistake, I'd have turned round and gone on my way. Instead,
I persevered and, half an hour later, we were allowed into the village.
The men at the checkpoint called the place what sounded like 'Clee
Artsy'. Not surprisingly, there was no such place on the map but, by
checking where I'd gone wrong, I figured I was in the village of
Kljaci.

The village was a one-street affair clinging to the side of a steep
hill. Every garden was beautifully tended and happy-looking children played in the road. They all seemed amazed to see UN Warriors
and ran along in front of us as we slowly drove through their village.
The road was very narrow and both Phil and I stood high in the turret to ensure we didn't damage any property. The track funnelled
into a bend where two houses overhung, rather like the Shambles in
York. The clearance on each side was only a few centimetres but we
were becoming used to tight squeezes and we barely checked our
speed. Eventually, the road widened into a village square and we
turned round and headed back. I intended to pass on through and
send one of the platoon commanders here later but my plans
changed when two old men blocked the way.

I dismounted again and shook hands with both men. One was
wearing a faded light blue beret, like my UN one, except incredibly

old. He had a jolly, red face and a huge grin that showed off his three teeth. He introduced himself as Mister Asim. The other man wore an off-white woven skullcap. He was Arib, Asim's cousin.

The two were the village elders and invited me to take coffee with them in Asim's garden. The garden was a little paradise of brightly-coloured climbing plants and wonderfully-scented roses. We sat at a wooden table and coffee was served by a tall, pretty, blonde girl. Unfortunately, she exploded from the neck downwards and would've made an excellent prop-forward. The coffee was thick, sweet and strong and was complemented by delicious biscuits.

We chatted and they said we were the first UN soldiers to visit the village. I hadn't the heart to tell them that it was all a mistake. We stayed for the best part of an hour and, as I left, I gave the elders a small quantity of baby food. This had been given to me by Mark Bower and was meant as a gift of good faith rather than an attempt to solve their food problems. This was the beginning of my bitter-sweet relationship with the village of Kljaci.

On leaving the village, I managed to find the right road to Grahovcici. We passed by a coal mine and up a narrow track. Snapper had been vague with the tasking on this patrol and I wasn't really sure what I was supposed to achieve in the village. The task had literally been to check if the village was Muslim or Croat. The Cheshires had been hampered by atrocious winter weather and had-n't been able to visit all the villages in the area. There was therefore a void of information and many of our earlier patrols were tasked with very simple objectives.

The villagers were Croat, and, again, were astonished to see UN vehicles. They were initially stand-offish, which was hardly surpris-ing as BRITBAT was not exactly viewed as the impartial face of the UN. Nevertheless, I was ushered into the HVO headquarters and met the local commander. The guy was about my age and gave me the normal line about how Bob Stewart hated the Croats. I assured him this wasn't the case and anyway, we were a new regiment who would be totally impartial.

This was the first time I'd talked in-depth to any Croat and he seemed a pleasant enough chap. He was concerned that the village received little aid. Apparently, they were in the Han Bila area and the distribution depot was BiH-controlled. I left them a similar quantity of baby food and said I'd look into the aid distribution.

It seemed a good area to show our impartiality. If we could provide some aid to the place the word would spread and maybe more Croats would start to trust us. So ended our first period on operations.

The nine-day period was a great start. The tunnel was a success and had freed more callsigns for other tasks. We were getting to know the area and nearly all my crews had received their baptism of fire. Already we'd managed to deter further Croat aggression by mounting dawn and dusk patrols. This was probably our greatest achievement in that first week. We were all ready for a change of pace during guard week.

The changeover day was fixed as Sunday for the rest of the tour. The guard involved two men in each of the four sangars: one each at the three entrances and one at the rear of the camp behind Press Row. There were also two NCOs manning the front desk in the main entrance to the school building. One of these posted a fresh pair of sentries every hour. The off-coming pair then had four hours rest in the guardroom. There was also an alert platoon of four AFVs. Finally, we provided a vehicle, and crew, to guard the BFI from would-be pilferers.

This was virtually half of the company and the remainder would be on guard the next day. Days off gave the boys time to catch up on their admin. It was also a chance to carry out our routine maintenance on the vehicles. In our case, it was time to replace the tracks.

'Track bashing' is the bane of every AFV crew the world over. The task took place outside the garage on the edge of the road. The tracks wear out every so often and are both replaced at the same time. Each track weighs two tons, costs twelve thousand pounds and is divided into eighty-two individual links. The first track is split by knocking out one of the pins that hold the links together. The Warrior is driven off the track leaving it like a tail behind the vehicle. This track is then broken into six-link segments, a two-man lift, and the new one constructed out of similar sections. Finally, the Warrior is driven onto the track. Ropes are used to pull the rear end over the running gear until the two ends meet at the front. Both ends are clamped together until a new pin can be inserted. This process is then repeated with the other track.

Sounds simple? Six hours later, Phil, Dobby, Donlon, Knight, Tookey and I finally finished. It was dirty, backbreaking work made worse by the baking sun and the ever-present dust.

That evening Jason Medley, one of the A Company platoon commanders, ran over a mine. He'd been sent to monitor the situation at Turbe and told to patrol right up to the front line. Unfortunately, it was dark and Medley's Warrior had hit a TMA 3. There were no casualties but the track was split and a road-wheel destroyed. Anyone could've predicted there would be problems driving along the front line at night. This was exactly what Richard was so worried I was going to do a few nights before.

There was an unpleasant surprise waiting for me in the mess. The latest papers had arrived and *The Times* of Friday 21 May was among them. On the front page, next to a picture of the group of us pulling the flour cart, was a headline telling the world that I was not prepared to get one of my men shot for the sake of a few sacks of flour.

Just in case anyone couldn't be bothered to read the article, a sub-headline named me as the originator of the quote. The text went on to describe the incident and how I handled it. I felt a slight burst of pride that I was not only mentioned in a newspaper but also on the front page of *The Times*. However, this euphoria was shattered when I read, with mounting horror, the last paragraph.

In this, the author described how Roy and I shared a room and how the Croats had threatened to mount an ethnic cleansing operation among our Muslim neighbours. In order to counter this we apparently slept with ... wait for it ... grenades under our pillows!!!

Well thanks a bunch mate! Talk about poetic licence. This paragraph had more licence than the DVLC. The fact that Roy had a grenade in his locker was hardly under the pillow. I mean, honestly, it would be like sleeping with a cricket ball under your head. The rest of the article was extremely positive and showed something of the difficult nature of the tasks we had to undertake. The reader could have nothing but sympathy with the UN given the immense problems we were facing. This last paragraph trivialized the whole affair and reduced us to the level of participants in a War Picture-Library Comic. I knew Colonel Alastair would be furious. His wrath was going to be like a visit from the mother-in-law. You know it's coming but there's bugger all you can do about it!

Sure enough, the next morning, Roy and I were summoned to see the CO in the mess. It was an informal bollocking, we got coffee. He was annoyed at what he considered to be my ill-considered and emotive comment about not wanting to get any of my men shot. I pointed out that I hadn't actually said that to a reporter and it was a misquote of what I'd said to Munib. It made little difference. He said

I shouldn't have made the comment within earshot of the press. I was about to say, 'Well that's all well and good but it's hardly practical to sweep the area for media before you hold a conversation' but there was no point arguing so I just said, 'Yes, sir' like a good little company commander.

The CO then turned to the issue of the grenades. I certainly wasn't going down for this one as well so I said nothing. The seconds ticked by and 'the look' was appearing. Eventually, Roy owned up to showing Evans the grenades and the CO asked what the hell the reporter was doing in our room in the first place. He wasn't pleased when Roy answered that Evans just knocked on the door and walked in. I was about to suggest we put a sign on our door saying: 'No tradesmen! No HVO! No press!' Fortunately sense, for once, got the better of me.

The colonel told Roy to hand his grenades in and not to carry them again. I kept quiet about mine and, in fact, carried them for the rest of the tour without once having them appear on the front page of a national newspaper. Besides which, they'd already proved their worth as a fist-deflector.

He warned us both about talking to the press. I argued this was the first time the regiment had appeared on the front page of any national paper since 1969. On that occasion we were the first troops on the streets of Ulster. The article showed the regiment in a good light and showed the commitment of the soldiers in a trying and difficult situation. Surely, the grenade comment aside, it was good publicity. Suddenly, it all went a bit frosty, and Roy shot me a 'Why the hell don't you keep your big mouth shut' look.

There is little doubt in my mind that the colonel was specifically told not to be another Bob Stewart. Bosnia Bob had become a public hero from an army that, traditionally, hides its heroes. He always had something sharp to say and the press expected more of the same from our CO. When all they received were bland statements they started to look elsewhere. The shift of press emphasis was subtle and Roy noticed it long before I did.

The day before, Roy had been asked to give a 'day in the life' interview for a Sunday supplement. He'd checked with James Myles and, sure enough, P Info had sanctioned the story. It never occurred to either of us that the CO might've already turned down an offer. They therefore came after the second best, the company commanders. There then followed a period of systematic targeting of Roy and me. Unfortunately, we were frequently involved in incidents, so our appearances became more frequent. The rise in the CO's ire was directly proportional to this.

At some stage the colonel should've told us not to deal with the press at all. Better still, James should've told them to leave us alone. Finally, we were to blame for simply not refusing to co-operate.

Unfortunately, I was singled-out for special attention from some journalists in particular. For a start, it was the name. Major Vaughan Kent-Payne was the sort of ridiculous handle Joe Public expected his officers to have. Somehow Roy Hunter seemed better suited to a Los Angeles private detective. Secondly, it was the rapidly-developing moustache of the sort that officers sported in films. Finally, it was the fact that whenever I deployed, something always seemed to happen. This, from a press point of view, was a godsend. While the CO was doing the really important business in smoky conference rooms, Major Vaughan was out saving lives and having a field-day. So were the press and, little did I know that I was heading for a fall.

Roy kept as quiet about his interview as I did about the grenades and the talk was over. At least it was for Roy.

The colonel asked me to stay behind and I knew, with that sinking feeling, that something else was wrong.

'How are you getting along with your CSM?'

This was unexpected and I didn't think there was a problem. Apparently, there was, however, and he went on to say that Zippy had complained to RSM Adair that I hardly ever talked to him, let alone confided in him. This was all I needed, my sergeant major going behind my back and complaining about me. Why the hell hadn't he broached the subject with me first? Now the RSM had told the CO and the boss clearly thought I had a morale problem in my company. This was all I bloody-well needed. Gritting my teeth, I thanked the CO for pointing this out for me and 'Yes, of course I'll sort it out, sir'.

Seething, I stalked out and went to find Zippy. I was going to flatten the little pipsqueak when I found him. At his house someone said he was in the shower and I settled down to wait. Still festering I bummed a cigarette off one of the sentries. The soldier looked surprised as none of them had seen me smoke before. I needed one now as my whole world was falling apart.

I sat in the late afternoon sun and drew deeply on the cigarette and started to think. When was the last time I'd seen Zippy, let alone talked to him? When was the last time I'd talked to any of the soldiers apart from my own crew? When was the last time I'd visited the lads in their rooms? The answer to all these was either days ago, or never. Why then was I neglecting my soldiers? The answer was that I didn't have time. Why didn't I have time?

The blindingly obvious hit me like a bolt from the blue.

Because I was too busy trying to solve the whole Bosnia problem single-handed. I was so determined to make a difference to this awful mess that I was neglecting the most precious asset that would help me achieve it, my soldiers.

Zippy returned and I stamped out the butt.

I asked him why he'd gone to the RSM and, as I suspected, it was the other way round. Adair had been snooping around, like all good RSMs should, and asked him why we didn't spend much time together. Now it was out in the open I was determined to put this right as a matter of priority. Bosnia could wait, this was family.

Zippy and I chatted for about two hours and the die was cast. We'd known each other for years and he spoke his mind. I knew I was stubborn and headstrong but I hadn't realized I intimidated people so much. Now was the time to lighten up a bit. From then on, we never looked back and I started to involve him in all company matters and, more important, listen to his advice. We started to forge a winning team that evening. I never did find out if the CO or RSM noticed a change. What I did know, however, was that they'd highlighted a problem and I'd moved to sort it.

When I returned to my room Roy was pacing around the room, beside himself with rage. Someone had stolen the flag from the front of the house. He'd obtained probably the biggest UN flag in Bosnia. Together, we'd nailed it to the upstairs balcony at the front of the house. It was visible from several hundred metres during the day and even stood out well at night. There could be no mistake that this was a British house come the next cleansing operation.

One source of irritation in our life at Vitez was the constant stream of visitors. There was at least one visit per week. Visitors ranged from the high-ranking, such as General Rose, to the low-level. We frequently hosted staff officers, up from Split to see how operations were at the sharp end. This was fine and should've enabled them to brief visitors on our tasks. However, we were rapidly developing a dislike for the base rats in Slipper City. After all, Split was in a separate country and their only danger was from sunburn. I'd heard these jokers telling their 'war stories' in the mess having spent a day in Vitez!

It so happened that two officers had stayed in the house that night and had left that morning. It was a pretty amazing coincidence that the flag should disappear at the same time. Now we were back to square one and this unthinking piece of theft could very well be putting our lives at risk.

So, if you're reading this – thanks a bunch, mate!

Zippy and I spent most of the next day touring the sangars and talking to the lads. The Jocks had settled in well and there were already some good friendships starting. Some of them sounded like Russ Abbot impersonating the cliché Jock. I couldn't understand a word they said so I just nodded and hoped it was at the right time. They probably thought I was daft.

We toured the Portakabins and chatted to the boys there. Most had made themselves cosy. We'd allowed them to pick their room mates as there's nothing worse than sharing for six months with three people you can't stand. Many had brought televisions and Sega Mega-drives and the whole area was alive with zaps and bleeps. They were all happy enough and, judging by the tan sported by Private Phillips, making the most of their days off. Finally, we toured the school. All the anti-tank and mortar boys lived in a large room. The company HQ lads lived in a dingy classroom downstairs. The windows were covered by blast screens and only a couple of bulbs lit the place. There were fifteen of them, all in bunk beds. No wonder the sign on the door proclaimed it to be the Swamp. The room had probably the greatest range of occupants, from Daz Erwin, who was nineteen, to Dobby and Mo, who were in their late thirties. The music in the room was a curious mixture of seventies rock, rave and everything in between.

I decided to have a snooze before dinner. Roy was back and was reading on the patio. There was a commotion outside and I ran out, to find Sonja in tears. She was distraught and told us that a sniper had tried to shoot her. Roy and I grabbed our rifles and followed. Sonja was living up in the unfinished upstairs part of the house across from ours with her husband and two daughters. She had a house in Grbavica but had moved closer to camp because of shelling on the village. Her husband was in the BiH and was away on the line. We climbed a wooden stairway and I saw the two girls huddled in a corner being comforted by an old woman. They were both dark haired, like their mother, and had beautiful, big brown eyes. Sonja told us that the oldest was called Leila and she was nine. Her sister, Larissa, was four.

The shot came from the Croat lines opposite the mess. Some sheets hung on a line, strung across the balcony, and the sniper fired through them. The bullet passed through the window, leaving a neat hole, before imbedding itself in the wall near where the girls had been playing.

I went to the window and located the hole. Outside, sure enough, was a small hole through the sheet. I peered through this and focused on the upstairs window of a smoke-blackened house over the road. This looked like the firing point but, to make sure, I moved back inside, peered through the hole in the window and lined it up with the hole in the sheet. As I was checking the alignment, another hole appeared in the sheet a couple of centimetres above the first. This was instantly followed by a 'pop' and a second hole in the window. There was barely a sound but I nearly jumped out of my skin. This was hardly surprising as the second round actually ruffled my hair. I'd taken my beret off when I entered the house and I felt the wind of the bullet as it passed just above the top of my head. I looked round and Roy, too, had jumped as the thing imbedded itself next to its mate a metre away from where he stood. This was too bloody close for comfort and we both cocked our weapons and followed-up. The boys in the front sangar hadn't heard a thing and probably wondered what the hell two majors were doing hard-targeting towards the main road. As we reached the corner of the mess I took aim on the firing point. Through the sight on my rifle, I glimpsed the gunman as he fled the room. The Croat emerged from the house carrying a bolt-action rifle. There was no chance to fire and he was gone before I could get my tongue around '*Stani ili put-sani!*' Serbo-Croat for 'Stop or I'll fire!'

The bloke was gone but I was sure he'd be back. We returned to the house and Sonja had prepared coffee for us. It was amazing how well the children coped with their narrow brush with death and they played happily on the floor. These little girls were to have another appointment with the grim reaper before the tour was out.

As we left the house there was another burst of firing, this time from the Grbavica Hill. The Croats replied and soon there was a full-scale gun-battle raging, with the rounds winging over camp. This couldn't go on and, sure enough, I heard shots from inside camp. Lance-Corporal Bingley from A Company had finished a patrol and was standing on top of his Warrior when rounds landed close by. There was no doubt he was being targeted and he fired three shots at a Croat gunman. He couldn't tell whether he hit but there was no further firing. These were the first shots returned during the tour. Roy and I saw the CO and asked him to speak to the Croats. This had to stop before one of our lads was killed. We also asked him to tell the Croats that any firing points used to shoot into camp would be destroyed. He agreed we had to develop a more robust approach to the gunmen.

Back at the house we found the sniper had been busy. Two rounds had hit the front door and one was imbedded in the wall of the hall, outside our room. We decided to build the wall up an extra half a metre. The house had now been hit several times and I cursed the git who'd nicked our flag. It was one hell of a rough neighbourhood, even for the heroes of Muslim Street.

Chapter 7
What Ford Escort, Phil?

The last weekend in May 1993 was the lull before the storm. Roy returned from a patrol and trashed a Croat bunker over the road. The log emplacement proved to be no match for thirty tons of Her Majesty's equipment. The Croats filmed the damage and protested. Roy told the CO, who didn't seem in the least bit worried.

Back on Muslim Street, Fered's dog had given birth. Jason, Tom and Stephen came round to choose a pup each. They were all going soft. Puppies with puppies, whatever next?

We changed over for our second operations week on 30 May and I was tasked to patrol the lines at Dubrevica, just north of Vitez. I took Jimmy Cliffe with a couple of Scimitars as some of the tracks were very narrow. We arrived in the area and I sent Jimmy on ahead. There was quite a bit of firing and the whole area was pretty tense with little sign that the cease-fire was holding. Suddenly the radio crackled and I heard Jimmy's cultured tones calmly report:

'Contact, two high-velocity rounds, wait out!'

The Scimitar is a small vehicle and, although armed with similar weapons to the Warrior, was considered an easy target by the locals. I told Tookey to make best speed and we hurtled down the narrow track. We reached the first Scimitar, parked behind a hedge. The NCO in charge, Corporal Hall, dismounted and told me that a sniper, hidden in a shed, had fired on the lead wagon. I briefed Jimmy to close down and slowly drive towards the firing point to try to encourage the guy to shoot again.

The Scimitar moved off and, seconds later Jimmy calmly reported the sniper had fired again and hit the Scimitar. This was it and we leaped forward, into a field. Phil was down in his seat and had selected Chain Gun; the sniper was in for a 7.62 mm-surprise!

Jimmy was moving towards the shed and we were speeding round to the gunman's right flank. At the last moment, as we were about a hundred and fifty metres away, he must've heard us because out he came, at the double.

The guy was sprinting across the field for all he was worth, trying to reach the cover of a thicket, a couple of hundred metres away. He carried a long rifle, with a telescopic sight. His other arm was pounding and he stole a quick glance over his shoulder. The look of horror was clear, even at a hundred metres. He knew he was never going to make it. Tookey had his foot to the floor and the automatic gearbox had gone up through all five gears. I reckon we were going about seventy kilometres an hour. I wasn't about to order Tookey to run him down but I was about to kill him. We were about fifty metres away and he still had over a hundred to go. I was just about to stop the wagon and give Phil a fire control order when the guy suddenly threw down the rifle.

The whole situation had changed. By the rules of the orange card I was still allowed to shoot him as he had fired at one of our vehicles, therefore endangering life. However, I wasn't about to shoot an unarmed man in the back. The Warrior slowed and I leaned out and gave fine corrections to Tookey. We didn't feel a thing as we ground the rifle into the dirt. The sniper was almost at the copse but there was a barbed-wire fence in the way. He was tiring with the boggy ground sucking at his feet. In desperation, he tried to vault the fence but became entangled in the top strands. The more he struggled, the more he became enmeshed. Gotcha! We slowed and halted about five metres from the man. I saw from the checkered badge on his sleeve that he was HVO. Bloody Croats! Phil traversed on and the guy ceased his struggles and found himself looking up the muzzle of the RARDEN. I was wondering what to do next when Tookey shouted: 'Sir. He's pissing himself!'

I looked down and, sure enough, a dark stain was spreading over the front of the man's trousers. This was the perfect end to the incident. I wasn't prepared to kill him and I couldn't detain him as we had no jurisdiction. We'd trashed his rifle and made him wet himself, there was little else we could do. We moved off and made as if to run over him. At the last moment Tookey swerved to the left and we splattered him in mud. We departed and Dobby and Knight jeered him until we were out of sight. I don't think we made much of a friend out of him but he was going to think twice about messing with the big boys again.

We followed the Scimitars back to where the track joined the mountain road. Here the Croats had built a road block. The track was blocked with three, very sturdy looking, star-shaped barriers made from lengths of railway line welded together. We slowed and I was just about to dismount and investigate when someone threw a grenade at us. The thing exploded between the rear Scimitar and us. Dirt and smoke rose from the ditch to the left. The wind was blowing towards me and I smelled the unmistakable marzipan stink of high explosive. There was no damage but the locals were obviously not friendly. I told Jimmy to get the hell out of it and both Scimitars sped round the left of the barrier. Hall's clipped the nearest star, which was almost as tall as his wagon, and one of the side bins was torn off. An oil can spilled onto the road but I wasn't about to get out and pick it up.

There was no way we could follow the same route and we were stuck with a building on the left and a ditch to the right. A guy ran out of the doorway and plonked two TMA 3 anti-tank mines in the gap and darted back inside. That settled it, we weren't going through that way and there was a chance he'd gone back for more mines, or an RPG. I ordered Tookey to close down, which was a waste of time, as he'd done so at the first sign of trouble. We advanced and hit the centre of the obstacle. 0B climbed up the barrier until we were at an impossible angle. I couldn't see the ground and my whole arc of vision was the bright blue sky. We were on the verge of toppling back on ourselves and I shouted to the guys in the back to brace. Suddenly there was a rending and scraping and all three stars collapsed under our weight. 0B fell to earth with a jolt that rattled my teeth. The tracks gripped the road and we were away. Looking back, there was a heap of railway lines in the road, but no barrier.

I was really hacked off with the Croats and looking for a fight. Outside the mess, the HVO was building another bunker. Four men were beavering away with logs and fertilizer sacks filled with earth. The emplacement looked onto the mess and Sonja's house and spelled trouble. The men scarpered when we arrived, which was just as well as their bunker went the same way as the barrier. I was just wondering if there was any other mischief that Mister Toad, master of the road-rage, could get up to when we backed into a telegraph pole. I was so busy thinking of cunning plans to annoy the Croats that I failed to give Tookey any directions. My last order had been to reverse and that was what we were still doing. The first warning was a shout of 'Whoa!' from the back, but it was too late. We hit the pole centrally, snapping it clean off at about head height. With a twanging of parting wires the top five metres or so crashed down on top of the turret. I ducked, just in time to save myself from the mother of all bangs on the head. Phil, Dobby and I threw the pole to the ground and we drove into camp. At least the HVO wouldn't have any telephones for a while.

In the afternoon, I was tasked to patrol to Guca Gora, to the west of Han Bila. The village nestled high in the hills and was home to a magnificent church and monastery. Well over a thousand years old, its twin towers dominated the valley. A conference was being held in the village and Tom had escorted some of the BiH leadership through the HVO lines to the meeting. I arrived during the break and met Djemo Merdin.

Tall, with grey hair and a bushy moustache, he looked like a Bosnian version of Anthony Quinn. Merdin was the deputy commander of Third BiH Corps. He'd been a colonel in the JNA and was clearly very bright. He'd also been a footballer of some note and we chatted for a while about the great players of yesteryear although he didn't seem to know much English other than the name 'Bobby Charlton'! Finally, I asked him how I could get to Han Bila as the bridge was blown and he told me there was a route through the river.

We headed east and, just short of Han Bila came to the bridge. Explosives had destroyed most of the concrete supports and a few planks were placed over the gap. It would probably take the weight of a car but definitely not a Warrior. We drove about and, eventually, found a place to enter the river. The water was about a metre-and-a-half deep but the bottom was firm. We forded the river without trouble and negotiated the bank, next to the bridge. Meanwhile, Erwin, in 0C, had picked a better route and was tanking along with a huge bow-wave cascading over the front decks. Despite the efforts of the factions we had opened up a new patrol route and messing about on the river became a regular feature of Bila Valley taskings.

I visited the village of Bandol and was turned back by the BiH. A short, swarthy man told me they didn't need any help from the UN and were perfectly capable of looking after themselves. Famous last words.

The CO's conferences had been rescheduled for six in the evening. This meant that most of the patrolling was complete and the results could be briefed-up. Only the tunnel remained out until around seven. The main talk was about how the UK press were crucifying Bob Stewart. Bosnia Bob had left his wife and gone off with Claire Podbielski. The *Sun* had christened him Bonking Bob! Having been the darling of the media he was now vilified and Colonel Alastair warned us of the dangers of trusting the press too much. Alongside the papers in the mess was the first issue of the *Dobro Donkey*. This was a lighthearted magazine put together by Steve Thatcher, the admin officer. I featured in one cartoon.

The boys in the company decided that if the Cheshires had Bosnia Bob then they would have Vitez Vaughan. There was a cartoon strip entitled 'Vitez Vaughan. He's Hard as F—K'. I didn't really need this, especially when I was trying to keep a low profile with the CO. The last thing I wanted was the boss thinking I was more aggressive than I actually was. Like all these things though, you can't complain without appearing a spoil-sport and the cartoon ran for a couple more issues until it died of lack of material.

I visited Kljaci in the early part of the week and was again stopped at the checkpoint. This time they remembered me and said they'd stop all UN vehicles except mine. I drew them a sketch of my callsign to assist them and they pinned it to the inside wall of their guard hut. I had coffee and cakes with Mister Asim and the local military commander, who was called Hajiya. The guy had a huge spade beard and wild, curly hair tucked under a dark green beret. He wore military fatigues and chain-smoked Turkish cigarettes. He was originally from the area but had lived for many years in Switzerland. He'd returned to fight in the early days of the War and fought for the Croatians against the BSA. He'd then been imprisoned in Croatia as a Muslim spy. He now, not surprisingly, hated anything Croat with a vengeance. Hajiya was an interesting chap but, unfortunately, seemed to have a terrible memory. I must've met him a dozen times since that first meeting and he told me the same story every time.

The next two days were the days from hell.

On 1 June I was tasked to go to the small village of Rijeka near Vitez. The Croats had given the Muslims in the village permission to leave the area and walk to Zenica, about fifteen kilometres away. This was just ethnic cleansing without the house-burning and I'd no doubt the Muslims had been threatened with dire retribution if they didn't leave. Perry Whitworth was going to be there to ensure they weren't ill-treated. He wanted to have two Warriors as backup in the vicinity. Normally I would've sent a couple of the NCOs but all my remaining callsigns were on other tasks.

We drove through Vitez and down the narrow road leading to Rijeka. About a kilometre from the village we encountered the civilians. There were about thirty of them. Old people, women and children, mostly carrying bundles of blankets and clothing. One old lady, who must have been at least seventy, carried what looked like a mattress. The load was tied up with string and the thin twine was cutting into her bony shoulders. She stopped every few metres to adjust it and then trudged on. At this rate it would take her days to reach Zenica, if ever. Another old woman was hobbling along on crutches. Her husband was bent almost double under the weight of two bundles. Even the children carried little burdens and the legs of a doll poked out from one. A couple of these poor people were pushing wheelbarrows piled high with pots and pans. None of them could remotely be classed as a threat to anyone and were being forced to move simply because they were the wrong religion.

The Croats jeered them from the safety of their upstairs windows and I was sure the Muslim houses had been looted already. These people had lived alongside each other for generations and now were laughing as their former neighbours were forced away.

Surely, there must be something we could do? I radioed back to camp and requested two lorries to transport the people to Zenica. David came on and said Perry had already asked for this and had been turned down by the UNHCR.

Perry was actually called Lee but we'd jokingly re-christened him on the basis that it wasn't a suitable name for an officer. Boris Cowan was another and I think his real name's Bruce.

Perry was standing next to his Land Rover. He'd taken his beret off in the heat and his normally unruly, curly hair was being especially unruly. His brow furrowed as he described the dilemma we were in. The UNHCR had been approached but wouldn't assist the Muslims. Apparently, the logic behind this was that they'd voluntarily left their houses and were therefore displaced persons and not refugees. The organization couldn't help as the Muslims still had homes and therefore couldn't be transported to a refugee centre and given a second home. To do so would be to assist in ethnic cleansing.

This seemed like 'jobsworth' to me. These people were not leaving of their own free will and it was inhumane to stand by and let them attempt to travel this distance. The double standards of the UNHCR were staggering as we assisted in ethnic cleansing every time we ran a SLAVEN. I got back on to David: 'Are you sure there's nothing we can do for these people?'

'Negative! Remember, we're here to support the UNHCR and our mandate doesn't include transporting displaced persons.'

The whole situation stank and our hands were tied. I was ashamed to wear the blue beret.

The least we could do was minimize the hassle from the Croats. Perry was doing a great job and was chatting away to the handful of HVO around. They weren't going to stop the Muslims. The best we could hope for was that we could alert the BiH who would send transport once the people had crossed the lines, north of Vitez. All this changed with the sudden arrival of a blue-and-white Volkswagen minibus. Approaching flat-out from the direction of Vitez, the vehicle was barely under control. For an instant, I thought it was going to drive right into the crowd. At the last moment it screeched to a halt. Dobby and I were forced to jump out of the way to avoid being mown down. I caught a glimpse of the driver's face, fixed in an inane grin, before the front passenger door opened and a small, bearded, geezer jumped out. Barging straight past me, elbowing me out of the way, he strode over to the Muslims and started haranguing them. The pitiful procession stopped and they started to turn back. Perry was attempting to talk to the guy and I moved closer to listen.

It appeared this ignorant git was the deputy chief of police in Vitez. He wouldn't let the Muslims pass because it wasn't safe for them to go near the front line. More like they were easier to keep an eye on where they were and could be used as hostages later. Perry tried to reason with him and some of the Muslims turned round again, sensing there might still be a chance. Bearded-git then pulled out his pistol and brandished it at the old people, who cowered and turned round once more. The LO was getting exasperated and finally said to the man:

'You are a wanker.'

Instead of a look of fury, Bearded-git just looked nonplussed, so Perry asked the interpreter what she'd said.

'Captain Perry, there is no Serbo-Croat word for "wanker" so I called him a self-abuser instead!'

I was instantly reminded of the tale of Field Marshal Templer in Malaya. When faced with a dishonest village headman he told him: 'You are a bastard!' The interpreter than translated this as: 'The field marshall knows that your mother and father were not married when you were born!'

There was nothing else that could be done and Bearded-git had achieved his aim. He turned and strode back to the minibus. I had said nothing and he just assumed I was another thick UN squaddie. Yet again he shoved past me. Here was a little man whose gun and position made him think he was something special.

Perry told me he was going to speak to Santic, the Mayor, and try to find a way for these people to leave. He asked me to stay in the area for an hour or so to ensure the Muslims weren't hassled any further. After a while, I went to have one last look at the Muslims, who I reckoned would almost be back at their homes. They hadn't gone as far as I'd expected. The fierce heat and the dashing of their hopes had taken a toll and several were sitting on their bundles, head in hands. We gave them some water and I saw the stares of hatred from the Croats. Here was the UN favouring the Muslims again.

We turned on our axis and headed back to camp. The lane was barely wide enough for the Warrior and I could only just see over the high hedges on either side. I'd forgotten about Bearded-git when I saw the minibus tearing towards us. He just couldn't resist another dig at the Muslims or maybe he thought we'd try to smuggle them away.

The VW was streaking along and the beauty was that the driver couldn't see me but I could see him. We slowed right down and I told Tookey to close down. The Croat driver saw us about twenty metres in front of him. His face turned from inane grin to sheer terror and his eyes widened and looked like they were going to pop out. They darted from side to side as he frantically looked for a way past. Too late, he hit the brakes and the smoke of burning rubber poured from the tyres. At the last second, the driver swerved and tried to go down our left side. There was a slight jolt and I glimpsed Bearded-git throwing his arms up as if to ward off the impact.

We slowed to a halt and I looked back. The bus had hit the Warrior and the whole left side had been peeled open, like a sardine can. There was a door lying in the road with a headlight and sundry other bits and pieces. The vehicle had flown straight through the hedge and Bearded-git had flown straight through the windscreen.

He was lying on the ground in a crumpled heap. As I watched he knelt up and then staggered over to the wreck where he leaned against it, looking very sorry for himself. The driver was moving as well, as were the two goons in the back.

Back in camp I reported the accident and filled in the numerous forms laying clear blame onto the reckless driving of the Croat police. The chief of police had already been on to the CO and, surprisingly enough, I was summoned.

I stood in the colonel's office and put on my best butter wouldn't melt in my mouth look as I expressed my concern over those poor HVO policemen. I saw Bearded-git about a week later in Vitez. He had a leg in plaster, an arm in a sling and a bandage round his head. I actually spoke to him and he'd absolutely no idea who I was!

Poor old 0B had a nice series of blue scrapes down the side. We also noticed a scar several centimetres deep and a metre long on the belly armour, the result of crushing the Croat barrier. That would have to be patched in a base workshop in Germany. There was no further time to admire our Warrior's wounds as I was called to the ops room.

Reports were coming in of a disaster involving a convoy escorted by two of my callsigns at a place called Maglaj. Jason told me the escort was led by Lance-Corporal Brown. Nine Platoon again! I feared the worst.

We drove to the UNHCR warehouse at Zenica where I was briefed by the field officer. Apparently, the convoy had been shelled at a road tunnel and there were several casualties. The Warriors were at the hospital dropping off the injured now. He wanted me to escort him north to recover the bodies.

Half an hour later the Nine Platoon Warriors arrived. In the back they carried four Danish UN civilian drivers. All were badly shaken and a couple were in tears. They were led away to the main building and I walked over to where Lance-Corporals Brown, Gillett and Grant stood. The three were obviously shaken as well and were spattered with blood. They described the events in the jerky, staccato manner of men who were on the verge of shock.

The convoy of ten trucks, a Range Rover and a Land Cruiser had halted in the tunnel a kilometre short of Maglaj. This area was close to the Serb lines and was frequently shelled. Because of this a drill had evolved where the convoy would wait in the tunnel and only two trucks at a time would go to the UNHCR depot to unload.

Brown had positioned his Warrior at the tunnel mouth in overwatch and the first two lorries had unloaded and returned. They then parked in the tunnel facing back towards Zenica. The Serbs waited until the next pair unloaded and the third pair had set off, then mortared the tunnel mouth. Sensibly, the four truck drivers hastily abandoned their vehicles and retreated to the safety of the tunnel. The mortar rounds came closer and one landed next to Brown's Warrior. He decided to move back inside but couldn't because of the other trucks blocking the entrance. The civilian drivers had then all crowded round to watch the mortaring in what was to be a fatal act of stupidity.

The Serbs then brought up a T55 tank and fired into the tunnel. Its first round impacted on the inside wall, fragmented and scythed into the drivers. There was carnage, four were hacked to pieces. The screaming alerted Brown and his crew who dismounted and gave first aid to the injured. Brown, Gillett and Privates Dainty and Nicholson saved the lives of at least two of the injured by their prompt action. The Serbs fired five more rounds into the tunnel. Despite this, the lads continued to give first aid. They could hear the 'whoosh' of the approaching rounds and ducked as they passed overhead. It was gallantry of the highest order.

Grant's Warrior was called forward and the injured piled inside. Brown then waited, under fire, for the UNHCR Convoy Commander to drive back from the depot. Apparently she parked in the middle of the road in her haste to reach the safety of the Warrior. He then commanded his Warrior down an embankment onto the railway track and then back through the adjacent railway tunnel. They linked up and took the injured to the hospital in Zepce before bringing the survivors back to Zenica.

I listened in admiration. Nine Platoon had, indeed, produced the goods when the chips were down. These young NCOs had displayed outstanding leadership and initiative. They described a scene from hell and said there was blood and limbs everywhere. I asked them if they'd come back with me and they all looked to the floor. I told them I understood and I'd get another two crews up to the tunnel. Gillett looked up and said:

'No, sir. We've started the job and we'll see it through.'

This was just the response I expected and I was proud of these lads. They might be the most unruly platoon in the whole of NATO but there was none other I would rather have on my side.

The field officer led, accompanied by the female UNHCR Convoy Commander. Once we reached Zepce I was on new ground and studied the map to get my bearings. The road and railway followed the Bosna River through a steep-sided valley.

We halted a couple of kilometres short of the tunnel and the field officer told me he'd accompany the ambulance to collect the bodies. He asked me to remain where we were with the Warriors in case the Serbs saw us and started shelling again. The woman came over to me and started to give me a hard time. She was looking down on me as just another thick squaddie. I don't know why it is, but some civilians have an annoying habit of treating all soldiers like we're complete dross.

She was upset because Brown had run over the Land Cruiser and demanded that we pay for it. I pointed out that it was she who'd abandoned the vehicle in the middle of the road. As a result, the only way for Brown to get to the railway was over the car. She wasn't having any of it and insisted she was going to lodge a complaint. I exploded:

'You ungrateful cow! That NCO just risked his life to give first aid to your drivers, who were injured through their own stupidity. He then waits around, under fire, for you to return from the depot where you abandon your vehicle, in the middle of the road. In order to get you back, because your drivers have blocked the tunnel, he takes the only course open to him. You don't offer a word of thanks and all you're concerned about is one poxy Land Cruiser. If you think I'm going to stand for your arrogant attitude you're very much mistaken. We're off back to Vitez and you can bring the dead back in your nice clean Land Rover. Now, if you'll excuse me, I'm off to find someone to help, who might just appreciate it!'

With that I strode off. The Nine Platoon boys were smirking and I got the impression she'd been arrogant towards them as well.

The enormity of her predicament hit her. She was just about to be abandoned, on her own, in the middle of nowhere, in a war zone. She ran after me clutching an extremely large humble pie. Not only did she eat plenty of it over the next five minutes, she was as nice as pie for the rest of the day.

Ninety minutes later the ambulance arrived back. The vehicle was painted a dark brown colour and looked rather like a hearse. This was apt as the three UN workers were all rather dead. I asked where the fourth man was and the field worker said he'd been a local interpreter and the ambulance had already dropped his body off.

The tail-gate was opened, revealing three, light grey body-bags. We opened the back doors of the Warriors and then started to lift out the first body. The bags were covered in blood. Some of this had dried, leaving long brown streaks. Most, however, was so thickly coated on that it clung in a semi-congealed mass. Our hands slipped and slithered over the smooth surface of the bag and we dropped the third one. It bounced off my knees leaving a sticky slick that immediately soaked through the thin material of my combat trousers.

All three were laid in a line on the road. The field worker had been unable to positively identify the bodies in the dark of the tunnel and wished to do so now. As the first bag was unzipped, Donlon confided that he'd never seen a dead body before. I told him to take a look, if he really wanted to. He was so close that he was virtually inside the bag. Talk about curious.

The first man had a boot sticking out of the side of his head. This struck me as just a mite unusual, so I, too, closed in for a better look. On closer examination I saw that one of his legs had been torn off and had been put in the bag upside down. No one seemed too keen to put it the right way round. I didn't suggest it as I could imagine Donlon would be only too happy to oblige. The boys called him Psycho Derek after a homicidal cartoon character in the magazine *Zit*. I could see why now.

A large, jagged lump stuck up from the middle of the second bag. All was revealed when the zip was opened. The lump turned out to be what looked like half a tank round embedded in the man's back. It was protruding about twenty centimetres. Goodness knows how much more of it was stuck inside the poor guy. Whatever, it was pretty clear he hadn't died of old age. The third bag was the worst. Donlon had gradually become more involved and was now the self-appointed man in charge of opening the bags. He drew the zip fully down with a flourish as if he were pulling the curtain back from the plaque at a new hospital. The most foul stench hit us and we all gagged (one of the boys ran off to puke up behind a Warrior) that is, all except Donlon, who seemed oblivious, and was pulling aside the halves of the bag to get a better look. The man had been disembowelled. His stomach was ripped open and intestines flowed from the gaping cavity. They looked like several grey and brown snakes twisting and entwining around one another. There were other organs poking through and it reminded me of a school biology lesson. The difference was, this was no laboratory rat. Having been trapped inside the bag, the gases were released in one reeking cloud when the zip was undone. Again, it wasn't hard to figure what'd killed him. The one merciful factor was that these men probably hadn't suffered.

The bags were finally loaded on to the Warriors. It was noticeable that the Nine Platoon boys didn't get involved and I figured they'd seen enough gore that day to last them a lifetime. I was feeling pretty queasy but I felt I had to show willing so I helped my crew to load them in. Donlon looked highly disappointed and I got the impression he'd rather be riding to the hospital with the bodies than coming with me. As the door slammed shut I quipped:

'By heck! There was more Gore there than in the US vice president's office!'

It was totally lost on them and Tookey gave me one of those 'Don't worry, keep on taking the pills' looks.

Nine Platoon disappeared back to Zenica with their sorry cargo and I asked what the UNHCR wanted us to do now.

'I wonder if you could recover any of the aid from the trucks in the tunnel? Also the road is blocked and it's vital for the supply of the town.'

I promised I'd do what I could to help.

We mounted up and drove north towards Maglaj. A sign above the entrance proclaimed the tunnel to be 1190 metres long. The right side of the road was chock-a-block with civilian vehicles of all sorts. There were mostly lorries, including some large artics. Most appeared to have been there for quite a time and were covered in a thick layer of dust. Several had flat tyres. The field worker had told me the locals placed them there for safe keeping rather than risk them being shelled down in Maglaj.

The line of trucks was solid bumper-to-bumper and there was only a metre clearance each side of the Warrior. I told Sergeant Barratt in 0C to wait at the entrance and we drove forward to investigate. Tookey asked to switch the lights on but I refused. The last thing we wanted was any lights advertising our presence with an unfriendly Serb tank about.

We drove slowly down the tunnel. The air was dank and very cold and our exhaust left a cloud of gases that hung in the still air. Soon, both Phil and I had handkerchiefs held over our mouths to keep out some of the fumes. I counted the civvy trucks and had reached over a hundred when Tookey called that he could see that old cliché, the light at the end of the tunnel.

We slowed and cautiously approached the northern end. About a hundred metres from daylight I halted the Warrior and dismounted. Tookey switched off and an eerie silence descended. I told the others to stay in 0B and Dobby and I walked slowly forward.

The end of the tunnel resembled a scene from Dante's *Inferno*. The right of the carriageway was totally blocked with civilian lorries nose-to-tail. Four UN trucks, facing away from me, obstructed the centre. These had been the rear ones in the convoy. The left, and also the pavement, was blocked with two other lorries, this time facing towards us. They must've been the first two that had unloaded. This meant there should be four more out in the open.

I was anxious to avoid being seen from the Serb lines. The last thing I needed was to end up in a body-bag with Donlon sticking his snout into it. We carefully crept forward and, as we reached the nearest truck, the smell hit us.

The stink of blood and faeces was thick in the air and we gagged in unison. There was more light now and, looking down, I saw a large pool of gore about five metres square. This must've been where the men were hit. I edged closer, my boots skidding and sliding in the coagulated mess. I studiously avoided the length of intestine lying there, I didn't need to guess which of the victims that came from. Something squelched under my right boot and I looked down. There was a dark blob lying on the tarmac and I bent to take a closer look. I didn't need to be a doctor to tell I'd just stepped on a human liver. There were bits of fat sticking to it and, with bile rising in my throat, I tried to kick it away. The organ ended up dangling from the toe-cap of my boot and only released its grip at the third attempt. I looked across at Dobby and we both burst out into fits of unnaturally loud laughter. A little further on I walked into the shadow of one of the trucks and stepped in something else. With mounting horror, I realized that whatever I'd trodden in had come right up over the top of my boot. It was like a scene from a horror film. What was it this time? There were only three bodies on the ambulance; was this the local and they hadn't moved him after all? Sod the Serbs! Sod the fact they might fire on us! I had to see, and I pulled out my Maglite. In the beam of the torch was illuminated what looked like meat, corned-beef to be precise. The blood had mingled with it and the red, sticky mass was ankle-deep behind the truck. Surely a man couldn't be blown into this many bits?

I cast the beam around and several tins glinted back at me. With a sickening feel of relief I examined one and the label read: 'Corned-beef. For aid distribution only. Produce of Argentina.' A tank round had hit the truck, which was laden with tinned meat. The cargo had been blown asunder and was, literally, oozing over the tail-gate. Somehow, this seemed worse than the liver.

We peeked out of the mouth of the tunnel and saw the four trucks. Two were still burning, abandoned just outside the safety of the entrance, presumably hit by the mortar fire. They were probably the second pair to return empty. The other two were facing away from us and had been abandoned just after setting off for the depot. One was about a hundred metres outside and the other about three hundred. Both were in full view of the Serb gunners and there was no way I was going to risk retrieving them. Finally, the Range Rover lay, shell-damaged, next to the trucks. It hadn't caught fire but looked a write-off. The Land Cruiser definitely was, and had a large track mark over the bonnet. It would require more than a respray. I sent Dobby back to get the others and told him to radio for 0C, we were going to need every bit of help we could get. Meanwhile, I wandered back inside, taking care to avoid the corned-beef.

Standing where the men had died, I tried to figure out how they could possibly have been hit. They'd been hidden from the Serbs between two trucks. Not only did the pool of blood indicate where they'd been standing but the cab of the one behind them was sprayed in the stuff. I walked over to the left wall and noticed a deep gouge about half a metre long. The round had entered the tunnel, glanced off the wall and probably fragmented before hitting the poor guys. It didn't need much imagination to envisage the carnage as it hit the group. One minute happy spectators in someone else's war, the next, torn limb from limb.

I wandered idly back towards where I could hear the Warrior starting up and kicked something hard. My imagination locked into overdrive and I expected to see a head lying there. Instead, I picked up about a third portion of a 100 mm tank round. It weighed a couple of kilos and bore the grooves made by the rifling. It was completely solid and had broken up, probably on hitting the wall. A remarkably similar piece had been sticking out of the poor guy's back and I hoped his didn't match my bit. When 0B arrived, I threw the chunk in the back and it later served as a rather tasteless paper-weight on my desk.

I gave Phil a quick guided tour and then asked his opinion on how best to recover the trucks. He and Dobby were my vehicle experts and I'd only mess it up if I intervened. I left them to walk round the trucks and assess the damage and they reported back about fifteen minutes later. Three of the lorries looked as if they'd be OK to drive but the other three would require towing. There was one major problem, however, none of the drivers had left their keys in the cabs. I shouted: 'I do not believe it!'

Only a Scandinavian would be so bloody tidy as to remove the keys before stepping out to watch the shooting. The damned things were either back at Zenica or still inside the body-bags. I asked if we could hot-wire the engines and Phil shot me a 'get a life' look. They might be DMIs but the art of auto-theft had yet to be included in the syllabus. There was only one other place to look.

I looked at Dobby and discounted him for the job. He might be a bloody good close-protection NCO but he was built more like Lennox Lewis than Carl Lewis. Donlon was the ideal choice and he jumped at the chance.

We gathered at the entrance, Dobby took up a fire position and Donlon and I zigzagged towards the first of the trucks in the open. I used the burning trucks for a little cover, a dumb move as the heat scorched the hairs from my left arm. There we were, running down the road, wearing bright blue berets, in full view of the Serbs. A flashing light would hardly have been a better aiming mark. Panting from our dash, we reached the first truck. I yanked open the door and groped frantically for the key. Sprawling over the seats, I clawed at the ignition and discovered that there was no key.

Why me? Why couldn't they have been Belgian drivers? They'd have probably left the engines running as well.

There was only one thing for it. We both drew deep breaths and nodded at each other. The two-hundred-metre dash took little short of the Olympic qualifying time. Donlon crouched by the front-left wheel, which I noticed had a flat tyre, and scanned around with his rifle in the shoulder. I pulled open the driver's door and saw, with sickening certainty, that there was no key.

Donlon joined me and stood there emitting a stream of expletives along the lines of 'The fucking fucker's not fucking there!' I turned to go as Donlon climbed up into the cab. He reached up and flipped down the sun-visor and, to my utter amazement, out dropped the ignition key. The streetwise little git, how many times had he done that back in Glasgow? I could have hugged him, but wisely refrained. I contemplated driving the lorry back but the odds weren't too good. The truck was facing the wrong way, with a flat tyre, and neither of us had driven an HGV before. Anyway, the tunnel was blocked and we'd still have had to park it in the open. We started to sprint back, slightly uphill this time. Both of us heard the distant pop of the mortar and redoubled our efforts. My brain was working overtime as I calculated that if the time of flight of the bomb was less than thirty seconds we weren't going to make it. I don't know how far the mortar was away but it must've been a fair distance. We entered the tunnel together and the bomb exploded at about the same time.

Looking back, I saw the rising cloud of black smoke a hundred metres away. They should've had the range better than that as they had, after all, spent half the day firing at the trucks. All I could think of was that they'd laid the weapon onto another target and been slack about readjusting. Thank God the Serbs weren't supermen after all.

I chivvied the boys back into the Warriors and we closed down and tensely waited for the incoming tank rounds. There was no further firing so, after about fifteen minutes, we emerged, helmets on this time, and set about our task. I warned everyone to keep away from the tunnel mouth but, funnily enough, they didn't need much persuasion!

I handed the key to Dobby and suddenly thought, what if it only fits the one truck? However, the wagons were Mercedes and, good old German engineering, the key fitted the first of the trucks facing south.

The rear of the lorry was badly splintered but the engine was intact and caught first time. The tunnel filled with grey smoke and I wondered if the Serbs still had the tank in the area. There was always the chance it may have moved and could be on its way right now. Dobby drove the truck off with a roar and a clashing of gears. I sent Barratt after him in 0C to park the truck in a safe place right at the end of the tunnel and to bring the key back.

The second empty truck had taken a direct hit. There'd been no cargo to absorb the splinters. Shrapnel had shredded the bodywork and ripped the canvas tilt in hundreds of places. The rear window of the cab was smashed but this lorry, too, started first time and Private Waltham drove it away. Old Wally had come along to escape from the stores for a day and was having a ball. Finally, the rear-most of the laden trucks was virtually undamaged and Dobby reversed this one off, with only slightly less gear grinding. That left the three non-starters.

The rear one had been hit by several large chunks of shrapnel and one piece, almost as big as the one I'd picked up, was embedded in the radiator. The coolant had leaked out and the green liquid was slowly mingling with the blood on the floor. Dobby prised the bonnet open and we surveyed the engine. Several of the hoses were severed and the battery leads had been torn off by flying shards of metal. It would need workshop assistance to get this running. Phil took charge and reversed 0B until they were back-to-back and we connected the towing bar. Then, with Waltham, the company HGV driver, at the wheel, dragged the truck back over a kilometre to join the others. The journey took over half an hour and, meanwhile, we looked over the penultimate lorry.

This was the one covered in gore. One rear wheel had been torn away and lay against the side of a civvy truck. One side of the cab had been hit, severing the brake pipes and bending the steering rod. The chassis was damaged too and the whole truck sagged in the middle, like a ship with a broken back. Shrapnel had peppered the front of the cab and coolant still leaked from the radiator. Finally, there was an ominous-looking pool of oil under the engine.

Dobby climbed in and inserted the key. The engine turned over a couple of times and then, miraculously, coughed into life. There was a horrendous rattle and thick blue smoke billowed out from under the bonnet. I made a note to buy a Mercedes if ever I could afford it.

Driving the truck was easier said than done. It obeyed no normal rules of the road and refused to steer and, of course, stop. Dobby peered through the starred windscreen and I signalled him left or right. He slowly reversed the rattling, sagging, truck back to safety. Every five metres or so, the wagon would veer off course and bang into either the wall or a civilian truck. As we made our slow progress, we left a trail of dents and scrapes and even more bits started to fall off our truck. I wondered if any angry posse of Muslim haulage contractors would be chasing me for compensation when all this was over.

I noticed bright lights heading our way and left Dobby, with the truck partially embedded in the cab of a green Raba. Now the tunnel mouth was almost clear these lights would be shining directly towards the Serb lines. I stood in the road and a white Land Rover halted a couple of metres away.

'Get those bloody lights out!' I shouted, and thought what a marvellous air-raid warden I would've made. The driver extinguished the lights and I stared at them as they faded. I was aware of two figures getting out. With my night vision gone, I blundered over to the nearest, actually bumping into him. In my best diplomatic manner I demanded:

'Who the hell are you?'

A shadowy figure introduced himself as somebody-or-other from Reuter's news agency. He'd hotfooted it up to Maglaj when he heard about the shelling and was here to film the clear-up operation. Not if that involved light I told him, only to be interrupted by a sudden glow that made both of us screw our eyes up in pain. I stumbled back to the truck to find another man filming with a TV camera. Mounted on it was a spotlight that looked like it'd been borrowed from the Eddystone Lighthouse.

'Get that bloody light out!' I yelled.

The cameraman looked at me as if to say, are those the only words you know? I was just about to pummel the guy when Dobby kicked the remains of the windscreen out. I don't know whether he did it to avoid the glare, for the benefit of the camera or whether he wanted to get the guy to move. Whatever, the cameraman was showered in glass and hastily switched the light off.

Having regained my cool, I politely explained the situation, at which the reporter agreed to film only at the safe end of the tunnel. The cameraman, he explained, was a local, and probably didn't understand me anyway. Well, one thing was for certain, the Serbs would definitely know we were here.

The truck sounded very rough now. An unpleasant burning smell pervaded the air and it could only be a matter of time before the engine seized.

We resumed our slow passage backwards and, in spite of the cool air, Dobby was sweating with the exertion of turning the wheel. Finally, after nearly two hours, we made it back to the others. Barratt had done a good job of parking the trucks in a neat line and we crashed ours into the tunnel wall roughly in the right position.

Dobby was still sitting in the cab, smoking a cigarette, when the rattling of the engine rose to a crescendo and suddenly ceased with a 'Thunk!'

'Vorsprung Durch Technik' was no more.

We walked back down towards the others and encountered OB towing the last truck. Phil was walking in front making small corrections to the line and keeping the towed lorry on a remarkably straight path. Waltham was in the cab and grinned, peering at us through his round, wire-rimmed spectacles. This truck was the worst of the lot, having been right at the entrance. It too was missing a wheel, this time a front one, and all the other tyres were flat. One had already been stripped away and bright yellow sparks flew from the hub. The cab was mangled and Wally was virtually sitting on a seat and little else. Donlon was standing on the running board next to Wally and their combined weight seemed to be preventing the front from toppling over on to the wheel-less side. The progress of the lorry was marked by a trail of corned-beef and mangled tins.

Well, that was it, we'd cleared the road and recovered most of the aid. We wandered down to take one last look at the scene and I was about to turn and walk away, when I remarked to Dobby:

'Pity we couldn't finish the job isn't it?'

'I was just thinking that myself.'

'Are you sure?'

'Positive, sir!'

'Come on then!'

We dashed out of the tunnel at full pelt like we used to when we emerged from bases in Northern Ireland. I sprinted and Dobby lumbered, with all the grace of an elephant seal, to the first truck. As I ran, I weighed-up the odds. It was like a kiddies potato race, should I go for the near or far truck first? Dobby had stopped for a breather at the first and that made up my mind for me. The road was fairly wide and he reckoned he would get round in a three-point turn. We had to move fast as we felt small and vulnerable in full view of the Serbs.

'Come on Dobby! For Christ's sake get moving!'

'I can't, sir, we don't have a key!'

I started to let out a stream of expletives, most of which started with 'F', when Dobby produced the key with a flourish, like a rabbit from a hat.

'Just joking. Naaaaa!'

Dobby was almost as good as his word and we turned round in five. We accelerated away into the relative safety of the tunnel and handed over the truck to Barratt. He'd never driven a lorry before either but was sure he could hack it.

What the hell were we going to do about the key? Dobby solved the problem by gripping it in his great paw and yanking it out. The engine missed a beat and carried on running. I never did find out whether all the trucks would do this. Whatever, we were back in business again.

We gathered ourselves and careered back to the last truck. It was down quite a sharp hill and Dobby's bulk seemed to accrue a momentum like an express train. We arrived together. The road was much narrower with a steep drop on the right falling away to the railway track. On the left was a deep drainage ditch. There could be no mistake on either side and I decided to marshal Dobby around. A civilian toiled in a field near by, apparently oblivious to the carnage around him. He wasn't oblivious to the mortar firing though. I wasn't sure whether I'd really heard it as it coincided with Dobby starting the engine. However, the fact that the civvy was scarpering back towards a cottage confirmed it.

'Dobby! We've got to get a move on. There's incoming!'

I started waving my arms, like a one-armed paperhanger, frantically trying to convey my directions to Dobby, who duly turned the wheel in exactly the opposite direction. The words of my grandma came floating back to me 'More haste, less speed'.

I drew a deep breath and calmed down. The next turn was better and we started to, ever so slowly, make it round.

We'd done about three turns when the first bomb landed. I couldn't hear a thing over the rumble of the engine and the first I knew was when I felt the slight shockwave. The round landed about two hundred metres away, between us and the tunnel. In fact, it was almost exactly where the earlier one had been. A cloud of debris flew skyward. I'd no idea when, or where, the next one would land. Dobby was blissfully ignorant as the truck was still facing away from the tunnel. The second round landed, a few seconds later, about fifty metres away from the first. The bomb impacted in a field and sent earth and green plants into the air. This was serious and, given the time between explosions, there must be at least two mortars. I started to look around me like a nervous rabbit. I'd no idea where the next two rounds would land and had no chance of hearing them coming. I felt oh so very vulnerable! I was so busy looking for the next explosion that I wasn't looking at the rear wheels of the truck. The lorry lurched and I saw that one wheel had gone over the edge of the ditch. Dobby's eyes widened and he hit the brakes. The truck was still at an angle across the road and would have gone in if it'd been any straighter. He rammed the Mercedes into forward, the wheels spun, and the wagon shot forward, almost mowing me down in the process. We shouted 'sorry!' in unison.

The next explosion was audible over the noise of the engine. I jumped and Dobby looked puzzled. The truck was broadside on to the road now and he was on the other side of the cab to the explosion. He didn't hear a thing. That one was close. Again, it was in the field and only around a hundred metres away. Its mate was even closer and only about fifty away, again in the field. I was way inside the lethal area but God was on my side and the soft earth plugged the bomb, absorbing most of the shrapnel.

We were still only half way round and we were going to get at least two more bombs before we were free. My legs began to shake uncontrollably. Glancing down, I saw the loose material of my trousers was actually shaking as my legs wobbled inside them. Pressing them together, I stood there like a man who's crapped himself – a character I was not far from becoming.

The fifth bomb landed in the field level with us but about thirty metres to my left. The shock wave hit me like a hammer and I wheezed as the breath was forced from my lungs. Something struck the side of the lorry with a metallic clash and I knew the next one would get us. Dobby had seen the last explosion and gave me a look as if to say 'rather you outside than me'. I couldn't have agreed more, though, in truth, the flimsy aluminium cab was little protection.

I heard the sixth bomb coming even above the noise of the engine. Hitting the deck, I prayed. This communication with the Big Man was starting to become a habit.

'Please God make it miss!'

There was a muted, surprisingly distant 'Crump!' and I picked myself up and tried to figure out what'd happened. A strong smell of explosives filled the air and I peered over the edge of the embankment. Sure enough, there was a smoking crater about a quarter of the way down the steep side. I wasn't about to get a tape-measure out, but the bomb cannot have missed the road, and me, by more than two metres.

We had about thirty seconds before the next one and our luck couldn't hold. We were almost there and another five turns should do it. I now had my back to the tunnel and the truck was at an angle, almost facing the entrance. The next round landed on the road about twenty metres behind the lorry and several things happened at once. The shockwave hit me on the shins like a blow from a baseball bat. Our lorry jerked under the impact of numerous fragments and Dobby ducked. Finally, both back tyres deflated with a bang.

I'd wised-up now and shortened the odds by positioning myself as near to the embankment as possible. The next bomb landed in the field but I didn't even see it as the truck was in the way.

With a final roaring of the engine Dobby was round and I vaulted into the cab. There was no way they could adjust that quickly and I knew we'd make it. The rounds would be already heading for where we'd been. I hoped.

The truck was wobbling with three flat tyres and Dobby was fighting the steering wheel. We'd covered a hundred metres or so with two to go and I was confident we were going to make it.

We both jumped as the green tracer flew over our heads. The rounds were from a heavy calibre machine gun or small cannon. They hit the hill above the entrance at an angle that suggested the weapon was slightly off to a flank. If only we could get inside the tunnel we'd be safe. I heard the distant bang of the next mortar round, way behind us. At least we didn't have to worry about that.

'For God's sake Dobby, can't you go any faster?'

I was going to suggest he zigzagged but thought better of it as we were all over the road anyway. The next burst initially passed very close over our heads and then the gunner corrected and we were hit. The truck shuddered and Dobby flinched causing us to hit the Land Cruiser. This unexpected movement caused the next burst to mostly fly behind us. Only a couple of rounds hit and then we were into the welcoming darkness of the tunnel.

We both whooped and yelled in a most un-British manner. We had survived!

The cab filled with the smoke from burning rubber and we had to slow down as we kept cannoning off parked vehicles. Dobby found a can of Pepsi, abandoned by the unfortunate driver, and we shared it with not the slightest pang of guilt.

We finally reached the others, parked the truck, in a manner of speaking, and climbed shakily out. The rear sides were splintered from the shrapnel and the canopy was holed in dozens of places. The rear had taken the cannon hits and the wooden walls bore nine, roughly twenty-millimetre holes. There was a trail of white powder leading back down the tunnel and a heap of the stuff already accumulating under the lorry. Sacks of flour piled high in the back had absorbed the energy of the rounds and none had reached the cab. We had saved the truck and it had, in turn, saved us.

The BiH looked after the aid and it was eventually broken down into smaller loads and taken into the town, at night, on farm carts. I called the crews together and gave them all a big thank you. Without their dedication, ingenuity, stamina and courage the whole sorry episode of the Maglaj convoy would have had a far worse ending.

When I returned to camp, I went to the Nine Platoon lines and told them what a great job I thought they'd done. They'd proved themselves under fire and I stood the two crews down from ops for the next day. The platoon, collectively, swelled with pride and would've probably become cocky if Zippy had not growled:

'The Boss might be soft but I'm still watching you!'

Afterwards, he confided that he, too, was proud of the way the lads had performed and would tell them in his own good time. Such are the ways of the Sergeant Major.

I too had intended to have a quiet day and catch up on some office paperwork. All was quiet until early afternoon when I was called to the ops room. The ops warrant officer, Sergeant Major Byrne, briefed me there'd been no mail for two days because of a troublesome checkpoint near Kiseljak. Two mail runs had been turned back by the HVO for no apparent reason.

The mail was collected by NCOs from the postal and courier section escorted by two AFVs from the ops company. Corporal Hutchinson had been one of those stopped and had been forced to spend the night at Kiseljak after being turned back. I found Richard and told him I'd carry out the mail run myself. I intended to take four Warriors because there were eighteen soldiers returning from leave as well as sixty bags of mail.

We formed up on the tank park and our little convoy consisted of 0B and 0C as well as 30 (Three Zero) with Tom Crowfoot and another of his vehicles, 32 (Three Two). Accompanying us were the posties in their Land Rover carrying the outgoing mail. I wasn't too happy about having a soft-skin vehicle with me but the NCO told me he was quite content to travel in it. This was also tempered by the fact that the HVO had simply blocked the road. There'd been no shots fired.

The mail we received from home was a vital part of everyday life in Vitez. The lads would hang around the company office for ages until the letters were sorted, and then scuttle off with their new arrivals. Mail was a major factor in the morale of the troops and, occasionally, the lads would be reduced to tears if an expected letter failed to materialize. With massive queues for the few telephones, many soldiers took to writing regularly for the first time in their lives. I'd been tasked to ensure the mail was collected and was determined to succeed.

I'd booked an interpreter, Andreana, a dark-haired Croat girl. I was furious to arrive at their office to find one of the LOs had nabbed her to go off on some 'vital' task. This was typical of their attitude, riding roughshod over the grunts in the companies. There were no others available.

We set off around five in the afternoon and reached the checkpoint about fifty minutes later. There was no sign of a barrier at the location, about three kilometres from Kiseljak. An elderly HVO militiaman was sitting on a stool drinking coffee from a small cup. He stood up and obligingly moved his seat so we could pass. This hardly seemed much of an obstacle. Still, Byrne had told me the barrier was an articulated trailer that only appeared on the return journey. We would have to wait and see.

Finally, we reached UN HQ and booked in for the normal fatboy's scoff. We had a mixed bag for crews and Zippy commanded 0C with the CQMS acting as gunner. I was happy with this as Goy was a good gunner in his own right. Above all, however, it was good for the lads to see the back-room boys getting a slice of the action.

After supper, we stuffed the vehicles with soldiers, their grip bags and the mail and left at just after eight, in the order: 0B, 0C, 3Zero, the Rover and 32. We clattered through Kiseljak and I noticed a superb red sunset to our left. Where the old man had been the road was now blocked.

A light blue artic trailer, of the sort used to carry sand or grain, was broadside across the road with its rear to my right. Further to the right was a house with a small garden surrounded by a wall. To the left, was a line of low offices and a depot of some sort. There was no sign of anyone about.

We edged up to the trailer and I saw there was no way round to the left. To the right was a gap that was just about wide enough for us. I climbed out onto the turret top and looked around. There was no one to be seen, in fact it was all a bit too quiet. There may have been some movement in the depot but it was impossible to see because of the glare from the low sun. The hairs started to prickle on the back of my neck and I dropped back inside as I gave the order to advance through the gap. As we approached, two HVO men appeared from behind the artic and started waving at us to go back. This was where we needed the bloody interpreter and there was no point in dismounting and starting a futile conversation in sign language. They were not actually stopping us and I was determined to press home our advantage. I was waist-up out of the turret, gently conning the Warrior through the gap, when the firing started.

The HVO opened with a fusillade of small arms fire, some rounds hitting the road in front of the wagon and the wall to my right. At least one hit the front of the Warrior and I distinctly heard the thwack as it connected with the armour. This was serious and I ordered Tookey to close down. We sped forward and halted about eighty metres past the barrier, taking another hit as we passed the depot.

Phil traversed to the rear and we covered Zippy through the gap. In his haste, he demolished part of the wall. We now had two through and the odds were more on our side. There was a lull and I stuck my head out and glanced around. To the right was a deep ditch. To the left, three soldiers hid in the doorways of the offices with a further three standing on the loading platform. Two carried 64 mm rockets and one, an RPG. This was rapidly becoming unfunny. I cursed my decision to bring the damned Land Rover, but for it we could all drive on and be home in an hour.

There was a slight commotion and another figure appeared, shouting at the soldiers. At this, one of them started to try to extend the 64 mm. I wasn't having this and I gave Phil a fire control order. The turret swung to the right and I shouted, 'On!'

'I can't see him!'

'You must be able to. You're pointing right at him!'

'I'm telling you, I can't see him!'

'Have you got your specs on?'

'Of course, but I can't see a thing. If you ...'

'Look for Christ's sake, Stevie Wonder, he's there in the sodding doorway!'

'There's no use swearing at me or being insulting. I can't see him!'

I dropped down into the turret, flipped to the times-ten sight and gasped as the glare hit me. The sun was shining right into the optics and dazzling Phil.

'Sorry mate!'

The guy now had the weapon on his shoulder and was fiddling with the arming lever. He was seconds from firing and I considered firing over his head. Warning shots were allowed by the orange card and now seemed a good time. I was about to tell Phil to fire a short burst when I noticed a row of flats behind the depot. Our rounds would strike these and could harm innocent people. Right, that was it, mind made up. Kill him!

I told Tookey to reverse about two metres and the glare cleared as the sun was masked behind the building.

'Got him! Laid-on now!'

There was a minute adjustment of the turret and the guy with the 64 leapt into view. He had lank, dark hair and was chewing gum. The tube was pointing directly at us. He looked threatening enough for me.

'Right, let's do it.'

I took one last look out of the top and was about to give 'Loaded Fire!' when I saw the car.

A metallic-green saloon car was rapidly approaching from the direction of Busovaca. I momentarily forgot the anti-tank threat, this car looked like it was on a course to ram us. The HVO weren't renowned for their suicide attacks but anything was possible. As the vehicle closed, I noticed it was, of all things, a Ford Escort. There were two HVO in the front, one had a black beard and I thought for a moment he may be the police chief from Vitez, out for revenge. At the last moment, the car swerved and screeched to a halt. Positioned immediately to our left, its rear doors were about level with our front-left corner.

The front doors opened and I heard one of them bang against our side. What was going on? The 64 man was completely forgotten as he was unlikely to fire with the car in the way. Just to be sure, I radioed Zippy and told him to keep an eye on them. A quick glance confirmed that his gun was laid on. I leaned out, feeling very vulnerable, and saw the two men open the boot. The next thirty seconds happened in slow motion, like a scene from a Sam Peckinpah movie.

One man, with ginger hair and a drooping moustache, reached inside and pulled out four TMA 4 anti-tank mines. The mines were about the size of a dinner plate and about ten centimetres thick with three pressure horns screwed into the top. Ginger rushed to the right of the Warrior and placed one a metre to the right of the right track. He was balancing the stack of mines like a baker with a pile of cakes. The pressure pads were touching the underside of the mine on top but clearly needed more than that to set them off.

He placed the second mine roughly in front of our right track and the third centrally. There was no doubt the last would be in front of the left track and we'd be stuck. The only way to go would be back to Kiseljak. Out of the corner of my eye I saw Blackbeard pull an RPG 7 launcher from the boot and then three missiles. It was now or never.

'Tookey! No questions! Forward, hard left stick now!'

The engine roared and we veered sharply to the left. Ginger dropped the last mine and dived out of the way. I couldn't see Blackbeard and didn't much care what happened to him. Our Warrior hit the Escort in the area of the rear door and we rode up slightly and then back down. I heard the windows pop out and a tearing sound and then we were free.

We pulled on another twenty metres and I looked back. The fight had gone out of the HVO and Ginger and Blackbeard stood in the road with open mouths. There was no sign of their RPG. Their expression portrayed a feeling of 'Hell! These guys really mean business'. The men at the depot just stood and stared, weapons by their sides. We'd regained the initiative and I wasn't about to let go of it again.

'0C, 3Zero and 32, form a box around the Rover and come to my location.'

The boys sparked well, especially Tom, who came crashing round the artic with the Rover hugging his rear door. Tom took the right, 32 the left, 0C the front, and they trundled towards me forming an armoured shield around the vulnerable Rover. There was no need, as the Croat bully boys were still in a state of stupor. At the last minute, 0C squeezed round the left of the wrecked Escort and the Rover followed. I told them to carry on round the next bend and wait for us.

The car was well and truly mangled. Our track had run over it diagonally from the front left door to the right of the boot. The

Escort's back was broken and the front wheels were both off the ground. As if on cue, the HVO melted away and I called the last two Warriors past me.

We rejoined the others and set-off back. When we reached the first BiH checkpoint the sentry waved at us to stop. One of our track-guards had been ripped when we hit the car and was hanging off. I thanked the guy, who drew closer and pointed at something else. Kneeling, I examined the damp, red stain standing out against the white of the belly-plate. Yes, it was definitely blood!

Zippy halted behind us and he and Goy dismounted.

'Bit of a problem, Sar'nt Major. Looks like we may have killed someone!'

'Aye sir. Didn't you see the bloke in the back of the car?'

This was all I didn't need but Goy gave me a wide grin and started to explain. He's one of those people who, when excited, talk in fast-forward. I could only pick out one word in three but the gist was that there had, indeed, been a third HVO in the car. He'd been trapped when we crushed the car and emerged a couple of minutes later reeling about and clutching his head. His mates then led him away into the depot. At least he wasn't dead but I bet he'd need a change of trousers.

I pointed to the blood and said 'Ha Vay Oh!' to the Muslim who recognized my atrocious attempt at saying Serbo-Croat for HVO. He went away chuckling to himself.

I reported the incident back in camp and there was a considerable post-mortem. One view was that taking four Warriors was too aggressive. I wasn't having that and pointed out that the alternative was to take an eight-ton truck for the passengers. I did agree that I should've left the Rover behind, but, again, we would've probably needed another AFV to compensate. There was, however, no hint there'd be trouble and the Rover had been used for the last seven months.

Some thought the trashing of the car was likely to bring down the wrath of the Croats. However, if I'd dismounted, I doubt whether I'd have got anywhere with the HVO. The last two patrol commanders had tried that and failed. We'd exploited a gap left by the HVO and they had fired first. The mines were also a threat to us as were the RPGs but, despite sufficient cause, we hadn't fired back. Yes, I'd taken an aggressive way out but it was better to damage property than people. We'd responded in a way that sent a clear message to the HVO. 'Don't mess with the big boys!' The alternative was to turn back and let the bullies walk all over us.

I felt sorry for the headquarters staff as it was they who would have to fiend the inevitable protests. No wonder they were keen to suggest other courses of action, amply aided by twenty-twenty hindsight. Alas, this is ever the conflict between the armchair tactician and the man on the ground. One has the luxury of making judgements in his own time, from the security of an office, while the other has split-second decision times. The funny thing was, the checkpoint was gone the next day and the HVO never attempted to interfere with the mail run during the rest of the tour.

This incident had a couple of amusing postscripts. The HVO sent the battalion a bill for 19,000 deutschmarks with a letter, framed in atrocious English. Blaskic employed the worst possible translators in his HQ. Part of the letter read:

'One of your Warrior he come upon a lorry broke down on side of road. HVO men try to stop Warrior because driver of lorry he work on repair flat tire. Your Warrior push passed them and through garden of innocent house. He mind not where he drive. Along come Ford Escort car driven by innocent civilian, Mr Ivica Bakovic of Busovaca. He take his sick brother, Anto and father, Stipo, to hospital in Kiseljak. On way, he find three RPG Rocket next to road stolen from HVO by Mujahideen extremist criminals. Being good man he not wish children to find this so he put in back of car to give to UNPROFOR in Kiseljak. Your Warrior he drive at Mr Bakovic and he squash car. The family Bakovic had to fly for there life. Your Warrior, he then drove off without stop to help these innocent civilians.

We therefore most respectfully demand that you apprehend this culprit and punish him for his reckless doings. We also demand that you pay the amount of DM 19000 to pay for car and the RPG which were property of HVO.'

We all had a huge chuckle at this but it was poor old Randy Rhodes who had to deal with it. Needless to say, I was not billed and poor old Mister Bakovic, his sick brother and aged father are still waiting! The HVO seemed to employ a special squad of Walter

Mittys to concoct these stories. Another favourite was to wait until we patrolled through Vitez and then send in a bill for damage to the kerb stones. All this from an organization who'd let a bloody great bomb off in the centre of town.

News of the incident soon spread through the school and we were known for a while as 'Wells Fargo Company – the mail always gets through!' There was also an upsurge in 'Vitez Vaughan' items in the *Dobro Donkey*, including this cartoon:

'Oops! What was that?'

I took the attitude that it was a bit of harmless fun and Roy and I submitted the following article:

The commanding officer has approved the following one-liners to be used by company commanders when dealing with the press:

OC A COMPANY	OC C COMPANY
Monday 'My men responded appropriately.'	'Eat lead Chetnik!'
Tuesday 'We operate in support of the UNHCR.'	'What can you expect from a bunch of civvies!'
Wednesday 'My vehicles carry a variety of ammunition natures.'	'I've got enough to blow the bastards to kingdom-come and back!'
Thursday 'The L2 grenade is a close-quarter weapon of the last resort.'	'Chew on this pineapple Slobodan!'
Friday 'There was an unfortunate break-down in the passage of information.'	'F—ing REMEs!'
Saturday 'Cunning negotiation often succeeds.'	'What Ford Escort, Phil?'

Chapter 8
Lowry on Acid

There was no time to recover from the mail run. Early the next morning, I was crashed out to monitor fighting reported in the village of Baje, up the Bila Valley.

The village was one of many in the area that had fragmented due to the fighting. The place was mixed, and the tension had caused all the Croats to gravitate to one half and the Muslims to the other. There'd been an outburst of sniping and we were shown a victim.

The local HVO commander, a young man wearing a red scarf round his neck, took us to a house on the outskirts of the village. The body lay on the floor covered by a camouflage groundsheet. A middle-aged woman, obviously the mother, sobbed in the corner. Muttering to himself, the commander pulled back the cover revealing a young man of about eighteen. He was dressed in camouflage trousers and brown vest. He'd been hit once, in the chest. The round had passed through him and the Croat turned him slightly to reveal a gaping exit wound, the size of my fist.

I asked if there was anything I could do and they wanted me to take the body to the hospital in Nova Bila. When I asked why the ambulance couldn't come to the body, they told me the BiH would fire on it. I said I'd broker a local cease-fire and set a rendezvous with the ambulance, at the broken Bila Bridge, for midday.

We then drove to the local BiH HQ and were told the Croats had killed four people. When I asked to see the bodies, they had, conveniently, been taken to Kljaci. I was beginning to get the hang of the Bosnian mentality and was starting to take all allegations with a pinch of salt. The four dead probably meant one. They blamed the Croats for shooting and claimed the dead man was the HVO sniper.

I remarked they must have a very good sniper of their own to kill the Croat one.

They insisted the BiH wouldn't tolerate the Croat violence and they'd soon be on the offensive. This backed-up all the Milinfo briefings. There was an atmosphere of cockiness that I hadn't seen before in the BiH. I was used to the cowering deference of the likes of Munib but this lot were very sure of themselves.

They finally agreed a route for us but this was too narrow for the Warrior. We had to knock a tree down to get past and this cost us yet another deflector plate. The body was loaded on and then the Croat commander asked if he could accompany it as he had to attend a conference. This was another, annoying, Bosnian trait. We'd do them a favour and they would thank us. Just as we were about to leave, they would invariably come up with a supplementary favour, usually involving something shady.

There was no way I was breaking my agreement. I told him I wouldn't carry him and he started to accuse me of siding with the Muslims. Bloody ungrateful gits! Here I was doing one of my first good turns for the Croats and they still wanted more. No wonder many of the lads referred to the Bosnians by the derogatory term of 'flip flops'.

'I am going now. I'm sure you'll find some other way to take this body to Nova Bila.'

I turned to leave and the Commander called me to stop, saying it was all a terrible mistake and of course we were friendly to the Croats. Perhaps this was not a good time to talk about Ford Escorts!

The broken bridge creaked and swayed under the weight of the vehicle but held, and the HVO man passed on his way to the next world.

We drove up to Grahovcici where the commander was friendliness itself. I'd asked Dominic Hancock to organize a small aid-drop to the village and this had arrived the day before. The villagers were worried the BiH would attack them. I tried to assure them there was still a cease-fire and the other side had said they wouldn't break it. I received their best 'and pigs might fly' look.

The CO's conference started with the news that three Italian journalists had been murdered near GV. In our area, the Travnik joint-checkpoints were now HVO only and there was increased tension in the town. Someone had taken a large BiH flag from a lamp post in Old Vitez and we were told to be on the lookout for it. Finally, there was a visit from the official war artist, a fellow called Peter Howson, and a BBC film crew making a documentary on him. I was tasked with hosting them.

After the conference I briefed the company hierarchy. Zippy saw me afterwards and said he thought he'd seen the flag. He took me down to the Portakabins and, sure enough, there was a large BiH flag in one of the Nine Platoon rooms. I summoned Tom.

'Couldn't we just give it back?' he said.

'No we bloody well can't! It's got "Mr Crowfoot is innocent, OK!" written on it!'

Secretly, I couldn't help grinning at their antics as it was a tacky flag anyway. In the end, I ate humble pie with Angus Hay and he produced one from the BiH in Travnik, to give to the BiH in Vitez!

That evening, we drove to Kljaci to check on cease-fire violations. Dobby, Donlon and I were dropped off by Phil and then shown into Arib's house.

We sat around the table, sipping coffee by candle light. Hajiya arrived and reminded me that he'd lived in Switzerland for twenty-two years. The same plump, blonde girl served coffee and he quipped that she should avoid the candles because if she caught fire, she'd burn all night!

The imam arrived and I was taken to see yet another body. Each mosque had a slab where the dead were laid to rest. The present incumbent was dressed in blue slacks and a green shirt. I was told that he was a miner who'd been killed in the Baje fighting as he walked to work. Hajiya insisted on showing me the five bullet wounds that peppered the corpse's torso. My stomach had become hardened to the sight of death but why this fixation with showing me the wounds? I could see he was dead. Both sides did it and, by the end of the tour, I must have seen more wounds than a Home Office pathologist.

In the event there was little sporadic shooting and although they blamed the Croats, it was impossible to tell which side was firing. In truth, I didn't much care. I'd tried to report cease-fire violations but knew it was fruitless. Neither side took a blind bit of notice of our protests. My being here wasn't going to shorten the War but I was gaining the confidence of the inhabitants of one particular village.

I awoke on the 4 June feeling a bit rough and decided to have a quiet day. There was a convoy of Muslims in four buses expected in our area and I sent Phil off to investigate. The people were mostly from Austria and Germany and were returning to Bosnia to be near their loved ones. Quite why anyone should wish to bring their family into a war zone was beyond me. This was exactly what the CO told the convoy organizer when asked for escorts through the Croat areas. However, they refused to heed his advice to turn back and carried on into our patch. The mandate was clear: we could not help organizations who were not part of, or approved by, the UN.

The convoy approached anyway and, when Phil returned, he reported that it was halted at the Novi Travnik T-junction. The Croats were demanding to see passports and told the people to wait until clearance was given from HVO headquarters. There they sat, meekly, on the buses, until someone shelled them.

I was called over the tannoy and rushed to the ops room. There was carnage at the buses and we had to cordon the area as soon as possible to prevent further firing. We'd need several callsigns to achieve this. I ordered Zippy and the S/NCOs to run round the Portakabins and the JRC to find as many of the lads as possible.

In minutes, the lads started to form up, some of them still pulling on uniform. I sprinted away to fetch my own kit and, when I returned, well over half the company was on parade. Zippy shouted out the callsigns and, when we had a complete crew, told them to stand by their wagon. Those remaining were then split into *ad hoc* crews. I then briefed the commanders on the situation. Using my map, I divided the ground up into areas and tasked pairs of vehicles to patrol these to prevent any heavy weapons from firing. All the high ground around the junction was covered leaving four of us to go to the scene. We rolled out of camp in a long convoy of seventeen vehicles. There were Warriors, Scimitars, 432s and the Spartan. I looked at my watch and the total time elapsed since the call on the tannoy was twenty-five minutes.

The locals came out to stare at this unexpected show of strength as we rumbled past. Callsigns started to disappear up the various tracks into the hills and, less than ten minutes later, I arrived at the buses. I deployed my two Warriors and Sergeant Smith's two 432s in a defensive circle and dismounted. The buses were parked nose-to-tail on the side of the road. As we neared the first we could hear the engine was still running, so I told Dobby to find the cut-off switch. Alone, I walked round the back and slithered in a pool of blood and something else. Looking down, I saw the something else was human brains and my boots had a coating of light-brown matter on the soles. Great, liver and brains, all in one week!

The owner of the brain was, not surprisingly, close by. In fact, he was lying under a cape, similar to the one used over the HVO man yesterday. I lifted the cover and stared in horror. The body was that of a woman with shoulder length peroxide blonde hair, cut in a bob. Shrapnel had entered one side of the head and out the other blowing the brains out. One side of the face hung off like a partially-removed rubber mask. Down below, a foot was almost severed, tenuously connected to the ankle by a thin thread of flesh. The poor devil must've been standing in the space between the buses when the first round came down.

Dobby joined me.

'This one's a woman!' I croaked.

'Not unless she shaves!'

He flipped the undamaged side of the face over with his boot and, with relief, I saw a distinctive five o'clock shadow. I don't know why I was relieved. It was still a dead human being lying before me. Somehow, the fact it was a bloke made it better.

The third bus was the worst hit and at least two rounds had landed close by. Shrapnel had pierced the thin coachwork in hundreds of places and shattered most of the windows. I stepped inside and gagged as the stench of blood hit me. The driver was slumped in the gangway with one leg still jammed under the pedals. I felt for his pulse but he was already quite cold. There was no obvious sign of injury but he was very dead. There was nobody else on the bus but the amount of blood spattered about the place suggested there must be several wounded. The belongings of the people were stacked high at the rear of the bus. Everything had been abandoned in the resulting panic.

'We've got company!' called Dobby.

Stepping down, I encountered two HVO men. Unusually, the Croats wore helmets. They looked very nervous. One told me it was the BiH who'd shelled the buses and pointed to the hills where the rounds had, apparently, come from. I'd sent Tom up there. He said the wounded had been taken to Nova Bila and I sent Sergeant Smith off to investigate.

When I asked why the BiH would fire on their own buses he presumed it was to put the blame on the Croats. I felt like punching the little creep. He was most insistent and again repeated that the BiH were the culprits. I didn't want to believe him but he had been in the area when it happened. It seemed odd he should cover for his own side if they'd just shelled him.

boys. I called the ops room and Richard answered. He'd spoken to the UNHCR and there was no mandate for us to move these people. They were not here with official blessing and we were not to get involved. I pointed out there may be trouble and was told Perry was at the buses. He was going to speak to the HVO local commander and try to obtain a guarantee for their safety.

I met Perry as he was supervising the loading of the dead onto an ambulance. As I arrived, the blond man was being peeled off the road and put onto a plastic-covered stretcher. His foot, unfortunately, didn't quite make it and dropped off *en route*. The appendage was scooped up by the medic and placed where it should've been, but facing inwards. It was wearing a white sock and grey loafer. I hoped I wasn't wearing white socks when my turn came.

Perry assured me the medic had scoured the area for bodies. This must've been difficult as it was dark, but I let it go. All was quiet at the junction and there'd been no shelling for over half an hour. There was, however, heavy fighting in Travnik and the coloured lights of tracer rounds were arcing from one side of the valley to the other. It looked like full-scale war had broken out in the town.

Perry had been ordered to try to persuade the Muslims to find transport to the nearest friendly village. He also told them we were unable to help. As usual, we were in a no-win situation. If we moved the Muslims ourselves, we'd be accused of helping the enemy, by the Croats. If we didn't help them and someone was hurt, then the BiH would accuse us of not caring, a charge they levelled after Ahmici. It seemed the UN policy was to do nothing and hope the problem was gone by morning. There was a possibility the people could simply walk to either Travnik or Grbavica where they would be safe. Both were within a few kilometres but this, of course, all depended on whether the Croats would allow it. I had an uneasy feeling and thought, perhaps, we hadn't seen the last of these people.

It was Perry's call and the CO had made it clear that negotiations with local commanders had to take place through the LOs. The shooting was over and I started to pull the callsigns in.

Most of the boys were back when I received a message from Sierra 21, a Scimitar, that they had a Muslim with them refusing to let go of the vehicle.

'Drive off then!'

'We can't, he's clinging to the sides!'

'Stop and prise him off then!'

'We've tried but as soon as we mount-up again he comes back!'

'Stay there. Delta 20 will come to assist.'

Stephen arrived and the Scimitars were able to leave. The man then clung to the Warrior and wouldn't let go. He wasn't in the least bit intimidated by the larger vehicle. The Warrior drove on for a distance but there was a real danger of the man falling off and becoming an extra track pad. Finally, I went there myself.

The man was middle-aged and had come from the convoy. He told me he was travelling to join his son in Tuzla. As he had no family on the buses he'd left the crowd but was then surrounded by HVO. They'd beaten him up and said they'd kill him when darkness fell. He'd hidden in a ditch until S21 had passed and then clung on. I examined the man in the light of the back door and one eye was, indeed, bruised and half-closed. I sent Stephen back to camp and told the Muslim the way to Grbavica. He was hysterical again and clung to the headlight guard at the front of 0B. He was like a limpet and, when Dobby prised one arm off he'd hook a leg up to try to hang on with that. His fear had given him the strength of three men. I called the ops room.

'Hello Zero this is Three Zero. I want your permission to bring one Muslim to the area of the camp. He's been threatened by the HVO and I believe his life is in danger.'

'Negative, we cannot get involved.'

'He's clinging to my vehicle.'

'Drive off then!'

'If I do, I'm going to have a human radiator mascot until he falls under the tracks!'

'Understood. You are the man on the ground, do what you think is best!'

We turned off the lights in the Warrior and we stood in complete darkness. I briefed the man.

'I'm going to break the UN rules now and carry you a short journey to the nearest Muslim village. When we get there, I'll point out the direction for you to go and you will not turn back. You will not tell anyone how you got there.'

The man looked at me in disbelief, as if it was all a big joke and we were going to hand him over to the Croats. However, Dobby bundled him in and, five minutes later, we were parked outside the mess. I took the man by the shoulder and pointed out the Croat houses and the Muslim ones. Finally I said:

'Now go! I never want to see you again!'

Instead of running, he fell at my feet and actually kissed my boots. It was all a trifle embarrassing as we'd hardly risked our lives for him. He proved almost as limpet-like round my ankles but, eventually, I was able to deftly step out of his grip and away he went. All in a night's work!

During the night the bus survivors started to congregate around the camp. Eventually, there were nearly a hundred of them grouped around the gate nearest the CO's house. They were hysterical and demanded sanctuary from the UN. The Croats herded them there from Nova Bila and hovered on the periphery firing the odd shot over their heads, occasionally closing in to threaten them.

The CO was anxious to avoid the same problems the French had experienced at Kladanj. Here, a crowd had gathered outside the UN base and demanded sanctuary. The French let them in and, weeks later, still had refugees living in the camp, refusing to leave. It reached the stage where it would be worse to now eject the refugees than it would've been to keep them out in the first place.

Our Colonel was determined not to let these people in and thus, we ended up with the bus-people camping on the track outside the gate. It was a freezing night and the anguished keening of the women was audible throughout camp. The CO sent an LO to tell them to disperse as we would not let them in. They had to find their own transport to Zenica as we could not help. These people were desperate for help and turned to the blue berets for assistance. All they received was the party-line that we couldn't help because they were not refugees. They should either return home or make their own way on. This was claptrap as there was no way the people could find their way anywhere. All were stuck in the middle of a hostile area and we were their only hope of salvation.

The A Company soldiers on guard had to stand in their sangars and listen to the cries of the desperate, and the taunts of passing HVO bullies. Eventually, the CO, correctly gauging the mood of the soldiers, went to the gate and expressly forbade Roy from giving any help to the Muslims. We were sticking to the UNHCR policy.

In the morning, I met up with the war artist.

Peter Howson was of medium height with hollow cheeks and sandy hair. He extended a hand that felt like a dead trout and I had to fight the urge to wipe my palm on the seat of my trousers. He was softly spoken with a strong Scottish accent.

The *Sunday Times* was paying him to come and paint as the 'official war artist'. In return for his expenses he was required to hold an
exhibition of his work in the Imperial War Museum. The supplement said his works sold for thousands and were highly prized.
Howson told me he would complete over a hundred paintings.

His work depicted grotesque, violent figures such as football
hooligans. They were all bullnecked with stubby fingers,
Neanderthal brows and snarling, twisted faces. Now this may sound
like your average Millwall fan but I could see no beauty to any of his
humans, even the children were grotesque. It was like concentra-
tion-camp art in reverse or Beryl Cook with violence. Nevertheless,
they were much in demand.

He should find plenty of material here as I could take him into
the JRC on a Saturday night and show him some hideous faces. He
laughed at this and said he wanted to see as much of the War as possible. That should be easily arranged.

I was also introduced to the BBC crew. They were making a programme in the '40 Minutes' series. The producer was a grey-haired
man who had a no-nonsense attitude and stressed that he'd not get
in our way. Not only did I have to look after Howson, I was going to
be filmed as well. There was scope for a nightmare.

We deployed to Travnik and into the middle of a war. The HVO
and BiH were going at it hammer-and-tongs. The town was being
shelled and a couple of the blocks of flats in the centre had taken
hits. One had blown a large chunk out of a room on the tenth floor
and a bed hung precariously out of the hole with a red quilt flapping
in the breeze. The town centre echoed to the sound of small arms
fire. We were supposed to be there to monitor whether there was
fighting or not. Yes! There definitely was. There was no point in
hanging around as duty target, so we made our way back.

The Dolac checkpoint was no longer joint. A surly group of HVO
ran the place and had placed a number of TMRP 6 anti-tank mines
on the side of the road. These were the best of the mines available
with a large hollow charge, which would easily pierce the underside
of a Warrior. They could be used with a long tilt fuse, which was set
off by the front of any vehicle. These, however, were the simple 'run
over and die' type. The HVO reluctantly moved the barrier and we
passed back towards Vitez. Howson was standing in the back with
his head out of the mortar hatches and wearing a radio headset. At
the T-junction, he asked if he could see the wrecked buses.

We stopped and walked over to the coaches. Looters had already been in action and a few suitcases were strewn around, their contents spilled on to the dirt. We stood between the buses and I explained how one man had died here. Howson blanched at the massive pool of dried blood and then made the mistake of asking what the brown stuff was.

'Oh that's brains!'

Howson retched and ran to the side of the bus. He appeared a few minutes later wiping his mouth and I said:

'Come on! We'll take a look in one of the buses. After you!'

The artist climbed into the coach and fell headlong over the corpse in the gangway. He literally recoiled in horror. His back arched and he threw himself off and out of the door. Bloody HVO and bloody LOs, why the hell couldn't they clear the area properly?

I asked the film crew if they were happy with the material they'd collected and they grinned and said what a great morning they'd had. Alas, our celebrity was not so happy and was strangely silent during the ride back.

Over lunch, the producer said that Howson was not too keen to go out again. Hopefully, he could be persuaded otherwise, and would we take them back to Travnik this afternoon! I made a noncommittal grunt and finished my lunch.

Sure enough, the producer led Howson out to the Warrior at two o'clock.

The CO had been earning his pay and had brokered a cease-fire with the local commanders. Travnik was a little quieter and our task was to show a reassuring UN presence to the frightened civilians. I wasn't sure if this would work as we had, after all, failed to prevent the morning's shelling.

There was only sporadic shelling but increased small-arms fire. We parked, in cover, under the steel and perspex awning of the bus station, and dismounted. The BBC filmed Howson and I talking about the War. I told him Travnik had always been considered a model town showing how Croats and Muslims could coexist.

As we were chatting, a gunman targeted us and a shot passed very close by. I was too busy gassing on and didn't really notice it. Dobby just looked bored but Howson ducked wildly. He picked himself up, looking very sheepish, and we carried on. The TV crew were consummate professionals and kept filming throughout. A minute later, a second shot passed even closer. Dobby and I were locked into a 'let's see who flinches first' competition and neither of us blinked. Howson was bobbing and weaving and looking very queasy again.

I then received a message from Tom, who was also in the town. His wagon had been hit by small-arms fire and I decided to pull Howson out. The relief in his eyes was obvious and I began to feel sorry for him. He liked to talk a mean fight, like many Jocks do. However, deep down, he was a sensitive man who was way out of his depth in the middle of a war. We escorted them back to Dolac and resumed our patrol.

Things started to hot-up and the locals tired of killing each other and started trying to kill us. Our task was to drive around the town, showing a presence. We were doing that, all right, and providing them with target practice into the bargain.

The first rounds cracked over our heads, well in the 'fuck me' zone. I heard one splat off the wagon but no amount of looking around could locate any gunmen. They were popping up, firing, and then laying low. We couldn't traverse the gun too much due to obstructions, such as lamp posts. I had both Tookey and Phil closed down and was crouched in the turret peering between the narrow gap between the two sight hoods. The calls were coming in that all of Tom's platoon, and 0C, had received hits. This was stupid and I called the ops room and asked to return. There was a long pause, and David came on: 'Are you sure you cannot stay in the area? Your presence is valuable.'

'We can stay here all day but you'll have six Warriors that look like colanders and we're about as much use as Rip van Winkle's bedside light!'

'Roger, point taken, return to base!'

We drove back to camp and examined the damage. We'd been hit on the left of the two back doors. The round, probably from an AK, had gouged a hole, about two centimetres deep, out of the armour. Our other hit was on the left-rear Chobham deflector plate. 0C sported similar hits and one of the Nine Platoon vehicles had four strikes on the rear door. The gunmen's tactic was to wait until we passed and then fire at the exposed rear of the Warriors. We were never in any great danger but it was just a pointless exercise in showing the flag to a bunch of twats who weren't interested in it.

I was summoned to the CO's office. He'd received a complaint about the telegraph pole, and I was in for another bollocking. There was no use trying to explain that it was, actually, an accident, as I had, of course, deliberately trashed the bunker. I decided to take it on the chin and say nothing. Roy had also been invited for an interview without coffee and had the misfortune to go in first.

The boss started on him the moment he entered:

'Did you take blankets and food to the crowd outside the gate last night?'

'Yes, sir.'

'You idiot! Why did you do that?'

'Because there were women and children, and it was cold.'

'You stupid sod! I ordered you not to!'

'Yes, sir, but they needed help!'

'You idiot. We'll never get rid of the people. Where did you get the blankets from?'

'All my soldiers volunteered to give one from their bed.'

'I can't believe it! How dare you disobey a direct order!'

'Sorry, sir.'

'Now you listen here. Those people came here of their own free will. It's none of our business that they're here. If we feed them they'll never go away and we'll be like the French in Kladanj.'

So it went on. Next door, in Tom Wagstaff's office, I didn't need to earwig, as the walls were paper-thin. Christ, it was my turn next!

'Right, now get out of my sight!'

Roy emerged, with a smirk on his face. He knew what he'd done was wrong, according to the rules. However, he probably felt he was morally right. I hoped I'd have done the same, given the circumstances, and Roy went up in my estimation, ten fold.

Feeling sick with trepidation, I knocked on the door.

'What do you want?'

'You asked to see me, sir.'

'Oh! Well I can't remember what it was for. Goodbye!'

That was a close shave and I beat it down to the mess to buy Roy a beer.

The Muslims were still here and I walked over to take a look. There were ninety-five of them, all crowded around the back gate. The first thing to hit me was the smell. They'd already been there for nearly twenty-four hours and the stench of human excrement hung in the still air. This wasn't the most powerful smell, however. The smell of fear was all around them. I recognized it immediately as I'd smelled it on myself when confronted with the mujahideen. It was a rancid, sickly, sweaty smell. When you're shit-scared, you can't help it. Your glands open and no amount of deodorant can hide it. The odour hung about them like a poisonous cloud. They were terrified and we were doing nothing to help.

I poked my head into the sangar, where two of Roy's soldiers stood, and asked how they were:

'This stinks, sir!'

'I know boys, they're a bit smelly aren't they?'

'No, not that, sir, the fact we're just letting them stand there, without helping.'

I nodded, non-committally, and he went on:

'It's arse this, sir. We're supposed to be the UN and protecting them from this sort of shit! Our OC nearly got sacked because we gave them blankets and food. That's what stinks, sir!'

I couldn't have agreed more and I assured them everything would be done to help. I hoped this was the case.

Outside the sangar, I surveyed the Muslims. Many were dressed in the thin summer clothes they'd worn on the buses. Harassed-looking mothers tried to keep tabs on bored and hungry children while others held babies to their breasts. Many of the old just sat in the dirt with the vacant stares of those who'd given up hope.

Dominic Hancock was talking to them, watched over by a film crew. He was trying to explain, probably for the tenth time, that the UN was not allowed to help because they weren't refugees.

'But we are in danger!' they cried.

'No you are not! We will look after you!'

The film crew moved in and the reporter tried to interview Dominic.

'Why is the British Battalion refusing to help these people?'

'Because they are not refugees and the UN High Commission for Refugees has no remit to assist them.'

'But surely, this is a humanitarian problem and you are morally bound to look after them.'

'There's no reason why these people cannot move to the nearest Muslim village if they so wish. Grbavica is only five hundred metres away.'

'The people believe they'll be shot by snipers if they walk along the road past camp. Why don't you let them walk through your base?'

'Because we cannot allow civilians into our camp.'

'Is it not because you are too scared of breaking the rules?'

'I don't want to answer that.'

'The people back home have a right to know what their soldiers are doing, or rather not, in this case.'

'No comment!'

With that, Dominic committed the cardinal sin, and thrust his hand over the camera lens. He was exasperated and was the unwilling front-man for a piece of inexcusable UN indecision. In his frustration he behaved like a criminal exposed by the 'Cook Report'. This film was broadcast and showed the military in an appalling light, as a bunch of people who could only follow rules, even when they were morally indefensible. The hand-over-the-lens epitomized our shame. I stormed off to find Richard. He listened patiently, as he always did, while I got it off my chest.

'Does the CO not know the damage this is doing to our reputation?'

'He does but he can't afford to let them in or we'll be left with a problem like the French have. He can't just disobey the UNHCR, you know.'

'We don't have to let them in. Why don't we just transport them to Zenica?'

'Roy's already suggested that. It's not that easy.'

'Oh come on! We could organize that in ten minutes.'

'But we'd be accused of taking sides.'

'So bloody what. We're not here to be popular. We're here to help people.'

'That's not strictly true. We can only help if the UNHCR ask us to.'

'I don't follow.'

'It's Friday evening and they've packed up for the weekend!'

'I don't believe it! No wonder the UN's a laughing stock!'

The following morning the Muslims were still there and the Colonel was interviewed and asked to explain his position. He talked about how the people were here through their own stupidity and how they'd been warned not to come to Central Bosnia. We couldn't help them and the UNHCR was working to find a solution.

The statements came across as bland, colourless and, above all 'jobsworth' and he was slated in many of the papers. One went as far as to call him heartless. This was unfair as there is no doubt that he must have agonized over the fate of these people. However, he wasn't about to go against the wishes of the UNHCR and he certainly wasn't going to allow his feelings to dictate his actions. He was a totally different follow-up to Bob Stewart who probably would've considered driving the trucks to Zenica himself!

To those of us who were out on the ground all the time, and couldn't see, or who didn't care for, the bigger picture, the whole episode reeked. We were in danger of forgetting our responsibilities as Christians and, as often happens, the soldiers were the ones who displayed true compassion. The poor old Colonel was stuck between a rock and a hard place, either disobey orders or be slated by the media.

Eventually, the UNHCR sparked and asked us to transport the Muslims to Zenica. This was accomplished on the Saturday morning with a minimum of fuss. By then the damage was done and, as one reporter put it, it was:

'Too little, too late.'

There's no doubt in my mind, that the bus saga was a public relations disaster for the UN, in general, and the battalion in particular. I was all for moving the Muslims and taking the flak later. From the MOD point of view, it was just as well I was only a lowly company commander!

At last, after a hectic week, it was back to guard again. Zippy and I discussed the R & R plot.

Rest and Recuperation was, basically, during-tour leave. We were all entitled to two week's worth. We discussed one of the young lads, Private Stow. He'd only recently joined us and wanted to get married on this first period. I tried to dissuade him as he was facing five months of immediate separation. He was adamant that was what he wanted and went ahead anyway. I decided to take the last period, to be home for my birthday.

All was going quietly when I was called to the back gate. The guard told me there was another group of six Muslims who'd replaced the ninety-five. Maybe the CO was right and they would all be at it now. I went to find an interpreter.

The only one available was the 'new girl' Sonja.

There'd been a crisis in the interpreter organization. Three of the girls, Andreana, Leila and Svetlana had been friendly with a few of the Cheshires officers. They'd obtained permission to leave Bosnia to attend the officers' mess ball in Fallingbostel. As they were all single girls, with few ties, they chose not to return. Funny old thing that! Of course, none of the Cheshires married them, and the last I heard was that they were all living in London. For them it was a way out of a hell-hole, for thousands of others there was no such chance. Sonja was one of these. Her husband brought home ten marks a month for being in the BiH militia. Nowhere near enough to feed four mouths. Mike Stanley's replacement, Ken Pickles, a Royal Army Education Corps major, was looking for new interpreters. Roy suggested that Sonja apply and she was taken on for a trial period. Her English was barely up to it so she spent most of the days learning the language and carrying out minor tasks.

The Muslims were standing in the same cesspit that the ninety-five had just left. They said they'd been threatened by the HVO and told that unless they fled, they'd be killed that night. There were two middle-aged men, a youth of about eighteen, his mother and an old couple. All were hysterical and refused to go back to their homes near Nova Bila. I was giving them the party-line about how the UN couldn't help them and how they should return to their homes, when the '40 Minutes' crew pitched-up. This was the last thing I needed. The producer, Michael something-or-other, had persuaded Howson that he really ought to go outside the mess. The artist was flatly refusing to leave camp so Michael decided to shoot some of his programme in the locality. A crowd of refugees on the doorstep was a golden opportunity.

I thought that familiar question: 'Why me?'

So here I was, with six hysterical Muslims begging to be taken to Zenica, a mandate that wouldn't allow this, and a bloody film crew watching my every move. I gave them the party-line and immediately realized I was committing all the sins Roy and I had railed against the day before. Here I was, going out on national television and about to win a 'That's Life' jobsworth award. Blow the mandate. These people needed help.

I asked them, again, if they could return home and they said they'd never do so again. I said I wouldn't take them to Zenica or let them into camp. However, I would walk with them down the road past camp to the mess where they could melt away into Grbavica. They pondered this and refused as they believed they'd be shot by the Croats occupying the houses along the road. I could see there may be some truth in this. There seemed no solution until Sonja drew me aside and suggested:

'Why don't you use a Warrior like you did to help the women collect the flour?'

This was it! I briefed the six:

'At two o'clock I will be leaving for a patrol. My Warrior will drive slowly from the back gate to the front gate along the main road. You may wish to walk alongside this vehicle, protected from the Croats. If they fire on you I will consider that they have fired on me, and we will kill them!'

They looked far from convinced.

'In England, we have a saying which is "take it or leave it!" The choice is yours.'

The old man was the first to speak up.

'We do not have a choice do we?'

'You could return to your homes!'

'We will be there at two o'clock!'

As we walked back across the tank park, Sonja said:

'Major Vaughan. I don't think this is a good idea now. I wish I had not suggested it. What if one of the Muslims is killed by the HVO?'

'We have many other sayings in England. The CO will "have my guts for garters"!'

This was a big risk. The boss was away at a meeting and I was in charge of the camp area; the decision was down to me. It should be relatively simple to help these people and, with a bit of luck, no one would be any the wiser. By the time the '40 Minutes' programme came out, this would be ancient history. I knew I should ignore them but I had this self-destruct button that said: 'They need help so isn't that why we're here?' If this went wrong I envisaged yet another talking-to.

In the event the operation went without a hitch. We deployed at two o'clock with a Warrior at each gate and 0B in the middle. The Muslims looked absolutely terrified and had to be cajoled into standing next to 0B. We then drove slowly down the road towards the front gate. The other two Warriors had their guns trained on the HVO houses but the Croats showed little interest in our activities. Those few soldiers that were visible looked on with a detached air of amusement. At one stage, Tookey had a bit of a rush of blood to the head and increased speed a little too sharply. In seconds we'd left the six a couple of hundred metres behind. The Warrior was like a magnet to them and I have never seen a couple of pensioners move so quickly. The old dear certainly ran the race of her life that day!

By ten minutes after two, the people were standing, with their fellow Muslims, around Fered's house. I walked 0B back to the tank park and went to check on the six. They were already being given coffee and would soon be on their way to Zenica. Their gratitude made it all worthwhile. Not quite so welcome was the limpet-man from earlier in the week who threw himself on me again.

It was a funny little operation. The situation was bizarre where six people had to be escorted a few hundred metres past our own camp. At the end of the day, they weren't harmed and moved to an area they considered safe. I had no qualms about my actions. It could be argued that I hadn't broken the mandate, merely stretched it. The Muslims hadn't entered camp and neither had we carried them. Another, albeit very minor, public relations blunder was averted.

The next day was to be Howson's last in Vitez. Michael came to see me in the mess and asked if I'd help him persuade Howson to deploy again.

'I don't give a toss about his bloody paintings. It's my programme I'm worried about!'

After two hours of persuasion, he finally agreed to come with us to Kljaci. I promised him there would be no shooting and no dead bodies, only the good side of the Bosnian people.

0B was in the garage having the new deflector plate fitted so we deployed in 0C with a Scimitar in tow. We were stopped at the village and I dismounted.

'You may not enter, we only let Circle 0B in!'

To emphasize the point he showed me the drawing of our callsign. I took my helmet off and he immediately recognized me.

'Ah! Major Vaughan. Why don't you come in Zero Bravo?'

'Bloody British workmanship, it's broken down!'

It wasn't true but it got a cheap laugh.

The village had been shelled with the mosque as the main target. Also, several small-calibre cannon rounds had pierced the minaret. I asked some local boys to collect fragments of shrapnel and they carried several chunks to Mister Asim's. The shells were home-made, probably in a small workshop. Most of the fragments were large, indicating a poor-quality explosive. The Croats were feeling the pinch as much as the Muslims and were having to resort to man-ufacturing their own munitions.

We had coffee and Hajiya appeared and was delighted to have a fresh audience to tell about his time in Switzerland. We stayed for two hours and Howson made numerous sketches.

I had an uneasy feeling that our recent visits may have prompted the shelling so I decided to visit more Croat villages in the next few days. If I could build the same level of trust with them, we may go a long way to improving their opinion of the UN. What we needed was a spectacular incident, such as the buses, where we could help a large number of Croats. This happened sooner rather than later.

Howson left us the next day. Back home, he was interviewed by a newspaper and wasn't exactly complementary about the Army. The gist of the article was how we were all unfeeling and insensitive, describing death in a matter-of-fact way. The whole War was a big joke to us.

This absolutely incensed the company, some of whom wanted to go up to Scotland on their R & R and give him a good stuffing! We'd gone out of our way to look after him and help him and, frankly, having him about was a pain in the arse. Yes, we did make light of the death and suffering but that is the natural defence mechanism of the soldier. To imply we didn't care was a gross insult and one that I took very personally. He didn't understand the mentality of the soldier and, seeing as he spent well over half his time in the mess, was never likely to. A few weeks later, the *Sunday Times* magazine featured his first paintings. Few bore much likeness to anything we'd encountered.

A few months after the tour, Patrick Bishop, a *Daily Telegraph* reporter, penned a scathing article about the grotesque nature of the paintings. To illustrate his point he wrote:

'In his sketchbook he attempts a likeness of a British Army Major, Vaughan Kent-Payne. I remember him as a cheerful, sun-tanned figure whose blond moustache made him look as if he had stepped out of "The Four Feathers". Howson gives him mad, staring eyes and a demented air.'

The subbies had a giggle at this and commented that the artist wasn't so bad after all!

Months later, Dawn and I attended the opening of the exhibition in the Imperial War Museum. We took Stephen Lees along with us. When he spied the paintings, he exclaimed:

'They're like Lowry ... on acid!'

Chapter 9
The Worm Turns

The BiH offensive commenced on 8 June. Spearheaded by mujahideen, the attacks took place along the Bila Valley. Maline, Brajkovici and Grahovcici all fell in the initial stages. The BiH kept a corridor down the valley free from attack, and the Croats fled in their thousands towards Nova Bila. Soon, reports of atrocities started to filter in from Guca Gora and A Company deployed.

Jason Medley was the first officer on the ground and, with great presence of mind, herded all the Croats into the monastery. He then disarmed all those HVO who turned up. The mujahideen were a little miffed and fired on Medley's Warrior, hitting it several times. Eventually Roy deployed and took charge of the situation. The Croats were kept in the church while the soldiers formed a perimeter and returned fire when they were sniped at.

A relief-column of trucks was organized but was turned back by the BiH, who now controlled the Dolac checkpoint. Roy was told to stay at Guca Gora for the night while efforts were made to halt the fighting.

Meanwhile, back in camp, my company sat around itching for the chance to deploy and have a slice of the action. This feeling, that we were missing out, reached down to the boys in the sangars who were not going to take any nonsense. The first time the Croats shot into camp, Private Barker returned fire and all was suddenly quiet. Next morning, there was still an impasse at Guca Gora. The BiH were refusing to let the UN in, or the Croats out, saying that several criminals were hiding in the church. I was tasked with leading the relief column and waited at the Novi Travnik T-junction with eight lorries waiting for the call-forward from the CO.

More fighting flared up and more A Company vehicles were hit. As we sat at the junction it became clear that several hundred rounds of Chain Gun had been returned. This was no place to take lorries so I drove to camp and started to assemble an armoured force.

Using the same procedures as we'd done on the night of the bus incident, we rustled up sixteen AFVs in twenty minutes. I deployed, and was told, over the radio, that the CO was at the scene.

Our convoy consisted of nine Warriors, a Spartan, 432 ambulance and five 432s. At the rear, was a four-ton truck to carry any baggage. We reached Dolac and the BiH had blocked the road with four TMRP-6s, probably the ones left by the fleeing HVO. They refused to let us pass saying there was heavy fighting. This was the normal bullshit and I was having none of it. Obviously, with so many vehicles we were going to evacuate Guca Gora. I told them we were going to pass and they could let us through or die!

'You cannot run over the mines and it is you who will die if you try!'

They were so bloody cocky now they were on the up. However, I'd devised a highly risky tactic that might just get us through without hours of negotiation.

I drew the nearest three Warriors up and they fanned out as best they could given the steep drop to the left and hill to the right. We then drove up to the mines and I carefully conned Tookey until we were parallel to the line of four, about ten centimetres away from our right track. The BiH had retreated to hide behind some logs and one had produced an RPG. They knew there were three Warriors covering them and relied on the mines to stop us. They raised themselves up a little, curiosity overcoming their fear of our guns. I closed Tookey down and then ordered:

'Very slowly. Neutral turn right!'

There was a slight hesitation and Tookey said;

'You're joking, sir!'

'Just do it. Trust me!'

The engine revved, a cloud of black smoke billowed out, and we slowly began to turn on our axis. The right track nudged the nearest mine and moved it a few centimetres. We halted for a second while I took a few deep breaths. In order to stop us, the moment we started to ride up one of the mines, I had to lean right over the side, to see straight down. You didn't have to be a physics professor to realize that if we set one off, the blast was going to go straight up the side of the Warrior. In milliseconds, I would be wearing the contents of the mine. This was dangerous stuff but I couldn't think of another quick way to shift them. Tookey would be OK as he had an engine to protect him and the others were fairly secure. If this went wrong there'd be nothing left of me to bollock!

We started to turn again, picked up the second mine, and it, too, started to slide to the right. The third mine was a little trickier and the track immediately started to ride up over the casing. Trying not to sound panicky, I ordered:

'Hold it there! Neutral back to the left a fraction. Well done! Now select forward and drive on a tad.'

Tookey skilfully executed the tiny adjustment and we tried again. This time we caught the mine on one of the sprocket tooth-slots and it started to slide, together with the other two. The final mine was a doddle and obediently started to scrape over the tarmac.

We now had all four and I had to resist the temptation to rush. Ever so slowly we shunted the four to the right until they met in a cluster. There was now room for us and we pulled back, smartly turned and roared through. The clearance took little more than two minutes and the BiH were hugely hacked off. One of them came running out as if to pick a mine up and throw it under the track. He soon thought otherwise as three turrets were, simultaneously, trained on him.

We were through and off, in a snaking column, towards Guca Gora! The next obstruction was a cream Lada abandoned in the centre of the narrow road. There was no way round so I decided to nudge it out of the way, down the steep slope to the right. We slowly approached the car and touched it. Instead of moving the vehicle, we started to mount up over the bonnet. I thought for a second of driving straight over but then remembered that the four-tonner couldn't do the same. Dobby and I dismounted to push it out of the way. I opened a front door to free the handbrake and noticed what looked like a bundle of rags on the back seat. I did a double-take, and, with horror, saw it was a little girl. She was dressed in a red-and-white gingham dress. Her feet were bare and her eyes stared lifelessly at me. Mercifully, there was no sign of how she'd died. She must've been about nine and I fought back the huge lump gathering in my throat. Together, Dobby and I carefully pushed the car to the right where the fence, thankfully, stopped it from plunging down the hill. We passed on and I hoped her parents could return and give this innocent little victim a decent burial.

I radioed ahead and asked for the road to be cleared of UN vehicles and we finally reached the monastery in mid-afternoon.

We ground past the twin towers and into the tiny square where I'd met Merdin a few days before. 'Sniffer' Clarke was on hand to do what sergeant majors are especially good at, organizing vehicles. Within ten minutes of shunting and turning, we were all facing the other way and I led the convoy back to the ancient church.

The colonel was there to meet us and warmly shook my hand.

'Great to see you!' he enthused.

Someone shouted:

'The cavalry's here!'

Roy was also there and took me for a quick guided tour of the place, while Zippy organized the evacuation. The church was huge, with great high beams and ancient wooden galleries. Unfortunately, the whole scene of thousand-year-old religious splendour was ruined by the fresco. Above the altar was a massive, gaudy mural about ten metres high by twenty wide. It depicted scenes from the Bible but was so bright it was tacky. It looked like it was painted by a bunch of hippies, with primary school painting materials. Quite why the abbot of the day had allowed his magnificent church to be modernized in this way was beyond me.

The Croats huddled in groups on the rows of pews, and nuns and monks moved among them giving them words of comfort. Roy showed me the library, which was renowned throughout the Balkans, and the courtyard. It was from here that his OC had returned fire on a mujahideen heavy machine gun.

He was absolutely shattered but there was something else he wanted to tell me. Eventually, he recounted how, in the small hours of the night, one of the statues appeared to move. It was probably tiredness and the flickering of the many candles playing tricks on his eyes. Nevertheless, there was no doubt that offering sanctuary to the people and then protecting them in such an ancient and holy place must have been a profound religious experience.

At the steps Zippy had attempted to count the Croats.

'There's over a hundred and fifty but it's impossible to count them as the buggers won't stay still!'

The BBC had appeared from somewhere and Justin Webb, the reporter, started to give a short piece for the cameras while we started loading up 0B.

We had to be absolutely brutal with the people. They were terrified and the sickly smell of fear hung about them. Had we let them, there would've been a rush for the vehicles and the only losers in the stampede would be the old and weak. I deployed that old cliché straight from 'A Night to Remember'.

'Women and children first!'

We sorted them out by size, not family. I was aware I had to jam them in as there would be, on average, a dozen per wagon. Thus, we split families and I know this caused some hardship and temporary anguish. Nevertheless, I had no doubt that if I was allowed to organize the evacuation my way, we would deliver all the Croats safely to Nova Bila.

We started to fill 0B.

'Right Sar'nt Major, first four!'

Two very fat old ladies were led forward by Dobby. They must've weighed seventeen stones each. One of them had a wispy moustache and looked like Gareth Chilcott in drag. The women puffed and wheezed as they were helped into the rear of the 0B and totally filled three seats.

'Woman and child next! Preferably a thin woman!'

A frightened young woman in her twenties was led forward, leading a boy of about seven. The child's eyes widened when he realized he was actually going to ride in the Warrior and his plight was forgotten. The woman carried an infant of a year, or so. Good, that was another one. As we helped them in there was a slight commotion and a man wearing combat trousers tried to elbow past. Dobby stood in the way and the man started shouting hysterically.

'That's my family, I will not leave them, I demand to go!'

I silenced him:

'Do Croat men always save themselves before women and children? I give you my word that you will be reunited at Nova Bila!'

My words stung his Latin ego and he nodded and rejoined the crowd. I was determined that, if we ran out of room, the vulnerable four-tonner would only contain young men.

0B was packed and Corporal Knight gave me a 'where the hell am I going to sit' look.

'Room for one more child, no older than ten!'

The crowd was starting to respond and a mother led her daughter forward. The pressing throng parted and a woman brought the child to the back, hugged her and then left her, without a backward glance. Many in the crowd offered words of sympathy and praise for her selfless action.

The Warrior was stuffed and Knight clambered in and squeezed himself onto half a seat.

'Drive up for three hundred metres, Phil, then stop and keep your eyes peeled. Corporal Knight out the back to guard the rear. Don't let the civvies wander about.'

0B roared off and we started on the next one. I selected the people and counted as each passed me; Dobby acted like a Tokyo train guard and packed them in. I kept a running tally in my notebook. We'd filled five vehicles when the colonel came over.

'Make sure that you count them in.'

I was about to say: 'Bloody Hell! That's a good idea. I never thought of that!'

Nevertheless, I bit my tongue and carried on. He then displayed the classic officer quality of wanting to get involved and started to give directions, which soon started to upset the plan.

'For God's sake! With great respect, sir, we're in danger of having too many chiefs. If you want to take over, I'll go and find something else to do!'

The colonel looked stunned for a moment and Zippy shot me an 'Oh no not again!' look.

'Yes, you're quite right, of course. I'll leave you to get on with it.'

Over the next hour, we continued to pack them in and soon the supply of women and children dwindled and we started on the old men. Our record was sixteen people in the rear of an anti-tank section 432. Finally, the abbot, who insisted on being the last, climbed into Tom's Warrior at the rear. Their cases were piled onto the truck with as many religious artefacts as we could pack in. We couldn't even make a dent on the books but we loaded several statues and the great, leather-bound, Bible. Altogether, there were 181 people evacuated that day.

Carson was the last one out and symbolically locked the huge wooden door. I wondered if the BiH would leave the place alone or whether they'd destroy it in revenge for the mosque in Ahmici.

The return trip was conducted without a hitch. At Dolac, we halted next to the mines again and I jumped out and asked if they would move them or me. They grinned and, obligingly, shunted them away. We finally reached the refugee centre in Nova Bila at about eight in the evening. The Croat authorities were on hand to receive the people who, gradually, disappeared inside the building. We hung on to the religious items as the abbot asked Carson to take them to the main church in Vitez.

As I stood by 0B, I was approached by three HVO soldiers.

'Why did you allow this to happen? Why didn't you protect our people?'

We'd just saved the lives of nearly two hundred people and these gits wanted more. I wasn't having it and said the first retort that came to me:

'If your army was any good, you could've protected them yourselves!'

This incident came at an ideal time for the battalion. The positive reports on television and in the papers went a long way to undoing the damage caused by inaction over the bus people. Above all, however, it showed the Croats that we were impartial. For the rest of the tour, whenever I received a hard time from Croats about our apparent bias, I always trotted out the line:

'But what about Guca Gora?'

The Three Corps offensive was brilliantly executed and took the HVO completely by surprise. Most of the Bila Valley was now in BiH hands. The Croats still controlled the southern part, that nearest the camp, and a section of the western side. Here, there was heavy fighting around the villages of Pokrajcici and Cifluk, the opposite side from Kljaci. The HVO had been virtually driven out of Travnik, and Dolac was in BiH hands. Most important, however, was the fact that the BiH, by capturing Guca Gora and Brajkovici, had linked their strongholds of Travnik and Zenica. This was a major strategic gain.

The Croats in our area had been squeezed into two narrow corridors. One ran roughly west to east along the Lasva Valley with Vitez as its main stronghold. The other was roughly north to south along the Kiseljak Valley with that town and Busovaca the main concentrations. To further complicate matters, Vitez still had a substantial Muslim enclave and Novi Travnik was divided, with the front line bisecting the town. It was into this battleground that the Muslims decided to bring the convoy of joy.

The convoy, arranged by the Mayor of Tuzla, consisted of several hundred lorries carrying food and fuel to his town. This was meant to supplement the UN aid reaching Northern Bosnia. The only problem was that the convoy had to pass through the Croat enclave around Vitez. The UNHCR adopted the same policy as with the buses. They refused to assist the convoy, saying it was not sanctioned and the safety of the drivers could not be guaranteed. Again, the battalion was in an impossible position. Had we assisted, we would be blatantly siding with the Muslims. If the Croats started to murder the drivers, what would we do then?

This, of course, is exactly what happened. The convoy was stopped and the first eight drivers dragged out of their cabs and beaten to death. A Company deployed but was not, initially, allowed to intervene. At one point, Corporal Bulmer watched a driver being stabbed with a pitchfork after he was set upon by a crowd of Croat women. He couldn't fire as there were several children there.

We were not required to deploy and spent a maddeningly frustrating day in camp. The firing kicked off after last light with the BiH in Grbavica deliberately firing into the camp, perhaps in retaliation for our inactivity over the convoy. The front gate Warrior was targeted from the house with the BiH flag. Using the night-sight, the lance-corporal in command returned fifty-seven rounds of Chain Gun. The firing stopped and, ten minutes later, two men transported a lifeless form out of the house in a wheelbarrow.

Finally, the UNHCR acted and the remnants of the convoy were split into packets and escorted through our TAOR to Zenica. The Croats were livid and accused us of siding with the BiH. The BiH accused us of not acting quickly enough to save the drivers and their cargoes. We were, again, in a no-win situation.

On the day before the next ops week, 12 June, I drove out to have a look at how the area had changed. A segment of the convoy drove past escorted by a couple of Warriors from A Company and then the CO pitched up. He halted next to 0B and hopped across. 'Oh crikey! What've I done now?'

He was happy, animated and bubbling over; I'd never seen him this enthusiastic over anything. He'd received a telephone call earlier from the Prime Minister congratulating him over the handling of the convoy affair. I was sure I would've thought it was a wind-up if someone had handed me the phone and said: 'There's John Major on the line for you!'

Our first task on operations was to investigate reports of atrocities in the village of Maline. The place was close to Guca Gora and several HVO prisoners were reported to have been tortured, and then murdered, by the mujahideen. We had several passengers with our patrol.

Randy Rhodes was coming along as it was his job to verify atrocities on behalf of the UN. Mark Bower was also with us to do the same for the military. We also had the media with us. Both sides had threatened the press, the HVO because they saw the media as biased against them. The BiH believed that film of their dispositions would be passed to the HVO to enable them to plan their attacks. Both sides were pathologically suspicious of the media and, for a while, it became impossible for press vehicles to operate freely. A system had to be found that allowed the press some freedom of movement for the time they were at the greatest risk.

James Myles therefore organized press 'mini-pools' to travel with our patrols. A pool might consist of a BBC reporter, an ITN cameraman and *Times* journalist. All parties had to agree to pool their material, to be used later by them all. This was bitterly opposed as each organization wanted the chance for its own scoops. They also distrusted us and believed this was the early stage of manipulating the media. On the plus side, they had access to three or four times as many potential stories. At least they were fairly safe as they travelled around the country. Unfortunately, for us, this meant we had the press riding in the back of our vehicles. The news from Bosnia therefore became centred on the activities of the battalion in general, and me in particular.

Each evening, James would show the patrol programme to the assembled press and they'd choose the one they wished to accompany. They soon wised up to the fact that little was likely to happen on a tunnel patrol. However, there was a fair chance of some action if they accompanied 'Vitez Vaughan'. There followed a period of intense media coverage. Being a media star soon became a pain in the backside as I started to receive flak over my frequent appearances. I didn't need more trouble from the boss and tried to avoid saying anything too controversial. Unfortunately, I didn't always succeed and on other times the reporters just made up the facts anyway. The mini-pool only lasted a couple of weeks. The soldiers loved it and some joked that Dobby had more time on the air than Kate Adie. For me, it was a period where every move I made was under the intrusive gaze of the world's press.

I returned to Guca Gora in strength. With 0B and 0C were Tom Crowfoot with two more Warriors, and two of the Scimitars. We halted outside the monastery and the situation hotted up immediately.

The mujahideen were using the place as their HQ and several came running out. Within a couple of minutes around thirty of them had taken up position around us. There were two heavy machine guns trained on us and several anti-tank weapons. Many wore Arab headdress and there were also a couple of hennaed beards on show. I divided the arcs and issued fire control orders over the radio. If they opened fire, I was relying on a withering blast from all our weapons to sweep most of them away. We were in a poor position as there was a steep drop on the right and a high bank leading up to the church on the left. This meant that many of the muja were actually above us and looking down onto the turret. This would be the ideal killing shot.

We had to move forward to re-deploy quickly.

I dismounted and walked forward to the square where a small, bearded man came to meet me. He was olive-skinned and wore a grey shemague around his head. From the look of him, I guessed he was a North African. He refused to shake my hand and spoke in halting English.

'You must send your interpreter away. I will not talk with a woman present.'

We stood alone, and I asked to be allowed to go to Maline.

'You cannot go on because it is too dangerous.'

'Who is the danger from, the Croats or you?'

'Both!'

'I would like to talk to your leader.'

'That will take time.'

'Please fetch him and I will move my vehicles to a better position.'

'Why do you have to do that?'

'Because, as a professional soldier, I cannot allow my men to be in such a bad position.'

'You are in no danger.'

'What about all the anti-tank weapons?'

'They are there to protect you from the Croats!'

Suddenly, a film cameraman and two reporters appeared. The reporters were Patrick Bishop from the *Daily Telegraph* and a free-lance, Anthony Lloyd, an ex-Royal Green Jackets officer. The muja went spare and started screaming at them, so I used the excuse to return to 0B and herd the three back inside. Bloody press, their thirst for a story would get us all killed.

Sergeant Barratt was in the turret and I climbed up to talk to him. This brought me level with a fellow in red-and-white Arab head-dress. I engaged him in cheery conversation:

'Good morning!'

'Fuck off!' he replied in a broad Bradford accent.

'How nice to meet a brother Yorkshireman!'

'Fuck off! I'm not your brother. Fucking UNPROFOR, fuck off home!'

'What an extensive vocabulary you have! Why don't you go home too?'

'I'll fucking kill you!' The Brit cocked his AK and pointed it at me.

'Brave, aren't you, especially when you shoot people in the back?'

I turned away from him and, with the familiar trembling legs starting again, briefed Barratt. I couldn't go on facing these people down. Sooner or later, I was going to be shot.

I turned round and the man's eyes blazed with hatred. They bored into me as I clambered off the Warrior.

OC also had a crowd of mujahideen looking down on it. Jason had his pistol cocked and resting in his lap. He'd also loaded six rounds of HE. I didn't blame him.

As I briefed him, one of the mujahideen fired his rifle. It was an accidental discharge and the idiot nearly shot himself in the foot. Six turrets immediately trained to the left and we were seconds away from opening fire. The Bradford man was screaming:

'Don't fire! It was an accident! Cool it!'

I told Jason to tell our callsigns to hold their fire. The situation markedly calmed down thanks to this opportune act of stupidity. Jason moved the vehicles into better positions and I was confident we could extricate quickly, if we had to. I returned to the square. The mujahideen leader had arrived and I recognized him as the man from Fazlici. I deliberately offered him my hand and he refused, again saying he wouldn't touch an infidel. This amused me as he clearly didn't recognize me and I could only think that it was because my moustache was bigger.

He, at first, refused to let us go to Maline. Then, I called up Randy and Mark to explain that we had to check the report of atroc-ities. Of course, it would be better for them if we looked. They refused to let any of the armour pass and we'd reached a stalemate. I had an idea.

'So the objection is to my vehicles and not the fact that you won't let us near Maline?'

'Of course, that is correct.'

'Good, then provide a car and the three of us will come with you. The only weapons will be our pistols.'

Randy gulped and looked distinctly queasy. Mark whispered: 'I hope you know what you're doing!'

The muja reverted to Arabic and Randy reverted to sensible mode.

'This is stupid. They'll kill us!'

'Maybe, but do you want to do your job or not? Maybe you'd better leave it to the military!'

That was below the belt and stung Randy, who'd only just retired from the US Navy.

The leader agreed and, minutes later, a battered white Toyota pickup truck arrived. I walked back to brief Jason:

'Thirty minutes, if we aren't back, head for Maline!'

I had a queasy feeling and I gave him my signet ring for safe-keeping. Randy and I sat in the back, with the North African in the middle and Mark in the cargo compartment with another Arab. The truck set off, backwards and straight into a telegraph pole. The leader slapped his driver around the head and I began to realize just why we'd won the Gulf War so easily.

We careered down the narrow lanes, clashing the gears as we went. At one stage the two in front said something and there was an exchange of cruel laughter. I imagined our deaths were being discussed.

We passed several groups of civilians pushing barrows full of looted goods.

'*Allah Akhbar!*' the leader shouted, shaking his fist out of the window, and the cry was returned as we passed. This showed the power of the mujahideen as such gestures were totally alien to the vast majority of Bosnian Muslims.

We reached Maline and had twenty minutes to poke around. There'd been plenty of time to remove any evidence and, indeed, the only dead were three pigs and a dog. Mark had been given a crudely-drawn sketch supposedly showing the site of the massacre. It bore no relation to the ground and was as much use as a chocolate fireguard. The Arabs followed us everywhere and there was the same, oppressive air of potential violence we'd sensed in the jeep. There was no way we were going to find anything. The trouble was that to find evidence we'd have to saturate the area with troops. We could well have to fight to achieve this and, without the full co-operation of the warring factions, we were largely ineffective.

The mujahideen leader dropped us off back at the square and the three of us let out a collective sigh of relief.

Back at the wagons Randy started on me.

'That was one helluva risk you took back there!'

I didn't need his moaning and I rounded on him:

'You ungrateful bastard! It was you who asked us to get you into Maline and you're now saying that it wasn't worth the risk. Just driving out of camp is a bloody risk. Listen, mate, if the task wasn't worth doing then you shouldn't have asked us in the first place. In C Company we pride ourselves on the fact we always get the job done. If you didn't want to succeed, you should've approached another outfit. Don't come to me in future unless you're positive you want to complete your mission!' With that I turned and stalked off to organize the withdrawal.

To his credit, Randy came up and apologized:

'Hey! Sorry pal. I haven't been so uptight since we invaded Panama!'

The morning's activities received coverage in several of the daily papers. The most memorable was an article in the *Daily Telegraph* of the 16 June. Auberon Waugh wrote the following:

'Mysterious reports of a Muslim offensive in Central Bosnia include references to an Islamic force wearing green headbands with Arabic script. It is composed of foreigners and a few local Muslim fundamentalists.

Some have long hennaed beards and Afghan caps with a variety of uniforms, including baggy khaki trousers and strange waistcoats. When Major Vaughan Kent-Payne of the Prince of Wales's Own Yorkshire Regiment accosted such a group in the Croat village of Guca Gora, near Travnik, its leader told him to "cool down", speaking in an accent from the North of England.

I suspect they belong to the Liverpool Foreign Legion. I suppose we are right to send Major Kent-Payne to keep an eye on all this. The forcible partition and reallocation of territory has been going on as long as human history. The only sensible attitude is to thank our lucky stars that we are not involved, but anything which provides jobs for Liverpudlians cannot be entirely bad.'

We continued to patrol around the area and a local asked me to go to Bandol.

The place had been systematically trashed. Every house had been burned, most of them to the ground. There'd obviously been heavy fighting and spent cases littered the ground like the devil's confetti. The map showed a mosque but there was no sign of it. Eventually we tracked it down. The Croats had paid particular attention to the building and had razed it. Only a couple of small portions of coloured mosaic flooring indicated that the building had once been a place of worship.

We searched the village and Donlon and I heard a slight noise in a shed. I covered him as he gingerly opened the door. There was an ear-piercing screech, and he jumped back with a cry of terror. A starving moggy gave him a quick clawing before it ran to safety. I laughed, a little too loudly, at his obvious embarrassment.

Dobby's shout alerted us and we ran to where he'd discovered the body.

The cadaver lay on a concrete path behind one of the houses. A mass of black flies covered the head like a grotesque beard. They rose, as one, into an obscene cloud and I gagged as they brushed past my face. The fellow was a BiH soldier and had been dead for a few days. He still wore combat trousers and black boots. Decomposition had set in and his bare torso was a waxy grey colour. There were several large purple bruises and I didn't need to be a doctor to recognize these as the results of a good kicking. I didn't need medical training either to recognize the cigarette burns. There were around half a dozen deep burns, mostly around his throat.

A wire clothes-line was wrapped around his neck and it looked like he'd been held by this in an upright position while the thugs worked on him. Finally, his torturers had become bored, or careless, and stabbed him a couple of times before shooting him.

A cluster of white maggots wriggled around his lips and I decided that I'd probably not be attempting mouth-to-mouth resuscitation. As I leaned over to get a better look at his face, Donlon stood on his chest.

The mouth opened with a stinking sigh and a jet of maggots shot up towards my face. I screamed and jumped back brushing the writhing creatures from the legs of my trousers. Peals of laughter came from Donlon who thought this was the best revenge ever. I resolved never to cross the evil little Jock again!

In the moment before the maggot attack I had a good look at what was left of the face. I couldn't be sure but I thought he may have been the swarthy soldier who'd sent me away a couple of weeks before. The words 'We don't need any help from you' stuck in my mind.

Later, I found the nearest HVO position and asked them about the village. They were the normal leering low-life and blamed the Muslims for torching their own village.

I reported the village to Milinfo and the consensus was that we'd been lucky not to have another Ahmici. The village was less than five kilometres from camp yet we'd been unaware of the place being cleansed. I suspected this had been one of the final straws that prompted the BiH offensive. I filled out a load of forms for the War Crimes Commission but doubted if the Muslim's torturers would ever be brought to justice.

That evening, I went to the mobile surgical team to see Private Holland who was recovering from an accident down at the garage. His crew had been track bashing and someone had swung a sledge-hammer with a little too much gusto. He was awaiting evacuation to the UK. The company was awash with jokes along the lines of:

'When I'm ready, I'll nod my head and you hit it!'

The MST was a godsend. It was like MASH from the TV series, with all modern surgical facilities and skilled surgeons on hand. They were, thank goodness, under-utilized but we all knew that if we were injured we'd receive the best possible treatment.

That evening we held our first company barbecue. The last time we'd tried to hold it was the night of the bus attack. This time the gods were only a little kinder and we were deluged in rain. We retired to the remnants of the tented camp and carried on anyway.

I was chatting to a few of the boys, Corporal Field, Lance-Corporal Danby and Privates Battersby, Cox and Shevlin and asked them how we could improve the lot of the young soldiers. They told me that their main problem was boredom.

We initially deployed with a full complement of seven soldiers for the rear of each Warrior. However, we only patrolled with two in the back, so four or five were always left in camp. This meant that some of the younger soldiers only deployed twice on an operations week.

A couple of NCOs said they wanted more action.

'What about if I take a section vehicle with me when I patrol, instead of 0C?'

There was a murmur of approval but not a full-blooded 'what a good idea, sir!'

'Unless, of course, you don't think you can handle the pace?'

The gauntlet was down and all agreed to accompany me on future patrols. The more I thought about the idea, the more I liked it. One great plus was that I'd be able to assess the performance of the other crews at first hand.

The barbecue was winding up when James Myles wandered over from the P Info house.

'Do you mind hosting a reporter tomorrow?'

'Who is it?'

'Maggie O'Kane of the *Guardian*.'

'Do I have to?'

'Fraid so!'

'Cheers mate!'

Maggie was a fiery Irish reporter, not renowned for being a lover of the military. I wasn't sure if I wanted her company for a day. She was doing a 'day in the life of' article and I was the poor guy who was going to be the subject. She wanted to report on the whole day and that included visiting our room at eight in the morning. Nightmare!

In the event, Maggie and her photographer arrived at 7.15. Roy was still in bed and I had an undignified scramble for my trousers, under the watchful eye of the press. She was very astute and toured the room taking in details, finally stopping at the bookshelf. Studying the books, she remarked how out of character it was to have an army officer reading a book on metaphysical poetry. I just blushed and kept quiet. Roy pulled his duvet over his head and giggled as she rummaged through the contents of his bookshelf. Mercifully, I managed to distract her before she reached mine. I think my collection of Sven Hassel novels would've confirmed her worst fears!

The task for the day was to take a representative of the UNHCR to visit Grahovcici. I stopped at the P Info House and was presented with my press for the day. As well as the *Guardian* crew, I had a BBC cameraman and Patrick Bishop from the *Telegraph*. Captain Peter Bullock accompanied us as the press 'minder'. Peter was from 7th Gurkha Rifles and was James Myles's assistant.

Finally, I picked up the UN representative. He looked bent as a nine-bob note. As soon as I arrived, he bollocked me, in front of the press, for being five minutes late.

'This is a most important task and I must get to this village today!'

All went well until we reached the Cajdras checkpoint, on the Mountain Road. Here, our progress was blocked by a tree trunk lying across the road. I dismounted and went to speak to the checkpoint commander. The time was 10.30 in the morning. The two BiH men were unusually well dressed for Bosnian soldiers. Both wore combat fatigues and dark-green berets, with BiH cap badges. They had short hair and carried the obligatory AK 47s. They looked the part and were, initially, friendly. However, they refused to let us through to Grahovcici saying that snipers had made the route too dangerous for us.

I negotiated for half an hour and got absolutely nowhere. They would not let me pass without papers from Three Corps Headquarters. I deployed the press in the hope that their presence might spur the guards into action. I pointed out that the world's media was here and that people would only think they were hiding something.

'We don't give a damn what the press thinks. We gave up on that a long time ago. We know we are on our own.'

Maggie and Patrick were in the background taking notes and none of the growing crowd of soldiers seemed especially bothered. However, when the cameraman appeared from the back of the Warrior and started filming, the mood changed instantly.

'Get him away or we will shoot him!'

As usual, the media appeared at just the wrong moment! A heavy machine gun was deployed in the top window of a house and trained on us. Phil traversed the cannon on to the window and the gunner ducked out of sight. The cameraman, not surprisingly, had made himself scarce, so I rounded on the Commander.

'Why are you threatening us? We have shown no aggression to you and yet now you threaten us with a machine-gun. If that gun opens fire, I will kill every man here at this checkpoint, starting with you!'

The Muslims would not be intimidated and one appeared with four TMA 3 mines and laid them around the log. These guards were displaying the same arrogance as the Croats had done a few days before.

All Bosnians seemed to be the same: when their side is on the up
they behave like swaggering bullies. As soon as they are losing, they
become servile and pleading. I had tried every form of negotiation
apart from force so I decided to call their bluff.

'I'm going to see the Corps Commander and I will return with the
piece of paper you require.'

This shocked them a bit and I was determined to drop them in it
if I could.

We drove to Three Corps and I went in. First, I was shown into
the deputy commander's office. Merdin greeted me like an old
friend and I explained the problem to him. He listened patiently and
then trotted out the same excuse about the snipers. I told him we
were hardly in danger in the Warrior and he hummed and ha'd
before knocking on the door of the commander's office. Two minutes later, I was taking coffee with the corps commander.

General Enver Hadzihasanovic possessed one of the most unpronounceable names in Bosnia. He was of medium height with silver
hair and looked a bit like Gregory Peck. His office was large with a
huge table covered in maps. It was here that the lightning BiH offensive had been planned. The General was friendly and listened to my
problem before promising me a police escort that, he assured me,
would be better than a piece of paper.

It seemed extraordinary that such a paltry decision had to be
sanctioned by the boss himself. This was a throwback to Communist
days where only the men at the top wielded any real power. The
General was involved in all decision-making, even over trivia such
as this one difficult checkpoint. I couldn't resist having a dig at this.

'You have to understand that we are a very new army. It will take
us many years to forget the old ways of the JNA. We are trying hard
but it is difficult to change our ways in the middle of the War.'

Well that seemed a fair answer and I thought how maddening it
must be to be virtually the only decision-maker in the whole corps.
As is the way of the Balkans, the simple act of rustling up a policeman took over an hour. During this time I mentioned the bad attitude at the checkpoint and Merdin promised to sort them out. I then
had visions of the Commander being thrown into jail and felt a bit
of a sneak. Well, for about three seconds anyway! Eventually, at
nearly two o'clock in the afternoon, we followed a battered old Lada,
with a broken blue light, back to Cajdras.

The guards looked surprised to see me again and probably

thought I'd be rodded off at corps HQ. They went all surly on us, but, faced with the military policeman, reluctantly shoved the log aside. Good old K-P, always gets the job done.

All went well until we reached the crossroads at Novi Selo. This was manned by soldiers from another brigade. They took not the blindest bit of notice of the policeman and refused to let us pass. These guys were from Seven Muslim Brigade and were only one stage down from the mujahideen. The Brigade was the most hard-line in Three Corps and part of its organization included the mujahideen itself. The remainder were committed Muslims and many were Bosnians who affected Arab dress. We called these 'plastic mujahideen'.

The brigade frequently led Three Corps operations and was still in the area following the lightning offensive.

I went to talk to their leader, who was in heated conversation with the policeman. It appeared that we needed papers signed by the commander himself and that the policeman's presence wasn't good enough:

'We have never seen him before and we think he may be a Croat spy!'

I had to laugh at the idea of us escorting a spy, complete with BiH police car. The whole situation was infuriating as we could see the rooftops of Grahovcici, about a kilometre away. I had my mule's head on now and I wasn't going to let this drop, so I promised the leader I'd return, and walked back to 0B.

The boys had been having a little fun with one of the 'plastics'. This guy had a red-and-white checkered shemague wrapped round his head, in what was supposed to be the Arab style. However, he hadn't a clue how to wear the garment and it kept coming undone and flopping over his AK. Seeing as he was standing on a bank level with the Warriors trying to look intimidating, this wasn't doing his cause much good. The lads were laughing and shouting insults at the poor guy who was red in the face and furious. He kept prodding his rifle at us and making cut throat motions with his other hand. Presumably we were supposed to be scared by this pathetic, macho posturing. After each prod, the headdress unwound and he had to re-wrap the shemague, and suffer yet more ridicule. I thought he might actually try to shoot someone but he turned and stalked off to an accompaniment of 'Why was he born so beautiful!' They say Satan finds work for idle hands; well the boys had certainly been idle so far this day. It was now four o'clock and I let their dangerous little game pass without comment.

We returned to Three Corps where the general was rather annoyed to hear we'd been stopped. He promised that the paper would be forthcoming. I somehow expected him to sign it there and then. However, this was, after all, Bosnia, and I was shown into a waiting room and assured that the papers would be here in a moment.

The minutes ticked by and, after an hour, I began to wonder if the general was personally chopping the tree down, to make the piece of bloody paper. Finally, after ninety minutes, Merdin arrived and presented me with a scruffy, badly-typed note, with a scrawled signature that looked like it'd been written by a doctor. I was tempted to stuff the thing in my pocket but instead, I thanked him profusely and left, holding it like it was a million-pound banknote. I was convinced that the whole delay was just to mess me about for being too persistent. There was also the faint possibility that Seven Muslim Brigade had been given the time to clean up the village. Nevertheless, we were on our way.

Still with our trusty policeman in tow, we sped back towards Novi Selo. Dobby hailed me over the intercom. The UNHCR man wanted to talk to me. We stopped and I climbed down into the rear of the Warrior.

'It is six o'clock and I have finished work now. Please take me back to my lodgings.'

'Run that past me again. You want to finish now, before the job's done!'

'That is correct. I am only under contract to work until five and it is after that time now.'

'What about the task that you told me was so vital this morning? We're almost there and I've spent all day making this happen!'

'The task will have to wait for another day.'

'No it bloody well won't. We're going to Grahovcici whether you like it or not.'

'You cannot make me go. Take me to my headquarters this minute!'

'We're going to the village now. If you want to get out you can jump off the top at any time. Now if you don't mind we have a job to do.'

'You are very rude and I wiil be reporting you for holding me against my will!'

'The Catholic church was intact'
Gornji Pecine shortly after capture by the
BiH, 19 June 1993. The Croats were on the
receiving end this time and elected to flee
across the front line into Serb territory
rather than face capture by the Muslims.
The Muslims were generally better at
respecting places of worship and the church
remained largely undamaged

'Dust bunny' Lance Corporal Ricky
Holtom comes last in a clean uniform competition. The soldiers in the back of the
Warriors had a thankless task providing
security to the rear. They were constantly
covered by the thick cloud of dust thrown
up by the tracks. Fortunately we had a
mobile laundry that worked flat out to cope
with the volume of dirty uniforms

'Built by robots, driven by Bosnians'   HVO Commander's car after a close encounter of the
Warrior kind on the road to Sarajevo, 23 June 1993. The driving of the locals was atrocious and
they would frequently play 'chicken' with the Warriors, swerving away at the last minute. This
individual, his senses dulled by slivovitz, misjudged the timing, with predictable results.
It was a miracle he escaped with little more than a broken ankle

C Company Headquarters, Grbavica, September 1993   *Front row, left to right:* WO2 (CSM) Clark, Maj. Kent-Payne, Lt. Calder.
Zero Bravo, left to right: Cpl. Mowforth, L/Cpl. Holton, L/Sgt. Watson, Cpl. Dobson, Pte. Erwin, Capt. Stainthorpe, Cpl. Commerford (pay staff), Cpl. Tooke.
Zero Charlie, left to right: C/Sgt. Goy, L/Cpl. Braithwaite, Cpl. Donlon, Pte. Allen, L/Cpl. Chapman, Pte. Waltham, Pte. McCloy.

'You are very unprofessional, and I don't give a stuff if you report me to Boutros Boutros Ghali himself!'

I was beginning to see why the UN in Bosnia was such a mess. As long as we worked for people with an attitude like this guy, we'd never realize our full potential. The military mind isn't the answer to everything but a few ex-soldiers would've certainly achieved dramatic results working for the UNHCR in Zenica.

The Seven Brigade soldiers were annoyed at us actually obtaining the paper but, eventually, let us pass. We finally arrived in Grahovcici after a day of negotiation that had taken eight hours.

I had no doubt that men had died in the village and that there may have been some prisoners killed. However, there was no sign of a massacre and it seemed as if most civilians had been allowed to flee to Nova Bila. The visit was an anticlimax. There were no bodies, apart from the usual pigs. Most of the houses were intact and only a few had been burnt. There was, however, evidence of fierce fighting and the Croat trenches were littered with spent cases. Casting an infantry eye round the place, it was easy to see why the village had fallen. The trenches were sturdily constructed but there was no mutual support between them. Each would have been captured in turn with the men in the others unable to offer any assistance. The whole HVO set-up in the village was thoroughly unprofessional and, frankly, they deserved to lose.

We spent ninety minutes in the place before the field worker virtually pleaded to be returned. I finally dropped off the press at their house at nine in the evening.

Maggie's article appeared a few days later. Entitled 'White Warriors lost in the ether' it described the day's events in some detail. She also commented on the mini-pool system and the Army's control of the media. The press may not like being 'managed' but the alternative was to have even more dead journos littering the country.

She then went on to describe me: 'Major Vaughan Kent-Payne, straight from central casting. At 34, he's blue-eyed, with a perfect moustache and at 5ft. 7, on the right side of short.'

Needless to say, I received a great deal of stick from the subbies over this description!

The article was fine and I was pleased that I'd managed not to say anything too controversial. I was especially glad that the altercation with the UN worker wasn't included. The only part that annoyed me was a supposed quote:

'We were given a job to do today and we got through to here with stubborn British bulldog determination.'

This was bullshit not bulldog. It's not an expression I ever use and seemed to have been included to lend a little colour to the story. This was like the 'grenades under the pillow' incident. Here was a respected journalist, from a quality broadsheet newspaper, writing things that only resulted in trivializing what was a bloody serious war. I awaited my summons to see the old man.

The events of the next day catapulted me further into the attention of the media.

Like all good days it started quietly enough. I was tasked with re-visiting Bandol, and again James allocated me one of the mini-pools. This time I had Justin Webb from the BBC as well as a cameraman and Anthony Lloyd. Patrick Bishop was along for his regular 'Vitez Vaughan' story with Peter Bullock as minder.

Bandol was still trashed but was, this time, occupied by the BiH. I wandered up to the Croat lines and found the soldiers there tense and on edge as if expecting an attack. We walked around their position and they suddenly became very friendly. One of them confided that they wanted us there because it would discourage BiH attacks. Well I wasn't prepared to do this bunch any favours. They'd been the ones who told me the Muslims had burned their own village.

We set off back to the Warriors and several high-velocity shots were fired at us. Thankfully, we were walking along a sunken lane and the rounds whistled harmlessly over our heads, cutting off small twigs from the hedges as they passed. As usual, it was impossible to detect a firing point. I wasn't sure if it was the HVO firing at us because we'd refused to stay or the BiH because they thought we were helping the Croats.

It'd been enough for one morning and I headed back to catch the best salads for lunch, spot on twelve. About 500 metres west of the Novi Travnik T-junction, a woman ran into the road, right in front of us.

I wasn't sure what she wanted and thought it may be the start of another human-wall protest, so I told Tookey to drive round her. Looking back, I noticed 0C had done the same and the woman now had her head in her hands. It didn't look much like a protest but the call of that salad was strong. Again, something made me hesitate, and we stopped, and reversed back to the house where the woman had come from.

I dismounted and went to talk to the woman, who was middle-aged with long blonde hair. She was wearing a white jumper and, when she stopped wailing for a moment, I found out that her name was Senada Senic. In between wails she told me she was a Muslim and her family was in the house. I went to look, and was confronted with three geriatrics, two women and a man. They were her parents and her aunt. I later found out that she was forty, the parents eighty-five and seventy and the aunt ninety.

The woman was wailing hysterically about how the HVO had threatened them and said they'd be killed that night. I couldn't see any Croats and the whole area seemed quiet. By this time, the press had congregated and I found myself, on camera, giving the party-line to the people.

'I cannot take you to Travnik as you are civilians.'

'Please help us as we will be killed!'

'No one is going to hurt you. Stay inside, and you will be safe.'

'It is not safe and there are HVO everywhere.'

'There are no HVO soldiers here. Whose house is this?'

'It is my parents. Please take us away, we will all be killed!'

'I cannot take you because you are not refugees. You have a house and you should stay in it. There are thousands of really needy people already in Travnik.'

Just to make sure I walked around the house and, sure enough, the area appeared free of HVO.

'I'm sorry, I am not allowed to take civilians in my Warrior. You are not in any danger. I will not be responsible for creating four more refugees.'

'Please help us, we are in great danger. We will be killed!'

'You are not in any danger. There are no HVO. They have all run away ...'

At that moment, an unseen Croat soldier fired an RPG 7 that hit the house, penetrated the wall and exploded in an upstairs room. Plaster showered around us and all three women started wailing in unison. Looking round, I saw several HVO soldiers had appeared in the gardens about a hundred metres away. One of them raised an RPG and fired again. The rocket flew past the house, trailing a shower of sparks, and exploded against the roof of the next door house. Bits of tiles flew into the air and a fire started immediately. I ran to the Warrior and yelled:

'Keep an eye out for those bastards, they're running around!'

Things had changed dramatically. Their house was right on the front line and the HVO was mounting a counter-attack. The civvies were, in my opinion, definitely in danger, and I wasn't about to leave them there.

We reversed 0B up to the door and, with Phil covering, we helped them in, one by one. The old folks were all cartoon geriatrics and could've been anyone's favourite grandparents. Peter gave them a cup of tea in the back of the wagon and, minutes later, we sped them off to Travnik.

In the town, we dropped them off at a relative's house. The woman embraced me in a bear hug, attempting to shower kisses over me. It was all a bit embarrassing, especially when Dobby called:

'Ey up boss! You've pulled there!'

The poor lady was so grateful for such a small act. Again, the smell of fear clung to her and I hoped she couldn't see me wrinkling my nose!

Justin Webb asked for a quick interview:

'Why did you first refuse to take them?'

'Because they appeared to be in no danger. They were not refugees and UN rules forbid us to carry civilians.'

'Why do these rules exist?'

'Our mandate is to escort convoys, not to intervene in the conflict.'

'Why did you carry them in the end?'

'Because I believed the situation had changed and they were now in danger.'

'Will you get into trouble for bending the rules?'

'I couldn't leave them there with the fighting. If I exceeded my authority I'm prepared to accept the consequences.'

As soon as I uttered that last sentence I wished I hadn't. Oh for the ability to grab the words back and gobble them up! Although I'd spoken the truth, and I didn't care about the consequences, I didn't need to damn well say so. A simple 'No!' would have sufficed. Here was the classic dilemma of the commander on the ground having to make split-second, life-or-death decisions, under the media spotlight. There was no time to ask for advice about whether to take them, just as there was no time to ask for advice when asked for a comment. In one moment of thoughtlessness, I'd fallen into the Bob Stewart trap and I knew I'd be hung out to dry.

The more immediate consequence was that the story was national news. The *Telegraph* covered the story, with a photograph under the headline: 'Rescuers bend the rules.'

The Times carried an article by Bill Frost telling how we'd rescued the Muslims.

The *European* carried the story and we even appeared in *Hello* magazine.

Sky news ran their coverage from the pooled film on the hourly news programmes for the rest of the day. However, perhaps the best report was on the BBC early evening news.

Justin Webb had taken over the reporter's duties from Martin Bell. A pleasant fellow in his late thirties with dark, curly hair, he was one of the up-and-coming new generation of reporters. He put together a striking report that, I believe, was nominated for an award for live news coverage. The piece where I was cut off in mid-sentence was pure theatre. It was a classic 'famous last words' to almost rival the American Civil War General Sedgewick at the Battle of Spotsylvania: 'Don't worry men! They couldn't hit a barn door at this dist …!'

The other result was a first in the annals of the early news. Webb wanted to include the bit where I shouted to Phil. The approval to use the word 'bastards' had to be sought from BBC head office and was, apparently, the first swear-word ever allowed on the early programme. That was all very historic but I couldn't see Colonel Alastair appreciating the accolade.

I knew the flak was heading my way and I went to see James. He viewed the tape and agreed the report showed the British Army in an excellent light. It was just the sort of item the folks back home wanted to see. I asked him to try to convince the CO of that.

Having missed our salad, we were sent straight back out to help with a body-retrieval operation. I wasn't that keen but, as usual, we were the only spare callsigns in the company. So, out we went to the village of Pokrajcici and into a relationship that was to last the rest of the tour.

At the HVO headquarters, I was met by a man who introduced himself as Drago Marjanovic. He was a small man, about five foot five, with a thin face, black hair and a well-clipped beard. He eyed me over with distaste. Clearly, he didn't think much of BRITBAT. He told me I'd assist in the removal of the bodies of two HVO soldiers who'd been killed several days earlier. Drago wanted me to go there and load the corpses into my Warrior. There was no way I was having this so I suggested we escort a civilian vehicle and his men could carry out the actual handling. This was refused on the grounds that the BiH would fire on them. I didn't like his attitude and I wasn't in the mood for being messed about.

'Look. Why should I take risks to recover your men? If you want them back so much you have to take a share of the risks. I'll escort you there and the enemy won't fire on you because we're so close. If that's not good enough then it looks like the bodies will have to stay there! I also suggest that you mend your attitude. The Croats are no longer the top dogs around here and, pretty soon, you'll want all the help you can get from people like me.'

He hesitated, so I started to walk towards the Warrior. Within seconds, he caught me up and apologized for his bad attitude. Yes, of course my plan was the best. It was just that he was used to a hostile attitude from the British.

The plan was set and we escorted a battered Mercedes van, with a crude red cross painted on the side, along the front line. This was an area where we'd not been allowed before. The line ran along the west side of the Bila Valley along the very crest of a steep, wooded, hill. A continuous line of trenches, interspersed with stoutly-constructed bunkers, ran along the roadside. The dugouts were made of logs with earth-filled fertilizer sacks acting as improvised sandbags. It was very reminiscent of the First World War and was the first line of defence for the Nova Bila stronghold. Across the valley to my right Kljaci perched on the far hillside. We passed a large pile of 20 mm spent-cases and guessed these had been fired at the Muslim village in retaliation for the recent offensive.

The first body was lying in a water-filled ditch, face-up with only the head and torso visible. Its face was already blackened with decomposition and birds had pecked out the eyes. His comrades must've abandoned him in a hurry as his AK was still lying, half-submerged and rusty, next to him. The two Croats jumped out and sprinted to the body. They hauled him out and both gagged at the smell and threw up in great projectile surges. Unfortunately, the stench drifted up to us as well and I pulled my scarf over my nose. The dead man's legs were twisted under him and set in rigor mortis. I watched as the two started to drag him by the arms, gripping the corpse by the wrists. They were halfway to the van when one of his arms fell off. It was like a scene from a slapstick comedy as one of the men staggered backwards clutching an arm. However, this was no dummy but a rotted human one with bits of sinew poking out of the soggy end. The Croat dropped the arm and retched again. A raucous laugh rang out from the back of 0C and Donlon's dulcet Glaswegian tones filled the air.

'Don't worry about him, he's armless!!!'

Donlon was cackling like an old crone at this piece of wit. It broke the ice and, although they probably didn't get the joke, the HVO started chuckling as well. They recovered their composure and, grinning, threw first the body, then the arm, into the van.

We drove on a little way and found the second stiff. This one was lying in the grass and the sun had also blackened the flesh. The corpse was starting to desiccate and the skin of the hands was stretched tightly over the bones like that of an old woman. There was far less smell. Unfortunately, this one too started to disintegrate. The two Croats had started to pick up the body when the head lolled back and then fell off. It bounced on the dirt track and one of them ran to retrieve it. Another burst of laughter rang out and Donlon shouted:

'It's not worth losing your head over!'

Dobby chipped in with:

'Hey Alan! D'yer reckon he's the Head Honcho?'

I was sure these two wits would have a sound future writing the jokes for the inside of Christmas crackers.

One of the Croats, by now grinning again, picked the head up. Holding it by a tuft of hair, he went through the depressingly familiar ritual of showing the corpse to the nearest UN, in this case me. The head was held up for me to inspect and the Croat gave a cut throat symbol. The ragged skin around the neck suggested that the throat had been cut with enough force to almost sever the head.

'Mujahideen!' called the man, fearfully looking around him. I'd heard they didn't take many prisoners and here was one unfortunate example. I tried to avoid gazing at the empty sockets. However, it was either that or look at the maggots that were wriggling out of his mouth and dropping onto the dirt.

Mercifully, the HVO man thought I'd seen enough of the atrocity and dropped the head into the van where it rolled over the metal floor until it came to rest against the other body.

Drago was gratefulness itself and thanked me for giving the men the chance of a Christian burial. He invited me into the dingy house that served as the headquarters and we drank coffee and Slivovitz.

The plum liquor was strong, probably about sixty per cent proof. It slipped down easily enough but left a disgusting aftertaste. I was still belching it up the next day. He invited me to come to the HQ another day when his battalion commander would be present.

As we were finishing the second Slivovitz, a huge bull of a man entered. The fellow was at least six-foot-four and probably weighed eighteen stone. His hair was close-cropped and he looked like the soccer hooligan from hell. He held out his hand with a surprisingly soft grip, which I squeezed hard. I then wished I hadn't as he gripped mine with twice the strength. I wasn't going to give him the pleasure of wincing so I gripped back and we stood for a few seconds eye-balling each other and squeezing the life out of each other's hands. Suddenly, he relaxed the grip and, with a roar, gave me a matey slap on the back. Fortunately, my flak jacket took most of the blow but I still staggered under the impact. Grinning hugely, he slumped into a chair and poured himself a Slivovitz. Drago told me the newcomer was 'Juti', a fact I'd figured out myself.

His name was Zarko Andric. Juti was a nickname meaning 'yellow', a parody on the fact he was anything but cowardly. He was the local criminal boss, somewhat akin to the Mafia. Juti was feared by the locals and was not above dishing out the odd beating. The Cheshires had some dealings with him as his men were believed to have hijacked a UN vehicle. He was rumoured to hate the UN but seemed friendly enough that afternoon.

Next morning we patrolled out to Guca Gora. I stopped at the monastery and was surprised to hear voices inside. There were no BiH about so Dobby and I walked right in. Inside the church we were greeted by a most extraordinary sight.

A gang of around fifty Muslim women was cleaning the Catholic church. The reason was immediately apparent. The mujahideen had wrecked the place. All the wood panels had been kicked in and the pews were covered in excrement. The frescos had either been daubed in paint or hacked out of the wall with shovels. To be fair, this was almost an improvement. The floor was covered in broken glass and the walls were dotted with bullet holes and daubed with Islamic slogans.

A red-faced and flustered BiH policeman appeared and tried to shoo us away. He was waving his arms as if to prevent us from seeing any more.

'In America, this is what is called a cover up!' I told him.

'We have been ordered by Zenica to clean up. It was the work of the mujahideen!'

I believed him, as to ruin a church was not within the psyche of the average Bosnian Muslim. Perhaps fearful of the adverse propaganda, Three Corps Headquarters had ordered a clean-up. They were always saying how it was only the Croats who destroyed religious sites and this must've been an embarrassment for them. However, no matter how hard they tried, you can't un-smash a 500-year-old window. We left the locals to continue their cover-up.

On the far side of Guca Gora I noticed a line of trenches on a hill, near the village of Cifluk. We drove up the steep side of the feature and halted. I was preparing to dismount when Phil exclaimed:

'Hey look! There's a body down there!'

Sure enough, there was a dead soldier lying just off the track. He'd been there for several days and it was impossible to tell which side he was from. A head appeared above the parapet of the trench and I hailed the fellow.

'Hello! Do you know there's a corpse down here?'

Two HVO scampered out of the trench and ran down the hill to join us. They peered down at the body:

'Not one of ours!'

With that, they doubled-back to safety again and we left the poor fellow there. They'd probably move him after dark and use him in a body-exchange.

The track took us along the Croat front line and I realized it was the same one we'd been on the day before. I'd discovered another way to get to Guca Gora without going through Dolac.

Back in camp, Roy and I were summoned by the Commanding Officer, yet again.

I sat in his office while he dressed me down.

'What did you think you were doing when you made that comment about the mandate?'

'I'm sorry, sir. It was careless of me, I'll try to keep my mouth shut.'

There, I'd apologized and, hopefully, that would be the end of it. I knew what I'd done wrong and was happy I could avoid the same mistake.

'You've appeared in the media far too much. It has to stop.'

'Fine, but, as you know, I don't task the press. James Myles offers them the choice of patrols to accompany.'

'Yes I'm well aware of that. Stop making the news so much.'

That was like saying 'Go and patrol around but don't do anything while you're out there.'

'Sorry. Things just seem to happen when I go out!'

'Yes, that's another point. You're out far too much. Spend more time in camp concentrating on administration.'

Before I could protest, he went on:

'And another thing. Your activities have been annoying the BiH leadership. Cut it out.'

'Come again sir?'

'Colonel Merdin has been on to me about your visit to Bandol the other day. You arrived just as the BiH was about to launch an attack. They had to call it off because you were there.'

I almost laughed aloud. At least that explained where the shots had come from. I could imagine the shock on Merdin's face when we pitched up out of the blue.

'Sorry, sir. But that patrol was tasked by the ops room. We only go where they tell us.'

His reply was lost on me as I thought, 'What the hell are we doing giving in to the wishes of Three Corps. There aren't supposed to be any no-go areas for the UN.'

'Right, get out, and shave that moustache off. I've told you before, I don't like them!'

Roy was in our room and we compared notes on our career interviews. Both had been strikingly similar.

'What are you going to do?' I asked Roy, as he was busy shaving off his moustache.

'What he says I suppose. If he doesn't want us going out as much I'll just stay in camp more. How about you?'

'Same as usual, I guess!'

The next day, 17 June, saw me back at Cifluk to check on reports of heavy shelling. James Myles asked me to take Patrick Bishop with me. I wasn't happy and told him so.

'Look, mate! I'm getting flak because you keep allocating me press people.'

'Yes, I know. I've said it's not your fault.'

'Some good that's done. I'll not take him unless you provide an escort.'

So poor old Peter Bullock was summoned.

The shelling had been heard from camp early in the morning and

Snapper was anxious to discover who was firing on whom. We drove past Pokrajcici, along the Croat front line and were flagged down by three very shell-shocked soldiers. Ken Pickles was interpreting for me and told me there'd been a bombardment of the Point 688 feature near Cifluk.

We stopped at the foot of the hill. All seemed quiet so I left 0C static and we ground our way up to where we'd stopped the day before. I climbed out and stood on the top of the Warrior calling out 'Hello!' in my best British accent.

A bald man emerged, gopher-like, from one of the trenches. He beckoned me to come, quickly. We all dismounted and set off up the last few metres of the track in the order: myself, Dobby, Peter, Ken and Patrick. Two more HVO appeared and, again, beckoned us.

We were about five metres away from the parapet of the nearest trench when there was an almighty bang! I was hurled to my right and ended up in an undignified heap in a very prickly gorse bush. I was totally deaf in my left ear and the stars in front of my eyes looked like a map of the Milky Way. The air was thick with dust and reeked of high explosive. I was obviously injured as my legs were numb and I couldn't move them. I shook my head and Dobby swam into view, lying sprawled across my shins.

'Are you OK, Dobby?'

'Yeah, but me ears hurt!'

'Get off my damned legs then, you big lump!'

Grinning, Dobby rolled off me and we ran back to check on the rest. Peter had a deep gash on one arm and blood over an eye. Ken looked OK and I doubled over to where Patrick was rolling in the dirt. He looked in a bad way and was covered in gore. Dozens of tiny wounds were oozing thick red blood. He looked like he'd been fired at by a shotgun. His blue flak jacket had taken a lot of the blast and was shredded in several places. Patrick's helmet had saved his head though his face was a mess. He was wearing shorts and his legs had been hit by dozens of pieces of shrapnel.

Altogether, he looked in a right state. Dobby and Peter started to patch him up and I looked around for where the device had landed. I'd heard no incoming sound and wondered if it had been a mortar round. Looking to my left I saw the cause.

Standing on four small legs was a type of Claymore mine. It was bright blue with a plastic case the size of a small shoe-box. A green-and-white striped cable led off to the Croat trenches. The mine was

an explosive charge into which were packed hundreds of ball-bearings. It was fired electrically and spread the shrapnel over a wide
area. There was a patch of bare earth with scorched grass around it
where the other mine had been. Casting around, I located the end of
the second wire which had been severed by the explosion and led off
towards another trench. There was no doubt in my mind that some
bastard had deliberately set the thing off. We were, fortunately, on
the edge of its arc and only poor old Patrick had copped much. Five
seconds earlier and we would all have been wounded, or worse.
What was, however, in the middle of the arc, was 0B, and I ran to
check if Tookey and Phil were OK. Thankfully, they'd been under
cover but the tops of the Chobham boxes had been blown off by the
blast.

A fat and balding HVO man, his eyes wide with alarm, ran out
from the trenches shouting:

'*Grenada! Grenada!*'

He started to make gestures to indicate that the BiH had fired
some form of grenade at us. I pointed to the remains of the Claymore
and the tell-tale wire snaking back towards the trenches.

'*Ne! Ne! Muslimanji!*'

I was getting hacked off with this trying to blame the other side.
The evidence was damning and there were only the Croats to blame.
I turned to check on Patrick. The Croat grabbed at my sleeve, so I
chinned him. The blow connected with the side of his jaw and he
went down like a sack of spuds. If I'd not been wearing gloves, I
would've probably broken my hand.

Gopher man was slowly picking himself up and I called Ken over.

'Tell him that if he ever touches me again I'll kill him!'

Ken hesitated, then saw I was in no mood for arguing and repeated the threat. The Croat's eyes started darting around, looking for a
way out. He gave me a wide berth as he stumbled back to his trenches.

I strode after him and over the nearest parapet into a long ditch
about three-feet deep, interspersed with bunkers. One of these had
clearly taken a direct hit. A man came running over and I recognized
him as the young HVO commander from Grahovcici. At least he
hadn't been killed when his village was captured. The guy tried to
blame the Muslims as well and I pointed to the Claymore wire. He
suddenly looked shamefaced and mumbled something that Ken
couldn't catch.

As if remembering why we were there in the first place, he asked me to come to a bunker. A shell had landed right on top of the log roof of the dugout, sending the wood flying. The two soldiers inside hadn't stood a chance. One lay face down. Both his legs and an arm had been blown off. The legs were close by, but there was no sign of the arm. The other soldier had half his head blown away. His face hung loosely now there was no skull to support it. I recognized him as the man who'd held the head up for me to examine, the day before. I was about to leave when I noticed the extra leg. It was lying, partially buried. Unless the HVO had recruited 'Jake the Peg', there'd been three men in the bunker.

The Commander wanted me to help retrieve the bodies and take them to the hospital.

'You must be bloody joking! You try to blow us up and then ask us for help! Do your own dirty work!'

I left Ken grappling with the sentence and arrived at the Warrior in time to see Patrick being gently loaded in. The boys had done a good job of bandaging him up but he looked in a bad way. I needed to get him to the MST, and fast!

As I climbed up the glacis plate three HVO dragged another out from the bunker with the wire leading to it. At my last sight of him he was lying in a ball receiving a sound kicking!

We reversed down the hill and sped along the front line. The track was narrow and several soldiers were forced to jump into their trenches to avoid the clanking tracks. We hit the metalled road, and Tookey hit the gas.

Careering down the track we were soon at the main road. I radioed on ahead and alerted the MST, giving descriptions of Patrick's injuries as best I could. I was genuinely concerned for his safety and told Tookey to 'Step on it!'

The Warrior rocked and bucked as our driver slewed it round the corners right at the edge of losing the traction and sliding off into oblivion. We came up behind a car and Tookey hesitated until I shouted:

'Go on! Take him!'

The occupants of the Lada Riva looked up in horror as thirty tons of metal passed them at ninety kilometres an hour. We were half way there, and I crouched down in the turret.

Corporal Knight was placing another field-dressing over Patrick's calf, which was still oozing blood. I was worried at the way the reporter was hunched over. He looked in agony and his face was screwed up. It was then that I saw that he was bracing himself against the motion of the Warrior and scribbling furiously in a small notebook. I could just make out: 'The Warrior sped along the narrow country lane. The Major radioed the base to stand the medics by. I was rocked from side to side as we slid round the corners. There was a grim sense of purpose in the rear of the vehicle.'

The man was writing his story! A true professional to the last and I knew he was going to be OK.

We drove straight into camp and I stopped outside the MST. The Medical Corps Colonel ran out, and Patrick was stretchered into the operating theatre. He had dozens of tiny pellets removed from his arms, legs and face. Despite the blood, none of the wounds were deep and he made a full recovery. Peter had his arm dressed and was especially lucky as another pellet had only just missed an eye. Ken declared a slight injury and had shrapnel removed from his backside. He had to endure days of 'pain in the arse' jokes. Dobby was slightly concussed. As for me, I only noticed the blood that had trickled from my left ear when Tookey pointed it out. My ear was ringing for days and the hearing never fully returned.

In just a few days the whole situation in our area had dramatically changed. After weeks of provocation, the BiH lashed out in a highly effective way. Despite the human suffering the general consensus was that 'The Croats had it coming'. I remarked to Dobby how different the situation was now, from when we first deployed. A man of few words, he agreed:

'Aye, sir. T'worm's turned!'

Chapter 10
Loose Cannon

I went straight back out and up to Pokrajcici. I was in no mood for negotiation and demanded to see the local commander.

A man in his late thirties, of medium height and sporting a ginger Nigel Mansell moustache came over. He held out his hand, but I refused it.

'How dare you? You ask us to carry out patrols of your front line and then you fire a mine at us. Two of my men are injured because of you. I will order my soldiers not to come into this area again. Until you can control your troops, there will be no more UN patrols to this sector.'

For the first time I saw a reasonable response from a Croat leader. His face was a picture of 'Shit, we've gone too far now. We need these guys on our side.'

I stormed off leaving him in mid-sentence. I never intended to return to the bloody place again.

After lunch, we escorted the padre to Guca Gora. With him, was the imam from Stari Vitez who was going to inspect the damage to the church. We were stopped short of the village by Seven Brigade soldiers. They refused to let us through and deployed a heavy machine gun to emphasize the point. Stephen was with me and I told him to remain with his two Warriors and keep negotiating. I was going to try something new.

We turned round and sped off, back to Dolac, along the Bila Valley and then up to the ruined bridge. Within thirty minutes we were approaching the outskirts of Guca Gora from the other direction.

Another checkpoint barred our way, just short of the church. The sentry said he'd shoot if I continued. I wasn't in the mood for his posturing, so I stayed in the turret, looked down at him and presented the caring face of the UN.

'You are hardly in the best position, with Warriors at both ends of the village. I only want to link up with my other vehicles.'

I could see his peanut-size brain trying to weigh up the options so I helped him:

'We can do this the easy way or the hard way. One is to provide a car to escort me through the village in exactly five minutes. The other, is that at five seconds after five minutes I will run over you!'

Ken, who'd gamely come out with us, despite having a large sticking-plaster on his backside, hesitated.

'Vaughan, you can't go around threatening people like that.'

'Look, mate! You might be the same rank but you're working for me. Tell him what I said. You can see it in his eyes, he'll back down!' Four minutes and forty seconds later a battered green minibus screeched into the square and escorted us to where Stephen was tensely waiting.

His face lit up and he told me he'd been on the verge of shooting the guys who had the machine gun. They'd told him to move but he'd obeyed orders and stuck to his task. He was a good kid and I admired him for his guts.

The BiH soldiers manning the gun were thoroughly cheesed off. They tried to point it in two directions at once before admitting defeat and slinking off. It was only a minor victory but our little action kept the road open for several more days before the BiH tried, again, to close it to us.

I went to the 'swamp' and suggested we go and see Patrick, who had, by now, been discharged from the MST. Donlon amazed me by producing a hand-drawn card with a jolly picture of a pirate on it. He really was a bit of a dark horse. Lance-Corporal Latus penned a poem about the incident, which was also very good. The hidden talents of the lads never ceased to amaze me. Myself, I had no such skill to offer, so I used the American solution to every problem. Throw money at it! Armed with a bottle of *Moet et Chandon* I strolled down to P Info. Patrick was sitting in the shade, swathed in white gauze dressing. He was remarkably cheerful and expected to return to reporting duties within a month. I shared a beer with him and Bill Frost of *The Times*. Frost was also injured. He was rather embarrassed when he told me he'd consumed a few too many beers and fallen over a step! Patrick seemed touched by our concern. His last article about the company appeared the next day.

Under the headline 'Caught in the stupidity of a slivovitz-soaked conflict' the piece described the incident. It was journalism at its best and used some marvellously descriptive phrases:

'Below them lay the valley, a picture of bucolic tranquillity.'

'As we walked towards the Croat fox-hole we were hit by a blast, like the opening of a furnace door.'

'Another figure appeared, a short fat man whose face was a mixture of fear and bovine stupidity.'

He was one of the best journos in theatre and I hoped he'd make a speedy recovery.

The HVO, realizing they needed every bit of support they could get from the battalion, organized an inquiry. I went along to their headquarters, at the Hotel Vitez, and picked up a couple of their leaders. We then drove to Cifluk and collected the brigade commander.

Ilya Nakic was about my age and height. He had fiery dark eyes and a stubbly black beard. He shook my hand firmly and looked me in the eye when I talked to him. My immediate impression was that he was a man of honour.

I always take particular notice of people's eyes. It's said they are the windows to the soul and I agree. I'd look locals directly in the eye when I talked to them. Soon, I became adept at recognizing the slight look away when they lied, the blaze of imminent aggression or the widening of fear. A penetrating gaze soon un-nerves those with something to hide.

We drove to Point 688. The place was like Hamburger Hill. There were trenches and bunkers covering most of the crest. The ground that hadn't been disturbed by the spades of the soldiers had been churned up by constant shelling. There was no doubt this was the cornerstone in the defence of the sector and its commander would be a man of some ability. This was borne-out by the fact that Nakic's men cheered him when he emerged from the Warrior. They scampered over like children anxious to shake his hand. He chatted with each before sending them away, back to their trenches. This was not stage-managed or contrived, his men genuinely worshipped him. I racked my brains to remember a time when I'd heard a British general cheered by his troops.

We poked around and, eventually, Nakic drew me to one side and admitted one of his men had been drunk and fired the Claymore.

He'd been disciplined, and was now in the hospital in Nova Bila! This merely confirmed what I'd already figured but I was grateful for his honesty. The other HVO leaders stuck to the BiH grenade theory, and I ignored the idiots. I was happy there was nothing else to be achieved. The HVO had shown willingness to co-operate and would no doubt blame the Muslims. I could report the true cause to the CO. In the way of Bosnia, an equitable compromise had been reached.

We dropped Nakic off and I walked him to his HQ. He asked me to pop in for a chat next time I was in the area.

'You wily old fox! You know that to do so I will have to break my vow not to patrol this area again!'

He laughed when he realized he'd been caught out. However, I'd already mellowed from the previous day and would return, when the mood took me. This just might be the break we needed and may enable us to bridge the gap of distrust between us and the HVO. I returned to 0B and climbed on to the vehicle. One of the boys passed up a can of Coke and I stood on the back decks, drinking the cool liquid. Without warning, a large-calibre mortar round landed about forty metres away. There was a deafening 'kerump!' and shrapnel buzzed past me together with a 'thwack!' as something hit the side of the Warrior. The blast hit me and knocked me into the turret cage where I lay, for a moment, clutching my head, oblivious to the Coke dripping down my legs.

That was bloody close. My left ear started to ooze blood again and was ringing big-style now. The biggest injury was to my dignity. A puddle of Coke had collected in my lap and it looked like I'd wet myself. I quickly jumped into the turret before anyone noticed.

That night, there was some shooting around camp, some of it close to our houses. Ten minutes later, I was woken by an anxious soldier.

'Sir, come quickly! Mr Lees has been shot!'

I threw on some clothes and sprinted to the MST. I barged through the door to find Stephen, sitting up on a bed, with a large plaster on his nose. He seemed to be OK and was busy chatting up one of the nurses.

'What happened? I was told you'd been shot!'

He recounted the story.

When the firing started, he dived out of bed and grabbed for his rifle. As he swung it up, the barrel hit the lampshade above him. The glass shattered and a large piece fell and embedded itself in his nose. Bleeding profusely, he stumbled to the MST passing the sangar on the way. The soldier on duty rightly associated the shooting with the sudden appearance of a wounded officer but added two and two together, to make five!

The BiH launched an extension to their offensive and broke yet another cease-fire. They attacked the Croat villages to the west of Novi Travnik, capturing them all. This time, the inhabitants were not left with an escape corridor. Rather than fall into BiH hands, they approached the Serbs and were allowed to cross their front line. As usual, there were reports of atrocities and hostage-taking.

I volunteered for the task of patrolling the area as this was somewhere none of us had been. The press soon caught on and requested an escort to the area. I therefore pitched up at P Info to be presented with Peter Bullock, complete with bandaged arm, Anthony Lloyd and an ITN team headed by David Chater.

Of medium height, with curly grey hair and a rosy face, Chater had already been wounded in the early part of the Balkan War. He must've been a glutton for punishment because here he was again, back in the firing-line. He'd been in Vitez for almost a week and had yet to have a story included on the news. This was always the reporter's nightmare. Every day, he had to produce a story good enough to compete for valuable air-time with the multitude of others from around the globe.

We transited through Novi Travnik and south-west until we were stopped by the BiH at the village of Sinokos. They were in a jubilant mood, but were local militia and not the fanatics we'd encountered in the Bila Valley.

One old man chatted to me. He rued the day the Muslim/Croat Alliance had broken down and predicted that the only winners would be the Serbs. He told me:

'We have an old Bosnian proverb: two thoroughbred racehorses and a donkey enter a race. If, half way round, the horses stop to fight, the ass will win!'

He was a wise old man and was proved correct within days.

We drove on and entered a world of deep valleys and steep wooded hills. 0B churned up a massive cloud of dirt from the parched track and every time we slowed, the trail caught us up and swamped the rear of the wagon. No wonder the lads in the back were affectionately known as Dust Bunnies.

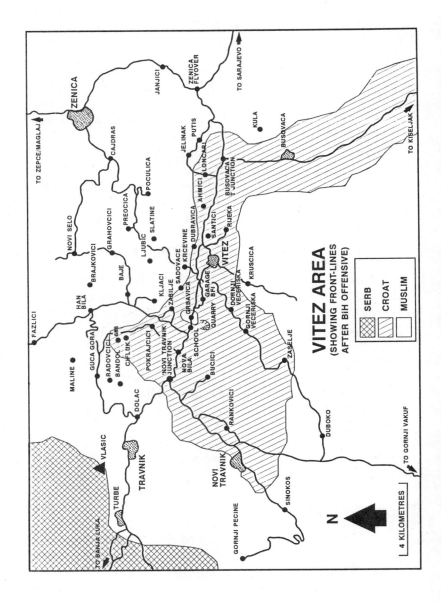

VITEZ AREA
(SHOWING FRONT-LINES
AFTER BiH OFFENSIVE)

There was no sign of conflict until we reached a small knot of soldiers by the side of the track. These were the BiH who'd actually done the fighting and were from our old friends, Seven Brigade. They tried to block our progress. I knew if I stopped they wouldn't let us past. However, as we were moving and they hadn't physically blocked the path I decided to press on. We nudged past them and they shouted their anger at us. As we started to speed up, one of them fired a volley of shots to the side of the wagon. It was more a gesture of macho frustration than an attempt to kill us. Also, they may have thought the firing might persuade me to stop. In any event, we were soon round the corner and out of sight. Phil conned the vehicle while I studied the map for other ways back. There were none. Unless we, too, asked the Serbs for asylum, we would have to return this way.

The road petered out into a dirt track, and we climbed steeply. There were several Croat-style chalets, all deserted. The track narrowed even further and presented a sheer drop of a hundred metres to my right. Our right track was centimetres from the abyss but I now trusted Tookey implicitly.

The houses in the first village were totally deserted. They'd been abandoned in a great hurry and food was still on the tables. The whole set-up was a looter's dream. We were going into people's homes with all their things to be had. We'd spread out so we were all on our own, any of us could've stolen anything. The sad fact was there was absolutely nothing worth pinching. There was never any chance of a moral dilemma. It was all cheap, worthless junk. The people were simple country folk and had neither the money to buy luxuries nor the range to choose from even if they had.

I was amazed how many homes had photographs of Tito still hanging. It was a level of the affection the rural folk held for the old dictator. We found a dog trapped in a cellar and the boys started a rescue operation, filmed by the TV crew. I wandered off alone.

In another part of the village, which, incidentally, had no name on the map, I found the school. Walking in, I entered an Aladdin's cave. Standing in the entrance hall was a brand new SPG 9, 90 mm recoilless rifle. The weapon consisted of a barrel about two metres long with one vented end to allow the gases to escape. The whole thing was mounted on a small, two-wheeled carriage. I sniffed the end of the barrel and it smelled of oil. This particular weapon hadn't been fired recently.

Further inside were two mortars, an 82 mm and a giant 120 mm. I was surprised at the size of the larger one. The barrel stood as tall as me, not that that's saying much. Scattered about were a few of the bombs. I lifted one and it must have weighed fifteen kilos or so. This was probably the type of round fired at us the day before.

The kitchen was packed high with food, most of it UNHCR, or EEC aid. This confirmed what I already suspected, that the majority of aid went to feed the military.

The next part of the school housed a fifteen-bed field hospital. There were, again, tons of medical supplies. We were fortunate enough to have Lance-Corporal Blinkhorn, one of the battalion medics, with us and I called him over. His eyes widened and he examined the piles and pronounced that they were all high-quality items. These were in desperate supply in the local hospitals. As far as I was concerned, this was a salvage law situation, finders, keepers. No one owned them now so I went outside and radioed the ops room.

'I've found several tons of medical supplies abandoned by the HVO. Am I OK to load some of this up and bring it back for distribution to needy hospitals in our area?'

'Roger, that's an excellent idea. Just don't get seen by the locals!'

'There's also a brand new recoilless rifle. May I bring that back too?'

'Negative to that!'

'Roger out!'

That was a shame as it would look nice outside the sergeant's mess back in Osnabrück, with the gun they'd brought home from the Gulf War. Still, one out of two wasn't bad.

Blinkhorn set about sorting out the most valuable kit and the lads loaded it into 0C. The cameraman had grown bored with filming the rescue of the dog and proceeded to shoot plenty of footage of them packing the supplies in. Lloyd also noted down my conversation with the ops room and it was likely he could sell the story to a daily newspaper.

If we couldn't take the weapons I knew what the next best thing was. Chater set the camera rolling and asked me to describe the weapons and then I finished by remarking:

'I'll make sure these are damaged before we leave!'

Chater then added:

'The Major was as good as his word!' as Tookey drove the Warrior over the lot!

This wasn't quite as easy as I'd hoped as the barrels refused to be squashed. It took several attempts before we dented the three sufficiently to ruin them.

We drove on to the village of Gornji Pecine and arrived to find the place apparently deserted. The Catholic church was intact and there was no sign of any damage. The door was open so we sauntered in to the deliciously cool air. All the lads automatically took their helmets off when they entered.

I couldn't resist it, so I rang the great bell. A couple of minutes later, two middle-aged HVO men appeared. They'd been left behind and were steadily getting drunk on Slivovitz. They were determined to defend the village to the death and, judging by the state of them, that wouldn't take long. I wasn't going to transport them out but I did suggest a route by which they could probably reach Novi Travnik. They argued the toss between themselves for a couple of minutes before nodding and staggering away into the hills. I wondered if they'd make it.

There had clearly not been any atrocities. The Croats had simply fled before the BiH had even arrived. There was nothing else to do; we had accomplished our mission, so we headed back.

We came upon the advance guard of Seven Brigade a few hundred metres past the school. They made a much better effort to stop us this time and deployed four men across the track. There was no way I was going to stop and let them see the medical supplies, so we increased to ramming speed and headed for them. A game of chicken between thirty tons of Warrior and a few blokes was only going to have one outcome. Sure enough, they flung themselves out of the way at the last minute. One brave soul ran into the road after we passed. He raised his AK and loosed off a burst. Most of the rounds hit the track, flinging up little puffs of dust. However, the last few found their target and two slammed into the turret cage. That was a little too close for comfort and missed me by less than a metre. He took more careful aim and was about to fire again when he looked over his shoulder and saw 0C bearing down on him. The 'Plastic' joined his mates in the ditch, in the nick of time, and there was no more firing. The soldiers were mightily annoyed, but not as much as they would be when they discovered the crushed weapons. We'd almost reached Sinokos again when the radio crackled:

'Hello Three Zero, this is Zero. Change of plan. We've given this some thought. Do not take the medical supplies. Leave them where you found them.'

Oh just bloody great! What was I supposed to do? Drive back to the school and say:

'Hello Mister BiH! I'm the man who just tried to run you down. Yes, I'm sorry about the weapons we actually did run over. I really didn't see them! Ever so sorry to hear about your men. Are they hurt? Oh yes, and by the way, would you mind if we put these medical supplies back? They seem to have somehow found their way into the back of my Warrior!'

I pondered for a moment and made up my mind:

'Hello Zero this is Three Zero. Roger your last, doing it now!'

We halted in a deserted lane and I called Chater and Lloyd to me.

'I've just been told to put these supplies back. You heard the trouble we had getting through the lines. I know a little village where they'll be well used. I realize you filmed us loading them up. Well I'm going to disobey the order and take them to the village and I'm asking you not to use footage of the incident.'

There was no hesitation and they both nodded in agreement.

I wasn't sure if I could trust them. Lloyd in particular could sell the story to a tabloid. It didn't take much to imagine the headline: Army officer disobeys order and takes medicine to needy Muslims!

It would make a great story, as would my subsequent court martial. I had no choice, and we trundled into camp and locked the stuff in the wagons overnight. The lads were a different matter. I wasn't going to give them an illegal order to ignore my action. Only their loyalty would prevent them from telling someone.

In the event, nobody did. Chater and Lloyd kept their word and the story never leaked. However, Chater did file a report on the rest of the day, and, finally made the 'News at Ten'. We took the supplies to Kljaci the next day, much to Mister Asim's delight.

'In England we say that these fell off the back of a lorry!' I said.

At last it was the end of another ops week and a time to escape from the limelight. I expected another summons from the Colonel. After all, the day after he told me not to go out so much, I go and get myself blown up in spectacular fashion.

During this time, the old man at Sinokos was proved right and the Serbs advanced and occupied Gornji Pecine, seizing it from the BiH. That must be a record for a village: three owners in a week.

I'd written to several firms specializing in the manufacture of baby products. I thought these goods could only be used to help infants and wouldn't be misdirected towards the military. This seemed like the ideal way in which we could play a small part in distribution.

The UN rules were, as usual, woolly, on this one. We were not supposed to get involved in the actual distribution of UN aid. However, the G5 Cell had a quantity of aid, mostly baby food, which it could dish out as small goodwill gestures. The CO declared that company commanders could also tap into this pool as well. The line to take was to tell the locals that this was not aid but a gift in return for hospitality.

Within three weeks of writing I received a letter from Jasmine Magee, the Humanitarian Aid Coordinator of Cow & Gate Limited. In it, she promised five thousand jars of assorted baby food.

Her latest letter confirmed that the aid would be delivered to the FTC Warehouse in Reading for shipment to Bosnia. In return, I promised to write an article for their company magazine and photograph the actual distribution.

Some of the lads were far more mercenary, writing, basically, begging letters:

'Dear Mister Reebok. I am a poor soldier serving in the terrible war-zone of Bosnia. We are allowed to run around the track in camp but it is covered with sharp stones. My training shoes have now disintegrated. There is no way I can get another pair and I was hoping that you may be able to help.

PS: I take a size nine.'

It was amazing how many firms sent items to the lads, such was the wave of sympathy back at home for the troops. There were more new trainers in Vitez than in Linford Christie's locker.

The next load of R & R personnel had returned including Jimmy Cliffe. That night, we held the second of our impromptu company parties in the mess.

The food in the cookhouse was very good but, inevitably, became monotonous. There were also few luxury items because of the vast distances they had to be transported. I therefore hit on the idea that whenever one of us returned from leave we'd bring a quantity of decadent food back from the UK. Tom had gone first and had returned with some delicious cheeses. We then all sat around one of the small circular tables in the mess and totally flaunted our delicacies in front of all the other mess members.

Jimmy, being cavalry, had to go one better and returned laden with smoked salmon, caviar and pâté. We decided to have our little get-together upstairs in the mess. Well, the evening became extremely rowdy and ended up with us pelting bread rolls down onto anyone within range. Richard came upstairs to tell us to calm down and met with a withering hail of stale buns. Hastily, he withdrew to cover, and scowled up at this affront to his dignity. Funnily enough, we were banned from any further company parties in the mess. The latest R & R group was due to fly back to Sarajevo. After weeks of negotiation, the Serbs finally allowed a convoy, escorted by Warriors, to take the next load of outgoing soldiers and collect the returning ones. Roy had been shown the way and invited C Company officers along as well. It was too good a chance to miss.

Sarajevo had been under siege for months. Constantly in the news, the plight of the Muslims in the City seemed to epitomize their struggle throughout the region. Their stoicism under constant Serb fire had won them many allies around the world. Our patrol had taken weeks of negotiation to organize and we were to be some of the very few from the Battalion actually to go to Sarajevo.

We left early in the morning of the 23rd June. The aim was to show the route to as many of the officers as possible. Roy led in his 0B and I followed in mine with Phil driving and Tom Crowfoot next to me. Next was the four-tonner carrying the outgoing personnel and finally A Company's 0C with Ian Crowley, one of Roy's subbies driving, and another, Richard Lockwood, in the turret.

Roy was tonking along when, just short of Kiseljak, a white VW Golf GTI careered round the corner, in the middle of the road. Built by robots, driven by Bosnians! Unfortunately, Roy was also in the same position and ran right over the top of the car.

The Warrior rocked slightly and carried on as if nothing had happened. I yelled to Phil to stop and was out, running down the glacis, even before we'd halted.

The car was almost totally flattened. One track had run right over it from bonnet to boot. I ran to the driver's door and found it squashed. However, the passenger side was slightly less flat and, after a lot of tugging, the door opened. The driver was flattened as well. His seat had collapsed and he lay, pushed back at an unnatural angle. The roof of the car looked like it was moulded onto his chest. He was in uniform and wore a pistol. Just our luck, an HVO commander. I leaned into the car and gagged on the smell of stale slivovitz and urine. The guy was obviously Harry Hissed and the liquid dripping from his legs told me where the other smell was coming from. I felt for a pulse but there was none. I thought he'd gone to the great distillery in the sky.

The others had arrived and Sniffer Clarke and I used a crowbar to try to prise the roof from his chest. We are both midgets and, eventually, Dobby and someone else took over and, with a great heave, they moved the roof a few centimetres. Freed of the crushing pressure, the guy spluttered and spasmed. They heaved again, cleared a larger space and the medic went to work.

Sergeant Hartwell was one of the MST nurses going on leave. Using a Warrior first-aid kit, she revived the guy. She inserted a pipe into his mouth and strange whistling sounds emanated from it. A crowd gathered and was rapidly turning nasty. It appeared the driver was, indeed, the local HVO leader. I wondered if he was the one who'd ordered the firing on me when I escorted the mail run. If he'd been in the Ford Escort as well he was seriously unlucky.

Roy kept the locals at bay while we extricated the driver. His feet were jammed around the pedals but, eventually we freed them. Sniffer did a sterling job working in the confines of the car amid the guy's legs. Someone pulled open his shirt and I saw he had track-pad marks on his chest. Only the fact that the seat collapsed can have prevented him from instant death.

Finally, we laid him on the pavement and Hartwell gave him full resuscitation at which he started breathing, more or less normally. She most definitely saved his life. The HVO police arrived and tried to arrest Roy's driver. There were a few tense moments but the atmosphere lightened when it appeared that the guy would survive. In the end he got away with a broken ankle and a few cracked ribs. He was one lucky drunk.

We booked out through UN headquarters and headed through the valleys until we reached the Serb line. This had been constructed just like a border frontier with red, white and blue bollards. It reminded me of a Loyalist area of Belfast. We had to submit to having our vehicles searched and all had to have our UN identity cards inspected by a 'customs officer'.

The UN rules forbade us from letting the locals search our vehicles. However, there were times where our job simply wouldn't get done if we applied this. The CO took a robust view and instructed us to comply if there was no other way of completing the task. I per-

sonally didn't have a problem with this. Both sides were always lev-
elling the ridiculous charge that we transported weapons and ammunition to the opposition. If allowing a quick peek in the back helped
to dispel these rumours I was all for it.

However, this particular checkpoint was an affront. The Serbs
had captured this territory by force and were attempting to legit-
imize their claims by creating an artificial inter-state border. They
held the upper hand. We wanted to travel into Sarajevo and had to
agree to this illegal checkpoint in order to do so. So much for the
power of UNPROFOR. It was no wonder the joke was that it stood
for UNPROFessional!

Eventually, we arrived at the heavily sandbagged terminal with a
sign that proclaimed 'Aer...rom Sar...vo' in splintered letters. Roy
and I walked inside and found the check-in desk and then wished we
hadn't. The aeroplane wasn't due in today. We drove back with a
sense of failure hanging around us. The leave people looked gutted
to see one of their precious days evaporate.

We checked back in camp and it turned out the officer in charge
of R & R hadn't read the date correctly. We'd been sent on a fool's
errand.

Our patch was far quieter due to the latest cease-fire between the
BiH and HVO. This one actually seemed to be holding but it was
obvious it wouldn't last. The BiH had halted to consolidate now that
they were facing renewed Serb aggression. They'd lost the support
of the HVO and now manned almost all the front line with the Serbs
in our area. There was no doubt they'd soon resume with the strategic aim of cutting the Vitez pocket into two, or preferably, three segments. The easiest place would be in the area of Santici where the
pocket was only two or three kilometres wide. There was scope for
another split around Kula near Busovaca. If they could achieve this,
they could destroy the Croats piecemeal. Their tactical aims were
the relief of the siege of Stari Vitez and the capture of the Vitez
ammunition factory.

The Croats were now reaping the whirlwind they'd created by
destroying Ahmici. It was hard to feel sorry for them and I had to
keep telling myself that the normal civilians were just as vulnerable
as the Muslims. Apart from suvival, their tactical aim was to secure
a route from Novi Travnik to Vitez. This ran past the school and was
almost totally in HVO hands. The one exception was the tiny
enclave around our houses and the village of Grbavica. Both these

harboured snipers who fired on to traffic.

The situation was confused in the extreme. One example of this was Stari, or old, Vitez. This was a Muslim enclave under siege within a Croat enclave, which was itself under siege in another Muslim enclave, which was also under siege in a Serb enclave, which was surrounded on three sides by Croatia. No wonder the politicians couldn't find a solution!

Proceedings in the mess were livened up by a fashion show. A few days earlier, the *Sun* had published a dress pattern that it reckoned anyone could follow. Jane remarked that there'd be few blokes who could manage to make a dress and Peter Edwards, Roy's Warrior captain, took up the challenge.

Peter slaved away for hours cutting out pieces of bedsheet with a pair of nail scissors. He then painstakingly sewed them together and his fingers were covered in sores where he'd jabbed himself with the needle. Finally, the garment was finished and Jane tried it on. It fitted everywhere but over the hips. The hem was slit and she wore shorts under the dress while she paid up her forfeit of champagne.

As our week on guard ended the BiH recaptured Gornji Pecine and Gary Payne from B Company ran over his third mine. The CO made it clear in his conference that this was careless and that all ranks had to be extremely vigilant for mines. I hoped he hadn't got wind of the way we'd cleared the mines at Dolac.

Two of my corporals had been promoted and had, fortunately, stayed in the company. John Hutchinson stayed in Nine Platoon and Stu Foote replaced Geoff Barratt in company headquarters.

The first day back on operations was also the first day for my policy of taking section vehicles out with me, and I deployed with D21. I had no tasks so I decided to visit the tunnel callsigns.

Everything was quiet so we returned and I retired to sit in the sun, on the verandah, and read a trashy detective novel.

Crump! There was a huge explosion on the Grbavica Hill around eighty metres away. The blast hit my left ear, which started stinging and oozing clear fluid. I rushed inside and found my helmet and camera and settled down to watch the barrage and take a few photographs. The nearest mortar round landed just the other side of the Bila River about fifty metres away. Unfortunately, I ducked as the roof of the house was showered in fragments and only succeeded in photographing my knee. The bushes on the side of the hill were ignited and burned merrily for a while. It was the HVO letting the

BiH know they were still in business. But the rounds were very close to the houses. It would take only a tiny error of correction, or sudden gust of wind in flight, to cause the bombs to drop either on us, or, worse still, on camp.

The 28 June was another day in the office. Snapper was interested in the extent of the BiH gains above Vitez and asked me to take a look. The main briefing board in the conference room had the numerous front lines in our area marked on. These were constantly updated to brief our many visitors. I took D23, with two of the anti-tank 432s under Sergeant Smith. Sergeant Pratt of the LAD asked if he could come along so we sandwiched his 432 between the Warriors.

We reached the area above Vitez and climbed into the hills. The locals were friendly enough as they rarely saw UN vehicles. We passed through Dornji and Gornji Veceriska and I sent the 432s off to satellite the area while we stopped in the village of Zaselje. This was high in the hills and afforded an excellent view down over Vitez and the garage. Through the times-ten I could pick out the white Portakabins in camp, glinting in the sun.

The village was seriously isolated and very poor. It was like stepping back into the 1920s with women in traditional Croat dress, beaded waistcoats and white headscarves. Many of them were heavily tattooed. The village was mixed Croat and Serb and only a kilometre from the front line. The people were, understandably, worried about the proximity of the BiH but trusted their HVO to protect them. Dobby mended a child's toy crossbow. He found some rubber tubing and fashioned this into a string. By the time he'd finished, the weapon would pierce Chobham at fifty paces.

I sent Smith along to probe the route through the lines of Muslim Duboko near Route Diamond. However, he was turned back by the HVO so I went to try myself.

The HVO were initially hostile.

'How can we monitor all the supposed BiH violations of the cease-fire if we can't patrol the area?'

They pondered on it and finally said they'd move their anti-personnel mines.

We were in a thick forest with the deeply-rutted track only just wide enough for the Warrior. We were, without doubt, the first UN vehicles to attempt this route. The HVO walked ahead and lifted their mines, which were dark green and about the size of a boot-polish tin. They waved us farewell and, fifty metres further on we ran over another one. There was a sharp 'crack!' and a small puff of smoke from under the front of the right track. I looked back and the HVO man was holding his hands up in a 'sorry!' gesture.

One of the dangers of wars such as this was the indiscriminate laying of mines. They were rarely recorded and then often on the back of a fag packet. Usually, they were laid by one or two specialists who retained the information in their heads. If they were killed, the information died with them.

I certainly wasn't going to dismount and wander around to check the damage so I lay on the glacis while Tookey reversed until the strike area was visible. Fortunately, the track was substantially tougher than the human foot and, although the pad had been ripped off, there was only a small amount of buckling to the link. We continued and the trees closed in overhead, blocking out the sun. I kept my eyes peeled for any other mines on the track and so almost missed the Claymore.

However, its blue body caught my eye and we halted. It was wired to the tree trunk and was about a metre-and-a-half above the ground. It would decapitate a man on the track. We were nearly on the BiH line now and I took the precaution of ordering drivers and gunners to close down. I crouched lower in the turret but needed my head out to keep an eye on the track ahead. We'd only just set off again when there was a blinding flash and a bang to my left, followed by a fusillade of small-arms fire. The blast hit me and deafened me in my left ear yet again. The ear shells of the helmet have little catches that open or close them to sound, enabling the wearer to concentrate on the radio. I knew I always had a signaller to listen out for me so I travelled with mine open. That way I could here shouts, and shots, above the noise of the engine. It also meant that I could hear loud bangs, rather too well.

As usual, the rifle fire was high and wild and probably from below the parapet of a trench. I was showered with twigs broken off from the trees above and Foote jumped when one fell through the open hatch and hit him on the shoulder. A couple of rounds hit the glacis and one ricocheted away with a whine. Foote immediately traversed left and we picked up a row of bare heads in a trench.

'Fire if they fire again! I'm going up top!'

I was livid and climbed onto the roof of the turret. The curly wire attached to my headset hung like an umbilical cord, snaking away into the open hatch.

'Oy you bastards! We're bloody UNPROFOR! Stop that shooting at once!'

The strange language, the word UNPROFOR and my 'how we won the Empire' voice brought them to their senses. A few stood warily up.

'Put those weapons down at once! Who the hell do you think you are?'

I shouted at them and they calmed down. It was like saying 'shut the fuck up' at meetings. They hadn't a clue what I'd said but the cross tone was evident. I wondered how often similar words had been shouted by men in scarlet tunics to tribesmen in the African bush.

Within minutes we were chatting away. I jumped down and Dobby joined me. I handed out a packet of Silk Cut and winced as they broke the filters off before inhaling deeply on the smoke. No wonder they all died young.

I surveyed the damage. The bullets had barely marked the thick steel of the engine louvres. However, the ball-bearings had punched a perfect pattern of dents over the front-left Chobham outer plate. None had pierced the mild steel but the pattern perfectly took in the driver's hatch, which was covered in scoring. I banged on it and Tookey emerged, blinking like a mole, into the gloomy light. He nearly fainted when he saw how close he'd come to a face-full of shrapnel. The driver is the most important member of the crew. Without him the wagon goes nowhere. I thanked God that I practised what I preached: 'When in doubt, always close the driver down.'

The BiH told me they thought we were an HVO tank!

'Aw come on boys! When was the last time you saw a tank up here, and a white one at that?'

They all looked at the ground and shuffled from foot to foot. Bloody Bosnians were incapable of telling the truth. Why they just couldn't say 'We didn't know what to do so we fired just in case.'

We chatted away and they were the most friendly BiH I'd seen in a while. They were from the local area and were militiamen holding a section of the line. It was unlikely that any further attacks would take place until they were relieved by outside troops. At least that was positive information to report to Milinfo.

We couldn't turn back and the damage seemed superficial so we

carried on towards Duboko. The track narrowed even more as we
started to descend and we were forced to nudge several trees out of
the way. They generally shifted with a sighing and tearing of roots
but the odd stubborn one required a sharp push with the centre of
the glacis. Soon all four deflector plates were torn off. The 432s,
being narrower, were making light going of what was most definitely not a Warrior route. I'd no sooner decided to designate this area
as a 432 or Scimitar-only zone when there was a loud bang and the
right rear-idler sheered off. The massive wheel flew several metres
into the air and went rolling down the hill.

'Bloody Hell!'

We stopped. Well we had to as the right track sagged and started
to fold up. I jumped down and examined yet more damage. The idler
had broken off at the axle and must've been under terrific strain. An
Eight Platoon lad scampered away to retrieve it and returned, red-
faced, reporting that he couldn't lift it. Dobby lumbered away and
returned, puffing and panting, carrying the immense wheel like a
baby. With a clang, he dumped it in the rear, on top of the deflector
plates. This was serious and recovery would take hours.

Sergeant Pratt arrived and I wickedly said:

'Over to you, Silver Bullet! You REME. Wagon broken. You fix!'

It was a challenge and he rose to the occasion.

'No problem boss. We'll half-track it!'

I posted sentries and, three hours later, we'd broken the track and
removed several links. The track was dragged over the sixth road-
wheel and reconnected. This was no mean feat in the narrow confines of the wood, but with enough soldiers most things are possible.
We were back in business.

The Warrior wasn't exactly manoeuvrable but could still steer,
after a fashion. There was nowhere to pass so we still had to lead.
Dobby walked in front, guiding Tookey, and I walked further in
front to spot any potential hazards. All was going well until the sky
darkened and the heavens opened in monsoon-like rain. Within
minutes I was soaked and, by the time I reached the Warrior I was
so wet it was hardly worth putting my Gore-Tex jacket on.

The track was awash as the floodwater cascaded down from the
hills and was soon several centimetres deep, resembling a fast-flow-
ing stream. 0B started to slither and slide and cannoned off several
trees. One of the Chobham boxes was ripped open and I was disappointed to see that the fabled armour inside didn't glow, like

Kryptonite. Tookey fought the steering to keep the wagon on a straight path and we slowly made our way down the hill.

Eventually, the track widened and then emerged from the forest into the fields above Duboko. Five hours after we lost the idler, we reached Route Diamond. We increased speed to thirty kilometres an hour and wobbled and rattled our way towards home. The track was far too slick as it had been impossible to remove the correct number of links. We had to, therefore, turn very gently to avoid throwing the track off and it clanked and banged whenever we cornered.

Just short of the Novi Travnik T-junction, as I was thinking we'd make supper, I noticed a pungent burning smell, like hot oil. Moments later, smoke started to pour from the front-left of the Warrior and there was a terrible rasping and grinding sound. We stopped and Tookey climbed out and stood, shivering in the rain like a wet puppy. The smoke was coming from the front-left road-wheel that was so hot the raindrops immediately evaporated with a hiss as they touched. I couldn't imagine why the wheel had seized until Dobby noticed the spyglass. The centre of the hub is fitted with a small window, a couple of centimetres in diameter. This enables the hub oil to be checked without removing the filler plug. One of the ball-bearings had smashed the glass and all the oil had gradually been flung out by the centrifugal force. It was a chance-in-a million hit.

I asked Dobby what would happen if we carried on and he shrugged and said:

'The wheel's knackered anyway, so we may as well.' So, on we went with stinking smoke pouring from the red-hot bearing until we reached the garage.

Our arrival caused a crowd of soldiers to congregate. The Warrior looked a mess. All four deflector plates had gone, together with two top plates. Leafy branches stuck out from every crevice. The right-side was missing the idler and the left was pockmarked and dented. Staff Mackareth arrived and surveyed the scene.

'We'll have her back on the road this evening!'

The garage cookhouse provided us with scoff and we worked through the night on the wagon.

I was sure there'd be trouble for getting Claymored for a second time. Unfortunately, the front line was a dangerous place. The troops there were on edge and inclined to shoot first and ask questions later. The mines were laid out to stop the enemy from coming

up the very tracks we were taking. I could see why we were constantly sent up to the lines to collect information to give Milinfo a
full picture of the area. However, I wasn't sure it was worth the obvious danger.

As I mused over this, I could see a major flaw in my character
developing. I couldn't say no to a task. No matter how hard it was, I
was determined not to back down from it and would go to any
lengths to achieve my mission. Today's activities and the brush with
the mujahideen were examples of taking excessive risks to get the
job done.

This would've been an admirable quality if we were at war. In the
Second World War Bomber Command I would have been called a
press-on type. However, this wasn't our war and the tasks, in most
cases, weren't worth the risks. I had to try to assess when a job was
worth risking lives for and I would put the Guca Gora evacuation in
that category. Equally, I had to assess when it wasn't and today was
such a case.

I tried to take all the risks myself but that was impossible when
you command a vehicle with several other people in it. The risk is,
inevitably spread around the crew. It was a measure of the champ-
ion team I had that they never complained or baulked at anything I
asked them to do.

I decided to talk to Richard about the tasks we were getting. In
the meantime, I resolved to try to steer the lads, and myself, away
from taking too many unnecessary risks. Nevertheless, that didn't
affect what the Colonel was going to say to me. What did, however,
was the fact that the boss, himself, ran over a mine.

Earlier in the day, he'd driven up to Zepce to try to negotiate the
release of some UNMOs trapped in the town. On the way, he'd
crossed some rubble, which had been strewn over the road, and det-
onated an anti-tank mine. Kate Adie was reporting on the episode
and the explosion was shown on the news. Mercifully, no one was
hurt although the Warrior was immobilized. That's what you get
when you have the 'Angel of Death' accompanying you!

Detonating someone else's mine cannot be simply dismissed as
carelessness. It could happen to any of us.

A couple of days later, I patrolled up to the villages around
Pokrajcici. I was determined to leave it a few more days before I
returned to speak to Drago and his commander. We noticed a bear
in a field, chained to a post. This was Juti's territory and, apparent-

ly, he used to wrestle with the animal. My mind was working over-time. This could be a way to rival the Cheshires great bear-rescue operation and reap some good publicity. I met a couple of women who said they were refugees from Brajkovici. After chatting for a while I asked them:

'Do you think it would be a good idea if we organized the removal of this bear and its evacuation to a zoo in Split?'

'I think it would be far better if you concentrated on feeding people instead of worrying about a bear!'

Of course, she was right. How crass to worry about an animal, for the sake of a bit of publicity, when people needed help all around me. It put the earlier bear-rescue into context and sowed it up for what it was, a cheap publicity stunt.

On 1 July, Milinfo asked me to find out who controlled Gornji Pecine now. As I was one of the few who'd been there I set off, in company with D11. John's platoon had joined us from Tuzla a few days earlier. They had had a great time and had to get used to being back in the fold. My company group now consisted of 14 Warriors, four Scimitars, six 432s and the Spartan and the three REME variants. All in all I had well over 150 men under command.

James allocated me David Chater's ITN team and Chris Bellamy, a reporter for the *Independent*. The village was seemingly deserted. Although the church was still intact, the priest's house had been totally ransacked. This was by far the biggest, and best-furnished, around and reflected the power and status of the Catholic Church in Croat villages.

A crowd of my favourite BiH soldiers from Seven Brigade appeared. One of them said he was going to burn the church in retaliation for Ahmici and Bandol. There was no way of telling whether he meant it or not so I called the ops room and obtained permission to remove as many artefacts as possible.

We were filmed loading statues and crosses into D11 and then all the priest's robes. They were quite garish but, nevertheless, works of art. Several had hand-painted panels depicting scenes from the Bible and others were intricately embroidered. We shoved them unceremoniously under the seats.

As we were loading the wagon, Dobby noticed an old woman looking down at us from the yard of a house. She was, I guessed, in her late seventies and tiny and frail. She wore a black shawl over her head and a long grey skirt. Her feet were stuffed into shoes that looked like Wellingtons with the tops cut off. When she talked, she exposed a mouth full of rotten teeth. They were almost two centimetres long where the gums had decayed away. Bosnia had to be the country with the worst record for dental hygiene in the whole of the West. She said her name was Ana Ghavric. I was to see a great deal of this funny little woman over the coming months. She was accompanied by her cousin, Anto Marjanovic. He was even older, possibly in his eighties. He wore a little Tyrolean hat with a faded red feather on one side. His shirt, waistcoat and trousers were varying shades of grey and he wore the same type of rubber shoe. His face was covered in snowy white stubble but his eyes were sparkling and bright.

They'd lived in the village all their lives and were too frail to follow the others when they fled. They were determined to live out the last of their days in their homes. That wouldn't be too long judging by the fact the BiH had stolen most of their food. They didn't want to come with me and I doubted if they'd last long in the refugee centre anyway. They were probably best off staying put, if they could feed themselves.

I promised to return and bring them some food and they gave me a 'I bet you don't' look.

We dropped the artefacts off in Novi Travnik and were told they would end up in the church at Rankovici. I hadn't been there and decided to visit it some time. Chater's report about us made the news again. No wonder he liked coming out with us.

Next day, we had our first war-wound in the Company. I'd patrolled right into the hills above Pecine. The scenery was almost alpine and I half-expected Steve McQueen to ride over on his way to try to escape over the wire. On the way back, as we transited Novi Travnik, a frantic message from D13 halted me.

'Stop now! We've been hit!'

0B slewed to a halt and I was out of the turret like a greyhound from the trap. Back at the other Warrior, the Seven Platoon boys were crowding around the rear. They parted as I approached and I retched at a rancid smell, like a public toilet.

Private Savage was nursing one arm and covered in foul-smelling liquid. Some kid had thrown a bottle of urine at the Warrior. It hit the top of the crew compartment and shattered, spraying the stuff over poor Savage. He was only slightly cut but was, understandably disgusted. We whipped him straight back for a tetanus jab.

The next day, Saturday 3 July, was the last day of a fairly quiet ops week. However, I knew before we set off that this was not going to be a quiet day. James saw me as I was booking out for a routine convoy escort.

'Hello Vaughan! How are you?'

My hackles raised. Beware P Info men bearing smiles!

'Fine thanks, but I've a feeling I soon won't be!'

'Oh, it's not bad news. I just want you to take Kate Adie with you!'

'Thanks a bunch mate! I'm glad I took out that extra life insurance!'

Kate had a reputation for making things happen. She had a nose for a story and was always in the thick of things.

'Come on! It'll be all right!'

'So you say! What do you think's going to happen when you put two trouble-magnets together? What's the boss going to say?'

'I tell you what. I'll come with you myself. That'll keep you out of trouble!'

'Cheers mate! But I'd still rather take Lucrezia Borgia!'

By now, the press were starting to venture out in their armoured Land Rovers. Frankly, I preferred it when we had them in the wagons as at least I knew where they were. We were told to ignore the press wagon and patrol normally as if it wasn't there. This was pie in the sky. If you had trouble at a checkpoint you could never forget the vulnerable vehicle behind you. You could drive across country with all guns blazing but the press would cop the lot. They may be old hacks but they were still Brits.

I shook hands with Kate and she gripped my hand like a bullmastiff. I then briefed her on the task and she eyed me with the critical look of the staff college directing staff. She'd been there and done it all before.

We set off with eleven trucks to Zenica, via the mountain road. After dropping them off at the warehouse I was told to take a look at an HGV blocking the road near the Busovaca T-junction.

Sure enough, there was an articulated lorry jack-knifed across the road. The wheels were surrounded by mines with the cab festooned with various wires and probably booby-trapped. The aim of the barrier was to stop aid reaching Muslim Zenica. This really was a futile gesture as we'd just proved that aid could still get through to the city.

None the less, we weren't going to get through so I decided to try to bypass it by using the small track through Jelinak and Putis. Kate liked this idea. Probably because this had been where Bob Stewart had his famous 'contact'.

We turned up the narrow track but had only gone a few hundred metres when we came across a white Lada car blocking the track. Its wheels were off so it clearly wasn't someone's pride and joy. I was about to run straight over it when I remembered the bloody Land Rover. We would have to try to shift the car by hand.

We dismounted and were about to heave the car out of the way when the BiH arrived in force.

'Bugger it!'

If we'd been on our own we'd have been over the barrier and past them before they knew we were there. The soldiers formed a line across the track in a gesture that said, You will not pass!

Their commander approached and I recognized him from weeks before. He was still wearing an ill-fitting East German helmet and scruffy brown vest.

'You may not proceed without papers.'

'I am here to help you. I must get back to Vitez to report the barrier so we can have it removed. When we do that, more aid will reach Zenica.'

'That may be so but you still cannot pass.'

Here we go again. More hours of fruitless negotiation under the baking sun.

'Why will you not let ...'

Crack!

I was interrupted by a high-velocity shot from somewhere to my left. The round struck a wall to my right and a puff of masonry dust floated away on the slight breeze. The BiH had all taken cover in a ditch and the film crew were crouched beside the Warrior. I had the reactions of a paralytic sloth and just stood there, rooted to the spot.

'As I was saying. Why will you not let us pass?'

'We cannot negotiate while we are under fire. Turn back before you are killed.'

'Certainly not! Come and talk to me and stop skulking in that ditch!'

The Commander started to raise himself up to join me when another shot was fired. This one was really close and scythed through an overhanging tree. A twig fell at my feet and I looked up and saw the freshly broken end a few centimetres above my head.

That was bloody close.

In front of me, the Commander was doing an impression of a mole, making sweeping motions with his arms trying to pile earth around him. To my left, were the Croat trenches about 400 metres away. The sniper was either hopeless, in which case he'd probably hit me eventually, or bloody good, in which case he'd have hit me already if he wanted to. I plumped for the latter.

'Now listen here! I'm not moving from this road until you've moved that car!'

'You are mad! He'll kill you!'

It was then that I noticed the interpreter had forgotten her flak jacket. She stood shaking with fear and trying to make herself as small as possible. Without thinking, I took my own body armour off and gave it to her. It was a reflex action, like opening a door for a lady. I heard Dobby mutter:

'You're soddin' mad!'

The next round hit the ground at my feet scoring a white track across the tarmac. I placed one foot forward and the strike mark was less than a boot length in front of me. This guy was toying with me like a cat with a mouse. The sweat was trickling down my back but I was, mercifully, free from the paralysing fear I'd experienced early in the tour. It wasn't bravery. I was simply getting too used to the danger and thinking, 'it won't happen to me!'

At least I had the Warrior to call on. The sniper probably couldn't see it through the trees. The sensible thing to do would've been to call it forward, locate the firing point, and ventilate the bastard. However, I felt I had a point to prove. I wasn't going to let this git humiliate the UN. If he wanted Latin bravado then two could play at that. I was endangering no one but myself so I decided to stick it out. It was like a game of Russian roulette, except I wasn't pulling the trigger.

Moving to the Lada, I sat on the bonnet, attempting to look as nonchalant as possible, in full view of the sniper. I was trying to negotiate with the supine figure of the Commander, in my best British voice, when the sniper fired his fourth shot. This was a belter, and the side window of the driver's door shattered. As I was leaning against the windscreen, this was centimetres from my back. My legs started to tremble as I imagined life in a wheelchair. That seemed far worse than a clean shot to the head.

I was about to bottle out as my nerves were shot to pieces. My brain said to me move now when some stupid, stubborn, streak made me change my mind. I'd already started to shift off the car and didn't want the lads to see I'd almost funked it. To hide this, I used the shift to reach into my breast pocket for my cigarettes.

Lighting one, with trembling fingers, I inhaled deeply before starting to talk to the Commander again. By this time, a crowd of about thirty BiH had gathered to watch the mad Englishman get himself killed. They squatted behind the safety of the wall and eyed me like a man in the tumbrel on his way to the guillotine.

The cigarette was between my lips when he fired again. I felt the round pass me at face level. The rush of air and the supersonic crack as it passed me were so close that the ash fell off the burning end. The cocky git couldn't resist it and had tried to shoot the cigarette out of my mouth! This was going too far. I stood up and bowed theatrically to the sniper. There was a slight stir from the trench and a man stood up. He was holding an outrageously long rifle and waved at me with his free hand.

Quickly, I beckoned the Warrior forward and there was a snort of exhaust as Tookey gunned the engine. 0B shot forward and Phil traversed left on the move. The sniper stared for a second and then saw the turret. He dropped the rifle into the trench and sprinted for the shelter of a building. Within seconds, he was gone. I knew Phil wouldn't fire without an order from me. Moving the Warrior had been the only way I could think of to get one-up on the Croat. It was highly dangerous and I was as pathetic as he for giving in to the urge to challenge the Latin ego. True, the adrenalin rush was exhilarating, but one that I wasn't sure I wanted to experience again. Helmet man looked at me and said:

'You are very brave!'

'No! I am very stupid!'

The whole incident definitely was stupid. I'd risked my life several times before, but always with an aim in sight. The aim of helping people. This was different. I was risking my life to prove a point. It was in no way a noble gesture, though the media coverage built it up as such. It was a pointless, childish game in a playground where it was very easy to get hurt.

I'd calmed down by lunch time and was looking forward to a quiet afternoon. I had just the sort of easy task that would give us all a good feeling, without any risk. I was going back to Gornji Pecine with a promise to keep.

After lunch I was sitting in the sun, when Dobrila walked over. We chatted for a while and she told me she was looking forward to spending her leave with her parents in Novi Travnik. I said I'd take her there if she needed a lift. I picked up a stone and was idly toying with it. She stood up to go and I absent-mindedly pocketed the stone.

Kate Adie was still with us. Did she ever give up? James had, wisely, decided to sit this one out and sent the new boy instead. Paul Sykes was a civilian working in the P Info world. About my height, with fair, curly hair and glasses, he looked like a teacher who'd inadvertently strayed into the war zone. He'd recently arrived to boost the team of minders.

I was warned of shelling in Novi Travnik and said I'd pull out if things were too hot. In the event, we arrived just after the bombardment, probably from the BiH. Their offensive had started again with the aim of driving the Croats from the town. This was a harder nut to crack than the isolated villages of the Bila Valley and the front line appeared to run through the centre of town. Novi is Serbo-Croat for new and the place was just that. The town was a jungle of colourless high-rises with none of the character of its namesake. There was sporadic small-arms fire but none of it directed at us.

As we clattered along the deserted streets we passed a four-storey apartment block that had obviously been recently shelled. The roof was ablaze but there was no sign of anyone about. It wasn't our problem, and soon we were into the suburbs. We trundled by the ammunition factory, firmly in BiH hands and rumoured to be recommencing production. Under Tito, most towns had an ammunition factory on the outskirts. It was part of his policy of creating a state that was a 'prickly hedgehog' with each region being self-contained. He wanted to ensure that his country was never again overrun in a lightning campaign. With each region able to fend for itself, he hoped there would be no need for a costly partisan campaign. His policy had, by chance, nicely given both Muslims and Croats the ability to manufacture their own ammunition in our little patch. No wonder the BiH set so much store by capturing the Vitez factory.

Presently, the suburbs gave way to the tranquillity of the countryside and we arrived at Pecine without incident. The old folks were there and seemed amazed to see us. My crew had been on the scrounge and had rustled up a box of food at short notice. They nicked a couple of loaves from the cookhouse and the rest was the contents of a few packed lunches. I wasn't sure if old people could live on Kit-Kats for long and decided to speak to the ration sergeant to provide something more substantial.

Kate filmed the people while they told me they'd been well treated by the BiH. They also told me there was another old couple in a nearby village who were refusing to move. Having heard this news, I felt morally obliged to try to find them, perhaps another day. We walked back to the wagons and Kate stopped me.

'Can we take a look; at that burning apartment block?'

'No! It's not on our tasking!'

'Just a little look?'

'No! If I investigated every burning house I'd never do anything else!'

'Just a quick look; we won't get out. I just need it for some library footage.'

'Oh all right then!'

I should've known better. No journalist of the calibre of Kate Adie spends their time wandering around collecting library footage. I should have just said no but there didn't seem any harm in it. Thanks to her persistence, we were about to embark on yet another news-making operation.

We arrived on the outskirts of the town and I stopped to listen.

There were a few shots but, if anything, the place was quieter than before. A thick pall of greasy, black smoke hung over the rooftops. We stopped on the main road opposite the apartment and I was shocked at the transformation. We'd only been away ninety minutes or so and the place was almost totally gutted. The roof had gone, the top two floors were well ablaze and the first floor was on fire in several places. Judging by the smoke billowing from some of the ground-floor windows it would be only a matter of minutes before the whole place was an inferno. I assumed the cameraman was taking his precious pictures and almost didn't notice the frantic signals from a window. I looked again and there she was. A woman waving a tea towel at us and, behind her, another beckoning us to come to her.

I didn't think it was an invitation for coffee but I couldn't figure why they'd stayed there. They were about to be burned to a frazzle. After my luck with burning buildings I wasn't keen on wandering into this one but I felt I had to at least warn them of the impending danger. There was a small ditch between us and the building. Little trouble for the Warrior but the Rover wouldn't make it. At least that was Kate out of my hair. We turned off the road, went down the bank, over the ditch and drove the last fifty metres across the courtyard of the block. As soon as we left the road, the firing increased, not at us, but all around us.

We halted outside and I jumped down. A smoke-blackened, and very frightened face appeared in the doorway and the woman gestured at me to come inside. As I walked towards the doorway, there was a shot, which I hardly noticed above all the others, and a lump of rendering flew off from near the doorway. The woman ducked out of sight. I noticed there were several similar splat marks around the entrance. No wonder they hadn't moved, they were pinned down. I entered the building and immediately smelled the same, throat-stinging, smoke I'd experienced over the road from camp. A shadowy figure emerged from the gloom and I jumped with the shock. More people appeared and the story began to emerge. The place had been hit and, every time they tried to flee, snipers fired on them.

'Why not go out the back!'

'Because there are snipers there too!'

'Hang on a minute! There can't be snipers shooting at you from both ends of town!'

'We are right on the ethnic divide. There are Muslims and Croats in here!'

Ah! This was, indeed, complicated. The gunmen didn't know who was who so they fired at anyone trying to leave, just in case. This could only happen in Bosnia.

'If I take you. How far do you need to go to be safe?'

'Only a few streets!'

'OK! I'll organize something!'

These people were in imminent danger and I was going to move them. I went to the door to get Phil to reverse up to us. It was then that I noticed the BBC crew sprinting across the waste ground. For a middle-aged lady, Kate showed a remarkable turn of speed. The sound recordist wasn't far behind. Not so the cameraman, who was burdened with his heavy equipment. He lagged well to the rear and a couple of shots were fired at him. This spurred him on and he arrived, his chest heaving and wires dangling about him. He scowled at the ace reporter and set about preparing his camera.

The Muslims had further to go so I decided to take them first. I told them to grab what they could but they fannied about for sever-

al minutes. I could hear the floors collapsing above. One particularly loud crash sent a plume of smoke sweeping down the passageway
from some unseen breach of the ceiling.

'Move now!'

I was about to yell, 'For fuck's sake move now' but, at the last
minute noticed the camera. Thankfully, I avoided adding the F
word to my earlier 'bastard' on the national news. The CO would be
proud of me!

Phil had been unable to get too close to the door because of a low
wall, leaving a gap of about ten metres between us and the Warrior.
This would be the risky bit. Tookey was closed down and Ricky
Holtom was out the top with his rifle trained on the nearest block of
flats. All the surrounding blocks were bigger than ours and made
ideal vantage points from which to fire on us. The only consolation
was that none of the gunmen could be too bold due to the risk from
the other side's snipers.

The Muslims, three women and a man, refused to cross the gap.
There was a crash from inside and flames started to appear from the
end ground-floor flat. There wasn't much time. I jogged into the gap
and began to walk up and down, trying not to look scared. The little stone somehow appeared in my hand and I started to throw it
from palm to palm in what I hoped was a confidence-inspiring manner. Dobby joined me and together we paced up and down the danger gap while Paul hustled the four across it. He was extremely
brave, especially as he was unarmed and wearing a brand new, and
very bright blue, flak vest.

The final Muslim was a smartly-dressed woman in her thirties,
leading, of all things, an Afghan hound! As if on cue, the firing
increased as both sides realized what we were doing and rounds
started to ricochet off the tarmac. However, it was impossible to
locate any of the firing points as the sound of the shots was magni-
fied by the walls of the tall buildings. The dog, not surprisingly, was
panicking. No wonder you're supposed to keep them indoors on Guy
Fawkes' night. It flatly refused to jump into the Warrior. Meanwhile,
the woman, from the safety of the interior, was tugging at a lead that
was threatening to snap at any moment. Suddenly the animal gave a
yelp as it was punted into the back on the end of one of Dobby's size
elevens!

The doors were closed and we drove for ten streets or so into a
quiet, leafy suburb where we decanted the Muslims. They were all

thanks except for the young woman who spat:

'Leave the Croats to die!'

I was tempted to turn the Afghan into a track-pad but there was no time to marvel at the niceties of Bosnian people.

It was the Croats' turn now. Three middle-aged women. We reversed as far as we could. Phil was whipping the turret this way and that, the power-traverse working overtime. With all the zipping from side to side, I totally cocked-up the reversing and we ended up about twenty metres from the door. I jumped down and began the stone-chucking routine again. The first two women made a dash for it and one of them cried 'Ay!' as she cracked her shins on the hard metal of the door rim. I'd never realized there could be a Bosnian word for ouch!

Holtom bundled her in, aided by Paul. The last woman was shaking with fright; I knew how she felt. She was about to make the run for safety when the gunmen really got stroppy. There was slightly less fire as the HVO must've sussed we'd rescued the other lot first. The BiH made up for it, however, and seemed determined to stop the last three getting away.

The firing intensified to a deafening crescendo and rounds hit the building. To cap it all, several bits of wall fell inwards, sending sparks flying into the interior of the block. The woman flipped and started to run into the open. Resolutely refusing to let go of a carpet bag, she waddled across the concrete, heading for the nearest building. Before I could even think about acting, Dobby was after her. I could almost feel the ground vibrating as he pounded across the yard.

He caught her as the BiH turned her into 'duty target'. Rounds splattered all around and it seemed impossible that she wouldn't be hit. Dobby placed his bulk between her and the gunmen, cocking his weapon as he ran. The firing slackened under his threat of retaliation and the two lumbered for the safety of the corner of the building. Dobby placed his free arm around the woman and propelled her flagging legs onwards. In the last few moments, the gunmen seemed to realize they were about to be robbed of their prey and commenced rapid fire. Rounds started to hit the wall around them and then they were safe. Looking over, there were so many strike marks on the wall it seemed a miracle that neither was hit. If life was a cartoon, there would've been a Dobby-shaped clear patch of wall amid the pockmarks.

The BiH gunmen then turned their attention back to the build-ing. I was so busy gawping after Dobby that I didn't notice the first rounds falling around me. It was only when a couple struck the con-crete skidding into the running-gear of OB with a metallic thunk, that I realized we were being targeted. Another then hit the concrete a metre to my left, and several slammed into the wall. This had to be defused quickly and there was no time for me to climb in. I yelled to Phil to take them away and the Warrior roared off in the direction of the town centre.

After what seemed an eternity, OB returned. Kate seemed deter-mined to get herself killed and sprinted off in the direction of the Rover. Her crew hesitated, then dutifully followed. There was no time to stop them so I shouted to Phil to put the Warrior between them and the BiH flats, then Paul and I doubled after them. I thought that after they'd deliberately targeted a UN soldier, we would be fair game. However, the Warrior proved to be a great deter-rent and there was only sporadic fire.

The ditch proved to be a little harder to cross going the other way and Phil had to line the wagon up carefully. This gave the BBC crew time to spring up the bank, in the open again, to the Rover. Hurriedly, the two blokes dived into the back and slammed the doors. Meanwhile, the spare crewman was in the driving seat ready for a quick getaway with the passenger door open for Kate. I then witnessed an extraordinary incident.

The reporter ran straight to the driver's door and yanked it open. I clearly heard the yelled conversation:

'Move over!'

'No! I'll drive! Get in the other side!'

'I said move over!'

'No!'

'Look, I'm in charge and I'll drive. Move over now!'

This last was emphasized with a shove, and the poor bloke, at last, slid over. Rounds were continuing to fall as the reporter's pert back-side finally disappeared into the cab! It was serious teddy-in-the-corner time.

As we rounded the block, and out of sight of the front line, the firing was still going on. I glanced back and glimpsed one gunman raise himself over the balcony of the tenth or so floor of a block of flats and loose off several wild shots. On the balcony of the floor above, a woman was hanging out her washing!

We met up with Dobby, who was sitting on the kerb, smoking. His face was red from the exertion of having to run for the second time during the tour. His face was impassive and there was no clue to his outstanding deed. Without a word, he ground out the butt and joined us.

The day received coverage from both BBC and ITV, who used the pooled film. David Chater put together a piece about it which captured the sound and atmosphere of the action in Novi Travnik well. It clearly showed me chucking the stone about with the caption 'Major Vaughan Kent-Payne coolly directs the operation under fire'. This was all rather flattering, if a long way from the truth. The incident had bordered on the too risky category. Nevertheless, we got away with it and saved seven people's lives. They really owed their salvation to Kate Adie and her library pictures.

The old man saw the ITN coverage of the day and rounded on me:

'How dare you go out on patrol without a flak jacket?'

'I didn't, sir. I took it off to give to the interpreter when we were fired at. If you look at the clip again, you'll see that they've used bits out of sequence. I go from wearing the flak vest, to not wearing it, to then wearing it again.'

'Hm. Be that as it may. You shouldn't take risks. I can't afford to lose a company commander.'

'But the civilians would've died!'

'I don't care, your life is more important.'

'Well, I'm very flattered, sir, but I don't think one human life is worth more than any other!'

Whoops! Me and my big gob!

'Why do you have to question everything I say? I'm telling you, stop taking risks!'

The coverage was excellent PR for the battalion, and, indeed the Army. It showed soldiers helping people in trying and dangerous circumstances, all in the best traditions of the British Army and of the United Nations. However, I was sick of all this angst over the media reporting of my actions. Initially, it was fun and, to be honest, good for the ego. However, when I had the Colonel constantly studying the results, it had reached the stage where I may as well take him along on each patrol. This had to stop and I went to see James:

'That's it. I'm refusing to take the press out again!'

'Come on Vaughan, you can't do that!'

'You're supposed to cover my back. Remember, I only take the press if you task them to me in the first place. Now the Colonel's saying I'm in the spotlight too much. If you won't act then I will!'

'But they ask to go with you because you're good for stories!'

'Maybe so, but they can concentrate on someone else now. If you allocate me any more press, I'm turning right back to camp!'

James knew there was nothing he could do, and that was the end of my media career. I remained friendly with several of the press but never took them on an operational patrol again.

I hoped for a quiet week on guard as I was worn out after the last few hectic weeks. The crew was suffering as well and we all had bags under our eyes, like Marty Feldman. The track mileage records for each vehicle showed that we'd covered more kilometres than any other Warrior at Vitez.

At twenty to nine on the evening of 5 July I was called to the captain's house. As guard company commander, I attended any incident. It surely couldn't be that serious, not at the captain's house.

I arrived just as the ambulance was leaving the school, its klaxon blaring. Fearing the worst, I rushed inside to find Cameron Kiggel. Kidge looked towards the sitting room and shook his head. I stepped inside, fearing the worst.

Dobrila lay on the floor attended by one of the MST officers. She was wearing a startlingly white jumper and white trousers. Her long hair spread around her but even it couldn't hide the pool of blood. I knelt down. Her brown eyes were wide open and staring. Her legs moved slightly and I looked at the nurse. The girl had tears in her eyes and she, too, shook her head. I took Dobrila's hand, which was fluttering lightly, and she gave one last gasp and lay still. I'd never actually seen anyone die before and never wanted to again. It wasn't quick, like in the movies, and it certainly wasn't dignified. She was already dead when I walked in but it took her body a while to catch up with the fact. The appearance of life was like the little glow that remains in a television set even after the power has been switched off. Just an illusion and nothing more.

Mercifully, she looked at peace, and relaxed. The round had entered and exited behind her ears and the wounds were covered by her hair. It was such a waste of a young life. The rest of the MST crew arrived and started to bandage her head. They tried, without success, to revive her in the hospital. I looked around and worked out where she'd been standing, next to the open french doors. The round had passed through her, the inner door, and through the door of a room across the corridor. The bullet was imbedded in the wall above Phil's bed. I prised the copper-jacketed 7.62 mm round out and pocketed it. It was easy to line the two holes up and they pointed to the roof of a wooden shed over the road. I'd seen HVO gunmen use this position before.

The lump in my throat was replaced by a cold, but strangely controlled, rage. Totally unlike my normal red-mist. The Croats had gone too far this time. I jogged down to the ops room where I briefed David.

'I'm going to patrol across the road and quieten things down.'

He started to say something and then changed his mind.

Out on the tank park, John Reeve was ready to go.

'Step aside John, I'll take the patrol out.'

'But I'm the QRF Commander!'

'Yes I know but I don't want you involved!'

I briefed the crew and jumped in. The light was fading as we roared the short distance across the road. The first port of call was the firing point. It was too much to hope the bastard would still be there. We hit the shed a glancing blow, knocking one wall clean away and sending the whole structure crashing to the ground. The time was six minutes to nine.

Target number two was a line of three new bunkers that overlooked the mess. These collapsed under our weight and we moved on to a couple of trenches. Militiamen were still in these. The three saw us coming and stood rooted to the spot. At the last moment, they realized we weren't going to stop and abandoned their weapons and fled. We halted over the first trench and neutral-turned to the left, then back the other way. The sandy soil collapsed inwards filling the trench in. The other Warrior was about to do the same but I called it to a halt. I'd carry the can for this myself.

We flattened the second trench and I spied a Croat running into a hut.

'Go! Go! Go!' I screamed.

Private Bowness, the driver, shouted:

'It's pay-back time!'

We bore down on the shed and the door opened as we approached. The HVO man raised his rifle and then figured an AK probably wasn't going to stop us. He flung himself to one side as we rolled straight through the hut, without checking our headlong rush. The Warrior turned into a mobile shed as we were covered with plywood panels.

'Emergency stop now!' I shouted.

We careered to a halt, rocking forward on the springs, and half a ton of matchwood flew forward and onto the dirt.

We spent the next ten minutes chasing every HVO we saw into cover. Just for good measure, I found the recently-repaired telegraph pole and trashed it again. Not a shot was fired at us. It was as if the Croats knew we were itching for the chance to kill them. As the light faded, so did my anger, and we headed back into camp, leaving behind several very shell-shocked HVO. I wondered if I should just go and pack now. The boss was sure to sack me.

I thought I may as well face the music.

The CO was in Richard's office. I tossed the bullet onto the desk.

'What have you been up to?'

'As I briefed the ops room, patrolling the area to quieten things down.'

'And what did that entail?'

'Oh you know, the normal, crushing a few trenches, that sort of thing!'

'Look, this isn't funny!'

'No and neither's the death of your interpreter!'

'We're not here for revenge!'

'No but we are here to do a job and we can't when we're constantly sniped-at by the HVO!'

'Do you realize what the consequences of your actions will be regarding our relations with the HVO?'

'Yes I do. I don't think they'll fire into camp for a long time. They've never seen gratuitous violence from us before; it's what they understand!'

'How the hell would you know?'

'Because I deal with these thugs every day!'

'Go away while I decide what to do with you!'

I wondered when he'd sack me and was surprised to find I didn't care.

I knew I'd really annoyed him this time. Aggressive patrolling was definitely outside the UN mandate. However, every time I replayed the incident back in my mind, I knew I'd do the same again. The HVO in our area had to be taught that we wouldn't tolerate sniping, by means of a lesson they would understand. It was outside the remit of UNPROFOR but, what the hell! I mused on the fact that for me the only meaning of the word career ... would be a country divided by the 38th parallel! I was likely to remain a Major longer than Norma!

Funnily enough, the HVO complaint was half-hearted and, as usual, they tried to blame the BiH. It turned out to be more than two months before they fired into camp again.

Next morning I went to see Richard.

'Vaughan, I've got to tell you something.'

'Let me guess. The CO's really hacked off at me!'

'Yes. How did you know?'

'Oh, just an educated guess!'

'He's asked me to have a word with you.'

'Why doesn't he do it himself?'

'Because he knows you always argue with him, like last night.'

'Sorry! I really don't try to be difficult.'

'But you're not just bloody difficult, you're a loose cannon!'

Chapter 11
Hearts and Minds

The HVO was noticeably more subdued and shooting in the area tailed off to virtually nothing.

Fered threw a birthday party for Dalma. She was seventeen, going on thirty. Mrs Fered cooked lamb and her husband provided the beer. Our landlord certainly wasn't short of a bob or two. He made a hefty rent from our house and had a finger in most of the local pies. Under the house was a large garage and a small, frosted-glass window led onto the hallway. It was open one day and I couldn't resist a peek. The garage was piled high with electrical goods and dozens of cartons of cigarettes.

His wife charged a few marks to do our washing. It came back, ironed without a crease in sight and she even gave my battered old smock a new lease of life.

The Puppies received their puppies. Tom's lived in a run in his platoon lines and the other two were at the house. James Hurley was threatening to eat them. The fact he'd jumped out of bed and straight into a dog turd may have had something to do with it. The pups stayed for a few weeks before Diddly Fawcett, one of the Provost NCOs started being a little over zealous. He started quoting health regulations and they had to go. This was a bit much as soldiers adopt animals wherever they're stationed on ops. These dogs were a harmless distraction for the Subbies and were actually well looked after. However, the local wildlife had its revenge on Fawcett a few weeks later.

Meanwhile, overhead, Operation Deny Flight was in full swing. This US initiative was supposed to discourage Serb air attacks. Consequently, NATO aircraft constantly patrolled the clear blue skies looking for attacks that never came. They had the authority to shoot down any aircraft violating the no-fly zone.

However, the best entertainment during this period was watching the antics of the helicopter. The HVO arranged for regular flights by a helicopter from Croatia. For about a month the Mi 8 Hip flew in most afternoons. The first time, he came at night to prove the route. Next day he was more bold and flew over in broad daylight taking everyone, us, the F-15s and the BiH totally by surprise. He landed in the Stara Bila quarry, unloaded weapons and explosives and picked up casualties. It was great for the morale of the besieged Croats.

The day after, the BiH was waiting for him.

The Vitez pocket was around five kilometres wide in the area of the school. However, the pilot knew this, and flew accordingly. Sitting on the verandah, I heard the faint drone of the engines. Shielding my eyes from the strong sun, I spotted the Hip several thousand metres up. It hovered and then began a series of lazy circles, gradually losing height. This seemed to be inviting fire and I wondered what he was up to.

Sure enough, when the helicopter was about a thousand metres up, the firing started. A withering hail of a green tracer arced from both sides of the valley. Much of it headed straight towards the, seemingly vulnerable, aircraft. The Hip must surely be hit. However, the pilot had done his homework and all of it fell short. The tracer reached its farthest point and then burned out. I knew the rounds would continue for a while but there was no way of telling where they were going. What was clear, however, was that it was all dropping short. The boys were up on the roofs of the ISOs watching the spectacle when the overs from the far valley started hissing around like angry bees. They rushed for cover, rendering the urgent tannoy message redundant.

When the chopper was about five hundred metres up, the BiH fired an AT-4 Spigot anti-tank missile from Grbavica. The rocket launched with a bang and the trailing flare snaked away on its erratic path as the operator gathered it in his sight-picture. This had to be curtains for Charlie Croat. The missile straightened and streaked towards its victim then, at the last moment trailed away and fell to earth. A muffled explosion in the village marked the last resting place of the Spigot. With the missile having a maximum range of two kilometres, the pilot was either lucky, or bloody good. The machine dipped out of sight and we waited for it to refuel and take off again.

A couple of hours later, it emerged and the process was repeated in reverse. The BiH fired another missile, with the same result, and the Hip slowly spiralled skywards. The jets arrived, probably only after the pilots had eaten lunch, and swooped about the azure sky, dropping decoy flares.

This is it, I thought. Scratch one Hip!

None of the jets fired but continued to buzz the chopper, presumably trying to frighten the pilot to death. After a while, the Hip reached its maximum altitude and headed south. So much for the, much vaunted, no-fly zone.

This process was repeated over a dozen times until the flights suddenly ceased. I later learned the pilot had made enough danger money to retire on. We missed our regular visitor and the attendant display of the NATO Paper Tigers.

One of my lads, Private Handley from Nine Platoon, was baptized in St George's Roman Catholic church in Vitez. He was hoping to marry in a church back in the UK and wanted to be, as he put it, a real Christian.

Carson conducted the service assisted by the priest. He was certainly living up to his nickname of Carson the Parson. It was great to see one of the lads discovering religion and I know he put up with a lot of good-natured ribbing over it.

Stephen Lees was really coming along well. He was one of the youngest officers in the Army and, like me, had joined straight from school. I gripped him right at the start when he attended a Muslim feast. The local BiH let Stephen and his soldiers fire their weapons. I became the crusty old company commander with him and pointed out the dangers. What if one of the guys shot someone, or the weapon blew up? Stephen had slunk away with an everybody hates me look and I couldn't help remembering it was just the sort of thing I'd have done as a subby. Now, he was establishing an excellent rapport with his soldiers and many of the locals as well. One day, he transported a pregnant woman to hospital and, somewhere in Central Bosnia, there's now a little boy called Stephen.

Jason was doing a brilliant job and I trusted him implicitly. He was only the same age as the other Subbies but had grown in stature with the extra responsibility. He ran a tight ops room and was never afraid to bollock the platoon commanders if he thought they deserved it. His father was a brigadier and I could see Jason bettering that.

I returned to Pecine on what the boys were now calling the Crinkly Patrol.

The old couple had been moved by the BiH to a house in the centre of the village to protect them from bandits. They said they were being well cared for and, understandably, wouldn't hear a bad word said against their captors. The soldiers were friendly and said they shared their food with the old folks. Here was a dilemma. Ana and Anto still refused to move and I had no power to make them. I couldn't take them too much food as the soldiers would only steal it. Also, they might stop feeding them altogether, and rely on me to do it for them. The best solution would've been just to drive away and forget them, they would probably survive. But what if they didn't? It was a problem of conscience and I decided to keep it up for as long as I could.

I also found the other old people I'd been told about a few days before. The woman was working in a field and her white blouse caught my eye. We stopped and walked up to meet her. She was in her late seventies and dressed in traditional Croat costume. Her hair was covered by a black, brocaded, headdress and she wore an embroidered waistcoat and long, black, skirt. Soon, she was talking, nineteen to the dozen. Her sons lived in the village but had fled with the rest, and she showed us their ransacked houses.

Her husband was more than eighty and very frail. He wore a little Tommy Cooper fez and sported an immaculate white moustache. He'd been a partisan in the war and proudly showed me a faded photograph of him in uniform, holding a long rifle. They were spotlessly clean as was their tiny cottage. Their names were Ana and Ivo Lesic. They too were determined to stay there until they died. The band of crinklies was growing.

Things were hotting up around the Novi Travnik T-junction in the second week of July 1993. The BiH was trying to capture the road to cut Novi Travnik off from Vitez. Understandably, the HVO pulled out all the stops to prevent this.

Shelling during the bus attack had cratered the road and the Sappers were tasked to fill in the holes. They pitched up in two Spartans and started work. As the weather was its usual sunny self, they stripped off. The BiH then mistook them for an HVO work party and started machine-gunning them. They were pinned down and Sergeant White saved the situation. He was on tunnel duties and returned fire with his GPMG. This drew the BiH fire and the Sappers remounted and beat a hasty retreat. White's action was particularly praiseworthy as he had to stand up, out of the exposed cupola of the 432, to operate the GPMG. He stuck to his task with rounds falling all about him and effectively suppressed the BiH gunner. Milinfo asked another patrol to the front line in the hills above Vitez. I sent two Scimitars because the tracks were so narrow. They were Claymored by the BiH, this time in a different location. Lance-Corporal Pirrie, one of the Gordons, had accompanied the Scimitars and was wounded in the arm.

This incident acted as a catalyst and caused the ops staff to rethink. At last, they recognized the futility of tasking patrols up into the hills, just to check if the front line was still there.

On the 15 July, I decided to take a turn on the tunnel. The soldiers hated this duty. It meant an early start and late finish with a boring day, either sitting at one end, or trundling up and down the same patch of road. The fact was, however, it worked, and dramatically reduced the incidents on Route Diamond. All the crews had done several days on the tunnel so I thought I'd better see what it was all about.

I teamed up with three Seven Platoon Warriors, commanded by Sergeant Huskisson. Leaving camp at six in the morning, we dropped off the other pair, and meandered down to the 81 Northing.

The day dragged by. We relieved the other two and sat for two hours while they patrolled the route. On the next leg I drove, to keep my hand in, while Tookey sat in the back and chewed his nails. We sat it out again and I wished I'd brought a book.

'Hello Zero Alpha this is Delta Two Two! We are held up by a human-wave road block three kilometres south of your position.' We arrived at the crowd, just outside Novi Travnik. About fifty women and children were blocking the road. I talked to them in my rudimentary Serbo-Croat. I think I understood they were demanding information about the whereabouts of several Croats, supposedly held by the BiH. They wouldn't let any UN vehicles through unless we found these people. This was obviously a very localized protest. I doubted if the HVO leadership knew what they were doing as, in effect, they were stopping all aid to themselves, as well as the Muslims.

The women were stopping every vehicle, including HVO cars.

This confirmed it was a civilian protest. They were redirecting the traffic down a narrow side-street, so small it wasn't marked on my map. The road emerged a couple of hundred metres past where we were parked. In other words, this was a block aimed against the UN and not their own side. I'd soon sort that out.

We drove to the narrow road and arrived just in time to meet a car full of HVO commanders. By a nifty piece of reversing, Tookey managed to block it before they could slip round us. They leapt out, furiously brandishing pistols. One of them spoke a little English and demanded that we move. I made a great show of lifting an engine louvre.

'Sorry old chap! We've broken down!'

'How long before you move?'

'An hour, maybe four!'

They were livid but realized we were beating them at their own game. I was learning to think like a Bosnian.

Cooky was running the ops room and sensed some sort of impending disaster. He thought I'd need all the help I could get.

'Hello Zero Alpha, this is Zero. I've got Delta Two-Zero and Two-One stood by in Travnik!'

'Roger, thank you for that.'

'I've also got Sierra Two-Two and Two-Three moving in from Vitez!'

'Roger, thanks for that but there's no danger and it won't be necessary.'

'I've also ordered Uniform Three-Two and Three-Two Alpha to move to the Novi Travnik T-junction!'

'Thank you but they really won't be needed!'

'I've also stood-by four more callsigns in camp!'

Hell! This was getting bigger than a Cecil B.De Mille epic.

'Hello Zero, this is Delta Zero Alpha. Can you fix for me to have a Polaris missile submarine sail up the Lasva River?'

'Zero, no need to take the mickey. Out.'

Poor old Cooky, he really meant well. No wonder the boys called him the General. I could imagine him moving little Warrior symbols all over the map board to converge on our peaceful little demonstration.

By this time, several very annoyed HVO soldiers were berating the women as well. They finally asserted themselves and the crowd let them through. However, D11 then blocked the main road and the

Croats were back to square one. They went back to the women and more finger-pointing followed. Ten minutes later, the crowd started to drift away and a pointless little protest was over.

The mess held an officers' dinner a few nights later. After the cookhouse had been cleared, the staff laid out the silver and we had a superb meal. During the port a mortar round landed very close by. The windows shook and everyone just carried on. I went to investigate after a second round landed and found both had exploded about thirty metres from the perimeter. Who fired them, and why, we never found out.

At the end of the ops week I returned to the crinklies. At Ana and Ivo's, yet another man had turned up. Nikola Tomic was in his sixties and had been the local communist party representative. It was plain that Ana didn't like him. His lift didn't quite reach the top floor and he kept drawing me aside to whisper about conspiracies.

After weeks of careful nurturing, my whiskers had reached their zenith and Ivo shouted out: '*Moja* Major *Brko!*' (My Major Moustache) Well, that was a new nickname!

He sat and smoked a cigarette I'd given him. He'd resorted to smoking newspaper in his pipe and the Marlboro was like ambrosia to him. I idly wondered if broadsheet papers were a more mellow smoke than tabloids.

Ana Ghavric had taken to wailing at us, much to the annoyance of Anto. She led us to the church crying: '*Miko! Miko*' (Mother! Mother!)

Inside the vestry were a number of robes and several books she'd collected. I took them, just to shut her up. She told me she was fifty-seven and had never married. As she looked eighty, I wasn't surprised.

A couple of days later I took my Land Rover and a four-tonner to the UNHCR warehouse in Zenica to collect three pallets of baby food. We now had our own company supply of aid.

I called in at the FTC house and exchanged some jars for a variety of baby products, including nappies. We weren't supposed to associate with the charity as they were a non-governmental organization only loosely affiliated to the UN. The battalion hadn't established the same rapport with them as the Cheshires had. One reason was that two of the charity workers had gone native. Steve and Lawrence were two drug users who'd gone on from distributing aid to distributing drugs. They were on the run and living in Travnik, courtesy of the BiH. Foreign mercenaries tended to have a short lifespan in the region, and it was probably only a matter of time before we recovered their bodies from some ditch. The new charity field worker was an honest fellow called Jim Ryan who was trying to recover the credibility lost by these idiots.

A second soldier of mine was baptized by the padre. Private Lee Ellerker, from Eight Platoon, was initiated into the church in Vitez. Carson and I took the items from Pecine to the priest. He wasn't keen on taking them as his church was full of the Guca Gora artifacts. He showed us his leaky storeroom and Carson decided to hang on to the items until a more suitable storage place could be found.

Back on guard company, I 'stagged on' in the ops room for a couple of nights. I enjoyed the night duties as it was a time to write letters. Also, I always phoned Dawn when I finished, at four in the morning. This was early in the morning for her too and it was like talking to a dormouse emerging from hibernation. It was worth it, as it was the only time there were no queues for the phones.

A couple of days later Zippy and I decided to do something different. We were briefed as part of the guard one morning and then spent four hours on duty. Each soldier rotated through the four sangars doing an hour on each. The front gate was the busiest with a constant flow of vehicles in and out. Its barrier was atrociously constructed. As we were both weedy midgets, it took both of us to lift it.

We received a good indication of the way some people treated the soldiers. One UNHCR field worker arrived as we were checking the pass of a civilian worker. He stopped outside the barrier, waited for a few seconds and then started to pump his horn. I walked over and he rounded on me.

'Get that bloody barrier open now! I'm late!'

'Well you should've got up a little earlier!'

'How dare you? Do you know who I am?'

'From here you look like some rude git in a white Land Rover!'

'You're in deep trouble. I'll report you to the Guard Commander!'

'I am the Guard Commander! When your manners have improved, come and apologize and I'll open the gate!'

There were several like this. All used to treating the soldiers like skivvies. It was a real eye-opener to the abuse the lads put up with. The difference was, we had the rank to give as good as we got. The temperature rose and we went to have a drink from the water jerrycan. One smell of the brackish water convinced me I'd rather go thirsty. I'd visited the sangars several times but you never get a feel for a problem unless you experience it yourself.

After a four-hour stint we retired to discuss our findings. Neither of us pretended we could know what the lads went through, stagging-on day after day. What it did do, however, was to give us a list of improvements that would, hopefully, make the duty more efficient and bearable. The first of these was to get a new barrier made!

Having learned so much, Zippy and I thought it would be a good idea if the rest of the company hierarchy stood a four-hour duty. Bad mistake! Neither of us had reckoned on the hassle this would create. One of the subbies and a couple of the seniors came to see me and told me they thought that doing a duty would undermine their credibility with the soldiers. I pointed out that Zippy and I had done the duty and had that undermined our authority? On the contrary, the lads seemed to think it was a good idea. I was about to add that they must be very insecure if they were that worried about what the soldiers thought of them. Anyway, one senior was prepared to resign rather than spend four hours sharing the soldiers' duties, which I thought was a bit over the top.

In the end, I'm afraid I took the easy way out and quietly shelved the idea. I didn't like backing down but didn't feel as strongly about it as they did and I rather pusillanimously opted for a quiet life. One Sergeant told me: 'It took me ten years to reach this rank and I don't see why I should go back to doing private soldier's duties'. I think he was missing the point of the exercise.

I finally returned to Pokrajcici on the 25 July and met the front-line commanders. Drago introduced me to his battalion commander, Marenko. This was the guy I'd snubbed after Patrick Bishop had been injured. He had an earnest face and immediately apologized for the actions of the drunken soldier. He was not half-witted but seemed it at first. He weighed up every sentence carefully before answering, very slowly. With his vast range of earnest expressions, and economy of speech, he was Bosnia's answer to Gary Cooper.

He was an electrician by trade and had rough, worker's hands. His character reflected his job and I guessed he was a no-nonsense, hands-on, commander.

Drago was his staff officer. With his immaculately manicured hands, dainty little pearl-handled pistol and leather satchel stuffed full of papers he was the epitome of the indoor man. It came as no surprise to learn he was a teacher by profession.

Ivica was one of the company commanders. A tall thin man with delicate hands, which fluttered as he talked, he talked of the day when there'd be peace. The others told him to stop dreaming of the impossible. He looked vaguely familiar and told me I'd rescued him from Guca Gora. At least I'd got off to a good start with this guy. He was a cabinet maker and musician. A man of creativity, the classic dreamer.

The final man, Davor, was the youngest and carried a large revolver and an equally large knife. He talked about how they should take the fight to the BiH and how he wanted more action. Davor was the hothead of the four and had been a student. I could imagine him at a poll-tax rally back in the UK.

It was striking how their personalities so strongly reflected their professions. We drank whisky and I arranged to bring a visiting army-training team to see them. The atmosphere was cordial and I knew we were helping to dispel the deep-rooted distrust the Croats had for us. Meanwhile, the lads outside at the Warriors were building their own bridges, playing football with the HVO soldiers.

That gave me an idea. I think it was Mao who said: 'Win the hearts of the people and their minds will follow'. Perhaps that would work here.

Next day I took a mixed-bag of three majors to the same headquarters, this time, to drink their brandy. Keith Kiddy was a fusilier who was helping to run Warrior training in Germany. Pat Butler was a para who was in charge of setting up a UN training centre in the UK. Finally, Simon Wolsey, a gunner who was planning the training for the Coldstream Guards, who were to relieve us. Forget the droves of visiting generals. This was, in my opinion, one of the most important visits of the tour. The Army had accepted that, in common with most of our wars, Bosnia would not be over by Christmas. At last, it looked like a decent training package would be set up.

We then went to see Ilya Nakic, who took us to see his position on point 688. While one of his officers showed the three around, we chatted, and I tentatively suggested a football match. He was dubious at first, worrying that his men wouldn't want to associate with the UN.

'They will if you tell them to. If you get them there, my men will build the bridges with yours!'

We shook hands and the deal was struck.

A disgusting stench hung all around and I guessed what it was.
'Have you removed the BiH body by the track?'
'What body?'
'The one that's making the smell.'
I asked for his help to arrange with the BiH to have the body
reclaimed. He wrinkled his nose and agreed.

I returned in the afternoon and unloaded some of the baby food
at Pokrajcici. Then, I fixed a drop-off point for the body with the
BiH Brigade Commander.

At Cifluk, the next day, we met up with two HVO soldiers
detailed to help us remove the body. We parked next to it and the
two scampered out from their trenches and hid behind the Warrior.
The BiH was expecting the exchange and had agreed to a half-hour
local cease-fire.

Both HVO donned thick rubber gloves, which we provided, and
each wrapped a white nappy round his face. They were the only
cloths we could find! Armed with a UN-issue body-bag, we
approached the corpse.

The fellow had lain there for at least two months. He was almost a
skeleton and the grass had grown through him and was sprouting out
of the gaps in his tunic. They gagged as they picked him up and there
was an obscene squelch as he parted company with the earth he'd rested upon for so long. Unfortunately, he then disintegrated. The Croats
retched and dropped the fellow who totally fell to bits. My knowledge
of human decomposition was a little sketchy and I rather hoped he'd
fit into the bag like a good little corpse. One of them held up the skull,
to shouts and jeers from those watching from the trenches. This went
into the bag first. His legs were laid out, followed by the arms, before
the torso was placed roughly in the middle. He almost looked like he
was positioned correctly on the bag. His legs were the wrong way
round, but it was only a minor detail. All was going well until they
zipped him in and picked him up. The body collapsed with a slither-
ing that was audible through the thick plastic. The repulsive mass
then accumulated in the centre of the bag. Like a sack of spuds, they
dumped him into the back of 0B. We bade the Croats farewell, drove
the hundred or so metres to the BiH trenches and dumped him on the
side of the track. Job done, we left and, ten minutes later, they all went
back to trying to create more bodies.

The incident reflected well on the HVO. Nakic didn't have to
agree to a truce and he certainly didn't have to detail his men to

help. He received no reciprocal body in exchange. It was done partly as a favour to me and partly as a humanitarian gesture. The whole
Croat attitude had changed from swaggering arrogance to helpful
co-operation.

On the way back along the Croat front line I was amazed to see
what looked like an empty jar of Cow & Gate baby food. The container lay, discarded, on the parapet of a trench. It was a long way
down from the Warrior but I was quite sure. The next bunker confirmed it. On top was a cluster of three jars. One of the Croats was
tucking in to pea and ham, specially formualated for nine-month-
olds. As we progressed along the line, I saw that every soldier had at
least one jar by his side.

The lying, cheating, stinking Croat bastards! I was livid and was
going to drive straight to the HVO headquarters and take the
remaining food back. We halted outside the deserted building.
Nobody was around. In frustration, I stomped up to a house where I
knew a mother and baby lived. Furiously, I banged on the door, and
she appeared, complete with child.

We went inside and I immediately saw a slab of a dozen jars lying
on a table. Another, opened, was on the unit. This was confusing.
'Do you know that the soldiers on the front line are eating the food
we brought for your baby?'

'Yes!'

'How can you allow that? The food is for children like yours.'

'You must understand that we live in a village under siege. We
have the BiH on two sides of us. Only the soldiers stand between us
and slavery. Therefore we give most of the food that comes to the village to the soldiers. They must be strong and well fed to fight hard
for our village!'

'But without good food your baby will not grow to be big and
strong!'

'Without the soldiers my baby will not grow up at all!'

It was a logic I'd never considered and a view given freely and
under no duress. The women of the village knew about the food yet
they were quite happy to share it with the soldiers. They'd received
their quota and the rest had gone up to the line. This tied in with
the HVO headquarters I'd seen at Pecine packed with food. It made
a mockery of the UNHCR aid effort and I wondered what percent-
age of food actually found its way into the hands of the needy. Very
little, I thought. It was surreal. The UN was supposed to be helping

the refugees but was actually feeding the soldiers to make them strong enough to create more refugees.

The HVO was not to blame. All sides were at it. The only way to feed these people would be to distribute the aid via soup kitchens. A total impossibility, given the scale of the problem. Even the baby food argument was flawed. A hungry soldier will eat anything, though I thought I'd have to be ravenous to eat pea and ham gruel. We would still distribute it but I'd just have to be far more careful where we delivered it. Another lesson about life learned in the crazy world of Bosnia.

The day of the match arrived and we drove to Pokrajcici in six Warriors, with about fifty of the company. Several overhanging telephone lines crossed the track leading to the field. At each one a child was stationed with a long pole. As we passed, they pushed the wires up and over our antennae. Someone had given this afternoon a lot of thought.

A similar number of HVO waited for us at a leafy glade. We provided several crates of beer, mostly out of the company fund. I also raided the LOs' fund. As it was the 31 July, I took the remaining allocation for the month, beating one of them to it by two minutes! The HVO provided brandy, Slivovitz and a whole roast pig and lamb. We played on a bumpy grass surface with helmets marking the goals. The difference in football cultures of the two nations was immediately apparent. While the Croats played skilfully, executing expansive passing moves, the Brits just fouled everyone!

In the event, they won, five–three, and it broke the ice. Within minutes, the two groups were mixing about. Singing started and Dobby led a chorus of the nonsense song: 'We're going on a lion hunt! We're going on a lion hunt! We don't care! We don't care! 'Cos we've got guns – and bullets!'

It means absolutely nothing and has to be sung in a manner that shows no teeth. However, the HVO Brigade Quartermaster was most intrigued.

'This song your men are singing. Is it a comment on weapon and ammunition re-supply in the British Army?'

'I hadn't the heart to disillusion the poor fellow.

The act, however, which brought them all together was when Ivica produced his guitar. Soon the fields of Central Bosnia echoed to eighty drunken soldiers singing 'Country roads take me home! To the place where I belong!'

After four hours Zippy tipped me the wink and we started to load the lads back into the Warriors. The drivers and sentries were a little miffed at missing the fun but knew their turn would come at the next match. I bade farewell to Ilya Nakic. It had been a superb afternoon, the lads had got on well and we left at just the right time. Later, whenever C Company Warriors drove through Nova Bila and Pokrajcici, the HVO soldiers waved to us like old friends.

A slight problem occurred as we arrived back in camp at the same time as our latest visitor, the Chief of the General Staff, General Sir Peter Inge. The General had a reputation as a hirer and firer and had started a tour of camp while we were trying to decant tiddly soldiers into the Portakabins. Dobby and Donlon were the worst; I blame it on the stress they'd been under. Donlon was being the typical stroppy Jock and wouldn't leave quietly. He was giving all and sundry dogs' abuse when the General's entourage turned the corner. Zippy slammed the rear door and locked it. Muffled sounds of: 'I'll kill you lot. Who wants a fight?' came from inside. Someone dived into the next Warrior and started the engine, drowning out the noise.

Dobby was a different problem. He was sleeping off the effects of an HVO Slivovitz attack and wasn't in the mind to move from his nice, comfortable seat. Four of the lads couldn't shift his great bulk. We locked him in too where he slept it off for the next four hours. Perhaps the General wondered why there was a group of soldiers, whistling suspiciously, when he passed.

The next day, 1 August, the General and his staff went to GV for a visit. Colonel Alastair led the convoy of four Warriors including the two from my company HQ. Phil commanded one and Jason the other. On the way back, the left-hand drive-mushroom popped out and 0C crashed. The drive-mushroom is the cap that holds the drive-shaft in position. When the shaft stopped driving one track it caused the wagon to swerve, flip and then roll onto its roof.

In the back of the wagon were two brigadiers, who were severely shaken, and James Myles, who broke his wrist. Jason and Erwin were bruised and shocked but the worst injury was to Corporal Orr, the gunner. Orr, one of the Jocks, was flung about with such force that he struck a loose 30 mm round that had become wedged in the turret. The head of the round pierced his shoulder at the back and came out the front leaving, not surprisingly, a 30 mm hole.

I couldn't figure why there'd been a loose round in the turret until Jason explained. When we were surrounded by the

Mujahideen at Guca Gora, he'd loaded six rounds of HE. He automatically tossed the clips out of the top of the turret, as he would do on the range. The rounds had sat, undisturbed, until the accident had thrown them out of their rack, with disastrous consequences.

I went to see Orr and he was in good form. The MST, mercifully, had few customers so patients received the full attention of all the staff. He was due to be evacuated back to the UK in a couple of days. For him, the tour was over.

For the rest of us, there was no way out. The latest in a constant stream of visitors was the Defence Minister, Malcolm Rifkind. He was accompanied by the Foreign Office Minister, Douglas Hogg. Both clambered over the Warriors like excited schoolboys. Phil used the opportunity of having Hogg semi-captive in the turret to buttonhole him over our UN pay. This was a constant gripe with the lads as our Government appeared to be the only one that did not pass the UN money on to the soldiers.

SLAVENs were still running and I went, with D31, to provide the security. We passed the Novi Travnik T junction and through the HVO lines. The Croats had constructed a stout wooden chicane across the road with just enough room for a Warrior to pass through. They could now cross the road without being seen from the BiH trenches.

As I passed the last HVO trenches, someone threw an apple at me. We were going about fifty kilometres an hour when the round, green object flew up from my front right. I had a brief glimpse of the thing before it struck me a glancing blow on the top of the helmet and sailed away over the back decks. Seconds later, I felt the shockwave of an explosion. Looking back, I saw 31 screeching to a halt and a pall of black smoke hanging above the road. I signalled the other Warrior to drive on, out of what could've been an ambush, and we finally halted after a kilometre.

D31's crew was already out and I joined them. The apple had been a hand-grenade. Lance Corporal Kehoe, the commander, was the worst injured. He'd been hit by several pieces of shrapnel on his left arm. None of the wounds looked too deep but all were bleeding profusely. In the back, Private Stow was hit on the end of his nose. A sliver of metal sliced off a tiny fraction of the tip, which was trickling a little amount of blood, much to the amusement of his mates. A couple of millimetres one way and the fragment would have missed him; the other, and he would've been severely disfigured. I wondered what his new bride would've made of that.

Thankfully, their flak jackets had absorbed much of the shrapnel. Kehoe's was punctured in several places and his back resembled a hedgehog, with dozens of razor-sharp shards sticking out.

They had to be seen by the doc so we headed back to the MST. As I remounted, I noticed the top of my helmet. A green stripe across the top of the blue cover marked where paint from the body of the grenade had been smeared off. It was a very lucky escape for all of us.

Kehoe was patched up and then insisted in completing the patrol. He had every reason to stay in camp and nurse his injuries but was having none of it. It was yet another example of the grit displayed by the ordinary soldiers.

The HVO soldiers at the front denied all knowledge of the mysterious grenade and blamed the BiH. Now there's a surprise. The Muslims must be bloody good throwers to toss a hand grenade two hundred metres. We never found out who threw the thing, or why. Whoever did it was probably drunk and would've forgotten about it the next day. It was all a big game to many of the locals, yet baiting the UN could have lethal consequences.

A few days later, Nine Platoon was in Santici. The BiH launched a minor attack and the Patrol Commander came under increasingly accurate mortar fire. He eventually identified the fire control team. After 167 rounds of Chain Gun, two men were dead and the mortaring stopped.

The BiH accepted responsibility with little complaint. The leadership of both sides tended to take a robust attitude whenever we returned fire. In a culture of guns and violence, being shot if you fired at the UN was viewed as an occupational hazard.

I went to see the HVO Travnica Brigade Commander about the grenade incident. Vlado Juric was a short, stocky man with dark, receding hair. He'd been a Galeb, ground attack aircraft pilot, in the JNA. His HQ was a house near the Novi Travnik T-junction, fortified with logs and planks of wood. We talked in a smoky room and drank coffee and Slivovitz. He didn't admit the grenade but then he didn't deny it either. At least he didn't try to blame the Muslims. We chatted for a while and then he said:

'I have heard that you are prepared to be friendly to us Croats.'

'I am friendly to anyone if it helps me to do my job.'

'I have heard that your men played football with the Bila Brigade. I would like to arrange a match as well.'

That was an unexpected opening and I wasted no time in fixing the details. Business completed, we chatted for a while and Vlado started to tell me about his time as a pilot. Like all fly boys, he talked a mean dog fight. I lasted for twenty minutes as his hands flew around the room strafing imaginary Serb convoys, before making my excuses.

Back in camp, Mark Bower came to see me. He was one of the best of the LOs. A sensitive man, Mark really cared about the people. He'd had one horrendous incident early in the tour. He'd been trying to negotiate the evacuation of a wounded boy from Stari Vitez to hospital in Zenica. The talks took several days during which time he got to know the boy and his parents well. Eventually, the lad was taken to the hospital where he, unfortunately, died. The parents, not surprisingly, wanted his body back. Mark went to collect him, believing that he'd be in a body-bag, distressing enough in itself. However, the place was in chaos and they were told to go and find him in the mortuary. The room was full of corpses, piled ten deep. It was only after sifting through several heaps that they finally located the poor kid.

Mark arranged for us to travel to Stari Vitez to deliver some of the baby food. We went in two Warriors, through the Croat lines, to the Muslim quarter. Here, we unloaded several hundred jars of Cow & Gate's finest. A human chain ferried the aid straight into the local midwife's garage. I had a good chat with her and got the impression this lot might just end up with the babies and not the soldiers. The lads thought it was great getting hands-on experience of delivering aid. Private Smelt told me: 'It's great this, sir! I really feel like I'm really doing some good now!'

Marenko and I had become quite good friends and he invited me for lunch. Zippy, Dobby and I went to his house on the outskirts of Pokrajcici. The place was spotlessly clean and resembled a Swiss chalet. His wife, Ana, two sons and brothers, Anto, Ivica and Miran, were also there as well as his parents, Mato and Ana. I tried hard to keep a straight face. I'd now met four Croat ladies and they were all called Ana. It was like going to a party in Australia where all the girls are called Sheila.

We ate chicken and roast potatoes and chatted about life in general. I didn't hear a single shot while we were there. We could have been a thousand miles from the War. They were good, honest people caught up in the horror of the conflict. Like in any civil war, however, the actions of a few fanatics controlled their lives.

We returned to Ana and Ivo's on the 12 August to find that a roving patrol of BiH had called on them and ransacked their house. I'd taken one of the Mortar 432s with me. While Ana prepared sour milk, sour yoghurt and sour cheese, the boys set to work. The food was totally inedible and, strangely enough, sour. I dutifully nibbled on a piece of cheese. The house was tidied in an hour and would've passed muster at the hand-over of a married quarter.

Their water supply had failed. Sergeant White and Lance-Corporal Braithwaite set to work with a Bosnian pick and shovel, both bent, and soon uncovered the pipe. I then sucked on the end of it. The first thing to come out was a large spider that I promptly swallowed, washed down with a mouthful of rusty brown water. As I coughed and spluttered, Braithwaite quipped: 'You'll 'ave to swallow a bird now to get rid of that spider!'

The water started to trickle but we needed an expert so I promised to bring a plumber next time.

We patrolled back through Novi Travnik. As we crossed the BiH front line, they fired three shots at us. We all ducked and I disregarded the incident.

At the Croat village of Zabilje we handed out thirty slabs of the baby food and took some photographs to pass on to Cow & Gate.

Whenever we visited these little villages, I always stressed the positive side of UNPROFOR. Croats, in particular, were wary at first but soon came round when they saw we were actually trying to help. We were well on the way to lifting the standing of the UN, at least in the eyes of one ethnic group. In many villages now, I arrived and introduced myself.

'*Dobar Dan! Kakoste? Ja se zovem Major Vaughan!*' ('Hello! How are you? I am called Major Vaughan!')

As the tour progressed, more and more local commanders would say: 'We have heard of you, and we know you are a friend to the Bosnian people!'

Well, we might not be solving the overall problem but at least we were getting somewhere.

I escorted Carson to the hospital in Nova Bila. The hospital was adjoining the church and the orderlies had turned the aisles into an extra ward, with beds laid across the backs of the pews. We met the doctors who showed me four children, severely injured in a mortar blast in Vitez. One had horrendous head injuries and was not expected to survive. Another had lost an arm and yet another, a leg. I had a lump in my throat the size of an egg as I talked to one seven-year-old girl. She'd lost a leg above the knee but was laughing and joking as if hospital was a great adventure. She told me the doctors would make her better. I had to turn away when she confided that she thought she'd wake up one day to find she'd grown a new leg. These kids were the real victims of the War. The maiming of inno-cent children playing in the street furthered no cause. The doctors asked me if I could evacuate them to the UK for treatment. This was an unfortunate consequence of the actions of some of our politicians.

Operation Irma had made worldwide news. The Government had bowed to media pressure and evacuated a seriously injured Muslim girl from Sarajevo to London. It was just one child and a blaze of publicity followed from the sponsoring newspaper. 'Look at how much Britain cares and how we are helping this poor little girl.' It was manipulation of the media at its very worst. At the very least, they should've evacuated a little Croat child as well. Instead, this gesture sent the signals to Bosnia that the British Government would help only the Muslims. It also focused the public perception on to Sarajevo and the fact the Muslims were under siege. That there were tens of thousands of Croats under siege in the Lasva Valley was hardly worth a mention.

Thanks to the desire for a quick publicity stunt, we, at the sharp end, had to answer for their follies. How could I explain to a moth-er that her child would die because it wasn't politically acceptable to be seen to be helping those nasty Croats.

The situation had hotted up in Novi Travnik. After a fresh spate of BiH probing attacks the Croats had fortified their line. Mines and a couple of wrecked trucks blocked the road we usually took, so I dismounted to look for a suitable way round. As I was casting about, a high-velocity shot came from one of the BiH-held tower blocks. The bullet slammed into the wall behind me and missed only by a few centimetres. It was probably just a stray round but was bloody close.

At Pecine Ana saw us coming, hitched up her skirts, and hopped over the fence into their garden like a schoolgirl. She was one amaz-ing woman. Sapper Holland, a plumber, fixed the pipe at the Lesic house. They now had access to a regular supply of water. Prior to this, Ana had been carrying buckets a kilometre from a small spring. Not bad for a woman of nearly eighty. Back at the BiH lines, we started to negotiate the minefield. I was waist-up, out of the turret, conning us through, when a round slammed into the side of the Warrior. I heard the thud of metal on metal and ducked, albeit a second too late. This was getting to be a habit and the BiH in Novi Travnik didn't seem to have a very high regard for the UN. They were getting frisky around camp as well. We'd stopped the Croats from sniping in the area but the other side was making up for it. As I was sitting on the verandah, writing, some scrote fired a burst from the top of the hill. Three rounds hit the roof of the house and one, the wall near my bedroom window.

Roy had gone to Tuzla for a six-week stint and the LD Squadron had now joined us back in Vitez.

We tried something new at Nova Bila. I arranged with Ilya Nakic to hold a children's party on the 17 August. The HVO selected a patch of grass and we pitched-up with two Warriors, a 432 and a Scimitar. We told the Croats we could cater for around eighty children. In the event, in true Bosnian fashion, there were more than 300.

The food came from the cookhouse, jelly, cakes, chocolate and crisps. Our idea was to give each child the same amount of treats, dished out from a line of tables. We also had juice for the kids and coffee for the mothers. After forming an orderly queue, the kids were supposed to await their turn.

In the event, when the first sweets apeared, there was a stampede, and it was a miracle none of the smaller kids were crushed. It also looked for a second as if Sergeant White was going to be buried under a mass of grabbing paws. The crush only abated when all the food was gone. On reflection, it was obvious what would happen when we were dealing with kids who hadn't had crisps for more than two years.

The kids then clambered all over the vehicles and we unloaded the weapons and let them hold them as well. All the boys instantly turned into HVO heroes. Stephen Lees organized face-painting and Jimmy Cliffe held a puppet show. The only man who didn't enter into the spirit was Dobby. Taking his job seriously, he spent the afternoon wandering around looking mean, while the rest of us enjoyed ourselves.

The BBC showed an interest and sent a crew under David Shuckman. Despite the problems, the whole afternoon was a resounding success. Colonel Alastair put in an appearance, fortunately missing the food scramble, and seemed to think the event was a good idea. We brought a small ray of sunshine into hundreds of little lives and, hopefully, the children and their mothers went away with a good image of those nice men in their white tanks.

Unfortunately, BBC news wasn't interested in the story but we did make Children's Newsround. I was horrified to learn it wasn't called 'John Craven's Newsround' any more. Another childhood bubble burst. Anyway, it was ironic the first positive publicity the Croats had received for months should be on children's television.

Operations finished for another week and we handed over to the LD. This was a problem as the Scimitars were too light for some of the more risky tasks. They also couldn't be used for ferrying local commanders about. Therefore, Richard Lockwood's platoon, from Roy's company, was attached to assist.

On Friday, 20 August, I had a brand new subaltern posted to the company. Stephen was due to fly back to England to attend his platoon commander's battle course and his replacement was straight out from Sandhurst. We decided to play a little spoof on the newly-arrived Second Lieutenant Adam Boothby.

I drove the Warrior down to GV to meet the incoming convoy from Split. We all swapped roles for the trip and I was Corporal Dobson. Zippy was Private Clark, Jason, Corporal Donlon and Donlon was the Sergeant Major. In fact, the real Donlon made rather too good a CSM. He spent ten minutes strutting around camp, wearing the rank-badge, and bollocking LD troopers. The poor guys hadn't a clue who this mad Jock was but they sure as hell jumped when he shouted at them. The final member of the crew was the interpreter. Corporal George Ward was the company jester and came along as George the gay interpreter.

The convoy arrived and Donlon brought Boothby across. Short and chunky, with vivid red hair, Adam looked like another stunned mullet, hardly surprising as he'd still been under training less than a week before. He looked even more stunned when I sauntered over, hands in pockets, and introduced myself: 'Ey up mate! I'm Dobby!'

His eyes flashed from the Corporal's stripes to my face and I thought he was going to bollock me. However, he let it pass as he did when Jason and Zippy were equally familiar. The gaff was almost blown when I heard a cheerful: 'Hello, sir!'

I looked round to be confronted by Chappy. He'd made a truly marvellous recovery and had pestered the system to let him join us for the rest of the tour. There would've been no comeback if he'd elected to recover fully back in Osnabrück. (Joanne later told me she was almost glad when he left. Apparently he talked of little other than how soon he was going to get better so he could be with his mates.)

I couldn't just kick Tookey out as he was doing such a superb job. However, it solved a problem as Erwin was still badly shaken after his accident.

Chappy bounded across to us and then caught my warning wink. He took one look at my stripes and immediately twigged. Without checking his stride he went straight past, to Donlon, and smartly braced-up in front of him. What an actor. Any doubts Adam may have had were instantly dispelled by this consummate performance.

Graham Binns arrived and handed Boothby an envelope. It was the ultimate cartoon package with 'Top Secret' stamped in bold red letters all over it.

'Make sure the CO gets this personally. It's the whole battle plans for the BiH offensive!'

We mounted up and Adam looked surprised when Donlon climbed into a black bin liner. He looked even more surprised when Georgio kissed him on the lips and then started to undo his flies. Donlon excused the interpreter's bizarre behaviour and handed the Subaltern a headset, instructing him to press the little switch if he wanted to speak.

We set off and Zippy and I started chatting over the intercom: 'Ey Dobby! Have you seen the state of our new Rupert? Does his mother know he's here?'

'Bloody officers!'

'Aye! What's 'is name?'

'Mister bloody Buzby or summat!'

'Just our luck to get 'im. He looks like a right stuck-up git.'

At this stage Adam had taken enough. He tried to assert himself and stop these slurs on his character. His platoon commander at Sandhurst would've been proud of him. However, Holtom had rigged the intercom so he could hear but not speak. He spent ten minutes frantically trying to interrupt as we continued: 'Just look at the way he was late as well. We've 'ad to do this run four times 'cos he couldn't be arsed to tell us he was on a later flight.'

'Aye, they're all the same them officers. The OC's no better, what a wally, with his puffy double-barrelled name. And as for the CO . . .'

Adam was beside himself with rage at this disloyalty to all and sundry and was desperately trying to shout at us to stop. He soon stopped when Georgio put a hand on his knee. He quickly retreated to the corner where he sat, like a frightened rabbit.

Suddenly, I yelled: 'Bloody kids!' and brought the Warrior to a track-rocking emergency stop. The newcomer had no idea what to hang on to and ended up in a heap on the floor. Ward fell on top of him, using the opportunity for a quick grope. Quick as a flash, Jason leaned down and stuffed the envelope down his smock.

We finally reached the school and halted on the tank park. Donlon climbed out of the bag and brushed a few specks of dust from his lapels. Adam, of course, was caked in the stuff as our dust trail had caught us up and swamped the rear when I stopped.

Donlon was about to take him to meet his company commander when Adam remembered the envelope. He started to look for it and was cut off by Jason: 'You idiot! Don't you know that all papers have to be secured due to the flow of air through the back? It could be anywhere between here and GV!'

The rest of us shrugged in a not my problem gesture and left him frantically searching under the seats.

My part was played by Sergeant Hibberd, an imposing ex-Guardsman who immediately plied Adam with a huge whisky. He was then taken to see the CO. Phil played the crusty old Colonel to perfection.

'There's three things I expect from a newly-joined officer. First, he must be neat and tidy. Look at the state of you! You're a complete mess. The Sergeant Major was in the same vehicle and he's managed to stay smart. Secondly, I don't expect my officers to drink, and you stink of spirits! Not a good start is it?'

'No, sir.'

'And thirdly, I expect my officers to look after their equipment. At least you haven't had time to lose anything yet. Anyway, I believe you have a top-secret document for me?'

Adam was finally put out of his misery when we all burst in. He'd taken it all in good humour and would remember his first day in the Battalion for a long time to come.

Next day, it was back to reality and we had more bridges to build. We drove to the concrete football pitch in Nova Bila for a five-a-side soccer match with the Travnica Brigade.

We took some of the newly-arrived military interpreters. These had undergone a three-month Serbo-Croat course. Most were quite good but we had to have the exception.

Giles Gittings was a Coldstream Guards officer who'd just been made redundant and was serving out his last few months. I really liked him but he must've been on a different course, and probably planet, to the rest of them. He was brilliant if you wanted six lagers and three deep-pan pizzas but I don't think he'd ever learned the word for checkpoint! He was also a hopeless goalkeeper and we lost twelve–three.

This wasn't as bad as it sounded as the Croats had packed their team with former league players. We retired to yet another leafy glade for yet another roast lamb. We slightly redeemed ourselves as Lance-Corporal Latus, a keen bodybuilder, beat all comers at arm-wrestling. I also chatted to their coach.

Mister Renic had been a Yugoslav international in the sixties. I asked if he would coach our team and he immediately agreed. He was, himself, a refugee. He'd been known as Rena, pronounced Rayna, in his playing days. I remembered seeing the football sign outside the fire-gutted Café Rena near the Dolac checkpoint. He immediately became known to the boys as Rena the Trainer!

I was concerned about the health of the old folks at Pecine, especially Ivo. On my next visit, I asked the Commander in Sinokos whether he minded if I took a Croat doctor to see them. He was quite happy for me to do this and thanked me for my courtesy in coming to ask in the first place.

We had, as usual, been shot at as we transited the BiH part of Novi Travnik. This was a contrast to the friendly commander I'd just spoken to only a few kilometres away. Back in the town, we were, again, engaged by accurate small-arms fire. Tookey had studied the pattern of mines and threw the Warrior round them at nearly fifty kilometres an hour. The unexpected movement threw the BiH gunmen off their aim and the rounds fell harmlessly to the rear. It was almost as if this were personal.

The next day I had to travel 0C as my wagon had deveoped a slight coolant leak. This was the only time 0B was ever off the road and the REME traced the fault to a perished rubber pipe.

We picked up the doctor, Zdenko Kranic. The doc was a ringer for Prince Rainier of Monaco, with a closely-clipped white moustache. Immaculate in a starched, white uniform he quickly settled into the unfamiliar interior of the Warrior. He examined all the crinklies. Ivo was diagnosed as having angina and given some pills. The couple both knew Kranic and pumped him for news of the outside world. Both stressed they didn't wish to move but wanted news of their family. Doc said he'd try to trace them through the refugee records. BiH soldiers were busy raiding the surrounding houses for firewood as winter was, again, approaching. The Lesic wood supply was on the edge of the road and likely to disappear soon. Zippy suggested we move the logs and then chop them to make them harder to carry off. I identified a place, next to the house, and out of sight of the track.

Ana Ghavric was even more daft and wailed her heart out. Kranic said he'd send her some antidepressants although I doubted if a Mogadon sandwich would be enough. She'd found yet more books and robes. I dutifully stuffed these in the Warrior. I'm sure she was knitting these in her spare time. The folks were all in remarkably good health and most of their ailments were a product of a hard rural life and not their present circumstances. Their best tonic, however, was meeting one of their own, with news of the outside world.

Back at Novi Travnik, we passed through the BiH lines without incident, for a second time. It was funny how the gunmen seemed to like firing at 0B better than 0C.

We stopped off at Rankovici. The priest, Father Ilya, showed me round his beautiful church. The ceiling looked as if it was held up with Doric columns that were, in fact, skilfully painted on to the walls. Father Ilya looked like a Mafia Godfather. He lived in style in a huge house and was, obviously a man of some wealth and power. He didn't want the rather tatty robes so I took them back to camp, hung them out to dry, and gave them to Carson.

Next day, 25 August, it was back to reality. Yet more peace talks were planned between the Muslims and Croats. The Bosnian Croats asked us to transport the leadership of the HDZ to Kiseljak where the UN would fly them to talks with the Government of Croatia. Hopefully, they were going to approve the terms of the latest Geneva accord.

The leaders were the most extreme of all the Bosnian Croats. Dario Kordic was there with Anto Valenta. This guy made Mussolini look like a trendy lefty. He'd written a Croat version of *Mein Kampf* in which he described the Muslims as a lower form of human being. Carrying this scum was distasteful but if it resulted in an end to the senseless slaughter, it was worth it.

The trip passed without incident. The BiH checkpoints had either been warned of our task or weren't interested. Our mortar hatches were closed so we decanted thirteen very sweaty Croats at the HVO Headquarters at Kiseljak. Driving back, I reflected that the HDZ seemed remarkably cocky considering their parlous state. What could they have in store?

At around eight in the evening, eighteen large-calibre mortar rounds fell on the hill above our house. One fell short and fortunately exploded harmlessly in the river. The Croats were becoming increasingly hacked off with the BiH in Grbavica. A new sniper was using the area and had already killed two men working in the fields. The bombardment was unlikely to kill the sniper but its purpose was possibly to try to frighten him off, or turn the villagers against him.

We returned to Ana and Ivo's taking twenty of the boys. Some carried the logs from the track up to the house. Others chain-sawed and then chopped the wood. Lance-Corporal Pirrie, a country boy, stacked the lumber next to the house in a pile that was so tall it defied gravity.

By the time we finished we'd created several tons of firewood. We also harvested plums and tipped them into a huge barrel in the shed. Ana was going to make Slivovitz that she would then sell or barter with. In return, she made us pumpkin pie. It was absolutely disgusting and the lads wouldn't eat it. However, none wanted to offend the delightful couple so we all nibbled a bit and then pocketed the rest when she wasn't looking. They, at least, now had the means to keep warm and cook throughout the winter. That could be the difference between life and death.

Back in Novi Travnik the BiH had placed a barrier over the road but Tookey swerved round it and we, again, evaded the usual shots. Those BiH didn't like us.

Two incidents on the 27 August brought me to the brink of disaster. The first was what should have been a simple good turn. Father Ilya told me he knew a man who'd hidden the Pecine parish records when the BiH overran the village. He asked for my help as they would help the ICRC to trace the displaced villagers. It seemed simple enough and I took Carson along to lend the day a little ecclesiastical weight. The priest also provided a guide in the form of the man who'd hidden the book. He turned out to be one of the drunken militiamen I'd seen on my very first visit to Pecine.

We reached the village after a departure from the norm in Novi Travnik. This time, we came under very accurate fire from a small-calibre mortar, probably a 60 mm. About eight bombs fell around us. Tookey worked up to warp speed after the first two exploded just in front of us and the change in pace caused the remainder to fall behind. The Commander in Sinokos was, as usual, affable and seemed to regard our interest in the church with some amusement. He was even more affable when I presented him with half a packet of Marlboro.

We dismounted at the church and took the man inside. He was shocked to see the damage to the place. Not half as shocked as he was when he discovered that his house had been torched. Still, at least we had the book.

Wrong again! The pile of logs where he'd, supposedly, hidden the records had been pulled apart and there was nothing. He started to shake and his eyes rolled around and I thought, for a second, he was going to have a fit. However, he quickly recovered and asked if he could visit his son's grave. Apparently, he was killed fighting in Novi Travnik and was buried in the same plot as his grandfather. I wasn't too keen on this as we were, after all, behind BiH lines. They'd sent a couple of soldiers along as minders who shrugged when I asked if this would be possible. We trudged up the hill to the little cemetery. The guy went straight to the grave and then collapsed, howling with grief.

I ran to join him and saw the grave had been opened. The BiH had exhumed the recent corpse, almost certainly to add to their quota for a body exchange. Worse still, the skeleton of the man's father lay scattered around at the bottom of the grave. Even I was shocked at the mentality of people who could dig up corpses to use as bartering chips.

We walked back to the wagons and the man was, not surprisingly, silent. Half an hour later we were back at the outskirts of Novi Travnik and the BiH mortared us again. The mortarman was good and the first round landed some five metres from the Warrior. Fortunately, a low wall took most of the sting from the bomb. Nevertheless, the blast was unexpected and deafening and we were showered with bits of masonry. Dobby's urgent voice cut-in over the intercom: 'We'd better get to a hospital quick. This guy's having a heart attack!'

We tore through the deserted streets and slewed to a halt outside

Doctor Kranic's. The stretcher bearers ran out and the poor man was carried inside. I felt totally responsible. His heart had just had enough shocks for one day. I should've told Father Ilya the task was outside our mandate and left it at that. However, I'd nothing better to do and just wanted to be helpful.

Fortunately, he survived.

That evening we progressed to stage four of the plan to win over the HVO. We'd succeeded with the barbecue, party and football match. It was time to try something even more ambitious.

I suggested to Ilya Nakic that we held an evening function. He liked the idea and tasked Juti to arrange it. The venue was a disused night club that was all boarded up. As usual, we'd provide the beer, and the HVO, the food. As something special, Juti had arranged for several local girls to attend.

Zippy and I hand-picked twenty of our most sensible single soldiers. I cleared the gathering with the CO, who thought it was a good idea. The ops room was briefed on our whereabouts and I tasked the QRF to patrol the area every half hour. We arrived to find a totally transformed club. They had painted the inside and all the tables had vases of fresh flowers standing on freshly laundered cloths. Best of all, the flags of the Battalion and the HVO hung, symbolically, side by side. The Croats had gone to an enormous effort. No mean feat in the middle of a war. They ushered us into a small room where we laid our helmets and flak jackets in a line and placed our weapons in a rack. The door was locked and one of my lads, and an HVO soldier, stood guard. I was happy we had minimized the risks. I was the guest of honour at the top table seated between Ilya and a lady. Well 'lady' was stretching it a bit. Vera was in her late thirties with peroxide blonde hair and a green dress, split to the thigh. It was very thoughtful of Ilya to provide me with a partner for the evening. The meal was superb. The ubiquitous lamb was complemented with a delicious salad. When the dancing started Vera left in search of easier prey.

Their live group was brilliant and played a mixture of country and western and traditional music. The dancing was like a cross between a barn dance and Zorba the Greek. All the lads had a great fling though, it has to be said, mostly with each other. Unfortunately, the language barrier was too much for most of them.

However, the HVO soldiers seemed to appreciate seeing their womenfolk dolled-up, probably for the first time in over a year. At

11.15, Zippy and I decided to call it a night. He started to round up the lads while I sought out all the commanders to thank them for what had been a stunningly successful evening.

I picked up my weapons and equipment, the last remaining in the store, and thanked the HVO guard. Outside, the boys were already in the truck. I climbed into the Land Rover and asked the driver if we were all in:

'Just the Sarn't Major to get in the back.'

I settled down to wait, smugly congratulating myself on an excellent liaison function.

Two minutes later Zippy's anxious face appeared at the window: 'Sir! One of the lads has had his rifle stolen!'

'You're joking?'

This is one of the silliest things any of us say when confronted with bad news. Of course he wasn't bloody well joking! The story emerged. The boys had been getting on to the truck when one of the NCOs had taken Vera round the corner for a quick grope. He put his rifle down and someone had walked off with it. This was a disaster. After all the security we'd arranged, one idiot, with his dick welded to his forehead, goes and ruins it.

We sent the truck back and Zippy and I stayed while two of the lads waited outside. Ilya held a conference round a table. Suddenly, we were all very sober. He started by blaming the soldier. I agreed he was foolish to leave his rifle unattended but, the bottom line was, it must've been a Croat who stole the weapon. The HVO reckoned they could find it within three days. This simply wasn't good enough. It had to be found that night!

'We must find the rifle tonight. If I return to the school without it, I will have to report the theft. The Commanding Officer will then ban all future liaison functions. All we have worked for over the last two months will be for nothing!'

With that, I folded my arms and said they may as well find a bed for me because I wasn't leaving without the rifle. I'd no doubt the HVO was not behind the theft. They'd nothing to gain and could've, if they really wanted weapons, stolen the lot from the storeroom. It had to be the action of an individual or small group. The enormity of the problem hit me. It was now after midnight. The thief was probably tucked-up in bed with the SA80 in one of the hundreds of houses within walking distance. If he had a car, he could be in Busovaca by now. A Company had already had three rifles stolen at a social function with the BiH in Tuzla. B Company had lost one in GV and the Engineers had lost half a dozen. This was one club I didn't want to become a member of. I began to experience that sinking feeling of despair and an old American saying came back to me: 'You build a thousand bridges, shag one sheep, and what do they call you?'

Ilya tasked Juti to go and search for the weapon and the big man lumbered out into the night. We made small-talk for an hour until there was a total eclipse of the door. In strolled Juti carrying the rifle, complete with magazine and rounds and I could have hugged the big git. I tried to look cool as if I knew all along he'd find it, but my thanks came out just a little too eagerly.

Juti was the ideal man. No doubt he knew all the local likely-lads and had gone around knocking on a few doors. How many people had been turfed out of bed in that hour? I asked who the culprit was and was told he was a sixteen-year-old. I then made the mistake of asking what would happen to him.

'We will deal with him in an appropriate manner.'

As we left, the youth was being appropriately dealt with. He was getting a good kicking. Three HVO were taking it in turn to stick the boot in. I thought about intervening and then, like the Levite, walked by on the other side of the road.

As we climbed into the Rover my conscience got the better of me, especially as the sounds of the beating had, suspiciously, subsided. The three had the lad up now, his wide eyes darting about looking for a way to escape. Suddenly he was roughly pushed into the road. He began to run at the same time as one of the three pulled a pistol and loosed-off half a dozen shots. The youth stumbled and ran on clutching his right shoulder, in an appropriate manner.

It had been a very close shave. I've no doubt we would've been banned from any more hearts-and-minds operations if the weapon had not been found. The HVO had nothing to gain from stealing the rifle and emerged from the incident, frankly, better than we did. In their eyes we were probably a bunch of incompetents who couldn't look after our guns. I was livid with the NCO and fined him a week's pay. His greatest punishment, however, was the fact that the whole company knew what a tosser he'd been. To his credit, he put it all behind him. At the end of the day, all it proved was that you can never plan for the actions of an idiot.

The HDZ leadership returned from Kiseljak on the 30 August.

The white-painted Sea King landed and a UN official checked thirteen persons off the chopper, then told me all was in order. Every Croat was carrying cartons of cigarettes and looked like he'd just returned from hoiday. Being Bosnians, they couldn't just get into the wagons nicely. First, they asked me to transport five cases of cigarettes to Vitez. It wouldn't have been so bad if they'd carried them off the helicopter. The tobacco, however, arrived in an HVO car from the barracks in town. What did they think I was, bloody Pickfords?

The next scam was to ask me to take an extra man who suddenly appeared. They explained he was an electrician and was needed to restore power to Vitez. Maybe so, but they didn't book him on this trip. Transportation of commanders was agreed weeks in advance with the other side and a list of those to be carried had been submitted. The credibility of all future requests would be undermined if we moved extra people. It wasn't jobsworth but a matter of trust, and I wasn't going to betray it.

Finally, we searched their bags. One man had a large quantity of ammunition in his rucksack. He was lean and fit-looking, not at all like the bloated, pasty-faced majority of the passengers. He complained when I confiscated the rounds. Again, I explained that, as Vitez was under siege, it would be betraying the trust of the BiH if I transported ammunition and supplies for the HVO. I didn't recognize the guy and decided to check the list. There was no Anto Valenta.

At this stage Dario Kordic entered the fray.

'This man is here in place of Valenta.'

'Where is Mister Valenta?'

'He is staying in Croatia for a few more days.'

'How will he return?'

'The UN will fly him here as you have done with us.'

'In that case, he will be the thirteenth person. I will not take this man as he is extra to the list.'

'You must take this man. He is my personal bodyguard!'

'I will take the twelve on the list, and no more!'

'You must take this man. You brought thirteen here, you will take thirteen back!'

'No! I will take the same thirteen back. When Mister Valenta returns he will make the number correct. This man must stay!'

'Why can you not take one more?'

'Because I will have carried one extra armed man into the Vitez pocket. That will destroy the trust the BiH has for these operations.

'I do not have time to argue. He will travel with us!'

With that, the man, whose name was Misha, climbed into the Warrior.

'Mister Kordic, if Misha doesn't get out of this Warrior, I will have him dragged out!'

'I am a very powerful man. I can make life difficult for you!'

'Mr Kordic. You can threaten me all you like. That man is not going to Vitez with us!'

'I am warning you. I know who you are and I can have you killed!'

'I find your threats the pathetic actions of a playground bully and will give you three choices. One, I take the twelve of you. Two I do not take any of you. Three, I take all thirteen of you to Zenica and drop you off outside the headquarters of Seven Muslim Brigade!'

There was a sharp intake of breath from Misha and the other Croat in the Warrior. Kordic's face turned scarlet and his 'Joe 90' glasses started to steam up. It was clear no one had ever spoken to him like that before.

'For that last remark I will ensure that you never see your family again!'

I deliberately mispronounced his name. 'Oh that's OK Mister Kor Dick. It looks like we'll be going to hell together! OK boys! Mount up! This lot want dropping off in Zenica!'

I pressed the close button on the rear of the Warrior and the door started to swing shut. A yell escaped from the gap and Misha's head and shoulders followed it. Kordic looked at me, his face a mask of pure hatred.

'I will have you broken for this. I will report you to General Briquemont!'

Now the threat of being reported to some Belgian General I'd never even met didn't exactly make me wet myself, even if he was the overall UN Commander. Slowly, I took out my notebook.

'Here you are, Mister Kordic. I've written my name out, just so you remember who I am.'

He flushed again and snatched the paper.

'You are a dead man!'

'I take it that means take me to Zenica. Or would you prefer the Mujahideen?'

His face drained of colour as he imagined what those jokers

would do to him. He made to climb out of the Warrior but found himself looking up the barrel of Dobby's rifle.

'No, I'm sorry Mr Kordic. I can't let you out. You see I have orders to take you to Vitez. Do you accept that your bodyguard stays here?'

He nodded imperceptibly.

'I'm sorry. I didn't hear that.'

'Yes!'

As I shut the door he was shouting: 'I'll have you killed!'

Obviously not a man of action. A real man would, at least, have said, I'll kill you.

I went to brief the vehicle commanders. When I returned, Misha had the interpreter pinned up against a wall. She was quaking with fear. This Cro-Magnon seemed to think it was the interpreter and not me, threatening his boss. Either that or he was taking the easy way out and intimidating the weakest member of the team. It mattered little; I strode towards him and shouted: '*Stani ili putsani!*

This guy, at least, showed a bit of character. Instead of stopping when I said 'Stop or I'll fire!' he took one look at the fact I was unarmed and went for his pistol. His hand groped for his holster as he pushed the girl away. In one fluid movement I pulled apart the Velcro fastening of my flak jacket, reached inside, pulled out my own pistol, cocked it, and shoved it into his face. He looked more than a little surprised to see an apparently unarmed man produce a gun, like a rabbit from a hat. I wondered if he knew that Paul Daniels was a Yorkshireman as well.

I roughly pushed the barrel into his mouth and he winced as it ground over his teeth. I'd cleaned the weapon that morning and it still had a satisfying amount of rather smelly oil on the muzzle.

'Now listen carefully to what I have to say. The interpreter only speaks my words. It's me you have the quarrel with, not her. If you threaten anyone, then be a man and say it to me. Now I want you to apologize to her!'

There was only a tinge of fear in his eyes. He gargled something and I removed the Browning. The interpreter giggled and told me: 'He says it's hard to apologize when you are chewing on a pistol.'

I grinned as well at this touch of gallows humour. It broke the ice and Misha apologized to both of us. Maybe he wasn't all bad after all. I somehow doubted if his boss would be quite so forgiving.

We eventually dropped the twelve off at the Hotel Vitez and

Kordic rushed inside, still clutching the page from my notebook. Funnily enough I never did hear from General Briquemont. Probably Kordic was too embarrassed to report he'd been threatened by an officer called Major Hugh Gerection!

Back at the school, the CO summoned me:

'Vaughan, I want you to stay out of Novi Travnik!'

'Why, sir?'

'Because the BiH Brigade Commander has placed a price on your head!'

'Come on sir, this isn't Dodge City!'

'It isn't funny either! He reckons you're taking ammunition to the Croats. He's promised a reward to any of his soldiers who kill you!'

'Thanks for that. You realize it's nonsense!'

'Of course I do. But stay away all the same!'

'Just out of interest. How much am I worth?'

'100,000 deutschmarks!'

I left his office in a trance. That explained everything. The BiH must know my callsign, 0B. No wonder so many shots were fired at my wagon. It also explained why there'd been no shooting when I used 0C that day. That was a king's ransom in these parts. It was about £40,000, over twenty years wages for a BiH soldier. Come to think of it, I'd better keep this quiet or one of the LOs would be bumping me off to claim the reward!

I retired to the mess to make an appointment with several cans of Mister Boddington's stress-remover. Well, it had been a very even sort of day really. Death threats from both sides. Who said the UN wasn't impartial? I could see I had to win over a hell of a lot more hearts and minds!

Chapter 12
Ethnically Cleansed

September began with a whimper rather than a bang. There was no indication this was going to be anything other than another quiet week.

We held our second children's party, this time in Kljaci. I took along a variety of armoured vehicles, Warrior, 432, Scimitar and a CET. We'd learned from the Nova Bila party. Zippy arrived half an hour before the rest of us and set out a wire enclosure around the tables with a small gap at either end. We pitched-up and parked in a line and then started to serve the food. The kids were held back by the village elders. They only let six into the pen at a time and the system worked a treat. There was no crush and we fed every child. Eventually we catered for nearly 400 children and were away within two hours.

I presented Mr Asim with a brand new blue beret, which he proudly clamped on his head at a rakish angle. As a parting shot, we distributed a quantity of the baby food. We'd, so far, brought a little happiness into the lives of 700 kids from across the ethnic divide.

I wanted to sort out this matter in Novi Travnik. It couldn't go on as the old folks still needed our help. Also, I didn't take kindly to being threatened. I decided to minimize the risk and leave 0B at home. We arrived in the Land Rover and parked outside the BiH Brigade HQ. Dobby made to accompany me but I told him to wait. He grumbled and reminded me why he was supposed to be there in the first place. A crowd of curious BiH soldiers gathered and I hoped none of them actually knew what I looked like. I turned and strode purposefully into the building.

Halfway up the stairs my nerve failed me. My legs started to twitch, then shake violently and I sat down, before I fell down. My vision was blurred and I had a curious ringing in my ears. This was probably the last stage before being frightened to death.

I was in a bit of a pickle. I couldn't go on because my legs wouldn't let me and I couldn't go back because my pride wouldn't let me. Finally, I couldn't stay there because it would take only one guy to recognize me and it would be bye bye K-P, hello one rich BiH!

Mister Marlboro came to my aid. I took one from my special packet, a Silk Cut wasn't going to do the trick. It was one thing giving them to the locals but I wasn't in the habit of smoking the things myself. I inhaled deeply and then coughed deeply. By the time I'd smoked the cigarette, filter and two fingertips, I was calm and collected. Well almost.

After what seemed an aeon, I arrived at the Commander's outer office. After a cursory knock on the door, I went in. His secretary looked up.

'I wish to see the Commander!'

'He is in a meeting with his battalion commanders. Come back this afternoon.'

'My name is Major Vaughan and I will see him now!'

The recognition flashed across her face and I hoped she didn't keep a pistol in her desk. She called for the guards and I had to act, so I barged straight into the Brigade Commander's office.

The Commander was sitting at the head of a long table with half a dozen, or so, other men seated around him. One was the boss from Sinokos. Suddenly, it all went very frosty. There was a flurry of activity behind me and four armed men charged in. They surrounded me and all cocked their weapons.

This was it. I'd really gone too far this time. The legs were still and I felt a strange resignation. My mind was, miraculously, clear and I idly wondered what would happen if I ducked; they might all shoot each other. After a slight pause I spoke, or rather croaked as I seemed to have swallowed a sponge.

'My name is Major Vaughan. I understand you have offered a reward to any of your soldiers who kills me. Well I'm here to save you the money. But before you, yourself, shoot me I would like to know what I'm supposed to have done!'

Twenty minutes later, the Commander, Hasib Belegic, and I were chatting like long lost brothers!

It had all been a terrible mistake. Belegic had heard rumours of

Croats who'd filtered through the Serb lines. Somehow, they were being supplied with ammunition and our constant, unexplained, activities had been linked to this. I told him we always visited his man in Sinokos and cleared the visits first. Belegic said he would deal with him later.

It seemed inconceivable that two commanders, situated only a few kilometres from each other, didn't talk about such an important matter. However, such was the intensely localized nature of the conflict, area commands often operated in total isolation.

The Commander smoked, using a long, carved, wooden cigarette holder. I'd bought one from a roadside trader and deployed mine to good effect. It was some ten centimetres long and was the sort of thing Bet Lynch might have used behind the bar of the Rovers Return. It was the Russian hat syndrome all over again. After an hour of coffee and Slivovitz we parted on most amiable terms and I agreed to take a BiH policeman with me on all future trips. They trusted me, but not that much!

I was feeling extremely relieved when I rejoined the others.

'Thought we'd seen the last of you then boss!' Dobby grunted.

I was still trembling as we mounted-up and I told myself I wasn't going to take any more stupid risks in future.

We set off for Pecine in company with the policeman, Enes Begic. Thereafter, he accompanied us on all our trips to the crinklies.

That evening, I visited the football squad's final preparation for our next match. Sergeant White was the manager, a pretty onerous task as he hated the game. Renic was also there and I watched the session for half an hour.

Coaching via an interpreter was comical, but, somehow, it seemed to work. The squad was drawn solely from the company group and, to be honest, there wasn't a great deal of expertise to call on. However, under the eyes of the former international, they were starting to look the part.

The match was a Saturday afternoon fixture against the HVO Military Police. We pitched up at the indoor sports arena in Novi Travnik. It would've been a credit to any large town in the UK and boasted a huge Astroturf pitch. We settled down, with several hundred HVO and civilians, and the match began.

Half an hour later, a mortar round landed about two hundred metres away. The windows rattled and the game, momentarily, stopped. Seconds later, the players shrugged and the match resumed.

Ten minutes later another round landed, much closer this time. Again, everyone stopped and looked around.

'Play on!' I shouted. Vlado Juric took up the cry and the crowd cheered the players onto greater efforts. The lads were inspired and putting together some nifty moves that would've shamed the England squad. Not that that's saying much!

At 2.50 there was a huge explosion and the windows came in.

That was bloody close! I nodded to Vlado and we called the match off. There's no doubt that, if we'd cried 'Play on!' again, the teams would've stayed. However, so would the spectators and I wasn't going to be responsible for the lives of so many civvies.

We sprinted for the waiting Warriors and beat a hasty retreat. No one owned up to the bombing. The BiH blamed the Serbs and the Serbs blamed the BiH. The other theory is the HVO shelled their own stadium. After all, we were winning six–four!

The BiH sniper on Grbavica was getting very good. Half of the JRC was still used as a bakery by the locals. Sammy sniper was using the early morning queues for target-practice and had, so far, killed six people and wounded several others. The Croats would, literally, stuff the injured through the toilet window of the JRC knowing that, once on our land, we were obliged to take them to the MST. This put the doctors in an impossible position. They were bound to help, but what if one of us was subsequently hurt and they had used the only piece of some equipment on a Bosnian? We tried everything to stop the locals bringing their wounded to the camp, rarely successfully. The MST was also treating a wounded BiH soldier, who was on the ventilator. I hoped if one of my guys needed that machine, there'd be no contest over who used it.

This sniper was killing people on a regular basis now and I couldn't see the Croats putting up with it for much longer.

Back in my room, my washing was neatly laid out on the bed. Good old Mrs Fered. I was back on ops for us and I couldn't be bothered to go to church. It was veg-in-bed time.

At 9.05 on the Sunday morning, 5 September, a loud explosion woke me. It had been close, probably a hundred and fifty metres away on the hillside. Bloody inconsiderate these HVO. How's a chap supposed to get his beauty sleep? A minute later a second explosion rocked the house. It sounded like it was on the flat ground near the river. That would make it a hundred metres away. I contemplated getting up. I thought I'll see if there's another first. Another minute later there was a huge explosion. This was close, around fifty metres I guessed. If this kept up, the next one was coming down the chimney. Pulling my duvet up over my head, I prayed and promised I'd go to church!

I didn't hear the inevitable mortar round approaching. I think I was actually praying aloud. The resultant explosion was enormous and rocked the whole house. The glass panels of the door came in and the whole room seemed to be filled with flying glass. Masonry clattered to the deck somewhere outside. Simultaneously, the room started to fill with dust and the sickly smell of high explosive. Then I heard the screaming.

A high-pitched squealing, like that from a stuck pig, was coming from somewhere just outside the door and my first thoughts were for Jane Brothwell upstairs. I shook the duvet off me and dozens of shards of glass clattered to the floor. The room was half-lit with shafts of light filtering from the holes in the blinds and still full of choking dust. I groped for my boots and then flak jacket and stumbled for the door.

'Is everyone OK?'

The Colonel's booming voice cut through the dust as he shouldered-open the door. He looked relieved to see I was uninjured. He'd been passing and seen the explosion. Just my luck to be caught in bed by the boss at after nine in the morning. There I was, standing in boots, flak vest and a smile!

'Check to see if Jane's OK!'

Colonel Alastair ran upstairs and I ran outside towards the screaming.

The round had landed in the alley between Fered's two houses. Mrs Fered had been standing only a few metres away and copped the lot. She was in a terrible state. One hand was severed and the other arm hung by a thin thread of flesh. She was covered in blood from dozens of wounds. God forgive me. My first thought was: Who's going to do my washing now?

I rushed back inside, grabbed a couple of field dressings and started to try to stem the flow of blood. She'd mercifully stopped screaming and lapsed into deep shock. Two of the mess staff, Corporal Robinson and Private Spotiswood, arrived and I yelled at them to fetch a stretcher. Spotty doubled-off and Robinson joined me. A couple of others arrived at the same time as the stretcher and we hoisted her on. This was no mean feat as she must've weighed at least twenty stone. The four of them staggered off to the MST. Apparently, they dropped her three times on the way.

I looked for where the round had landed. It had struck the concrete and the fragmentation had been awesome. The walls of both houses were peppered by hundreds of pieces of shrapnel. Most of the windows had been blown in, which explained why the screaming had appeared so close. Using my bayonet, I dug out the tail fins of a 120 mm mortar bomb.

An ITV crew arrived and I fled back to my room. An immense clear-up operation commenced and it took an hour just to sweep up most of the glass. After this, the sappers boarded up all the windows turning the place into a gloomy prison. Still, it could have been worse. Another three metres and the whole house would've gone up.

Mrs Fered died the next day.

After a quiet day, it seemed as if this may have been an isolated incident. The CO, David and Carson disappeared off on leave, leaving Richard in charge. We had the French General, Cot, visiting us and I was tasked to fetch him from Kiseljak on the 7 September. As we approached Vitez, I could hear the noise of battle.

Camp was at red alert for the only time during the tour. The HVO had fired a concentrated mortar barrage on Grbavica and was preparing to attack. We arrived to find everyone was either in the shelters or closed-down in the Warriors. Several rounds had dropped into camp and Private Ellerker had been slightly wounded.

I found the injured soldier sitting in the ops room, wrapped in a blanket. He was deathly white and had been given pain killers. He'd been struck on the back of the thigh by a piece of shrapnel just as he was climbing into his Warrior. I spoke to the doctor, who said it was just a flesh wound.

Poor old Richard had the General and also Brigadier Searby to deal with just when the camp was under mortar fire. I'd nothing else to do and no soldiers to do anything with, so I decided to go and take a look. I sprinted to 0B, standing on the tank park, with the crew still inside. The camp was totally deserted as everyone was under cover. We drove to the camp gates and out onto the road, where we parked outside the bakery.

The HVO was assaulting Grbavica in an extraordinarily courageous manner. Dozens of men were scrambling their way up the steep, scrub-coated hill. They rushed over the lip, and, minutes later, were beaten back. Back down they came, dragging several wounded. They gathered again, just below the crest. Whistle blasts echoed across the valley and, like the First World War, they went over the top. Four times this happened before the Croats finally gained a foothold.

The first house to be burned was the one with the BiH flag from which the sniper had wreaked so much havoc. Other houses soon followed as the soldiers fought their way into the village. Nobody shot at us and the HVO seemed far too concerned with their objective to bother about the one, solitary, UN witness.

Evening was approaching and I asked Richard if I could deploy a screen around our houses. There was little danger of the Croats attacking camp but there was a very real threat of our houses going up in smoke. It would be only a matter of time before the HVO consolidated in the village and dealt with the little pocket of Muslims they had surrounded on our street. If this happened at night, it would take more than a few flags to protect our property. Richard agreed but stressed that we were not protecting the Muslims, they would have to fend for themselves.

The perimeter had to be organized in daylight so I rounded up Zippy, Tom, Jimmy Cliffe and Splash Lockwood. We sprinted round the area with stray rounds zinging all over the place. After a breathless half hour, we had all the positions worked out and the first of the eleven armoured vehicles started to deploy. We reckoned this should keep our houses, and the Muslims, safe.

Back at the school, I was approached by Sonja and Alija, one of the male interpreters. Sonja was hysterical and screaming: 'My babies! My babies!'

Leila and Larissa were in the village being looked after by a relation. She could see the burning houses and, understandably, feared the worst.

'Please help my babies Major Vaughan!'

Alija's problem was a little easier to solve. His wife, who was eight months pregnant, and little daughter, were stuck outside somewhere. He thought the girl might be sheltering in the front sangar.

I went to Richard, who was talking to another officer. 'We've a bit of a problem with the families of a couple of the interpreters.'

'What sort of problem?'

'Two little girls are trapped in the village and Alija's family is in the area of the front gate.'

'That's not really our business!'

'Well I think it is. They work for us and they carry a UN ID card the same as us. They're just as much part of the UN as we are. We owe it to them to try to help their families.'

'There's a danger it'll open the floodgates and we'll have all the locals wanting to come in.'

'I understand that, but these people are different. Who's going to want to work for us in future when they hear how we treat them?'

Richard seemed about to agree when the other officer butted in. 'It's too risky to go to Grbavica. There's a bloody battle going on. Why do you think we're at red alert?'

'We know where they are and I think we're morally bound to help these children!'

'Just forget them. They're only a couple of flip-flops!'

Richard and I stood, mouths agape, hardly believing that two human lives could be dismissed so easily. I wanted to come back with a stinging retort but could think of nothing to express my disgust.

I found Alija and Sergeant Rod Thornton, one of the military interpreters volunteered to come too. Dobby was on leave and I couldn't find Donlon so I took Ricky Holtom. We gathered at the back of the school, drew a collective deep breath and ran into the open. A surprising amount of fire was still coming into camp. Most of it 'overs' from the battle on the hill. As we charged through the rows of Portakabins, the odd round drilled into the flimsy walls. We bobbed and weaved and finally reached the front sangar. Sure enough, a crowd of around ten terrified Muslims milled around the barrier. The sentries had spread barbed-wire across the road to stop them entering camp. Thornton and Alija ran to collect the pregnant woman from a house next to the Captain's, while I went to the san-gar. The tiny wooden structure was jammed full of humanity. Six Muslims were squeezed in with the two soldiers. The BiH militia were firing on the Croats from positions around our houses and the HVO were shooting back. These people had fled their homes to seek shelter from the bullets.

I shouted for the girl and a beautiful, blonde-haired child of about three was hoisted up. She was wearing a white mohair coat and was wide-eyed with terror. I grabbed her and she clung around my neck, hugging me so close I could smell the shampoo in her hair. We started to trot down the concrete road towards the school. Unfortunately, the Croats, in the fading light, mistook us for a couple of BiH and started firing on us. Several rounds whizzed past but they were lousy shots and most hit the road leaving white scars on its surface.

'They're aiming for the white coat!' shouted Holtom.

I pulled open my flak jacket and tried, as best I could, to wrap it around the child. The firing slackened and we pounded into the school. Alija was already there having also run the gauntlet with his wife. She looked like she was ready to have the baby at any minute.

Richard called for me: 'We've got to get rid of those Muslims crowding round the gate and in the sangar.'

'Fine, why don't we just let them in?'

'We can't do that, they'd never leave again!'

'Well we can't leave them where they are or we'll have bodies outside our own front door before long!'

'Get them back to their own houses then.'

'It's not that simple. Their own militia is still fighting from those buildings. I'd be taking them into the middle of a battle!'

'Will you go and see what you can do?'

'On my way!'

I grabbed Thornton and Splash and we ran back to the front sangar. The light was fading fast now. I tried to explain to the people that they had to move and would they return to their houses? No one budged and they pleaded to be let into camp. It was a stalemate broken by a Croat sniper.

The crack and thump of the high-velocity round were milliseconds apart. The guy was very close and the round slammed into the wall of the sangar.

'Sniper! Follow me!'

I started to run for the Muslim house where Alija's wife had been. If I could herd them in there, we would, at least, have some control over them. One by one, they started to follow. The sniper fired again and the bullet slammed into the wall of the subbies' house. We had to get off the concrete road fast so I headed for what little cover was available.

We crowded into the front garden of the captain's house and I sent Holtom to the civilian house to ensure the door was open. He shouted back and we started to herd the terrified civilians towards the door. Splash, Thornton and I tried to put ourselves between the civilians and the sniper. We had over half of them safely away when the sniper seized his chance. An elderly couple were hobbling towards safety when there was a deafening crack!

The round passed between Thornton and me and hit the old man in the back of the head. I was a pace away and Thornton actually had his hand on the man's shoulder. The sniper had a gap of less than a metre between the two of us and it was a very difficult shot. Either that or the bastard didn't care if he hit a UN soldier. The bullet hit the man, with a squelching sound that I will never forget, and he fell at our feet.

We had to act fast. The three of us shoved the remaining ten, or so, into the nearest hard cover, the garage of the captain's house. The wife was sobbing and I gingerly stepped outside to check her husband. I didn't need to be a doctor to tell he was dead. The bullet had exited from one of his eye sockets and a pool of dark red blood surrounded his head like a halo. Apart from the eye, he looked at peace. An old man, with a neat white moustache, killed for no other reason than he happened to be the wrong religion.

I went back into the garage and found a tarpaulin to drape over the body. I shook my head to the old woman and she seemed to age by ten years in an instant. Two other women began to comfort her and I turned my attention to the problem of the BiH militia. They were still firing at the HVO on the hill and it was only a matter of time before the attack switched direction our way.

'Splash, take Sergeant Thornton and round up all the militia, disarm them, get them inside here and take their uniforms off them. When it's dark, take the lot into the Muslim house to join the rest. Put a guard on the door. They'll be under our protection!'

Splash was a good kid and would find a way to get the job done. Holtom and I doubled back to 0B, where the crew waited patiently. The crews of the headquarters Warriors were a mixed bag. Tookey was there and Donlon had also appeared. Corporal Wildon, from Nine Platoon was in 0C with Chappy and Private McCloy, our tame Argyll. For some reason Lance-Corporal Braithwaite was there, living up to his nickname of Combat Clerk! Finally Lance-Corporal Latus was in the turret of 0B.

'Who's on for a dangerous task?'

To a man they all nodded and I gave them a quick brief before we thundered out of camp.

Grbavica was in flames. The HVO were assaulting each house and clearing it, before torching the building. Dozens of fires lit up the dusk. With full headlights blazing we headed for the centre of the village.

The track was narrow, with high hedges on each side. Only the top of the turret poked above the branches so we couldn't use the guns. We halted and I took stock. Through my binoculars I watched an assault on a house a hundred metres away. It was textbóok house-clearing. Each room was grenaded before two men rushed in, spraying automatic fire as they went. Four bodies lay in the dirt and I felt, with a sickening lurch, that we were too late. I told Tookey to make best speed and we clattered along the track towards the firing. We were almost upon them before I saw the mines.

Tookey saw them too and slammed on the anchors. Four TMA 3s blocked our path. Evenly spaced across the road, there was no way of avoiding them. We would run over at least two. It was impossible to slide them away or turn off the track. The hedges were scraping the sides of the wagon and grew out of a steep bank that we wouldn't get up. It would take ages to reverse two Warriors back and then I'd have to find another way in. Unless . . . .

I hoisted myself out of the hatch and stood for a second on the turret. Latus swears that I crossed myself. To my left I saw five Croats, about fifty metres away. They saw me too and looked astonished to see a dark figure in uniform, apparently standing on top of the hedge. They raised their weapons and I skittered down the glacis and leaped down. At the last moment, I saw I was going to land on a mine and spread my legs, landing awkwardly. The mines stared malevolently at me and I really didn't want to touch them. I didn't want to even move when I saw they were wired together with green-and-white flex.

Both sides rarely booby-trapped their mines and I'd seen Beba moving other TMAs at Turbe. However the CO had, quite rightly, forbidden us to touch them. It was up to the locals to risk their lives. The trouble was, there were no friendly Muslims around, just a very frightened me.

I gingerly poked one mine a couple of centimetres. It scraped across the tarmac and I held my breath. I probably wouldn't feel it if they went off but the Warrior would need one hell of a hose down. Nothing happened so I slid all four into the middle in a little huddle. My mind idly told me they looked like a giant four-leafed clover. Feeling rather pleased with myself, I went to slip round the side to get in the back door. Kate Moss wouldn't have been able to squeeze through. The only way back was up the top again. Of course, if I'd kept a clear head, I could've wriggled under the Warrior to the back in complete safety. I climbed onto the engine-decks and crouched down, like a sprinter on the blocks. After a short pause, I ran like hell up the sloping louvres and jumped onto the turret. At the same time, the Croats saw me and all five opened fire. The air seemed full of whizzing bullets as I dived into the hatch, scraping both my shins in the process. As I ducked below the armour, rounds struck the wagon and passed perilously close overhead. Later, I found two bullet-holes in our UN flag. It had been centimetres from my head. There was no point in hanging around so I urged Tookey forward and over the mines.

The next obstacle was the forward Croat troops. They were assaulting the houses on my right, several of which were already ablaze. Two blokes stood in the track and were then shot at by the BiH behind them. They forgot us and dived for cover. We thundered past and one started to fire at us. Donlon stood up in the rear of the wagon, in full view of the Croat and raised his rifle. The HVO ducked behind cover again.

We stopped outside the house and Donlon and I jumped out. He knelt, again in full view of the Croats, and covered me as I ran to the house, shouting for the girls: 'Leila! Larissa!'

There was no answer and I assumed they'd fled. On impulse, I ran inside, still shouting. The place had been abandoned in a hurry and food was still on the table. Two small coats hung on a chair. A bullet crashed through the window and I redoubled my efforts. The firing was terribly close and I expected to hear the chatter of Chain Gun at any minute. This was madness and the Croats would have no idea why we were here. No wonder they were hacked off at us. I was in the sitting-room now. It too was empty. Giving one last shout, I decided to sack-it and save my own skin. As I turned to flee, a tiny head popped up from behind the sofa. It was Larissa, her huge eyes wide with terror. I rushed over and found the two of them cowering in the little space. I should have thought of it. I always used to hide behind the furniture when I was afraid.

I hoisted the smallest under one arm like a roll of carpet and she wriggled as I squeezed her hard. Dragging the elder behind me, we ran for the Warrior.

'For fuck's sake hurry up, sir!' cried Donlon, who was still totally exposed, covering the rear doors of the wagon. I threw the children into Holtom's arms and piled in after them. As we roared away, the HVO were throwing grenades into the house next door.

Minutes later, after a hair-raising journey through several gardens and part of the graveyard, we were back in camp. From start to finish, the whole operation took less than twenty minutes.

Darkness fell and the Croats halted and consolidated. The firing abated and, by the light of dozens of burning houses, Zippy, Cooky, Holtom and I toured the perimeter. Splash had done a superb job. In the garage was a pile of nine rifles and fifteen grenades. A heap of uniforms festered in the corner. He'd disarmed the militia without too many problems and had them all, under guard, in the Muslim house. His prompt action undoubtedly saved dozens of lives. Free from the flanking fire, the Croats lost interest in our little group of houses. We could hear them digging trenches fifty metres away across the river.

Inside the school I sought out Ellerker. He was in a bad way and was shaking uncontrollably.

'I can't move my leg!'

The field dressing was soaked in blood and I went to find the surgeon.

'Ellerker needs help. He's losing blood. Can you operate to take the shrapnel out?'

'Don't be silly! We're at red alert. All the equipment is in the MST. I'd be mad to risk going in there!'

'But he needs help now!'

'It's too dangerous and he's in no danger. I've already told you. It's just a flesh wound!'

Too damned dangerous! What had the Medical Corps come to? Noel Chavasse, double VC, would be turning in his grave.

I stalked off and Zippy and I continued our rounds. Mortar bombs were still landing about the place, probably from the BiH in retaliation. The lights were on in the MST and we entered, to be confronted by an extraordinary sight.

Sitting around a prostrate figure on a bed were two young nurses. One was wearing a helmet, flak vest, Snoopy pyjamas and pink, fluffy, slippers. These girls were looking after the wounded BiH soldier on the ventilator. Every few minutes they turned him over and went back to chatting to each other. When the firing started they'd gone straight to their post with the injured man. There they'd remained, for several hours, in a flimsy Portakabin, with mortar rounds falling all around. These two were true angels and the only people in the whole camp not under hard cover.

I confronted the doctor again and he agreed, reluctantly, to look at Ellerker again. To his credit, he identified the problem straight away and operated on the wounded man on a table inside the school. The fragment had severed Ellerker's femur and the surgery probably saved his life. Lee Ellerker was evacuated some days later.

Zippy and I spent the night touring the perimeter vehicles chatting to the lads. They were all fired up and itching for a fight. The Croats knew we were ready for them and stayed their side of the river. Zippy was a tower of strength as I began to flag in the small hours of the morning. I kept going over in my mind how I could've acted differently to avoid the old man being killed. If only I'd herded them into the mess, if only I'd put them all in the captain's house. We'd saved several lives but all I could think of was the desolate face of the widow.

'Come on, sir! Let's go and see the lads again!'

How such a small man could have so much energy was beyond me.

In the morning, the HVO kicked off again to finish the clearance of the other half of the village. Richard asked me to deploy and monitor the fighting.

'Don't get involved!' he warned me.

I drove into the village with 0C. Adam had two wagons on the main road. He'd taken a crash gunnery cadre run by Sergeant Barratt and was now thrown in at the deep end.

The fighting was as intense as the night before. The HVO was determined to capture the remainder of Grbavica and the BiH had drafted in reinforcements to try to prevent this. We slowly patrolled through the village. Over half the houses were torched and the Croats were three-quarters of the way through the place. Most of the Muslims appeared to have fled although there was heavy fighting in the north. The Croats were taking no chances and were still clearing every house as if it were occupied.

They paid little heed to us and we trundled around watching other people kill each other. I didn't see the woman run into the road and cursed Tookey for the emergency stop. I dismounted and a hysterical woman approached me. She was a nurse and with two others was manning a dressing station. A middle-aged man was also there, as an orderly. They, like our nurses, had stuck to their post and had been cut off by the HVO. It was only a matter of time before they were discovered. If they were lucky, they would get away with being gang raped. They begged me to take them and I thought this was probably their only chance of life. The orderly was dressed in a camouflage waistcoat and I told him to remove it and I'd take him as well. He was beyond the age where he could be classed as a combatant. The firing was getting closer again and I called to the four to hurry up. One nurse, a hard-faced woman in her late twenties, came to me.

'You must take this man as well!'

Out of the building emerged a BiH soldier. The guy was dressed in camouflage fatigues and brown Timberland boots with purple socks folded over the tops. He carried an AK and wore a set of leather chest webbing stuffed with spare magazines.

'I cannot take him. He is a soldier!'

'You must. He is wounded!'

The man held up a bandaged hand. A small amount of blood had soaked through the white linen over the palm.

'Tell him to remove his webbing and jacket, lay down his weapon and I will take him.'

'He cannot do that, he is a soldier. Now we must go. Now!'

With that, the soldier made to climb into the back but Donlon barred the way. They glared at each other and the Jock flexed his fingers ready to drop the guy.

'I will not take this man. He is still capable of fighting the enemy. If he moves now, he can evade the HVO.'

'You will take him with us or we will not go!'

This bossy woman was beginning to annoy me. First she asks me to help and now she starts demanding conditions.

'Fair enough! Right boys, let's go!'

I started to walk back to the Warrior. The sound of explosions filled the air about fifty metres away. If the guy put his weapon down, I would take him. Otherwise, I'd be interfering in the affairs of the two forces. That was way beyond the mandate. It wasn't just a question of sticking rigidly to the mandate. It was their attitude. They just wanted a taxi to ferry them away from a situation caused by their own failure to move quickly enough in the first place.

The woman cast a look of hatred at me and started to give me a hard time.

'Why did you not stop the HVO? Why do you only help the Croats? Why have you allowed them to burn this village?'

'Lady, I haven't time to talk to you now. Either you get in now or you can all take your chances with the HVO.'

The old man and the other two women didn't need any more per-suasion and were already climbing into the wagon. Donlon followed them and started to shut the doors. At the last moment, the woman bottled out and, with a contemptuous toss of her long black hair, joined them. The soldier shrugged and trotted away towards the BiH lines.

We carried the four a couple of kilometres through the lines and dropped them off with a BiH patrol. None thanked me and they shuffled off without a backward glance. Ungrateful sods. I almost wished I'd left them there.

We returned and the same house was ablaze. The place had been grenaded and shrapnel scars pitted the doorway. My anger subsided and I was glad we'd moved them to safety. The Croats weren't, and started to fire at us from the windows of a nearby building. Richard had told me to stay out of trouble so we roared away.

As 0B slewed round a corner, we clipped a wall and ripped the door off one of the back bins. A voice screamed over the intercom: 'Stop!'

I thought we'd run over someone and we halted in an instant. Donlon's voice cut across the static: 'I've got to get oot. The grease-gun's fallen oot the box!'

'Don't be silly. We'll get another one!'

'You must be joking! It's on me flick. I'm no paying for the bas-tard!'

With that the little Jock was out and haring down the road. The Croats couldn't believe their luck and opened fire. Rounds struck the tarmac around him as he hefted the grease gun and doubled back to the wagon. Beaming like a child who's just rescued a puppy, he dived into the back.

'Right, drive on!'

The cheeky Jock git!

It was a bit hot for us in the village so I drove out to join Adam. Boothby had been having his own slice of the action. As he watched the Croat assault, three BiH broke cover and ran across an open field. They were cut down but the third ran on. They finally hit him as he crossed the road. He fell, wounded in the leg, and became tar-get practice for an HVO sniper. First, he was hit in the arm, and then in the other leg. At this stage, Adam put his Warrior between the wounded man and the sniper and his lads hoisted him into the back.

They drove him a few hundred metres and left him safely with his own side.

The Croats were furious for they knew we were forbidden to intervene in the battles. Adam had, effectively, stopped them from killing an enemy soldier. The HVO targetted us in a fit of pique and we left them to it.

I returned to the village and went to the mosque. The HVO Commander arrived. Foolishly, I dismounted to talk to them. Their leader had a Vandyke beard and black hair. He looked like a slightly up-market version of the Yorkshire Ripper. His name was Zvonko and he was, like all his men, fired up on adrenalin. This was not a good time to hold a rational conversation as his men kept loosing off their weapons at every dog and cat they saw. I pleaded with him to spare the mosque but he spat that it was Muslim, and therefore evil. I was achieving nothing so we headed back to camp. As we patrolled through the village for the last time, gangs of Croat civilians were looting the few undamaged houses. They didn't even have the grace to look shifty as they shuffled past us, pushing wheelbarrows piled high with our neighbours' possessions. To the victor the spoils was the only rule of war that applied in Bosnia. As we turned into the school, Kljaci was burning. We neutralled-round and stormed off up the Bila Valley. Twenty minutes later a very hostile crowd of BiH soldiers surrounded us. They swarmed around like angry hornets and I closed Tookey down. All about, were burning houses and the place had received a pasting.

'Go away! We do not want you here!'

'Come on! You know me. What has happened here?'

'Go back to where you came from. We do not want you here!'

'What has happened?'

'You already know!'

'How can I know what has happened?'

'We have been shelled from Pokrajcici!'

'What's that to do with me?'

'We know that every time you drive along their front line you are delivering them ammunition!'

'That's rubbish!'

'We have been hit by the same shells as you carry!'

'Show me one of these!'

'They have all been taken to Zenica where they will be used as evidence against you in a people's court!'

These young Seven Muslim Brigade soldiers were not from the village yet they had, effectively, taken control. They were using the shelling, and the uncertainty created by the bombardment, to put the blame on to us, successfully turning many of the villagers against the UN. For the only time during the tour, I didn't dismount, negotiating instead from the relative safety of the back decks. Mister Asim arrived.

'I see you, old friend! What has happened and why are you blaming me?'

'Major Vaughan. I know this is nothing to do with you but I am powerless against these people who poison our minds!'

With that, he was roughly jostled away. I tried one last time: 'You know who I am. I am Major Vaughan. I have visited your village many times. I brought food for all of you and baby food for your children. I brought you medical supplies when you had none and I organized a party for your children. Why should I do all this if I were not your friend?'

'Because you wanted us to drop our guard so you could shell us!'

'Oh! I see! It's me that's been helping the Croats by shelling you!'

'Yes! We have seen your Warrior on the hill! Now go, before we kill you!'

'You are the most ungrateful people I have ever met. From now on, I will ensure that no UN vehicle ever comes near your miserable little village again!'

'Go home UNPROFOR!'

With that, they started firing in the air and shouting *Allah Akhbar*! The hard-liners had come to town.

I was shocked at how quickly a few armed hotheads could take over the place and wondered how many people actually believed their lies. As we left, one of the soldiers waved me down and posed the usual Bosnian supplementary question: 'Can you provide a fire engine to put out these fires?'

My answer was unprintable!

The day still wasn't over and I was crashed out to take the thirty Muslims from the house near camp to Travnik. We couldn't keep the perimeter secure forever and already the HVO was starting to venture over the river. We formed a human wall of soldiers and herded the frightened Muslims into the Warriors. Here were all our former neighbours. People whom we'd drunk coffee with for the last four months, children we'd watched growing up. Fered was there a broken man. In less than a week he'd lost his wife and both his houses. The last man out was a smartly-dressed man whom I knew from the earlier committee meetings. He locked the door of the house and offered me the key.

'Major Vaughan. Please take my house. Perhaps one day there will be peace and I can return. If not, I would rather the UN had it than the Croats!'

We were stopped at Dolac by the BiH who accused us of carrying a raiding party of Croat infiltrators!

'Fetch Beba Salko!'

'That will take time!'

'You have five minutes after which time I will drop all these people on the road here!'

'You cannot do that!'

'You have now used one of your five minutes. I hope Beba has a fast car!'

Beba arrived in just under the five minutes. He tried to accuse me of helping the Croats to cleanse the Muslims out of the area. He was technically correct.

'Would you rather they become prisoners?'

There was nothing he could do. He didn't like me one bit. In fact, I was about the only UN officer who didn't like him. Most treated him like a long-lost brother. To me, he was a little weasel who was trying to wring every last concession out of the UN. He knew I'd carry out any threats I made and finally escorted us, with our sorry human cargo, to the refugee centre.

I'd been on the go solidly for two days and I finally returned to my musty, dark room. The place was still a mess and I cut both feet on tiny shards of glass before I rolled into bed.

The BiH soldier in the MST died and we took him, and the old man, to Travnik. The medics wanted the bags back so we had to scoop both bodies out onto the mortuary slabs. The old man had brains leaking from the empty eye socket.

Sergeant Smith reported a headless corpse in the village and I went to look. By the time I arrived the victim appeared to have been hacked to pieces. Bone fragments and bits of cloth lay around a bloodstained felling axe. A dog was chewing on something that it dropped when chased away. It was a human stomach. However, there was little evidence of the body.

'Not to worry, sir! One of the lads took a video of the stiff!'

We sat in front of the TV in the guardroom and the corpse appeared in glorious Technicolor. Sure enough, there was no head. I froze and felt suddenly sick as the camera panned over the rest of the body to linger at the feet. Brown Timberland boots with purple socks tucked over the top.

If only I hadn't been so intent on obeying the bloody rules, the man would be alive. I could've forced him to leave his weapon or just damned well let him bring it. I'd been so annoyed by the attitude of the bloody woman that I lost sight of the danger he was in. For the first time on the tour I'd stuck to the book and now some guy was hacked to pieces.

Adam Boothby, on the other hand, had disobeyed the rules and intervened in the battle. The difference was, his Muslim was alive and mine wasn't. There was no place for a rule-book in life or death situations. The heart has to rule the brain for only it knows the true difference between right and wrong. It had taken a newly-joined second lieutenant to show me the meaning of the word compassion.

Zippy asked me to come to the gate. A cardboard box had been found containing a human head. I didn't need to go, to see whose it was.

We withdrew the perimeter and the HVO filled the void. Just after first light, I heard a noise outside my room and then someone fell against the door. The cardboard over the missing panes bulged inwards and then fell to the floor. The door swung open and an HVO soldier lumbered into the room. He didn't see me in the dingy light but, silhouetted against the door, I definitely saw the AK. The man staggered and fell against my metal locker and I used the commotion to leap out of bed. I charged across the room and cannoned into him, knocking him back against the locker. His AK clattered to the floor and I yelped as it landed on my foot. He yelped as well as I cocked my pistol and tried to ram the muzzle up one of his nostrils.

I hadn't a clue what to say to him so I just shouted at him in English. 'Piss off out of here! This is an UNPROFOR house. You are not allowed in here. Go away now and don't come back!'

I backed off, a merciful release as he stank of stale tobacco and Slivovitz, and pointed my pistol at his head. He looked terrified, in a drunken sort of way, his eyes spinning like tops as he frantically tried to focus on me. I gestured down to his rifle and he gingerly picked it up. Nodding to the door, I waved him out and he lurched off into the morning sun.

I went back to bed, shivering with the adrenalin letdown, but not for long. A few minutes later someone smashed the window in the hall. Several Croats were in Fered's garage, looting the cigarettes. It was time to move. This was two violations of our property in a few minutes and, knowing the HVO, it wouldn't stop there. There was no way we could have the same degree of trust we'd had with the Muslims. Then, we left kit all over the room including half our uniform. With this lot I wouldn't leave my underpants out. In truth, we would need a soldier permanently on guard.

I went to put the problem to Richard but found he was away at a meeting. I decided in his absence.

Using the key I'd been given, I opened the Muslim house and stepped inside. The place reeked of humanity. Hardly surprising as thirty people had hidden there for over a day. However, it was bigger than Fered's and in much better nick and I quickly worked out where everyone would stay. The place was infinitely better from a security point of view. It was on the concrete road looking across to the Portakabins. In a line with the other officers' houses, it could be fenced off from the rest of Muslim Street or Croat Street as it had, sadly, become.

I locked the door and returned to our house to be confronted by the Croat commander who'd led the assault on the village. Zvonko demanded the keys to the Muslim house to give to Croat refugees.

'If you have so many refugees why did you burn the village?'

'Because there were snipers in every house.'

'You know that is rubbish. I was there, remember?'

'That is of no consequence. You will give me the key to the house!'

'I cannot do that. We are going to move into it!'

'That is theft!'

'What do you call frightening the real owner away then?'

'We must have that house!'

'I'm sorry. That house will improve the security of the UN and we are going to take it. The house we are in now will be left empty!'

'But that is damaged!'

'Would your refugees rather have this house or no house?'

'You are threatening me!'

'No. But this is a threat. If you don't agree I will increase the perimeter of the camp to include all these houses and you will have none. Which is it to be?'

The Croat replied and I didn't need the interpreter to translate. I heard the word *blato* which means mud, or anything else murky. He knew I held all the cards and his position was indeed muddy. A gang of soldiers emptied the Muslim kit out of the new house and moved ours in from Fered's. Roy, Carson and a couple of others were away so we had to gather up their kit as best we could. Our padre still had the robes and books from Pecine stuffed into a couple of boxes. The priest in Vitez didn't want them so Carson hung on to them until he could find a home for them in a Catholic church.

Within three hours we were firmly ensconced in our new accommodation and the old place was empty. The boys wired off the four officers' houses. We were still outside the camp but now, at least, we had a reasonably secure perimeter.

Zvonko was far too slow off the mark.

'I have changed my mind. We want the Muslim house!'

'Sorry, old chap! We've already moved in!'

'You cannot do that. It is criminal!'

'If you are so concerned about the law, I'd better fence off all the other houses as well. Better nobody lives in them than you break the law!'

'You leave me no choice!'

'That's right, pal!'

'I demand the furniture from your old house!'

'That was Army furniture.'

'You are lying! I know that all the Muslim furniture was carried to the new house!'

Now unless Fered had bought a load of Army lockers and beds in his local MFI this was pure rubbish.

'By calling me a liar, you have made up my mind. My engineers will wire off this street within the hour. I'm sure you can explain to all your poor refugees why they have no home to go to! Now unless you are going to apologize, I have some wiring to organize.'

He knew, as a macho Croat, that calling someone a liar was serious stuff. Zvonko was going to have to grovel and I was loving every minute of it. Eventually, he apologized and we never had any other problems with our new house. A young Croat family, from a village captured by the BiH moved into our old place. Old Zvonko had a brain the size of a pea as he never questioned that if all our furniture had gone into the Muslim house, where had their things gone? For the rest of our tour, the local furniture was safely stacked in an open shed.

Thus ended ten days of intensive operations. Richard did an excellent job in the CO's absence. Meanwhile, the rest of us pulled together to make the best of our rapidly changing environment. The Croats had achieved their aim and the road from Novi Travnik to Vitez was clear of snipers. Above all, however, it was a great morale booster to the HVO after their pathetic showing in the Bila Valley. The Muslims in Grbavica fled to Zenica to join the thousands of other displaced persons in the city. Their predicament was mostly caused by the activities of one, solitary, sniper. As for me, I'd witnessed, at close hand, the ethnic cleansing of our friends and neighbours. The area would never be the same again. The lads joked for days about the officers being ethnically cleansed.

Chapter 13
We Made a Difference!

The fighting died away and Zippy and I toured the area around camp meeting the new Croat occupants. We suggested a few ground-rules, mostly involving the carriage of weapons on the periphery of camp. The Croats were generally on-side and just wanted to make the most of the chance to settle down somewhere. We were all dog-tired and had witnessed too much killing. The lads mostly coped in their own different ways. For some, however, it was too much. The Army had learned well from the experiences of the Falklands and Gulf Wars and recognized post-traumatic stress disorder. One of the MST officers was a trained psychiatrist. The lads were all briefed they could go and chat to the 'shrink' anytime, in total confidence.

The original 'trick-cyclist' left to be replaced by a female captain, with blonde hair and legs up to her armpits. For some reason the instances of self-referral increased. This caused Zippy and I many problems. For a start, the medical people wouldn't release any details of those who asked for counselling. By that, I mean absolutely no details at all. They wouldn't even tell us the names of those who'd been seen. This left us totally out of the loop and we had no idea if we were working with human time-bombs. Unfortunately, when the tour ended the, instantly-available, psychiatric help disappeared. Any soldier wanting treatment had to report sick, along with everyone else. The Army sick parade is designed to discourage malingerers and isn't exactly a quick and efficient process. It puts off many of those wishing to be referred on by the doctor to the psychiatrist. Their problems then fell to the company to deal with, where, in my opinion, they should have been kept in the first place.

The influence and effectiveness of the chain of command should not be underestimated. Company commanders and their staff are used to dealing with soldiers' problems. We take his debt, marital difficulties and moral welfare seriously so why not his mental welfare as well? A sympathetic chat with either Phil, Zippy or I could've nipped many of our later problems in the bud. In fact, Phil had become like a father figure to us all and I valued his advice above all others.

There's no question of undermining the experts. Rather the two should be separate links in a chain of mental care. As it was, PTSD almost became a status symbol. Regrettably, some soldiers enjoyed the chance to talk to a totally unattributable source about just about anything. Perhaps we were reflecting the counselling culture of the nineties but I felt we'd swung too far the other way.

One of my young NCOs didn't even give the psychiatrist a chance. One evening, he totally flipped and screamed that he was going to kill himself. He started to fire his rifle through the Portakabins. It was a miracle none of the boys were hit. The youngest of the Waltham brothers disarmed him. Deploying his considerable bulk, Wally junior, showing great presence of mind, and not a little courage, wrestled him to the ground. I sent the NCO home immediately. With him, it was a combination of pressures in Bosnia and trouble at home that caused him to crack. Mercifully, most of the soldiers kept their problems to themselves and dealt with them in the time-honoured way, by dispatching them to the file thirteen of the brain. This incident was a reminder of just how fine the line is between normality and temporary derangement.

Sonja's husband had survived and reached Zenica. I went to take her and the girls to Sadovace, a couple of kilometres from Grbavica, from where she could catch a farm-cart to the city. We were back on guard and I didn't want to put the crews of the Warriors out, as they were all shattered. I therefore took Dobby and Tookey in the Land Rover through the Croat lines. In no-man's-land, we were shot at from close range and two rounds passed through the body of the Rover. How no one was hit, I'll never know. We also collected another hit on the way back. It was the first really dangerous mistake I'd made and, for the sake of a little inconvenience, nearly got someone killed. It was temporary derangement of another sort. We returned to pick her up the next day in two Warriors. The area was quiet as soon as we appeared with armour.

Later that night I was called to see an HVO soldier who'd been caught pilfering from the JRC. He'd scaled the perimeter wire, which was an indication of how things could become with our new neighbours. There were no police to hand him over to so we roughed him up a little before ejecting him from the camp. We had no jurisdiction over the fellow and had to hope he'd be too scared to return.

A few nights later they raided us again. Privates Dainty and Colley were on sentry duty, armed with the time-honoured weapon of the sentry, the pick-helve. They encountered three Croats armed with the time-honoured weapon of the bandit, the AK 47. The Croats threatened the soldiers and were surprised when the two charged at them. A struggle followed and ended with the result Yorkies three, Croats nil. I confiscated the weapons and booted the three out of camp. Losing their rifles would've been a considerable loss of face for them and I doubted if they told anyone they'd been overpowered by two unarmed men. Dainty and Colley were battered and bruised and displayed great courage and devotion to duty. Colley later told me: 'It were just like a Leeds United away game!'

A locum padre arrived and was put up in Carson's room in the new house. When he arrived, he asked someone about the boxes of religious artefacts.

'It's a bit embarrassing really! You see Carson's been looting these and he's in the process of sending them back to Germany!'

We all had a giggle at this cheap laugh at Carson's expense and thought nothing more of it. However, a couple of weeks later I was on patrol in Zenica and had Carson with me. We received a frantic radio message.

'Hello Three Zero this is Zero. You must return the padre immediately as he has to telephone the Brigade Commander.'

Back at the ops room, the story unfolded. The locum reported Carson to the Military Police for criminal activities. They told the Commander, who was an old colleague of our padre. After a few minutes babbling down the phone, Carson the Parson managed to convince the boss that it was all a terrible mistake. Needless to say we kept quiet! Carson took the artefacts to Rankovici the next day. I still can't get over the idea of one padre grassing on another!

The BiH launched several retaliatory attacks on the 19 September and I was sent out to monitor them. At Bandol I sat, with the MFC Spartan, and watched a full-scale attack involving hundreds of men. The HVO fired several 105 mm rockets from Nova Bila. Beba appeared and started to shout at me.

'Why have you not asked permission to be here? You must go now, you are not allowed here!'

'Why's that then Beba? All I'm doing is watching some soldiers breaking the latest cease-fire. Now I wonder who they could be?'

'You are in the BiH security-zone. You must go now!'

'Oh I don't think so. I'll go when I'm ready!'

'You will be shot if you stay here!'

Then, as I was about to respond to yet another threat, the HVO came to my aid. There was a whistling, like a huge firework, and then a huge firework landed about fifty metres away. The Croat rocket impacted with a tremendous explosion and the shockwave rocked the Warrior. Beba had taken cover and pulled himself out of a very muddy ditch. He was plastered in the stuff and we all laughed openly at him. Another ear-piercing whistle assailed our ears and another rocket exploded. Beba dived for the ditch again and managed to get mud over the bits he'd missed first time.

'I think you'd better go before someone shoots you!'

He stormed off and I realized I was going to get one less Christmas card that year.

The Croat barrier near the Novi Travnik T-junction had been mortared. I hadn't noticed the Serbo-Croat words scrawled on it before and asked what it said.

'Alija! Screw your mother!'

This was a reference to the Bosnian President, Alija Izetbegovic. The slogan must have been a red-rag to the BiH and they'd spent most of the day trying to flatten the barrier.

That evening, we had a visit from the travelling entertainment show. Richard cried off so I attended the event in the garage in his place. The artists were superb. A fellow called Chris Luby did sound impressions down the microphone including a Spitfire taking off and landing. The comedian, Bradley Walsh, singled me out.

'Who's in charge here? Who the hell's Vaughan Kent-Payne? What a stupid name, he could only be an officer. I bet his real name's Derek Smith!'

The lads loved it and I thought how wise Richard was to bale out. In the mess afterwards, Walsh came straight over, shook my hand and apologized. He bought me several drinks and it was hard to believe he was the same foul-mouthed git who'd been up on the stage. He later hit the big time on TV and we appreciated seeing these rising stars taking risks to entertain the troops. It was all in the best traditions of ENSA.

The BiH was still trying to cut the Lasva Valley at Santici and had made some gains. Milinfo wanted to find out the extent of these changes to the front-line as the CO was due back soon. Unfortunately, it'd been some months since we'd carried out front-line patrols and we'd forgotten why we stopped them in the first place.

We arrived in the area of Dubravica, just north of Vitez and immediately heard the fighting. Two rows of trenches faced each other, a couple of hundred metres apart. The armies were exchanging thousands of rounds of ammunition but no one was actually doing any attacking. The lines hadn't moved for months and the Croats actually seemed to outnumber the Muslims. After a few minutes observing we turned and headed parallel to the line. A woman suddenly appeared in the doorway of a house. Thinking she may be trapped by the fighting I dismounted and sprinted over. She was far from trapped and invited me in for coffee. Dobby and I were soon joined by her husband and son, who trotted back from the line for their elevenses!

This was just Bosnia all over. People trying to continue a normal life while a battle raged around them. The BiH, as usual, didn't appreciate our presence and started to mortar the area. A couple of bombs landed close by, showering 0B with mud. We'd almost finished our coffee when a round exploded just outside the door. The logs laid over the entrance absorbed the shrapnel but the blast travelled round the sides. It was like being kicked in the chest and we all sat there, winded. Our coffee cups lay on the mat where the blast had lifted them off the saucers. It was time to go before our presence caused these people to lose their home. Laughing hysterically, Dobby and I walked with deliberate slowness back to the wagon. The adrenalin surge was like a drug and some little alarm bell rang to tell me that maybe I needed a rest.

I warned the company to stay out of the area.

The mortars and anti-tanks were sporting smart new vests emblazoned with the slogan: 'Real men don't wear Chobham!'

They had a point as they trundled about in thirty-year-old museum exhibits while the rifle platoons were protected by the best armour money could buy. Sergeant Smith asked me one day:

'What's the difference between a 432 and a sheep?'

'Go on, tell me!'

'It's more embarrassing to be seen climbing out the back of a sheep!'

I went out the next day, to pick up the Divisional Commander, General Dennison-Smith. In my absence, someone tasked two of my anti-tank 432s back to Dubravica. Inevitably, the BiH mortared the patrol.

Shrapnel hit Private Jones in the throat and Lance-Corporal Wignall in the shoulder and back. Wignall commanded the 432 back to the school as the lads patched Jones up as best they could. The surgeon operated on Jones, who was later flown back to the UK, where he made a full recovery. Wignall was particularly steadfast and insisted on reporting the incident in full before having his own injuries seen to. Once again, it highlighted the folly of unnecessary tasking.

Private Farnsworth was the last of my company to be casevacced. After heavy rain, he slipped off the duckboards around the Portakabins and broke a leg. He was Ellerker's best mate and ended up in the next bed in hospital!

We deployed up to Guca Gora on the 22 September where the mujahideen appeared to be grouping again. A soldier stopped us and I dismounted to talk to him. He was African, possibly Ethiopian. I discovered that he spoke no English or Serbo-Croat, only Italian. Now my Italian stretches to 'Just one Cornetto', so we weren't going to get very far. The guy was extremely offensive and kept pointing his AK at me. In the end I couldn't even make him understand that I wanted to speak with his Commander. I left him saying: 'The BiH must be hard-up if they have to employ men who can't even speak their language. I suggest you move because we are coming through!'

He hadn't a clue what I was saying but soon got the message when the Warrior started to lumber towards him. He stood his ground until the glacis hit him in the chest. The muja desperately clung onto the bolts of the radiator grilles as we increased speed. On my signal, Tookey stood on the brakes and the guy shot off into the ditch. He lay glowering at us as the lads in the back jeered him.

We parked on a small knoll from where I could observe a huge section of countryside. I dismounted and sat in the sun sipping coffee and studying the area through my binoculars. A wasp buzzed angrily past my head and I idly swatted at it. Another flew past, presumably attracted to the sugar in my drink. Suddenly there was a loud thud and, with a start, I realized that the wasps were bullets fired from a great distance. We mounted up and, from the safety of the turret, I looked back towards Guca Gora. I could hardly hear the weapon firing but assumed that our Ethiopian friend had borrowed a sniper rifle. I finished my observations through the sights and we left him to it.

At the bottom of the Bila Valley, the Croats had fortified the checkpoint with TMRP 6s, fitted with tilt fuses. I climbed down and chatted to the sentry. He daren't touch the tilts but moved the TMAs to create a narrow chicane. The BiH started to fire at us and, with renewed vigour, I guided Tookey through. Unexpectedly, I was grabbed by the shoulder and flung to one side. The Croat had assaulted me and I was about to assault him back when I realized that I'd almost stepped backwards onto a tilt fuse. The guy had saved my life.

Juti was waiting for me at the camp. I wondered when he'd try to call his favour in. He said he was in some kind of danger and wanted to travel to Croatia. It was either an internecine feud or he felt the BiH would try him as a war criminal if they ever captured him. Either way, he offered me half-a-million marks. This was a vast amount of money and equated to about 200,000 pounds. The funniest thing was, he actually had the cash with him and showed me a blue sports bag stuffed full of banknotes.

All he wanted was to be taken to Prozor from where he could hitch a lift south. It was such a simple request and I was sorely tempted. I could arrange a patrol to GV and just keep going. If I told the lads we had to transport an important Croat commander to a meeting they wouldn't even think it was unusual. No one would ever know.

'No thanks Juti. You can't buy me!'

'I will ask again in a week!'

I never did see Juti again. A couple of days later, he was gunned down by a Croat rival in Novi Travnik. Shot in the back, he was paralysed. The Hip made an appearance and he was flown down to Split. He finally made it to Croatia, albeit in a wheelchair. I kicked myself for not taking the money!

Back at the house 'Diddly' Fawcett was desperately searching the bushes in the garden of our new house. He stood and saluted, with a bandaged hand.

'What happened?'

'I was picking up bastard litter and a bastard kitten bit me! I've got to find it so they can send the bastard to Split for analysis. I may have bastard rabies!'

We searched for a few minutes but there was no sign of the offending bastard.

The next day, I noticed a small, tabby kitten scuttle into the shed where the Muslim furniture was stored. I cornered the animal and dispatched it with a blow from a broom handle. I felt guilty but at least Fawcett would be put out of his misery. When I presented him with the little corpse, you'd have thought I'd given him the crown jewels.

A few days later, I was passing the shed when I spotted yet another tabby. Inside, four identical kittens stared down at me from the rafters. I never did have the heart to tell him!

On 23 September, Ana Ghavric had decided she wanted to go to Rankovici and I said I'd try to arrange it. That seemed to please Anto who was patently sick of her.

We'd been trying to arrange another children's party but were having no success with the BiH. Everywhere we went, they refused. It appeared that an edict had gone out from Three Corps banning villages from openly associating with the UN. How the situation had changed from the Cheshires' time and we were now in the way of the BiH plans for further conquest.

The Colonel was back and warned us all to avoid FTC.

The charity wasn't exactly flavour of the month with the CO as he'd had to negotiate the release of Steve and Lawrence. The BiH had tired of the pair and imprisoned them in the condemned cell in Travnik. They were a couple of arseholes but were still British and we couldn't just let them be killed. They were eventually released into our custody to be transported down to Split. I saw them in the guardroom. Two scrawny nobodies who'd crapped themselves with fright.

The reconnaissance party of the Coldstream Guards arrived and the end of the tour was in sight. I hosted the two company commanders, Other Windsor-Clive and Richard Margesson. I'd hoped to show them a children's party and only one Muslim village would allow us to hold one. Cap in hand, I went to see Beba, who was even more weaselly than usual. He refused to let me go back to Radovcici to run the event. Despite the village leaders wanting us to go there, the HQ refused. Good old Beba, everyone's friend, depriving 300 children of a day's fun. It was as if he wanted the kids to believe the UN was against them and therefore couldn't be allowed to see the caring face of the battalion.

In desperation I headed for Rankovici. Father Ilya virtually took my arm off when I suggested a party. Three hours later Zippy had the place set up and we were bringing a little happiness to nearly 500 children.

I took the Coldstreams down to Kiseljak, via Busovaca, and then back via Visoko. Chappy was driving and, on one of the halts, climbed out to check the oil levels. It had rained and he slipped on the greasy decks and fell off the wagon into a ditch. We all laughed until I realized he was hurt. He'd damaged his ribs again and I decided to get him checked out at the MST. We reached the Zenica flyover and the BiH guard asked to see inside. This done, we drove through and halted next to two Warriors from Splash's platoon. A senior officer jumped across on to 0B. I recognized him and greeted him cheerfully but he instantly started on me.

'How the hell did you get through that checkpoint?'

'I opened my doors to the sentry.'

'Fool!'

'I beg your pardon?'

'You're an idiot! That is in direct contravention of UN policy. Do you know why we don't do it? I'll tell you. It's because of the murder of the Bosnian Deputy President. The French opened their doors and the man was shot. You are an idiot.'

'Sir! My driver is hurt and I want to get him checked out as soon as possible!'

'That's no excuse. You are not to open your doors for anyone!'

'Sir, we do it all the time. What about every time we go to Sarajevo? The Serbs wouldn't let us through unless we opened the doors.'

'That is simply not true. I've been sitting here for over an hour because I won't let them see in the Warrior!'

'I think you'll be here a lot longer then, sir!'

'Now listen to me. Being in the UN is not about taking the easy way out. We have rules to abide by and this is one of them.'

'Sir, you've been to the Battalion. The CO must've briefed you that we open the doors when we're not carrying commanders.'

'That's absolute nonsense. Now bugger off out of here!'

I was so embarrassed to be dressed-down in front of my own, and

A Company soldiers, never mind the two guards officers. I told the CO what had happened and he immediately phoned the Brigade commander in Split to ask him to speak to the fellow. The senior officer was hell-bent on proving his point and refused to budge. The BiH just sat there and would've done so all day. Bosnia is a country where people are used to waiting. Eventually, David saved the day by sending two Land Rovers to the flyover to take the chap to Kiseljak. As the BiH could see into the Rovers, the man's honour was salved. Never mind the risks to the soldiers who drove him around Bosnia, in a soft-skinned vehicle, for no good reason.

The postscript to the incident was that a couple of days later, I received a call from the fellow. I was out but the CO took it. He apologized for his attitude explaining he'd been in Bosnia for only a few days and hadn't fully absorbed his briefings. Would the Colonel please pass on his apologies to me?

Hasib Belegic gave me permission to move Ana from Pecine. We poled-up and she started her usual wailing. Anto pleaded with us to take her away. We gave her an hour to pack her things and she emerged wearing a fur coat, despite the temperature being in the seventies. She also had more of the bloody robes. Goodness knows where she was finding them. I decided to eliminate the middleman and take them straight to Rankovici. I figured Carson wouldn't want to see another vestment as long as he lived! Finally, we had the little woman safely caged in the Warrior and we made our way to Father Ilya's. Ana was overjoyed at reaching civilization and kissed my hand.

At the end of September 1993, some sappers played a blinder. While on a route reconnaissance, north of Zenica, they came across some mines. As no one was around, and being keen engineers, they put them in the back of their 432. The idea was to deactivate them and send them back to the UK for training purposes.

They arrived at the flyover and the BiH asked to search the wagon. The Muslims saw the mines and detained the sappers for hours. For weeks afterwards, whenever I denied accusations that the UN favoured one side or other, the locals would trot out: 'But we know that a UN vehicle was stopped when it was carrying mines to the Croats.'

The thoughtlessness of these soldiers had made life infinitely harder for the rest of us. Memories are long in the Balkans and the same story is probably still being told now. They also have a tendency to exaggerate and, by now, the Brits will have had a cruise missile in their wagon.

On 2 October I travelled south to go on my R & R. The company had a quiet two weeks and Jason coped admirably. It was a measure of the quality of this young officer that he was left to run a rifle company on operations. While I was away, he and Zippy managed to persuade the village of Janjici, near Zenica, to accept a party. The local commander had heard of our activities and told Jason that his HQ had forbidden contact with the UN. He was very pragmatic and said that sometimes his leaders forgot the needs of the people in their search for political statements. This was a real coup by Jason and Zippy and redressed the balance of our failure to hold another party in a Muslim village.

My magnificent handlebar moustache failed to survive the first contact with my children:

'Daddy, it's all horrible and tickly!'

I returned to Bosnia on 20 October as Major *Nema Brko*! It was amazing how many people didn't recognize me. At Pokrajcici, Drago refused to let me into his headquarters.

'I will only talk to Major Vaughan!'

There were only three weeks of the tour remaining. The Lasva Valley had quietened down and patrolling was cut to a minimum. These last few weeks saw us concentrating on hearts-and-minds operations as there was little else to do. The CO ordered an end to front line patrolling and, free of this burden, we did our own thing. We visited the orphanage in Zenica. There were over 180 children there, most with no hope of escape. The official policy was to allow adoption only by Bosnian families. By this, they hoped to prevent the drain of orphans to Western European families. The trouble was that few Bosnians wanted to take on an extra mouth in the middle of a civil war. There the children remained until they were old enough to leave at sixteen. As the majority were under seven, it was like a life sentence for them.

The place was well-run and Ginner Burton had built up an excellent rapport with the staff. We took along a karaoke machine and the lads sang to the children. Zippy had a go too, and certainly shouldn't give up his day job. The kids sang to us as well. Their offering was about a mother, working in an ammunition factory, who is grieving for her husband and son who've been killed in the War. It was more depressing than listening to country and western. We gave them a large amount of baby food and a load of other stuff from the rations sergeant. The children craved attention and, at one stage, I had four beautiful little mites sitting on my knee.

It was my turn to provide the food for the company officers and we had prawn cocktail followed by duckling, courtesy of Messrs Marks and Spencer. We ate in the sitting room of the Captain's house, in the same room where Dobrila had been murdered all those weeks before. As we had to wear uniform all the time we livened up the mess by holding hat parties. Adam Boothby was a clear winner at one of these with a carefully sculptured papier mâché Warrior perched on his head.

On one tunnel duty, in late October 1993, Sergeant White drove slowly past a group of BiH soldiers returning from the front. Some of these were drunk and one decided to play chicken with White's 432. The result was that the guy put his arm into the track and got it caught. Before the crew realized, the limb had been dragged around the sprocket and ripped off. The BiH tried to blame White but met with a very unsympathetic response from me when I visited their headquarters. After all this angst, I went to the small Croat village of Bucici, near the Novi Travnik T-junction. The priest, Father Jozor, was surprised to see us as UN vehicles rarely ventured off the main roads now. I offered him baby food and the chance of a children's party. He took it all in his stride and we soon had the details finalized.

While I was back in the UK, I'd collected some toys and baby clothes donated by friends of my family. Father Ilya arranged for ten mothers and babies to come to his church. We laid out ten piles of clothes, toys, milk, food and nappies. The people arrived and were overwhelmed that folk in England should send things for them. It was one of the few times during the tour that I knew what we'd given would actually stay with the people we'd given it to.

Sonja had lost all her possessions when her house was burned. I took her over to FTC and Jim Ryan gave her a small box of items donated by a family in Exeter. She wrote to thank these unknown people for their kind gesture and, months later, visited them when she qualified for leave.

On 26 October I was visiting Mister Renic in Novi Travnik to present him with a regimental plaque, when the BiH mortared the town. We rarely used the Warriors now as the lads were preparing them for the move back. The first round landed fifty metres from us, blowing Donlon and me off our feet. The area was alive with flying shrapnel, and a chunk hit the Rover. Two civilians were caught in the open and we carried one woman to the medical centre. She had several cuts to her legs but would survive. As we were stumbling along with her, a second round landed close by. We dropped the woman, and both dived on top of her as we were showered with dust and bits of brick. The sirens started to wail, as did the woman, and it was how I imagined London had sounded during the blitz. Once we'd safely delivered the woman to Doctor Kranic, we beat a hasty retreat.

The advance party of the Coldstream Guards arrived on 28 October and twenty-seven of my company left on the first flight out. The train-set was starting to break up.

We took the Guards Subalterns to Bucici for the party. The church was large and extremely cold but the priest had succeeded in absolutely filling it. Every pew was jammed full of children. Zippy counted more than 800 of them. They sang for us and Father Jozor said a few words. He then asked me to address the throng. This was a bit of a fast ball. I asked them all to remember why the UN was in their country and I told them we were there to help everybody. This was aimed at their mothers as much as the kids. Finally, I asked them never to run in front of the Warriors and always to wave at us when we passed. I felt like the village bobby lecturing at the Tufty Club. Nevertheless, if only a few kids went away with the message that UNPROFOR was good, it was worth it.

The priest was a masterful organizer and we filtered the kids through without fuss. He didn't stand for any nonsense and clipped a couple of older boys around the ear and sent them to the back of the queue.

The BiH couldn't leave us alone and lobbed a shell about four hundred metres away as we were packing up. It was my worst nightmare, that a stray shell would land in the middle of a party. However, the locals just viewed it as all part of the rich tapestry of life in Bosnia.

The guards were interested to hear about our tour. It had been an incredibly busy time and I estimated there had been only three times I'd stayed in camp all day. There had always been something to do and someone to help and we took the attitude that since we were here we may as well keep trying.

Despite what I'd vowed early on in the tour I was still trying to solve Bosnia's problems singlehanded. However, I was spending far more time with the company and a strong team had developed. This team stayed together for nine months after the tour and we wiped the floor with the other companies on exercise in Canada. This commitment had its price, however, and I ran myself, and my crew, into the ground. Even 0B suffered and ran twenty-five years' worth of peacetime track mileage in six months. The only things on the wagon we hadn't used were the guns. Above all our achievements this is the one of which I'm most proud. We found ourselves in some pretty hairy scrapes and nearly always had cause to return fire. However, I took the attitude that there was always another solution and we never added to the Bosnia body-count. It was ironic that 'Vitez Vaughan...He's Hard as F—k!' should never fire a shot in anger.

My crew was outstanding, as were most of my soldiers. Bosnia is an officer's war and they had no choice over where I took them or sent them. However, when the chips were down, they displayed aggression and compassion in equal measures. These qualities set us apart from the rest of the UN.

Dobby epitomized these qualities. He was thrown into a role for which he received little training yet he consistently displayed the utmost gallantry. He was later awarded the Military Cross, the first other rank ever to be so. After the tour he returned to the backwater of the vehicle stores, modest and self-effacing to the last.

The reader may have gathered that I enjoyed a 'special' relationship with the Commanding Officer. Colonel Alastair had a great deal on his plate dealing with high-level meetings and senior visitors. The last thing he needed was a wilful and headstrong subordinate. I know he debated sacking me and perhaps the last word on this should be that dozens of Bosnians owe their lives to his restraint. In common with many officers, I was drinking and smoking far too much. The mess at night was a place to forget the horrors. Richard Margesson commented that we were all barking mad. Now where had I heard that before? It brought home to me the fact that we were nothing special. We'd reacted to the surreal nature of our existence in the same way as the Cheshires. Poor leadership was not a factor. The shrink thought I was barking as well and one day buttonholed me after dinner.

'Have you ever felt the need to talk about your experiences with a psychiatrist?'

'Not really doc. There are far more needy people.'

'I guess you're right. I wouldn't know where to start with you any-way!'

The surreal taskings continued. On the 29 October I was sent to Travnik to pick up the Hay brothers, who'd been saying farewell to Beba. I told David I thought it was madness to send a patrol through two front lines in the dark. Quite apart from the danger from mines, we rarely patrolled at night and were bound to be fired upon.

'Can't they just stay the night there?'

'It's far too dangerous!'

'You seem quite happy for them to be there now though! Anyway, what the hell are they doing swanning around after dark? Why did-n't they just tell their driver not to drink? That's what normal peo-ple do when they go out!'

'The function's been sanctioned from on high.'

'It doesn't matter if John Major himself sanctioned it. It's asking for trouble to send troops into Travnik, at night, to pick up two pissed-up LOs. How many people's lives is their bloody party worth?' In the end, there was no point in arguing.

The Croats at the Novi Travnik T were jumpy and surprised to see us. I chatted for a couple of minutes and they agreed to move their mines. We were slowly picking our way through when Tookey suddenly cried out: 'Shit!'

'What's wrong?'

'I think we just ran over a mine!'

'Hold it right there!'

I jumped out and, sure enough, a TMA 4 lay half under the left track. The mine looked like a big round cheese and had three pres-sure-horns screwed into the top. The track had run over one of these without detonating it. It was an absolute miracle. The other two horns were still sticking up from the body, the nearest being a cou-ple of centimetres from the edge of the track. If we continued, there was every chance the rest of the mine would be dragged under the track. It would be too much to hope the other two detonators would malfunction.

The headlights from the following wagon gave me plenty of light, in fact a little too much. I hoped the BiH didn't try to ventilate me as I crouched there. Again, I couldn't think of a better solution so I took hold of the nearest horn and gave it a gentle turn. It was quite loose and soon I was unscrewing the thing. Donlon had climbed out to give me cover. Now, he crept up behind me.

'BANG!'

I shrieked and jumped back. Donlon's cackle filled the night as he picked up the helmet he'd dropped behind me. Still, at least it wasn't maggots this time.

The second detonator was more stubborn and, at first, refused to budge. I could only just get my fingers between the body and the edge of the track. The mine was jammed solidly under the track; at least I didn't have to bother about holding the thing steady. I was terrified of pressing down on the top of the horn and being blown into that school in the sky for failed mine-clearers. My hand was starting to sweat and slip on the smooth plastic suface so I put one glove on. This gave me the extra purchase and the detonator started to unscrew. Minutes later, having survived what was probably our closest shave of the tour, we were on our way again. As we drove through no-man's-land, a gunman fired a burst of automatic fire at us from one of the BiH trenches. The fire was high and wild but I clearly saw the muzzle flashes as we swept past.

Travnik was quiet and the streets deserted. The power was off with the full moon the only light. The pick-up was supposed to be at Beba's HQ at midnight. We were five minutes early so we dismounted and huddled round the back doors while Holtom produced coffee. Winter was near and our breath hung around us in the still air, reminding me of my first night in Bosnia, eight months before. Someone produced the cigarettes and soon we had our own little pea souper around the wagon. At 12.10 there was still no sign of the LOs so I went to fetch them. I felt like a taxi driver calling to collect drunken ravers on a Friday night. Funny old thing that.

The HQ was deserted as well. Where the hell were they? Travnik wasn't that big so we formed a little foot patrol and went for a wander. The only sound was our boots on the tarmac. We listened for any sign of a party but could hear none. Out of curiosity, I took the lads past the house of the Nobel Prize winner, Ivo Andric. He wasn't at home. Probably because he'd been dead for some years. He'd be turning in his grave over the state of his beloved Bosnia.

Finally, at well after one, a car screeched to a halt and out poured Angus, Colin and Beba. The Bosnian had a tartan cloth wrapped around him, clearly a gift from the brothers.

'Nice blanket, Beba!'

He glowered at me as the two staggered into the Warrior.

Back at no-man's-land, the BiH was waiting for us. This time, a heavy machine gun opened up on us from the high ground across the Lasva to my right. The green tracer was bright against the dark backdrop of the surrounding hills. Their first rounds were well high but the subsequent burst flew dangerously close to the front of the Warrior, nicely at turret height.

'Kill the lights, Tookey, and slow down.'

Instantly, the road ahead was plunged into darkness and Tookey stood on the brakes. 0B swerved, causing howls of protest from the passengers in the back. Zippy shouted to them: 'Shut up you lot! It's your fault we're here in the first place!'

The gunner was totally thrown off his aim and the next burst whipped past, about fifty metres in front of the wagon. The moonlight glinted off the damp road and Tookey had no difficulty in following it. We increased speed again and were soon back through the Croat lines.

By the time we reached the school, both LOs were fast asleep.

The guards were going to try a different system of LOs. Roy and I explained our frustrations to their company commanders and they'd proposed a change to their CO. They were to try a system where the LOs for a particular area worked to a company commander and the majors worked to the CO. That seemed like a sound idea and, funnily enough, is how everything else worked in the Army. It seemed a better system than one where captains virtually ran the show and majors had little to do but take food to old people. I suspected the Coldstream's system would work rather well.

There were rumours of fighting around the Dolac checkpoint and Milinfo reckoned they needed the exact situation to brief the incoming unit. I drove up there and the HVO, obligingly, moved their mines. The BiH was not so friendly and a heavy machine gun, probably the one from the night before, fired at us. It was only six rounds and we had increased to warp speed. Fortunately, the rounds fell nicely between the two Warriors. At Dolac, nothing had changed and the Muslims were sitting at a table, playing cards. Yet another pointless trip to the front line and yet more unnecessary risk.

The element of risk was ever present but most of us became more acutely aware of it during the last few days of the tour. A few soldiers became reluctant to go on patrol as their last week in Bosnia approached. The general feeling was that the safest place to be was in the school. Yet it was in the school that the last casualties of the tour occurred.

The Guards were soon to take over operations and asked for our pistols, to issue to their commanders. They had also taken over our offices so they could start to plan their opening moves. We, therefore, had to find alternative locations for our briefings. Roy was holding his conference in a huddle in the corridor when enter, stage left, one LO.

Colour Sergeant McFadden was about to take the pistol off him and asked for it to be checked. The LO pulled back the action, checked there was no round in the breech, let the working parts slide forward and squeezed the trigger. The drill is fool proof but not, unfortunately, idiot proof. The guy forgot to take the magazine off.

The pistol shot was deafening in the enclosed space and we all ran out to investigate. It looked like a grenade had gone off. Seemingly dozens of people were lying on the floor clutching their legs.

The bullet hit the marble floor, broke into several pieces that flew, like shrapnel, at the legs of Roy's men. Roy, Splash, Jason Medley and four sergeants were injured, as was Dominic Hancock, who just happened to be passing. Splash was the worst hurt and required surgery to remove fragments. The LO was probably the only man to wound eight men with a single shot. His street-cred was also severely wounded as was, later, his wallet!

We ran our final party, on 4 November, in the village of Dornji Veceriska to the west of Vitez. More than 500 children attended and one little girl gave me a bunch of flowers. The weather had turned bitterly cold and few of the kids hung around after the food was dished out.

Richard Margesson asked me to sum up our achievements. The most obvious were the parties. We'd catered for over 4,000 kids, giving them a few hours of fun, in a life that was anything but fun. This represented about 20 per cent of all the kids under ten in the whole of the Lasva Valley. Some people tried to trivialize these events and indeed, when weighed against all the other problems in Bosnia, they were of little consequence. However, we organized these besides our normal duties and I believe they fell well within the liberal interpretation of the mandate. With more time and resources, we could have done so much more.

We'd made great inroads into the distrust the Croats felt for the UN and proved we were, indeed impartial. I believe that this provided an excellent foundation for the Guards to build on.

We finished the tour with a winning team with everyone working together for the common good, helping people. Throughout the period we were given sterling support from battalion HQ who fulfilled the true functions of the staff. They fielded the big picture while we got on with the business on the ground.

Outstanding throughout was our fitter section, keeping our wagons on the road despite our best efforts to trash them. The Warriors were extremely robust, rarely broke down and absorbed all the punishment the terrain and warring factions could throw at them. Above all, however, the locals respected them. The MOD has truly provided a world-beating vehicle for the infantry.

Thankfully, we brought everyone home. The company and battalion had several soldiers wounded and injured but, mercifully, all survived. We all had some incredibly close shaves but luck was always on our side.

Above all, however, we saved lives. Indirectly, we helped people by just doing our job. The escorts and the tunnel all ensured that the aid kept flowing. We also saved dozens of people just by being at the right place at the right time. Most of us didn't care what the mandate said and we always tried to do the Christian thing. It was a moral rather than a religious attitude and we attempted to be the good Samaritan wherever we went. There were scores of Bosnians who owed their lives to the timely arrival of the Great White Warrior. The tragedy was there were hundreds of others we never saw in their hour of need.

It was time to say my goodbyes and I went the rounds of Ilya Nakic, Vlado Juric, Hasib Belegic, Doctor Kranic, Father Ilya, Marenko and others. I could only visit two in a day as the events tended to degenerate into a maudlin binge. I'd sussed out a way of appearing to drink the locals under the table by carrying a plastic cup with a sponge inside it, in the pockets of my flak vest. I must have tipped about a gallon of Slivovitz into them during the last days. It meant I allowed Mister Boddington the privilege of killing my liver.

I was sorry to see these people for the last time but I wasn't sorry to leave Bosnia. We did what we could but were constantly hampered by the mandate and the lack of a clear statement of exactly what we were there to do. We did not have the backing, or teeth, to peacekeep and the locals knew this. Most of the time, we were powerless to stop the killing and the standing of the UN fell to an all-time low. True, we were only supposed to be escorting convoys but even these had slackened off by the time we left. The fact that few, if any, people actually starved to death in Bosnia was only partially due to the UN. Aid reached the country from other sources and people grew food in the fertile soil. Indeed, the ground was so good that a discarded box of matches would probably become a copse in a few years. I remarked on this to one commander and asked why they didn't concentrate on farming instead of fighting: 'Why should we? We know the UN will not let us starve!'

This attitude, I'm afraid, typified the Bosnian people. A race whose only similarity with Western Europeans was physical. Kate Adie had been right all those months ago. Mentally, they were poles apart from us and treated each other with a brutality that bordered on the bestial. Geographically, the region was where the hot-blood-ed Latin merged with the brutal Slav and the results were often odi-ous. The UN failed to appreciate the nature of the people and deployed with a structure and mandate fit for operations in the Netherlands. The Bosnians only respected power and when they realized that we had none, they walked all over us.

The British deployed as part of UNPROFOR not out of any great national interest but to be seen to be doing something. Seeing how we managed to withdraw would be interesting as quitting while we were ahead seemed an unlikely scenario. To those of us doing the something the situation was frustrating in the extreme. By the end of the tour most of us wanted just to go home and leave them to it. True, we'd made a localized difference but, to the leadership of all three sides, we were a nuisance to be used, and abused when it suit-ed them.

On the 7 November, I took the Warriors on their last patrol, down to TSG. The low-loaders were waiting and soon the wagons would be on their way to Split. Tookey stayed but the rest of us had to return up country as the Guards still didn't have enough men in Bosnia to guard the camp.

I went to see the old people for the last time. Ana Lesic cooked pork for us on a fire made from the logs we'd chopped and gave us Slivovitz made from the plums we'd picked. It was a fitting end to our involvement with these dignified old people and I was confident they'd survive the winter. As we left, Ana and Ivo were crying.

The HVO and BiH were having a little bijou battle in Novi Travnik and several rounds passed perilously close to the flimsy sides of the Land Rover. A solitary bullet passed through the wing. It was our last contact of the tour.

I left Vitez on the 14 November. After 202 days, the tour was over. Heavy snow was falling and winter had arrived with a vengeance. In GV, Warriors from the Coldstream Guards escorted us through the town and I snuggled into my smock and started to doze. Before I fell into a deep sleep I reflected that after six months of living on the front line we may not have shortened the War by one second. But, by God, wherever we went, we made a difference.

Appendix

Honours and Awards to Men of C Company Group

Corporal Dobson	Military Cross
Corporal Gillett	Mentioned in Dispatches
Corporal Donlon	Queen's Commendation for Brave Conduct
Lieutenant Calder	Commander in Chief's Commendation
Sergeant White	Commander in Chief's Commendation
Lance-Corporal Grant	Commander in Chief's Commendation
Lance-Corporal Holtom	Commander in Chief's Commendation
WO2 (CSM) Clark	United Nations Commendation
Lance-Corporal Brown	United Nations Commendation
Private Nicholson	United Nations Commendation
Staff Sergeant Mackareth	Director General REME Commendation

Glossary

Adjutant	Officer, usually of the rank of captain, advises commanding officer on discipline and military law.
AK 47	Soviet 7.62 mm assault rifle. Weighing 3.4 kg it has a distinctive, curved, 30-round magazine.
AFV	Armoured fighting vehicle.
AP	Armour piercing.
APC	Armoured personnel carrier.
Battalion	Infantry formation consisting of around 600 men.
BFI	Bulk fuel installation. Sited near Vitez Garage, it held all the military fuel in the area. Diesel stored in large inflatable tanks and petrol in jerrycans.
BGT	Battle group trainer. Training facility for exercising unit headquarters. Basically a large wargame with models moved around a map table to simulate movement of troops on the ground.
BiH	Army of Bosnia Herzegovina. Official army of the state of Bosnia Herzegovina. Mainly Muslim. Divided into corps with regional responsibilities. Three corps operated in the Vitez area.
BRITBAT	UN terminology for British battalion. Hence, SPANBAT, CANBAT and FRANBAT.
Browning	British Army 9 mm semi-automatic pistol.
BSA	Bosnian Serb Army. Army of the Bosnian Serbs. Separate from the army of the state of Serbia. Commanded by General Ratko Mladic.
CAB-F	Confirming accuracy of fire. The first time the RARDEN (q.v.) is fired on the range. The three round shoot confirms that the gun and sights are working correctly.
Casevac	Casualty evacuation.
CET	Combat engineer tractor. Tracked armoured vehicle weighing 18 tons and with a crew of two. Large

356

front bucket used for clearing obstacles.

Chain Gun   7.62 mm Hughes Chain Gun. An electrically fired machine gun, the secondary armament of the Warrior.

CGS   Chief of the General Staff. Professional head of the Army. In 1993, was General Sir Peter Inge.

Chobham   Composite armour developed at the research establishment at Chobham, Surrey. Added to the Warrior, it provides additional protection against hand-held anti-tank weapons such as the RPG-7 (q.v.). The actual armour is hidden inside mild steel cosmetic boxes.

Close-down   Closing the hatches of an armoured vehicle to provide maximum protection for the crew.

CP   Close protection. Military euphemism for bodyguard.

Cpl   Corporal. Non-commissioned officer. Normally commands a section of eight men.

Compo   British Army field rations.

CQMS   Company Quarter Master Sergeant. Normally a colour sergeant. In charge of the stores and administration for the company.

CO   Commanding Officer. Officer in overall charge of a regiment. Usually a lieutenant colonel.

COMBRITFOR   Commander British Forces. Officer in overall charge of all British forces in Bosnia, former Yugoslavia. Based at Split in Croatia. For most of 1 PWO tour he was Brigadier Robin Searby, followed by Brigadier John Reith.

Coy   Company. Military grouping of around 120 men. Divided into three platoons (q.v.) and a headquarters and commanded by a major. Can swell to nearer 200 men on operations.

C/Sgt   Colour Sergeant. Senior non-commissioned officer in the infantry. Employed as CQMS (q.v.) or as a platoon commander.

CSM   Company Sergeant Major. Senior non-commissioned officer. The senior enlisted man in a Company. Will normally have at least fifteen years experience. Responsible for discipline and administration.

Deflector plate   Mild steel plates fitted to the front and rear sides of the Warrior. Their purpose is to prevent the Chobham (q.v.) boxes being damaged.

D30   122 mm howitzer of Soviet origin. Maximum range 17,300 m.

DMI   Driving and Maintenance Instructor. NCO who has attended a special course to teach him to instruct on a particular vehicle.

ECMM   European Commission Monitoring Mission. Employed by the EEC to monitor the situation in former Yugoslavia. Unarmed, and wearing white uniforms, they brokered local ceasefires and negotiated the release of hostages.

F-15   Two-seat fighter aircraft in service with US Airforce. Maximum speed, mach 2.5.

Fitter Section   Ten man group, attached to each company, responsible for repair and maintenance of vehicles. Manned by REME soldiers (q.v.).

432   British tracked APC weighing 15 tons. Obsolescent by 1993, it still equipped the anti-tank and mortar sections. Can carry twelve people and is armed with a GPMG (q.v.).

FTC   Feed the Children. Small charity based in Reading, England, specializing in delivering aid for young children. A non-governmental organization and therefore not sponsored by the UN.

Glacis Plate   Sloping armour plate at the front of an AFV.

GPMG   General purpose machine gun. Belt-fed, gas operated machine gun firing standard 7.62 mm ammunition. Can be carried by soldiers in the light role or mounted on vehicles such as the 432 (q.v.).

GRAPPLE   British code name for the deployment of troops to Bosnia in support of the UN.

GV   Gornji Vakuf. Town in Central Bosnia about 65 km south of Vitez. Scene of heavy ethnic fighting between Muslims and Croats in 1993. B Company 1 PWO stationed in town throughout tour.

Hard-targeting   Zig-zagging from cover to cover to confuse the enemy.

HE   High Explosive.

HDZ   Bosnian Croat political party. In Vitez area,

headed by Dario Kordic.

Hip   Mi-8 Hip Helicopter. Of Soviet design it can carry up to twenty-eight passengers or 4500 kg of freight. Maximum speed, 250 k.p.h.

HOS   Bosnian Croat political police. Extremist right-wing paramilitary police force.

HVO   Bosnian Croat militia. Organized into Brigades and controlled by a headquarters in Vitez. Commanded by Colonel Tihomir Blaskic.

ICRC   International Committee for the Red Cross. Civilian organization primarily concerned with providing medical support to the needy. Activities included negotiating release of hostages, monitoring conditions of prisoners of war, organizing the evacuation of the seriously ill to hospitals.

JNA   Jugoslav National Army. Army of Former Yugoslavia. Equipment formed backbone of the warring factions. Most militiamen had some experience of conscript service with the JNA.

JRC   Junior ranks club. Social club for all ranks of Corporal and below.

L/Cpl   Lance Corporal. First stage on the promotion ladder. Usually commands four men.

LAD   Light Aid Detachment. Detachment of around fifty REME (q.v.). personnel provides inspection and repair support for a Battalion (q.v.).

LD   Light Dragoons. Cavalry Regiment. Provided one Squadron of a hundred men to support 1 PWO.

LO   Liaison Officer. Officer with the rank of captain, drawn from within the regiment and responsible for liaising with local commanders in a particular area.

L2   British Army fragmentation grenade.

MFC   Mortar Fire Controller. Soldier responsible for calling down and adjusting mortar fire.

Milinfo   Military information. UN euphemism for intelligence.

MSR   Main supply route. Route used for transport of aid, supplies and personnel. Named and marked by UN, i.e. Route Diamond, and maintained by military engineers.

MST	Mobile surgical team. Small military hospital to provide routine medical and dental care to troops. Capable of performing life-saving surgery to stabilize casualties before evacuation to the UK.
MT	Motor transport. Collective term for all military soft-skinned transport.
Neutral turn	A turn, within the axis, made by a tracked vehicle.
OC	Officer Commanding.
Ops	Operations.
P Info	Public information. Military organization responsible for briefing the media.
Platoon	Organization of around thirty men, commanded by a subaltern or colour sergeant.
Pte	Private. Enlisted man, the lowest rank in the Army.
PWO	The Prince of Wales's Own Regiment of Yorkshire. Infantry Regiment formed in 1958 from an amalgamation of the West and East Yorkshire Regiments and recruiting from those areas. 1 PWO is the first Battalion of the Regiment.
QLR	Queen's Lancashire Regiment. Infantry regiment, based in Berlin in 1993. Provided around thirty soldiers to bring 1 PWO up to strength. The majority served with A Company.
QM	Quartermaster. Officer responsible for the overall administration of the equipment in the battalion. Commissioned from the ranks and will have at least twenty years experience.
QRF	Quick reaction force. An ad hoc organization created to provide an immediate reaction to any unexpected events. In Vitez, this was based on a platoon.
RARDEN	30 mm cannon. Fires single shot or automatic bursts out to 2000 m. Can fire high explosive or armour piercing ammunition. Main armament on Warrior and Scimitar (q.v.).
REME	Royal Electrical & Mechanical Engineers. Soldiers responsible for the maintenance and repair of military vehicles, weapons and equipment.
RPG-7	Soviet hand-held anti-tank rocket launcher. Weighing 6.9 kg, it has a maximum range of 500 m.
R & R	Rest and recuperation. Leave taken during or after an operational tour.

RSM	Regimental Sergeant Major. Senior non-commissioned officer in a battalion. The commanding officer's personal advisor on discipline and all soldier matters.
SA80	British Army service rifle. 5.56 mm calibre. It has a thirty-round magazine and a x4 magnification sight.
Sangar	Fortified sentry position.
Scimitar	British Army light tank weighing 8 tons and with a crew of three. Armed with one 30 mm RARDEN cannon and one GPMG (q.v.).
Sea King	Helicopter operated by the Royal Navy. Can carry up to twenty-eight passengers or 3600 kg of freight. Maximum speed 225 k.p.h.
2/ic	Second-in-command. The deputy to commanders of any rank.
Sgt	Sergeant. Senior non-commissioned officer. The next step up from corporal. Entitles the holder to membership of the sergeant's mess.
Shemague	Arab-style head-dress. Usually of a checked pattern.
Sight hood	Steel shutter that can be lowered to protect the gun sights on a Warrior.
64 mm	64 mm anti-tank rocket launcher. A Soviet copy of an American system. Weight 2.7 kg and effective range, 200 m.
SLAVEN	UN codeword for convoys crossing the Serb front line near Vitez. SLAVEN was for refugees and SLAVEN 2 was for food aid.
Spartan	Small, light armoured, British tracked APC, weighing 8 tons. It can carry six people and is armed with one GPMG.
Spigot	Soviet anti-tank missile system. Wire-guided with a maximum range of 2000 m.
S/Sgt	Staff Sergeant. The same rank as Colour Sergeant in non-infantry unit.
Staff College	Army establishment at Camberley in Surrey. The army staff course is a year long and is attended by officers between the ages of 31–35.
Stag	Military slang for guard duty.
Tank Park	Open ground where all armoured vehicles are parked.

Tank-round	Shell fired from a tank gun.
TAOR	Tactical area of responsibility. Area designated by headquarters within which a military unit can operate.
TMA-3	Small anti-tank mine. Operated by central pressure pad that detonates high explosive charge.
TMA-4	Large anti-tank mine. Operated by three pressure horns that detonate high explosive charge.
TMRP-6	Large anti-tank mine. Operated by central pressure pad or tilt fuse that detonates shaped, armour piercing, explosive charge.
TQM	Technical Quartermaster. Works alongside the QM (q.v.). Responsible for technical equipment within the battalion. Usually a captain.
Track Bashing	Replacing the tracks on armoured vehicles.
Track pad	Rubber pad fitted to armoured vehicle tracks to reduce damage to road surfaces.
TSG	Tomislavgrad. Town in southern Bosnia. Site of British administrative base.
Turret cage	Wire storage basket fixed to the rear of the Warrior turret.
UKLO	United Kingdom Liaison Officer. Armed military officer responsible for assisting with liaison in battalion area. Reported to the COMBRITFOR as well as the CO. (q.v.).
UNHCR	United Nations High Commission for Refugees. Part of the UN, responsible for the care, feeding and housing of refugees.
UNMO	United Nations monitor. Unarmed military personnel recruited multinationally and working to UN headquarters.
UNPROFOR	United Nations Protection Force. Multinational UN force, specifically created for operations in Bosnia.
Zero Bravo	Radio callsign of the company commander's Warrior.
Zero Charlie	Radio callsign of the company second-in-command's Warrior.

Index